Brahmacharya
Gandhi
&
His Women Associates

Brahmacharya Gandhi & His Women Associates

Girja Kumar

Vitasta

Vitasta Publishing Pvt. Ltd.
New Delhi

Published by Renu Kaul Verma for
Vitasta Publishing Pvt. Ltd.
2/15, Ansari Road, Daryaganj,
New Delhi – 110 002

ISBN 978-81-89766-60-3

First Edition 2006

Fourth Reprint 2020

MRP ₹ 499

Typeset by Vitasta Publishing Pvt. Ltd., New Delhi
Cover design by Prabha Singh

Contents

Preface

Eleanor Morton brought out her book *Women behind Mahatma Gandhi* in 1954, and since then there has been no book on the subject. Gandhiji's close association with women constitutes one of the most fascinating chapters of his life, especially as viewed through the spectrum of his philosophy of *brahmacharya* or celibacy. The present work is to be considered a biography within biography—of the man behind the man.

There were more than a dozen women who were closely associated with him at one time or the other. The saga of Kasturba constitutes a separate chapter in his life. She is the Mother Courage of the Gandhian era. These women must have been viewed by him as little replicas of his redoubtable mother Putlibai and his omniscient *ardhangini* Kasturbai.

Six of his women associates were of foreign origin and one of them was an NRI (Non-Resident Indian). Some of them like Millie Graham Polak, Nilla Cram Cook and Mirabehn could be an intellectual match for any woman of his times. They were daughters, sisters and mothers to him. Saraladevi Chowdharani, however, was an exception. He called her his 'spiritual wife'.

The theme of *Brahmacharya, Gandhiji and Women* is fascinating. The author's treatment of the book is based on his painstaking research over eight long years. *Collected Works* brought out by the Publications Division, Ministry of Information and Broadcasting, Government of India, New Delhi (in collaboration with Navajivan Trust), has been his Bible for this entire period and has been extensively quoted.

There is never a dull moment in reading Gandhiji. He is unpredictable, unorthodox, innovative, humane and brutally frank. Additionally, he puts on an impish though deceptive smile on his face. He had suffered resistance to his ideas all his life, especially from his inner quarters. His classic statement to Mrs Polak that she was born to suffer applied to him and to other women associated with him as well. He must have achieved inner peace through his own suffering.

Romain Rolland proclaimed him the second Christ. Just like Christ, Gandhiji's passion was also epitomised by his sufferings, death and resurrection. Equally, Passion Plays in their contemporary Indian context could be a rich raw material for our version of secular Passion Plays on the life and times of Gandhiji.

The book is primarily a celebration of womanhood as seen through his eyes. He was one of the very few to have decimated the line of demarcation between the sexes by daring to call himself a self-made eunuch.

Gandhiji was always relaxed in the company of women. They responded to him in an equal measure. *Brahmacharya, Gandhi and His Women Associates* is a faithful record of dialogues that took place for nearly five decades between him and a bevy of women who encompassed the entire range of *rasas* (human emotions) as depicted in the aesthetic tradition of India.

Girja Kumar

Acknowledgement

— Navajivan Trust, Ahmedabad and Publications Division, Ministry of Information and Broadcasting, Government of India, New Delhi.
— Nehru Memorial Museum and Library, New Delhi.
— National Archives of India, New Delhi.
— Gandhi Peace Foundation Library, New Delhi.
— Mr S K Bhatnagar, Librarian, Gandhi Samarak Granthalaya, New Delhi.
— To all authors who have been quoted in the present work.
— Mr S K Sharma of Teen Murti Library for providing an unending stream of references for the past eight years.
— Renu Kaul Verma, my publisher, for keeping me on 24-hour vigil to bring the book to its present shape.

SECTION I

Brahmacharya in Theory and Practice

CHAPTER 1

Ode to *Brahmacharya*

For Mohandas Karamchand Gandhi, the personal was not the political. At least, not in the same sense. Arguably, modern history's most extraordinary figure, a political leader who fired the imagination and stiffened the resolve of a poor, colonised society, Gandhiji's politics was, above all, about passion. But in his ideal of his personal life, and in how he wanted others to organise their lives, passion had no place.

What is remarkable about Mahatma is not so much the thesis—many, before and after him, have found virtue in abstinence—but his extraordinary efforts to obtain this ideal, efforts that, inevitably perhaps, produced contradictions, affected the lives of his closest associates and produced a vision, a passionless society, that looks curiously naïve, and not a little discomfiting, when compared with his still-inspiring political programme.

This forces us to ask certain questions. Did the man, who led a movement that brought political freedom for so many, go wrong on the issue of personal freedom? Do we need to re-evaluate Mahatma in this light? After all, given the importance he attached to restrictions on personal conduct, it would be illogical to ignore that aspect of Gandhiji's life and assess him on the basis of his politics only.

There isn't much in Indian historiography that deals with these issues. Whether this is because we tend to revere our icons or because, culturally, we are uncomfortable with public inquiry of personal details is not important. What is important is that our understanding of the greatest modern Indian will always remain incomplete if we do not read and understand what he himself said about the conflicts between mind and body.

Ironically, even though the Indian tendency is to shy away from this topic, Gandhiji was awe-inspiringly and fascinatingly frank about his struggles to banish passion.

Perfect *Brahmachari*

The Mahatma started practising *brahmacharya* in 1901. For him, *brahmacharya* was a wider concept than mere celibacy or continence. It constituted an entire philosophy and a moral imperative to be observed in thought, word and deed—a sure road to nirvana. Sexuality, in his world view, was to be banished to the nether regions for eternity. He took a vow of lifelong celibacy in 1906. From then till his death, his personal life was a mission and its goal was to become a perfect *brahmachari*. All through, he sought to explain his quest.

To his friend and benefactor GD Birla, Gandhiji had this to say: "Today I am a better *brahmachari* than I was in 1901. What my experiment has done is to make me firm in my *brahmacharya*. The experiment was designed to make myself a perfect *brahmachari* and if God so wills it will lead to perfection."[1]

Everyone should abjure passion, Gandhiji thought. His thesis of a passionless society was explained in a letter to his devoted follower Krishnachandra: "The idea is that a man, by becoming passionless, transforms himself into a woman, that is, he includes the woman into himself. The same is true of a passionless woman. If you visualise the state of passionlessness in your mind, you will understand what I say. It is a different story that we do not come across such men and women."[2] The primary discordant note in this abstinence-dictated harmony is, of course, that not even Gandhiji claimed to have reached that state.

Parade of Women

Historians are surprised to see that the man who abhorred bodily temptations was surrounded by women who constituted his entire world at one level. They walked in and out of his life. From his days in South Africa to the end of his life, he maintained close relations with them.

Millie Graham Polak was the first. She was a lady in every sense of the term. Gandhiji established complete rapport with her soon after she arrived in South Africa. Her husband Henry was also one of his closest friends. Sonja Schlesin was another woman from his South African days. She was the best secretary he ever had. She led from the front and was the only woman Gandhiji was afraid of. She was domineering, aggressive and opinionated but she delivered.

Two women entered his life after his return to India—Saraladevi Chowdharani and Madelene Slade from England. The former was a cultured and cultivated *bhadramahila* of Tagore lineage. She was Gandhiji's only true infatuation. In a rare confession recorded in his diary, he talked of "one exemption" to physical passion in his entire life. The tall Slade was a British Admiral's daughter whom Gandhiji re-christened Mirabehn. She was, as the irreverent modern expression would have it, obsessed with Gandhiji. Her whole life may be described as a pilgrimage in the cause of Mahatma. He teased her and played little games with her. In the end, she forsook him for Baba Prithvi Singh Azad, and later for Beethoven, her first true love.

There were three other western women who came in close contact with him but quickly left. The American Nilla Cram Cook was Mahatma's most vivacious woman associate. He was fond of calling her the 'fallen daughter'. She appeared and disappeared like a whirlwind. The German Jewish Margarete Spiegel was dull, boring and slow-witted but totally in awe of Gandhiji (and Tagore). Gandhiji was being gallant when he told her: "I shall love you in spite of your faults." The Danish missionary Esther Faering had an intense personal relationship with Gandhiji who treated her like his favourite daughter.

Gandhiji had high respect for Premabehn Kantak, Prabhavati and Rajkumari Amrit Kaur. Prema was known as the field marshal of the Gandhian army and was a true defender of faith. She often debated on *brahmacharya* with Gandhiji. Prabhavati, wife of a distinguished socialist leader Jayaprakash Narayan, practised *brahmacharya* even after marriage. She was the subject of discord between Gandhiji and JP. She was torn between two loyalties but ultimately preferred Gandhiji over her husband. Rajkumari Amrit Kaur, the Kapurthala princess, had also established a remarkable degree of rapport with her mentor.

There were several minor characters who survived a long association with Gandhiji. The "crazy daughter", Bibi Amutussalaam of Patiala, was asked to bring peace to riot-torn Sind. She was commissioned by her mentor to go to the riot-ridden region to bring about normalcy. She was, however, given to frequent bouts of depression. Gandhiji's ashram companion, Lilavati Asar, nicknamed "a limpet" by him, divided time between her studies and keeping her mentor company. Kanchan Shah, Mahatma's role model for practising *brahmacharya*, was as defiant as her husband Munnalal was submissive.

The younger women associates of Mahatma included Sushila Nayyar and Manubehn Gandhi. Sushila was his personal physician and in constant attendance. Sushila, her brother Pyarelal and Gandhiji constituted an "unstable triangle" with years of association dotted with prolonged periods of quarrels, recriminations and reconciliations as reflected in their correspondence. Manu Gandhi, the granddaughter of Mahatma's brother, was the youngest and most lovable of his woman associates. She was ready for the hard grind of *tapasya* throughout Gandhiji's sojourn in Noakhali. She was his closest associate during his last few years.

Above all others was the towering figure of Kasturba Gandhi, the 'mother courage'. Popularly known as 'Ba', she was the stabilising factor throughout Gandhiji's life. She was overwhelmed by his personality in the initial years of their relationship but gradually came into her own. She exercised subtle control over him at critical moments in his life. While the other women were sisters and daughters, Ba was his *dharmic* wife who subsequently substituted his mother. The most difficult years of Mahatma's life were after her death in 1944.

Women in *Brahmacharya* Experiment

In the 1920s, Gandhiji had started resting his hands on the shoulders of young women during his morning and evening walks. He affectionately referred to Manu Gandhi and other girls as his "walking sticks." The next step on the same road was his elaborate daily massage, performed by young women.

The massage was followed by bath with the presence of a woman attendant almost essential. Sushila Nayyar was the usual fixture on such occasions. She would take her bath at the same time. On such occasions, Gandhiji would keep his eyes closed to save him embarrassment. Gandhiji gave a graphic description of the bathing ritual after it gave rise to "bathing gossip" among the ashramites.

The next step on the road was the ritual of young women sleeping next to him, close to him or with him. What started as a mere sleeping arrangement became, over time, an exercise to obtain the nirvana state of perfect *brahmacharya*. Gandhiji was brutally truthful about his "experiment". He shared information with his closest associates, knowing fully well that the world would come to know about it.

Munnalal G Shah received a full confession of his experiments. An amazingly frank missive that Munnalal received, said: "I don't wish to exclude anybody. I have mentioned four.* Perhaps they will say, 'We were not objects of your experiment; we slept with you as with a mother.' I would not contradict them. It is enough here to mention that such a thing has happened. I don't consider Abha [Gandhi], Kanchan [Shah] and Vina [Patil] as part of the experiment. If we distinguish between sleeping together and the experiment, the difference between the two in my view is big one."

He went on to add: "Abha slept with me for hardly three nights. Kanchan slept one night only. Vina's sleeping with me might be called an accident. All that can be said is that she slept close to me. If Abha had continued, her case would have been an altogether different one. Kanchan's case was rather tragic. I didn't understand her at all. What Abha and Kanchan told me was this; that she had no intention whatever of observing *brahmacharya*, but wished to enjoy the pleasure of sex. She, therefore, stayed very reluctantly and undressed only for fear of hurting me. If I remembered rightly, she was not with me for even an hour. I then stopped both the women from sleeping with me, for I realised that Kanu [Gandhi] and you were upset. I myself advised them that they should tell you both and also Bhansali. You will thus see that these three names cannot be included in the experiment. Lilavati [Asar], Amutussalaam, Rajkumari [Amrit Kaur] and Prabhavati are not here. I have deliberately included Pra[bhavati] in the experiment. May be I should not. She often used to sleep with me to keep me warm even before I was conscious that I was making an experiment. I used to draw her to me when she lay on the floor shivering for my sake. This is an old, old story… Kanchan's labouring under a misunderstanding pained me, but I was helpless."[3]

The female partners in the Gandhian experiment were listless, disoriented and subservient. Gandhiji freely admitted to Krishnachandra on this score: "What I mean is that I have done naturally. Almost all of them would strip reluctantly. I have written—haven't I?—that they did so at my prompting. If I wish to be a *brahmachari* under all circumstances

---

* Rajkumari Amrit Kaur, Bibi Amutussalaam, Lilavati Asar and Prabhavati.

and want the women also to be such, this is the one way. Now leave this matter alone and watch what happens."[4]

Hostile and swift reactions followed from many quarters. Kanu Gandhi was upset because his wife Abha and his sister-in-law Vina Patel were reluctant participants in the experiment. So was Munnalal Shah because he did not want to be dragged into a controversy. Obviously, Gandhiji had a premonition of the events that followed. He sent two more letters to Munnalal on 6 and 7 March 1945. In the very first letter he asked him rhetorically: "What else may I give up? I cannot give up thinking. As far as possible I have postponed the practice of sleeping together. But it cannot be given up altogether."[5]

His humility was tempered with aggressiveness, with one following the other in cycle. In his very next letter to Munnalal, he dared those who disagreed with him to leave him. Similarly, he told Krishnachandra on 7 May 1945 that he would not bend beyond a limit to placate his friends. This would be like sacrificing principles for purely temporary tactical advantages.

Gandhiji could very well appreciate sensual matters. As C Rajagopalachari observed: "It is now said that he was born so holy that he had a natural bent for *brahmacharya* but actually he was highly sexed... Everything he achieved was through extraordinary self-discipline and renunciation."[6]

Joint Family Incorporated

Gandhiji had no daughter of his own. He had adopted a young harijan girl, Laxmi, as his daughter. She was, however, marginal to his existence and forgotten immediately after she was married off. The other women were far more important. They flattered him, laughed with him, cajoled him and endorsed every word he spoke. They were totally besotted by him.

They sought his attention all the time. He was definitely a father-figure to them. Possibly a few of them viewed him as a mystical lover. He was very informal and carried on voluminous correspondence with many of them. With a rare exception, all of them volunteered to live as spinsters and those who were married chose the path of physical *brahmacharya*, denying conjugal rights to their spouses.

Professor Nirmal Kumar Bose had watched Gandhiji from close quarters during his Noakhali days. He had a Freudian explanation to offer. The games young women played with Gandhiji were not so innocuous. They must have viewed him as an unstated 'object of love'. Professor Bose addressed his mentor directly on the subject and in most unambiguous terms: "When women love men in normal life, a part of their psychological hunger is satisfied by the pleasure which they derive in the physical field. But when women pay their homage of love to you, there can be no such satisfaction, with the result that when they come close to you personally, their mind becomes slightly warped."[7] In other words, he discovered a number of neurotic women surrounding Gandhiji. The common element that united them with him as well as divided them from the rest of the world was their neurosis. They shined in his reflected glory. No wonder, perhaps, they were forgotten soon after he died.

Charismatic Gandhi

Gandhiji, many thought, wasn't blessed with much physical appeal. But in the eyes of his female associates he exuded considerable charm. Perhaps his male companions failed to notice it.

When Millie Graham Polak met him for the first time, she thought Gandhiji's sensuous lips, probing eyes and his ramrod physical frame spoke of his unspoken sensuality. He laughed, joked and felt totally relaxed in the company of young females. The renowned feminist Margaret Sanger interviewed Gandhiji in 1936 and she said: "He has an unusual light that shines in his face, that circles around his head and neck like a mist with white sails of a ship coming through. It lasted only a few seconds but it is there."[8] It is interesting to note that his charisma was widely diffused. It rested not only in his eyes, but it was also ingrained in his ramrod body, his artful gait, his perpetual toothless smile and his gentle and meandering style of conversation.

Gandhiji was, what today would be described as 'compulsively tactile.' There is a mountain of Gandhian literature on the subject of touching or not touching women, or being touched or not being touched by them. The Hamletian situation of "to be or not to be" hounded him for decades. Professor Bhikhu Parekh has been perceptive enough to take note of his acute tactile faculty*: "Like most Indians, he was a highly

---

*This is a trait that he must have shared with another charismatic personality of modern India. Sri Ramakrishna Paramahansa was also given to touching his

tactile person and found physical touch irresistible. It is hard to find an informal picture of him in which his hand does not rest on someone's shoulder or he is not patting someone on the back."[9]

---

devotees and disciples. He provided a rationale for his tactile faculty. His touch had the magic quality of removing "impurities of the mind", with truth flashing and visions dawning with electrifying effect at the receiving end. On his second visit to Dakshineswar, Swami Vivekananda found the seer placing his right foot on Vivekananda's body in a flash. This magic touch was the beginning of a lasting bond between the two of them.

CHAPTER 2

Celibacy in the Indian Tradition

The endgame of Gandhiji's experiment was the abolition of the distinction between the male and female. His sleeping quarters were his laboratory. And he pleaded the cause of the unisex much before the term became popular or fashionable.

Ideal Eunuch

As early as 1914, in a letter to Raojibhai Patel, he had stated that killing the senses did not "do away with the impulses in the mind",[1] so much so that eunuchs are full of senses and therefore 'they have been known to be guilty of unnatural acts.' He was trying to be in line with the Indian tradition, best personified by the image of half-man and half-woman *Ardhanareswara,* carved in the niches of Hindu temples.

Gandhiji's inspiration came not only from Hindu traditions but also from Christianity and Islam: "There are many eunuchs, who were so born from the mother's womb, some were made so by men and some who made themselves so far for the Kingdom of Heaven." (*Bible*, *Matthew* 19 : 12). Similarly, he drew upon Islamic traditions. In a public address at Amishapara, during his Noakhali sojourn, Mahatma said: "The Prophet had discounted eunuchs who became such by an operation. But he welcomed eunuchs made such through prayer by God. His was that aspiration."[2] Thus, his ideal world was populated by 'natural' eunuchs. Indeed, the decimation of mankind was his road to *moksha* (liberation). After all, the state of nirvana means liberation from the cycle of multiple births.

Gandhiji had decided to wage a war against *Kama* (the God of desire). He hoped to succeed where others had failed. He was, however, a worthy combatant, who loved to put up a fight. It was a relentless fight and a costly one. After all, he was fighting against Nature.

War Against Senses

Gandhiji was always comfortable with women. But sensuality had no place in his worldview. The 'natural affinity' between men and women was to be limited to "the attraction between brother and sister, mother and son, or father and daughter." By 1926, he was confident enough to assert that: "If a Gandhi ... can today live as friend and brother to his wife and can look upon the fairest damsel as his sister or daughter, there is hope for the lowliest and the lost".[3]

Here is an example of Gandhiji in danger of losing the plot. His claim about "[this] natural attraction that sustains the world" begs the question: What about the natural affinity between man and woman (or husband and wife) that sustains the world both in metaphorical and physical terms? Rehana Tyabji once said that: "[Gandhiji] became my father, my mother, my girlfriend, my boyfriend, my daughter, my son, my teacher, my guru."[4] She came from the distinguished Tyabji family and was one of his most enthusiastic loyalists.

Ba was the earliest instrument in his experiments. In a letter to his son Manilal Gandhi, from Sabarmati Jail, the Mahatma had written: "If, at this moment, I get enamoured of [Kastur] Ba and indulge in sexual gratification, I would fall the very instant. My work would go to the dogs and I would lose in a twinkling all that power which would enable one to achieve *swaraj*. My relation with Ba is that of a brother and sister, and the fame I have is due to it."[5] Gandhiji considered it very important that he had restored Kasturba her autonomy of her body by giving "to her all her rights by dispossessing [himself] of all [his] so-called rights as her husband."[6] Doing this wasn't easy, though. Neither for him nor for others.

Collateral Damage

R P Parasuram, Gandhiji's secretary-cum-typist, quit on 1 January 1947 during the Mahatma's Noakhali sojourn. Parasuram's resignation letter was a handwritten 10-page long critique, with a 5-page long typed supplement. His limited expressive ability—Pidgin English—didn't detract him from the content.

Pyarelal was another strong sceptic. He asked Gandhiji whether the latter was seeking to emulate the ancient *rishi* Shukadeva, who was 'passionless' and abjured clothing. Pyarelal's description of quotidian Ashram life makes his disaffection clear: "There were no 'walls' in his (Gandhiji's) ashram, either at Sevagram or at Sabarmati. He had no 'private life'. His most intimate functions were not performed in privacy. Thus, he had his massage practically naked with young girls as his masseurs ... Similarly, while having hydropathic treatment, he allowed both men and women to assist him, and almost everybody had free access to him in his bath."[7]

Breaking Conventions

The Mahatma had an answer to that, however. You can't change conventions without breaking them, even though it is not always possible to avoid tactical errors in this struggle. In an interview given to his associates Swami Anand and Kedar Nath at Patna, on 15–16 March 1947, Gandhiji candidly admitted that he did not favour secrecy in his *brahmacharya* experiments. He, however, conceded that he should have avoided publicly speaking about women sharing his bed at the very initial stage of his experiment. When queried about his unorthodox practices, the Mahatma responded that without such initiative no progress was possible.

This is a thesis more common in western thought than oriental culture. It was no surprise, therefore, that Gandhiji looked up to the West for some inspiration. He was influenced, in particular, by thinker-philosopher Bertrand Russell's and psychologist Havelock Ellis' ideas. Especially, their faith "in the possibility and desirability of purity in life independently of ... institutions and usages."[8]

For this ideal, Gandhiji was ready to challenge taboos: "I can imagine circumstances when I may feel it my clear duty to go against the established rules. In such circumstance, I cannot allow myself to be bound down by any commitment whatsoever."[9] However, as was often the case in Gandhiji's experiment, contradictions emerged. Swami Anand and Kedar Nath, having been told of Western influences on the first day of their meeting with Gandhiji, were given this to contemplate over the next day: "I am as ancient as can be imagined and hope to remain so to the end of my life."[10]

Those near-irreconcilable statements made to his interviewers demonstrated an important fact: Gandhiji did have a personal philosophy of life but pragmatism was as important as ideology in his conduct. Indeed, pragmatism was his strongest point, as strong as his belief that he, and he alone, knew how to strive for the ideal; others like his associates, simply needed to follow. Gandhiji admonished his ashram manager Munnalal G Shah (the usual butt of his ire), who had asked him to consult his closest associates before taking any momentous decision: "If I consulted my friends in carrying out my experiments [in *brahmacharya*], it could not be said that they were undertaken with God's permission," and added, "More or less all my important experiments were single-handed and co-workers came in later."[11]

His pragmatism-laced ideology was formed largely by his early personal experience. He was, self-admittedly, obsessed with sex in the early years of his married life. The about turn came in 1886, with the death of his father. He was in his conjugal bed at the time of his father's demise. Thereafter, his antipathy to sex grew stronger. He warned his second son Manilal of finding "no happiness in marriage." "I cannot imagine a thing as ugly as the intercourse as a man and a woman," Mahatma once said.[12]

Impressions formed a large part of Gandhiji's views on *brahmacharya*. He visited the Trappist monastery near Pinetown in Natal in 1895. He was impressed with the spartan existence of Trappist monks in South Africa. Their vows of celibacy and silence left a lasting impression on his mind; they were the role models for him in communal living. He always regretted not transposing the strict discipline of the monastery in the Sabarmati Ashram.

Gandhiji claimed to have killed all his desires for worldly goods and personal gains. His ego beckoned him to new challenges. It was deeply ingrained in him as is in all charismatic personalities. He craved to be immortalised so that his name could be recorded on the sands of time. He greatly drew upon Indian tradition for his inspiration. His most favoured ideal was *Rishi* Shukadeva. Gandhiji wanted to emulate him and become a perfect *brahmachari*, even though he did not want to "go to the Himalayas as the *Rishi* did."[13]

His idealism was not shared by some of his influential associates like Kishorelal Mashruwala, Narahari Parekh, Kakasaheb Kalelkar and Swami

Anand. Even the saintliest of them all—Vinoba Bhave—differed with him on the subject. Vinoba had quit the editorial board of the *Harijan* group of newspapers along with three other editors. Independently, he made his disagreement public in his letter of 10 February 1947 to Gandhiji by pointing out: "any consciousness of the difference between man and woman was contrary to *brahmacharya.*"[14] It was his diplomatic way of telling his mentor that the very experiment of sleeping with Manu Gandhi rendered the concept of *brahmacharya* infructous.

Married *Brahmacharya*

Gandhiji sought to expand the parameters of *brahmacharya* by formulating the new concept of married *brahmacharya*. He had always been anxious to extend celibacy to the married life and had started practising it himself by 1906, i.e., after 23 years of 'marital bliss'. He actively worked to extend the scheme to the rest of the community.

Here he had a Christian sense of sin attributed to sex. He was flattered to find support from the unlikely quarters of the ancient lawgiver Manu, who had termed the first child as *dharmaja* (born out of duty), and the children born thereafter as *kamaja* (carnally born). He was happier still when he unearthed information from the *Smritis* in the cause of married *brahmacharya*. The new interpretation was that "married, who strictly observed the injunction of the *Smritis*, were as much *brahmacharis* as those who never married."[15]

Gandhi was so preoccupied with the concept of *brahmacharya* that he attributed all kinds of virtues to it. There seemed to be no life beyond *brahmacharya*. There was an element of exaggeration in his assertions on the subject. Obviously, he appeared to have had a guilt complex about his sexual proclivities during his younger days. He wanted to go to the other extreme, perhaps, through an act of expiation. He was bold enough to admit to the lacunae in him several times in his writings. In 1932, he confessed: "I do not claim to be a perfect *brahmachari* with 'evil thoughts' having been held in restraint, but not yet eradicated."[16]

Brahmacharya was, no doubt, his ideological weapon. In his framework, it was no longer limited to mere denial of sexuality. It had to be practised in thought, speech and action. Indeed, Gandhiji did not claim the status of a perfect *brahmachari* for himself. He had chosen to tread a lonely path. According to him, even the greatest of seers had transgressed the prescribed rules of the game: "It is like swallowing poison in imitation of Shiva, who [himself] strayed from the path, so we can succeed only *if we are unremittingly mindful of it.*"[17]

Didn't Gandhiji have his doubts about achieving perfect *brahmacharya*? After all, he was like any other human being burdened by doubts! He must have drawn some satisfaction from the story of Rishyashranga, a character portrayed in Valmiki's *Ramayana* (somewhat like Gandhi): "who feels joy in self-restraint, but will remain indifferent to them."[18] The young ascetic had never set eyes on a woman while leading an isolated life in his ashram. He was completely floored when he set his eyes on the first woman. The ancient parable has a contemporary implication about it. Was Gandhiji an amalgam of Shukadeva and Rishyashranga at the same time?

Inspiration from the Indian Tradition

Gandhiji's lifelong preoccupation with *brahmacharya* had turned into an obsession. There were striking ideological similarities between Sri Ramakrishna Paramahansa and the Mahatma. It has been said of Ramakrishna: "[His] entire spiritual discourse is a sermon about sex .... There is not only a deep preoccupation with sex, but the axiom of his sermons, reveals his obsession with what is called 'displaced sexuality.'"[19]

Ramakrishna and Gandhiji were one while accepting the improbability of banishing *kama* from their realm. Gandhiji often asserted that perfect *brahmacharis* existed only in imagination. He never claimed to be a perfect *brahmachari* himself. Ramakrishna admitted as much: "Ah, lust does not vanish till God is realised. So long as the body lasts, a little of it continues even after that realisation, but then it cannot raise its head. Do you think I am myself all together free from it?"[20]

Ramakrishna drew upon a long Vaishnav tradition in Bengal for inspiration and Saivite Sakta cult influences were predominant in his preoccupation with *Kali* worship. The Gandhi family had a Vaishnav background, but it was influenced by the Jaina tradition also, so prominent in the Gujarati ethos. Indeed, his two major formulations—*satyagraha* and *brahmacharya*—had a distinct Jaina influence on them.

Mothers and Sisters

Gandhiji had a great desire to be a woman. He told Manu Gandhi that he was a mother to her. Manu wrote a book titled, *Bapu: My Mother*,[21] on the subject. His cousin Maganlal Gandhi was his closest associate and when Maganlal died he received the greatest tribute for having 'widowed' Gandhiji after his demise.

The Polaks and Henry and Millie Graham, were closest to him in South Africa. Millie had the sharp instinct of a woman to note 'the love of many women for his womanliness'. Elaborating on the same theme, she attributed to Gandhiji all the qualities: "associated with women—great faith, great fortitude, great devotion, great patience, great tenderness and great sympathy."[22]

The vow of *brahmacharya* gave him a sense of freedom in transcending the sexes. However, the desire was more intense in case of Ramakrishna than in Gandhiji. Ramakrishna transcended male passion by assuming to be a female; he went to the extent of stimulating menstruation. His biographer has candidly admitted: "If a man can so inoculate himself with the idea that he is not a man but a woman as to be to all intents and purposes, a woman, that idea in turn may be made to give a way to a higher one—that there is neither man nor woman."[23]

Gandhiji saw in women his mother, sisters and daughters. While he saw his mother in his wife, he categorised his female associates as sisters and daughters. Ramakrishna saw the Supreme Mother in Goddess *Kali* and mothers in the entire womankind. The sceptics are bound to be cynical in viewing female veneration as nothing but an expression of male chauvinism. Women are venerated as mothers but they are feared as lovers. It is hard to ignore that mothers could be lovers in other situations.

Unfortunately, a veil of secrecy has been thrown on actual happenings. The diaries of Ramakrishna contain a meticulous record of his day-to-day doings but are off limits to discerning critics. Gandhiji was an open book with a difference. While he is on record about his *brahmacharya* experiments, he has withheld certain crucial facts, because he felt that the time was not yet ripe for making uninhibited confessions on the subject. Except for Abha Gandhi who conversed with Ved Mehta, other participants have remained silent on the subject.

Rajchandbhai

If there were striking similarities in the outlook of Gandhiji and Ramakrishna, they were merely coincidental. The greatest influence on Gandhiji was of Shrimad Rajchandra, popularly known as Kavi. His real name was Rajchandra Rajivbhai Mehta. By profession, he was a connoisseur of jewels and diamonds.

Gandhiji was fulsome in his praise of Kavi. He was the only one who could be described as Gandhiji's guru. Kavi greatly influenced Gandhiji during his early twenties though he was almost the same age as Gandhi. His father was a Vaishnavite and his mother a Jain and his family residence was next to a Jain monastery and a Vaishnav temple. Kavi was an amalgam of Jain and Vaishnav virtues.

Here was a marriage of Vaishnavite sensuality and Jaina denial, which equally characterised Gandhiji. He attributed the virtue of 'his living contact' to Kavi. His wide knowledge of the scriptures and his 'burning passion for self-realisation' had enabled him 'to see God face to face.' Gandhiji proclaimed that he was 'the living embodiment of the religion of compassion.' Like Gandhiji, he was unconventional in many matters. He asserted that: "If Jainism had not fallen into the hands of the Jains, it would have filled the world with the marvels of its truth."[24]

Gandhiji paid rich tribute to Rajchandbhai by acknowledging the influence he exercised over Gandhiji: "I have since met many a religious leader or teacher. I have tried to meet the heads of various faiths, and I must say that no one else has ever made on me the impression that Rajchandbhai did. His words went straight home to me... In my moments of spiritual crisis, therefore he was my refuge."[25]

As early as 1909, he was able to recall the great influence of Kavi on his thought processes. His book *Sandhya* became a *Bible* for Gandhi. It was Kavi who inspired him to take his vow of *brahmacharya* in 1906. His passion to see God face to face was transmitted to Gandhiji in his rigorous practice of *brahmacharya*.

Jain virtues of *brahmacharya* (purity), *ahimsa* (non-violence), *asteya* (non-stealing) and *aparigriha* (non-possession), therefore seem to have come directly from Kavi. It was also from Rajchandbhai that he learnt about passion stimulating properties of milk, because of which he forsook cow's milk for life. He talks of eschewing milk and *ghee* in 'the interest of self-assertment'. He believed it would subdue passion. It was at Ba's instance that he was persuaded to take at least goat's milk. He regretted the decision for the rest of his life. Similarly, Gandhiji was to build nine 'hedges' which turned into 'eleven disciplines' by 1947: Non-violence, truth, *brahmacharya*, non-possession, 'bread labour', palate control, fearlessness, religious tolerance, *swadeshi*, non-stealing and un-touchability removal.[26] Elsewhere, he placed *satyagraha* and *brahmacharya* on a high pedestal, with 'truth' being the primordial 'hedge'.

Women and Sexuality

The strand that held Ramakrishna, Rajchandbhai and Gandhiji together was their uncompromising concern about women as the embodiment of sexuality. Gandhiji was the mildest critic of them all. The other two seers suggested stringent indictment of sexuality as a whole.

Surely, God must have had the last laugh in this matter. That would not deflect Kavi, the ascetic, from prescribing hellfire for uprooting physical desire, the human body with its 'physical site of sex' and indeed, he thundered that it was: "a place which is not fit even for vomiting on. Whatever things are revolting in their nature, why, those are all present in her".[27] There is thus no hope of regeneration for those born of the womb: "Having come from that prison of infinite darkness, [the female body] weary of it, what prompts you to make friends with it yet again."[28]

It is, indeed, a declaration of war against womankind and God himself. Gandhiji was never able to resolve the dilemma in his mind. Sri Ramakrishna was no less compromising than Rajchandbhai: "But it is not so harmful for a wise man to have sex with his own wife. Discharge of the semen is just like ridding the body excreta—it's like going to the toilet, not to be remembered."[29]

The sculptures on the walls of the Belur temple in Karnataka made a lasting impression on Gandhiji's mind. It depicted lust or passion in the form of a scorpion, crafted in stone by master craftsmen of medieval India. The sensuous depiction of a scorpion stinging a woman was realistic and indeed: "its intensity had made her naked and thereafter lifting its tail and lying at the woman's feet in the pride of its victory, it smiled at her."[30] 'The scorpion of passion' was none other than the male of the species. Now, Gandhiji was in full flow, inspired as he was by the piece of art depicting a lowly scorpion. He went on to compare sexual desire with a scorpion: "One never knows when it will sting. It is *ananga* [without form]. So we cannot see it; we cannot catch it, even if we try."[31] He must have spoken from his personal experience. The elusiveness of sexual desire bothered him right from 1883 (the year of his marriage) to 1948 (the year of his demise). The battle waged against *kama* remained inconclusive for sixty-five long years.

Sexuality as a Roadblock

Essentially, Ramakrishna, Rajchandbhai and Gandhiji thought along the same wavelength. For them there was just a thin line of demarcation between women as mothers and as lovers.

For Rajchandbhai, sex was nothing short of disaster, being ugly, unhygienic and unaesthetic. For Gandhiji, sex was the main roadblock in the attainment of spiritual liberation. The state of nakedness seemed to unite Gandhiji with Ramakrishna. Both of them were barely clothed. Gandhiji used to walk about his living room in a state of complete nakedness. Like Ramakrishna, he viewed the state of nakedness as something natural to man, which helped him shed his inhibitions in matters relating to sex: "For Ramakrishna, nakedness was a natural expression of mystical state. It was not unusual for the Master, to go 'naked unconsciously and hold conversation with his devotees'.[32] When he lost consciousness 'his cloth, the only garment he had on, might drop off.'"[33]

In essence, all three of them were true representatives of the same strand of the Indian tradition. Gandhiji breathed, talked and practised *brahmacharya* for over four decades. However he never came around to defining the concept. His was a world populated by the male of the species. His women were passive spectators. His world view of *brahmacharya* was based on his laboratory experiments conducted in semi-secrecy and strictly on a person-to-person basis. It was essentially one man's obsession. To his credit, he had very unconventional views about *brahmacharya* with no sanction in either religious texts or social conventions.

The most comprehensive explanation ever, was provided by Gandhiji in his letter to Rajkumari Amrit Kaur. The apology offered to his close associate and sympathetic observer was in the nature of a personal testament rather than a straightforward definition; it mirrored the true state of his mind after his unhappy departure from Noakhali.

"One who never has any lustful intention, who by constant attendance upon God has become proof against conscious or unconscious omissions, who is capable of lying naked with naked women, however beautiful they may be, without being in any manner whatsoever sexually excited. Such a person should be incapable of lying, incapable of intending or doing harm to a single man or woman in the whole world, is free from anger and malice and detached in the sense of the *Bhagvad Gita*. Such a person is a full *brahmachari*."[34]

The practice of *brahmacharya* required the imposition of a set of rules and regulations. They were draconian in nature and were essentially do's and don'ts that he himself practiced before imposing them on the rest of the community. His associates hardly had any choice in the matter. Being married, it was easy for him to frame a set of rules for married couples. He redefined marital relations and reduced the importance of sex: "The true purpose of marriage should be and is intimate relationship and companionship between man and woman. There is in it no room for sexual satisfaction."[35]

These edicts could be traced as far back as 1928. His set of instructions had been raised to the level of 'marriage laws' by him. He advised married couples to sleep in separate beds and preferably in separate rooms. The set of 1928 regulations was supplemented by another set of regulations in 1935 wherein he recommended the break-up of marriages: "Even if either husband or wife desires their relations to be like those of a brother and sister but cannot live like that in the same house, it will be their *dharma* to separate." He further suggested an extreme proposition to a potential but harassed *brahmachari*, who was unable to segregate himself from his wife on account of having to live in a single room: "If you are living in only one room, you should go elsewhere or send away your wife or have a relative to sleep in the same room."[36]

Torture Chamber

Normal marital or conjugal relations were taboo in his eyes. All this was in the cause of retaining the life-giving bodily fluid, which was never to be used but retained for life for physical strength, health consideration and to subserve physical needs in the overriding practice of *brahmacharya*. Erik Erikson, the distinguished American psychiatrist, who interviewed him at length, charged him with sadistic tendencies: "Your sadism sometimes comes through in those utterances in which your revulsion against sensuality turns, for example, against women as a source of evil, against food intake as no better than defecation, and against milk as a dangerous substance."[37]

Such criticism did not bother Gandhiji. He was obsessed with *brahmacharya.* The disciplining of the palate through controlled food habits and thereby the preservation of "vital body fluid" was the road to *brahmacharya* and ultimate liberation for mankind. Even cow's milk became a casualty in the cause of *brahmacharya.*

Gandhiji talked of the so-called vital fluid that was God's gift, to be preserved, stored and retained under all circumstances.* This was the traditional Indian view that he adopted though medical theories completely contradicted it. Related to this obsession was his preoccupation with disciplining of the palate. He discovered a direct relation between food habits and *brahmacharya.* Fasting was an extreme measure that he advocated. A true *brahmachari* was expected not only to be moderate but abstemious while eating. He was always experimenting with his food habits. The poor but nutritious pumpkin was the most favourite dish served in the kitchens morning and evening, on all seven days of the week.

Gandhiji had started his experiments in South Africa. He would not take tea or coffee, but would allow Ba to have it. He also employed enema regularly for lightening the burdens of the palate not knowing that at the subconscious level, sensuality and enema have been related to sexual propensities by psychologists.

Sensuousness and Cow Milk

The most famous of his injunctions was against taking milk because of its sensuous potential. Millie Graham Polak, a close friend of his, whom he met during his stay at South Africa, mocked him for hitting out at cow's milk and asked him as to what did he think about milk flowing from the mother's breasts that sustains young babies? He would argue back and forth with Millie and tried his best to convince that milk stimulated 'the lower passion of man's nature.' She also shot back at her vitriolic best and said: "If that be so... then young children who are principally

---

*In his famous article "How did I begin it" on *brahmacharya*, published in *Harijan* of 2 June 1947, he went poetic in defence of 'the vital body fluid' by asserting: "who can measure the creative strength of such sublimation, one drop of which has the potentiality of bringing into being a human life?"

(Source: CW: 88: 2 June, 1947: 58).

fed on milk, would be nothing but horrible little brutes, and you do not certainly believe this to be the case."[38] The diffused sensitivity is a two-way traffic between the mother and the child. Gandhiji was right without knowing about it.

The apathy for cow's milk was a lifetime phenomenon. He also forsook buffalo's milk at about the same time. It was with great difficulty that Ba persuaded him to take goat's milk on the specious plea that the injunction by Kavi did not extend to it. He accepted the plea but regretted all his life that he had been tricked into a situation that was hard to defend. He continued to take goat's milk regularly. His hosts during his extensive tours, were greatly inconvenienced because they were expected to search for goat's milk for him.

As a practising *brahmachari*, he was greatly concerned about his palate pressuring involuntary discharges. He confessed experiencing involuntary discharges and 'dirty dreams' during 1927, 1936, 1938 and 1940 to his confidants Premabehn Kantak, Mirabehn and Amritlal T Nanavati. He was a worried man because he had involuntary discharges during his sixties and seventies. In admitting his culpability, he demonstrated a high degree of moral courage.

Such happenings naturally come to a normal and healthy human being. For Gandhiji, these were indications of defects in his *brahmacharya* practice. He would find faults where none existed. He fought against natural instincts all his life. If he was successful in his vigorous discipline of *brahmacharya* during working hours, there was no guarantee of impure thoughts invading the subconscious during his nocturnal hours.

He had found a direct connection between *brahmacharya*, food habits and involuntary discharges. He had assumed the functions of a self-proclaimed dietician. He made this clear in a letter to Harjivan Kotak: "*Vaids* say that even when impure thoughts are absent such discharges occur because of pressure in the bowels. But, instead of believing that, it helps us more to believe that they occur because of impure desires."[39]

Never pamper the palate! Avoid intoxicants and spices! Like a true Vaishnavite, he advised against the use of garlic and onions. Non-vegetarian food had been on his taboo list ever since he had savoured the taste of goat meat in the company of his Muslim friends. The liturgy of rules and regulations and of do's and don'ts from him kept imploding in gay abundance.

Public Openness

Brahmacharya is too sensitive a subject to be debated in the open, yet Gandhiji was at ease while doing this. Infact, he conducted himself too openly. There was no privacy worth the name. He slept either in the open or in the corridors, halls or rooms with doors open. He would be surrounded by a bevy of ashram women during his sleeping hours. They slept on cots next to him. Very often, they would sleep in the same bed to give warmth to his shivering body which was hardly clothed, save for a half dhoti which was his distinctive brand.

By no means should this experiment be considered maverick on his part. It was a part of his exploration in the cause of *brahmacharya*. In this brave new world, his experiments were meant to probe the limits to which a man could endeavour to intrude upon the domain of *Kama*. He had been raising the level of experimentation gradually. He was also in the process of exploring new ethics regarding the concept of *brahmacharya*. Absence of scriptural sanction for his unorthodox explorations did not deter him.

The last phase of his life, beginning late 1930s, was full of controversies. The *brahmacharya* practices were the talk of the town. The Indian press was full of gossip and critical references. Word spread fast across the oceans. A noted historian, Professor Edward Thompson, talked of malicious gossip about Gandhiji's so-called sensual adventures with women. The *Bombay Chronicle* published a report from its Allahabad office: "Startling revelations have come to light regarding what has been going round the House of Commons about Gandhiji. It is reported that Mr Edward Thompson, the noted British historian who visited Allahabad recently, threw some light on the curious mentality prevailing in England. Mr Thompson, who met political leaders here, is reported to have told them three things going around the House of Commons regarding Gandhiji." "...and there were various stories about Gandhiji's spiritual life, it being the impression that Gandhiji had ceased to be a saint."[40]

Much later, Koestler was to employ a witty phrase about Gandhiji having seduced many young ladies into chastity. Even he was not above sensation mongering: "On one of these occasions when British came to arrest him at night, they found the Mahatma in bed with a girl of eighteen. Unaware of the purely spiritual nature of the experiment, they made an indignant report, which the British authorities wisely kept secret."[41]

Mystical Experience

Even his closest associates were foxed. So much so that they began to have doubts about the efficacy of subverting sex through universalisation of *brahmacharya*. Vinoba Bhave, who was one of his closest associates, speculated: "Gandhiji was a great man; nevertheless, he had laid bare his mind in its fullness before the world. For his part, he had permitted no secrecy. Even so I must confess, the last chapter of his life, which I have called the '*Swargarohan Parva*', or the chapter of the 'Ascent to Heaven', remains a mystery to me. Indeed in my eyes, it stands equal to the last phase of *Krishna's Leela*. To unravel its mystery, it may be necessary for Gandhiji himself to be born again."[42]

In Saivite tradition, sex is considered a mystical experience. Some of the Saivite Sakta cult indulge in ritual sex. So is the tradition among the Vaishnavites. Radha and other *gopis* represent sensuality, but their love for Krishna is viewed as a mystical experience. Antithesis became thesis in case of Gandhiji. Indeed the denial of sex became his metaphor for realising the mystical experience. In one instance it was sensuality, and in the other its denial became the essence of the mystical experience.

Anti-Sexuality

There were several incidents in the life of Gandhiji that made him hostile to sex. Margaret Sanger interviewed him and immediately found herself in a titanic clash with him. She was sure that the sexual incident coinciding with the death of his father was "so shocking and self-blamed that he could never accept sex as anything good, clean or wholesome."[43] When she asked him whether he saw any difference between 'sex love' and 'sex lust', the answer was an instantaneous and emphatic 'no'.

Gandhiji outrightly rejected her formulation about two kinds of passions, one of man for woman and the other for God - which could be categorised as spiritual love? He asserted that his spiritual love for Kasturba began after he eschewed sexuality in 1906. He, however, rejected the Christian and Jaina practice of mortifying body. His object in practicing *brahmacharya* was limited to getting rid of sexuality for the sublimation of his personality.

A little known incident in 1907 strengthened his vow of *brahmacharya*. After his arrest on 30 November 1907, he was placed in Transvaal jail in the company of Kaffir and Chinese criminals. He spent horrifying nights with them. He underwent the mortification of watching a Chinese and a Kaffir 'uncovering each other's genitals' and "they played with each other sexually, and at least [on] one night Gandhiji had to stay awake the whole night to protect himself from homosexual rape."[44]

This must have been a contributory factor in his distress of sexual mating, human genitalia, physical passion and physical closeness of opposite sexes. It is, however, easier said than done. Passion was a subject that would not go out of his mind easily. He readily admitted to Rajkumari Amrit Kaur: "The sexual sense is the hardest to overcome in my case. It has been an incessant struggle. It is for me a miracle how I have survived it."[45]

It must be said to the credit of Gandhiji that there was nothing squeamish about him. He called a spade a spade. He talked freely of sexual passion, lust, animal desire and sexual congress without a whimper on his face. He found no virtue whatsoever in marital congress. It was in his opinion merely the harbinger of "momentary excitement and satisfaction", but resulted in physical exhaustion, spiritual disgust and dissatisfaction. He scoffed at the unnamed correspondent who had reminded him that man was essentially an artist and creator who liked to explore the subterranean nooks and corners of physical love: "I am not aware of any benefit, mental, spiritual, or physical out of sexual congress."[46]

The maximum he would concede in a man-woman relationship was "the state of married *brahmacharya*, the true purpose of marriage should be, and is, intimate friendship and companionship between man and woman" and in such a state of ideal being: "There is in it no room for sexual satisfaction."[47] He preferred an ideal relation of a sister and brother between husbands and wives and advocated this as the model. He was happiest when in a meeting at Colombo, Ba was mistaken for his mother.

The frank expressiveness about human genitalia could be distracting for a discerning observer. His writings of the thirties were full of livid expressions. In his view the practice of *brahmacharya* could become very easy, provided "the genital organs are not intended for self-gratification."[48] To his close ashram associate Premabehn Kantak he wrote about reducing the functions of genitalia to the bare minimum of excretion of human refuse. He decided to spread his message in the true missionary spirit.

Bombay Incident

After he had a stroke due to overwork, he was forced to move to Bombay. It was all play and no work. In his own words, it was the period of "my pampering the body with food while doing no work".[49] The result was described by him as a "wretched experience" with no parallel in his thirty-six years of attempting to practice *brahmacharya*. He wanted to confess in order to bring relief to himself. And, there he wrote *Nothing without grace*[50] published in the *Harijan* of 29 February 1936.

It raised the curiosity of ever-forthcoming Premabehn Kantak. He confessed to her that: "I had a discharge, but I was awake and the mind was under control."[51] He once again attributed the cause to "the pampering of body with food" and additionally to his enforced state of rest. Only a fortnight had passed before he began to have his self-doubts. He attributed it to residual sensuality resting in his mind.

A remarkable confession followed by which discussed a series of 'involuntary misadventures', termed by him as 'involuntarily discharges'. Again Premabehn prompted him and the result was his letter of 21 May 1936 to her: "You have put the question very well. You could have put it still more plainly, I have always had involuntary discharges. In South Africa they occurred at intervals of several years. I do not remember exactly. Here in India they have been of months. I have mentioned the fact of my getting discharges in a few articles of mine. If my *brahmacharya* had been completely free from discharges, I would have been able to place before the world very much more than I have succeeded in doing. But it seems practically impossible that a person who has indulged in sex gratification from the age of 15 to 30, may be with his own wife only, can, on taking a vow of *brahmacharya*, control the discharge of his vital fluid completely. One whose capacity for retention has progressively weakened from day to day for fifteen years cannot recover it fully all at once. Both his body and mind will have become too weak for that. I, therefore, consider myself a very imperfect *brahmachari*... The experience which tormented me in Bombay was a strange and painful one. All my discharges so far had occurred in dreams and they never troubled me. I could forget them. But the experience in Bombay occurred while I was fully awake and had a sudden desire for intercourse. I felt of course no urge to gratify the craving, there was no self-forgetfulness whatever. I was completely master of my body.

But despite my best efforts the organ remained aroused. This was an altogether strange and shameful experience. I have already explained the cause. As soon as that cause was removed the state of remaining aroused came to a stop, that is, during the waking state."[52]

The 1936 incident was not the end of the matter. Gandhiji had actually begun to doubt the efficacy of his *brahmacharya* experiments. There was another bombshell in store for him. He had an involuntary emission on 14 April 1938 also. He described his predicament to his long-time associate Amritlal T Nanavati: "I was slave of passion for thirty years and tried to satisfy it. Moreover, I recently discovered that I have not been able to subdue it all. I don't remember having had an emission while awake at any time during the last fifty years. I am not referring here to the emission in dreams or those brought on by desire. But I was in such a wretched and pitiable condition that in spite of my utmost efforts I could not stop the discharge though I was fully awake."[53]

He had no hesitation in admitting to Mirabehn: "The degrading, dirty, torturing experience of 14 April shook me to bits."[54]

The 'bad dream' of 14 April 1938, haunted him for long. For once, he had a "desire to see a woman" and also ejaculated in the process. He shared his innermost thoughts with Mirabehn: "I must not interrupt the [*brahmacharya*] experiment, but there is room for revision. My problem: 'Had the awful experience of the 14th anything to do with my contacts or has it another meaning?'"[55]

This led him to question his *brahmacharya* practices, albeit temporarily.

Triumph in Tragedy

Gandhiji's obsession with continence made him and celibacy interchangeable terms. He found virtue in continence which others were unable to see. He also propounded the thesis that morality, ethics and religion were interchangeable terms.

Nature meant ethics and morality. He denied the existence of any artistic design in Nature's construction. He was a part of the Indian mainstream and at the same time he was out of it. Though he was sure of himself, he had his doubts. Success made him too confident and failures unnerved him. In his letter to Rehana Tyabji, he confessed his self-doubts. When complimented by her on his achieving perfect *brahmacharya*, he confessed to her: "I am trying to lose that consciousness [about sex]. But

I have not lost it. Loss of that consciousness cannot be relative; it must be absolute." He threw his hands in despair by telling her: "I do not know any historical instance [of perfect *brahmacharya*]. It is difficult, I know, for history to record such instances."[56]

Gandhiji was functional on the frontiers of an uncharted territory* which were laced with land mines. He would not listen to his friends, associates and well-wishers. Trouble was in store for him as he experimented in sleeping with young ladies: "Sleeping together came with my taking up of *brahmacharya* or even before that can you understand it now."[57]

The year 1945 was the year of crisis for Gandhiji. The following two years were horrendous. He was forced into his shell, defending himself from all and sundry. None of his associates was prepared to stand by him. He told Mirabehn: "The way to truth is paved with skeletons over which we dare to walk."[57] In his last years of life he was treading the path full of 'thorns, stones and pitfalls'. To retreat did not match his determination to march ahead. Hence, he kept assuring himself: "We dare not turn back."

By 1947, Gandhiji was a lonely soul left to his own resources. It was like a Greek tragedy. He was cheating himself without realising it and all for the cause of *brahmacharya*. A stage came when he was all but disowned by his closest associates. J B Kripalani wrote to him about his practice of employing women as his subservient agents as means to service his ulterior purpose. Nirmal Kumar Bose had watched him from close quarters during his sojourn in Noakhali [1946–47]. He had no hesitation in being critical of him: "I felt it was subordinating a human being to a purpose not determined independently by the person concerned."[58]

In the end, nobody except him felt cheated.* While the world was lionising him for his epochal achievements, he was no more than an ageing lion licking his gnashing wounds without any succour in sight. He went on record about the agonising minutes and seconds of his life.

---

*He would never say die. His invincible faith in *brahmacharya* remained unshaken. His role model remained Shukhdeva, the son of legendary Vyasa of *Mahabharata* fame, who is considered an ideal *brahmachari* in Indian traditions. His *brahmacharya* was thus his road to turn into a eunuch not only as per Indian tradition but also as Described in *New Testament, St. Matthew, XIX,12.*

Source : CW:62: May 21,1936:429

The great man was like a sieve leaking all over, but it didn't help in rescuing his tortured soul. His own words were a testimony to his grief. While talking to a friend in 1946, he mentioned 'a nameless fear' that seized him and paralysed him completely. He found the pressures from his close associates too overwhelming. The inaudible whispers were turning into loud cacophony and reaching him in Noakhali. He would often wake up at night and see shadows lurking in his path. He saw falsehood enveloping him and, indeed, threatening to destroy him. Death seemed to be around the corner. So he wrote to a friend that he did not rule out Manu Gandhi and him being killed during sleep at the hands of a lurking assassin in Noakhali. Still he did not lose hope: "I would rather die, if need be, at the hands of an assassin. But I do not want to court [death] much less do I wish it."[59]

In its evolution over the years, *brahmacharya* had transformed itself from mere sleeping together to an experiment (or *prayog*) by 1945. By 1946–1947, it had reached the highest stage of *yajna* or *mahayajna* and the highest manifestation was to be observed during his Noakhali sojourn. His grandiose design of *brahmacharya* left him in lurch in the end. According to Vinoba Bhave, he was to be born again to fulfil his obligations to the cult of *brahmacharya*.

CHAPTER 3

Brahmacharya in Practice

To Gandhiji's critics, *brahmacharya* was not a philosophy of life but an obsession with women. Sceptics questioned his formulations about the special brand of celibacy: "An unmarried woman marries the whole world, makes herself a mother and a daughter to all people" and the sceptic in him added: "May be there has been no such unmarried woman."[1]

In practice, things did not work out the way he had envisaged. He persisted in the belief that such experiments involving one-to-one relationship needed to be conducted openly. Several inmates of the ashram told him that his practice was likely to set a bad precedent. But his constant refrain was that if the girls associated with him in his *brahmacharya* experiments consented, why should it bother others. It was with much reluctance that Gandhiji gave up his experiment for the first time in August 1932. It, however, didn't last. He resumed and stopped the practice repeatedly, in 1935, 1936, 1938, 1939, 1945 and 1947.

There is but a rare photograph of Gandhiji in a group when he is not in physical contact with another person. His daily ritual of morning and evening walks in brisk steps, while resting his hands on the shoulders of two young girls, was an unforgettable experience for his visitors. This was the first step in his practice of *brahmacharya*. The genesis of this practice may be traced back to 1891 when soon after his return from England, he took charge of the children of the family. He loved walking with them while resting his hands on their shoulders. It became a habit and persisted even after he returned from South Africa. This practice attracted criticism in the twenties: "I was unconscious of doing any wrong, so far as I can recollect, till some years ago at Sabarmati an inmate of the ashram told me that my practice, when extended to grown-up girls and women, offended the accepted notions of decency."[2]

Daughters and Physical Touch

Gandhi argued that all his women associates in the ashram were his adopted daughters: "I have never felt that I am committing the slightest wrong in putting my hands on the shoulders of girls, for I know that they are daughters to me... I have felt that through such intimacy I have entered their heart and that in consequence they have become purer in their feelings towards men."[3] But this logic had few takers and by the middle of August in 1928, he claimed that he had given up the practice. This was in deference to public criticism: "Putting one's hands on the shoulders of girls cannot be a matter of principle, and therefore as soon as the issue was raised... [I] gave up the practice."[4]

In 1932, Gandhiji resumed the practice. Protests followed immediately even from ashram inmates. So, there was another change of heart. In a letter to Premabehn Kantak, Gandhiji wrote: "I believe that I must stop taking the freedom which I do with the girls if that shocks the inmates of the Ashram. There is no reason which makes it a moral duty for me to take such freedom, nor my taking it violates morality."[5]

He would get back to the practice again and again. It was unusual of him to remind Premabehn Kantak in the same letter: "As long as the relations of men and women have not become natural in our society, one should certainly be careful in one's behaviour... One should not deliberately try to shock society, arguing that all conventional restrictions are bad."[6] By 1933, he had even begun to think of disbanding the ashram. After all, ashram inmates had hindered his *brahmacharya* practice. He admitted to Mirabehn that his experiment was disturbing because of its sheer novelty: "Mine is a novel experiment, dangerous and, it may be, even impossible of achieving."[7] He decided to turn his back on Sabarmati Ashram in March 1930, vowing not to return till India became independent.

Wall of Protection

Developments came to a head in 1935. Two of his associates visiting him at Wardha had warned him of setting a bad example. They saw the danger of others emulating the practice. He refused to see the virtue in their pleadings. However, he decided to appoint a two-man committee of ashram inmates to examine the whole issue. The inevitable came to pass. A young couple staying at the ashram began to employ the ungainly Indian-English expression, taking liberties. The incident set Gandhiji thinking and he decided to roll-back the experiment. On 12 September 1935, he made up his mind to build a fresh wall of protection around him: "Whilst I do not believe in a *brahmacharya* which ever requires a wall of protection against the touch of the opposite sex and will fail if exposed to the least temptation, I am not unaware of the dangers attendant upon the freedom I have taken."[8]

He decided to renounce the experiment to set an example for others: "Every act of mine is scrutinised by thousands of men and women, as I am conducting an experiment requiring ceaseless vigilance. I must avoid doing things which may require a reasoned defence."[9] The confession was published in his famous editorial entitled '*A Renunciation*' in the *Harijan* on 21 September 1935.

After the September 1935 incident, he had to go through a two-day 'searching interview' on the subject of *brahmacharya* with Margaret Sanger. They were a study in contrast. She responded to him with vigour and rebutted him on all points: "Yes, sex expression is a spiritual need and I claim that the quality of this expression is more important than the result, for the equality of the relationship is there regardless of results."[10] Gandhiji was so overwhelmed by the interview that he felt totally exhausted and had a major breakdown. He moved to Bombay for rest and recuperation. He wrote to Premabehn Kantak on 6 May 1936: "The truth is that my discontinuing the practice of resting my hands on the shoulders of girls has nothing to do with my sensual desire. It had its origin in my pampering the body with food while doing no work. I had a discharge, but I was awake and the mind was under control."[11] This came to be known as the Bombay Incident.

Ravana's Harem

The resistance to his practices had affected Gandhiji. To Mirabehn, he confided that he was in real trouble for attempting 'to climb craters in the moon.' His novel experiment had run aground. He sought the advice of Mirabehn about what to do next: "Should I deny myself the service rendered by Sushila? Should I refuse to have *malish* (massage) by Lilavati or Amutussalaam for instance? Or do you want to say that I should never lean on girls' shoulders?"[12] He took her advice seriously on another point: "About Lilavati [Asar] I cannot recall anything of what you say. But once I felt that I had put my arm around her neck. I asked her in the evening. She said she had no knowledge of any touch. Nevertheless, from that date I asked her to sleep at a proper distance."[13]

In his moments of despair he would turn to Rajkumari Amrit Kaur for advice. She belonged to the princely family of Kapurthala (a convert to Christianity)and had a special place in his scheme of things. She was always ready to listen to him whenever he ran into troubles. He would share his innermost thoughts with the Princess. He began to attribute his troubles to his 'lack of faith' in himself. The dissatisfaction that affected him was foreign to him. He was, however, sure of coming out of the well of despair: "Moodiness... creeps over me now and again. I suppress it by constant work... But I have not lost faith... If it is to be a new birth, a regeneration all around, it must be preceded by adequate travail."[14]

His long-time associate, Mirabehn, tried to be too realistic for his comfort. Her colourful imagery in depicting the association of Gandhiji with his women associates was attributed to her 'jealousy' as she had begun to feel friendless. She was jealous of Sushila, her brother Pyarelal and his secretary Mahadev because of their close association with Gandhiji. She even spread 'poison' about them. But Gandhiji had a soft corner for her. He pared a left-handed compliment to Mira: "Robbed of Mira's hysteria [her ideas] are sound."[15]

Gandhiji was instantly reminded of incidents in the *Ramayana*. It must have crossed his mind, if Mira was not placing him in the same class as Ravana in the harem? He would have a hearty laugh at his own expense: "Is not Mirabehn's description similar to that of Ravana's palace by Tulsidas? Ravana is lying unconscious and his numerous queens are reclining around him in various states of undress. I laughed and cried when I read it. How could I be affected in that way? Disregarding Mirabehn's exaggeration, I was affected by what remained in the letter and I wrote that I would change my practice. What if the suffering witnessed on the 14th [of April, 1938] was the result of these physical contacts."[16]

A careful reading of his letter indicates that Mira was not exaggerating. Her jealousy was one factor in the situation. But she was also speaking on behalf of the silent majority of ashramites who were concerned about the whole series of developments involving Gandhiji's proximity to a group of young girls and women. The group included Sushila Nayyar, Prabhavati, Rajkumari Amrit Kaur, Lilavati Asar, Bibi Amutussalaam and Premabehn Kantak among others. There was a virtual revolt in the making against him at the ashram.

To Ashram Inmates

Gandhiji's despondency soon returned due to unforeseen developments in the ashram. There was a churning discontent against him. He was forced to issue a public statement in the form of an *Ashram Note* on 2 June 1938. He signed an abject order of surrender, disowning all that he stood by in the past:

"… Yesterday it became clear to me as day that it had been wrong on my part to forbid my co-workers to avail themselves, during my lifetime, of the freedom I had given myself. I cannot understand how I could have put up with it all these years. I feel my action was impelled by vanity and jealousy…. My experiment was a violation of the established norms of *brahmacharya* ."[17]

Never had such an apology been extracted from him during his public career. Obviously, there were signs of open revolt in the Seagaon Ashram. Now, he was prepared to listen to Rajkumari Amrit Kaur on the subject: "You are again right in saying that even a woman's proximity, speech, look, letter, etc., may work the evil as her touch might. But I had to think of myself. If I scented danger then I might put out my eyes, rather than have the animal in me aroused."[18]

This was short-lived and soon he went back to his practice. He even tried to wriggle out of his 1935 vow, explained in the famous editorial *A Renunciation.* In his letter of 11 June 1938 to his close associate Balvantsinha, he asserted that he did not find anything wrong in placing hands on the shoulders of women. He resumed the practice effortlessly. He continued to maintain that Sushila Nayyar and Ba were exceptions to the general rule, all in a good cause and in deference to their hurt feelings. Indeed, his discontinuation of the practice had caused Ba 'much pain'. He tried to discontinue taking personal service from Sushila, but resumed it due to her supplications. All this reversal occurred after discussions with the girls and 'after some laughter and some cajoling'.

Balvantsinha's sceptical nature forced Gandhiji to send a detailed response: "Once I intended to give up all personal services from Sushila but within twelve hours, my soft-heartedness put an end to the intention. I could not bear the tears of Sushila and the fainting away of Prabhavati… Sushila has been present in the bathroom while I have bathed in the nude and in her absence Ba or Prabhavati or Lilavati [Asar] have attended on me. But I see nothing wrong in it. It was necessary for someone to be there. I could call a male co-worker, too. Pyarelal has been in attendance occasionally but I have never felt any embarrassment in being seen naked by a woman whose relations with me cannot come under any kind of suspicion."[19]

All the same, the protests lodged with him yielded results. He promised not to take the support of girls during his walks. He also vowed not to have any contact with grown-up girls except for personal services rendered to him by Sushila Nayyar and his wife. The new experiment had started on 2 July 1938: "But it is only the beginning as yet. The ship has set sail and is slowly leaving port."[20] He, however, confessed to Chhaganlal Joshi of difficulty in sailing in different kinds of weather, used as he was to favourable conditions.

Amrit Kaur's Advisory

There are limits to human patience and Rajkumari was no exception to the rule. She had a feeling that the troubles of her mentor were of his own creation. He had, indeed, gone too far in his person-to-person physical contacts. The change in the attitude of Amrit Kaur irritated him to no end. She was asked to shut up and not bother him over the subject again. He went on the offensive but pardoned her for her 'folly' in rendering unsolicited advice to him. As a clever ploy, he overwhelmed her with his tyranny of love: "[Love] is little worth if it cannot stand the heart pourings of loved ones."[21]

He was back to square one in his dealings with the Princess from Kapurthala for the simple reason that she, like Mirabehn, was employed as a mere sounding board for his *brahmacharya* practice. He decided to share his troubles with her in his letter of 25 June 1938. He had stopped all physical contact with his woman associates forthwith, but for the exception of Sushila Nayyar who had become an expert masseur by that time. His critics would have none of it. He had to forego the services of Sushila also but he intended to resume them at a later date. He tried to justify his reversal to Amrit Kaur: "A new phase had commenced in my search. I do not know where it will end."[22]

For Amrit Kaur, he took a different line: "My misery is superficial if there is any yet left. My peace cannot be permanently taken away by anything or anybody. You simply do not know me if you think that my experiences have undone me."[23]

But the reality was different. Chhaganlal Joshi, for one, was not impressed. He was a Gandhian with a difference who did not hesitate to oppose him and be counted. He reminded Gandhiji about the conclaves at Sabarmati Ashram and Wardha. Obviously, his reading of the Sabarmati Ashram conclave was quite contrary to the interpretation put forward by Gandhiji. Chhaganlal believed that the first meeting had opposed the principle behind *brahmacharya* as practiced by Gandhiji.

Chhaganlal Joshi's Offensive

Gandhiji sidestepped on the issue raised by sceptical Chagganlal Joshi as a diversionary tactic and confessed his Himalayan error of denying the privilege to other ashramites. Chagganlal once again reminded him of his public undertaking of keeping away from women. He, however, persisted: "My memory is that I had decided to maintain the *status quo*."[24] Since Sevagram was presumed to be a community of the like-minded, he should have consulted the ashramites before pronouncing his *ex cathedra* judgment (which had kept changing with the direction of wind on moment-to-moment basis).

One incident highlights the twists and turns of Gandhiji's experiments. The women of the ashram usually walked in a single file. Once, they called on his hut and took him along. Gandhiji described the scene thus: "I walked with my hands on their shoulders by turn. This was observed by some people and became the subject of comment… It was not in my mind at all that I would never place my hands even on the shoulders of girls who live with me, for after writing that article I continued to use Manu and other girls as my walking sticks. But that procession stopped, and the practice has not been revived and will not be revived."[25]

Not many of Gandhiji's male associates (who actually mattered) were ever convinced of the correctness of the *brahmacharya* practice. Gandhiji argued with Munnalal Shah when he expressed his doubts: "Is there danger of my being pierced with Cupid's arrows in my letting myself be massaged naked, or in a thousand naked women bathing by my side when I am blind? I do feel afraid of myself in letting the pure-minded Sushilabehn massage me."[26]

Critical Jivraj Mehta

The subtle criticism of his *brahmacharya* experiments had affected him adversely. He confessed to 'an inner longing for loneliness'. He turned into a recluse and no longer argued with his associates. He confessed to his besieged mentality in his *Ashram Note* of 24 May 1940: "Owing to certain irritations, big and small, I have entered on a period of silence today. The silence will continue indefinitely ..... At present there can be one *sadhana* for me. For this silence is essential."[27]

Gandhiji was also assailed by his personal physician Dr Jivraj N Mehta. His light banter about the experiments pained him greatly. The problem compounded when some Marathi newspaper published disparaging comments. Gandhiji told Dr Mehta: "My life is an open book. I have never had any secrets, so you can ask me about anything you wish to."[28] He was extremely unhappy that Lilavati Asar, who was the centre of controversy this time, did not defend him: "Why did you take quietly what Dr Mehta told you?.... You could have asked whether a daughter sleeping by the side of her father and girls in an institution falling on one another are the same thing. I think your keeping quiet itself implies your admission of guilt."[29]

Barely a week had passed when they made up with each other and it was business as usual. There was a stream of childlike queries to be answered. "Would you object if I had a massage in the nude at the hands of a man? Do you believe that it is injurious to health if people slept side by side even in the open air? Please examine this question independently of the supposed impropriety of a woman sleeping by the side of a man."[30]

The competition to serve him resulted in bad blood between the young ladies. Lilavati Asar and Amutussalaam were on a warpath against Sushila, the current Queen Bee. Lilavati kicked up a row. Gandhiji was left with no choice but to post an angry epistle to Lilavati: "I have noticed that you and Amutussalaam cannot tolerate S [Sushila] sleeping with me. Whatever may be the cause, I do not want to carry on my experiment by displeasing you two. I, therefore, want to tell both of you that I have discontinued my experiment for the present. The fault is not yours. I believe it is entirely mine."[31]

Sardar Patel

By January 1939, Gandhiji had been compelled to stop taking service from his women associates. This made the affected females including Lilavati [Asar] and Amutussalaam, unhappy. Prabhavati Jayaprakash Narayan, who had recently returned to the ashram, also felt disoriented. Sushila Nayyar had, however, continued in her service during his illness in her capacity as his doctor. He felt guilty of singling her out and began to think of dispensing with her services too.

On 2 February 1939, he issued his latest *obiter dicta* ordering the girls to spread their beds at a respectable distance from him. There is a graphic description of the night scene at the ashram in his letter to Sardar Patel: "This is to tell you that as from today, I have been compelled to stop taking service from girls. Lilavati [Asar], A. S. [Amutussalaam] have certainly not liked it. Sharda [G Chokhawala] and Vijaya [Pancholi] have not liked it either... Prabhavati came yesterday. She may be doing something or the other but even she is looking on in silence. Sushila [Nayyar] is continuing to serve. She has not the heart to stop doing it. While I am ill... As from yesterday, I have stopped sleeping close to them. That is, the girls sleep far enough to be out of reach of my arms. Sushila [Nayyar] hardly slept near me. Now no girl or man sleeps close to me. Sushila spreads her bed perpendicularly at my head. So does Rajkumari [Amrit Kaur] near my feet. I am not at all sorry about these changes... I say 'may be' because that is not the impression I get. It is my way to abandon things for the sake of my colleagues. I like to make such sacrifices, because thereby I can know myself better."[32]

Questions Unanswered

Gandhiji, however, found sympathetic audience among women. His charisma worked with them in all situations. Ba, Sushila Gandhi (his daughter-in-law) and Manu Gandhi (Harilal's daughter) never raised their voice. He told Sushila, wife of his son Manilal: "All of you can say so long as Bapu is not free from passion, let him be served only by Sushila and Ba? Or you can say: 'When he puts the burden on us, we do wish that he would let us touch him. What effect can his passion have on us? Either stand can be justified. The first is safer from all points of view.'"[33]

At another level, all these queries were relevant because those concerned his person. The seemingly innocuous questions were relevant to his ongoing *brahmacharya* experiments. For once, life was so peaceful that bliss was around the corner. He was happy to report to Rajkumari Amrit Kaur: "I have now come back [to Sevagram] and you will occupy your usual corner.... Amutussalaam sleeps by my side, fans me and covers me when I need more covering."[34]

Heaven had practically been established on earth but only for a fleeting moment. He was to inform Amrit Kaur from distant Peshawar (now in Pakistan) about his decision to discontinue his experiments in response to public pressure. He had also issued an *Ashram Note* but the fact remained that his practice had to be discontinued under public pressure. The larger questions remained unanswered. Why was it necessary for Gandhiji to be in physical touch with his women associates? Why did he have to be massaged by them fully stripped? Why did he have a woman present when he took his bath? Was the laudable concept of *brahmacharya* so fragile that Gandhiji had to resort to laboratory experiments?

His practice of physical contact had, in fact, become his second nature. Gandhiji's motto was 'never say die', as seen in his note of 19 September 1938 intended for his ashram associates: "The stopping of the experiment does not mean that things will go on the way they did before. I cannot say that I shall remove myself somewhere...This, however, I can say that I will not deliberately renounce the service of the few sisters in the ashram, sisters who are close to me. I shall take from them the service I require. I had never renounced such physical contact with them as I consider necessary for taking service from them. My practice of resting my hands on their shoulders will continue as before. The restriction that I had been observing during the period of experiment will be slackened."[35] Obviously, the change promised by Gandhiji was not intended to be substantive.

A conspiratorial silence prevailed over his *brahmacharya* experiments conducted at Sevagram ashram and subsequently during his Noakhali sojourn termed as *mahayajna*. He would not talk specifically but would give vague hints. He did not consider the time ripe for public disclosure. Manu Gandhi agreed to provide details to Professor Nirmal Kumar Bose that were never put on record. Abha Gandhi talked to author Ved Mehta with some hesitation. She told him that: "It was common knowledge that Sushila Nayyar slept next to him."[36]

When did it translate into common parlance? The precise dates have not been mentioned. Whether it was sleeping with him or participation in the *brahmacharya* experiments, it was not clear from the statement of Abha. Ved Mehta also talked to Sushila. Her version of the event makes a very interesting reading: "But long before Manu [Gandhi] came into picture, I used to sleep with him, just as I would with my mother. He might say, 'My back aches. Put some pressure on it'. So I might put some pressure on it or lie down on his back and he might just go to sleep. In the early days, there was no question of calling this a *brahmacharya* experiment. It was just part of the nature cure. Later on, when people started asking questions about his physical contact with women—with Manu [Gandhi], with Abha [Gandhi], with me, the idea of *brahmacharya* experiments was developed."[37]

Parivar's Revolt

Enough was enough. Eventually, Abha's husband Kanu Gandhi had to intervene. Kanu, Munnalal Shah and others volunteered to warm up his cold body whenever required. Vinoba Bhave had the last word on the subject. In case Gandhiji was a perfect *brahmachari*, he did not require his credentials to be tested. And if he was an imperfect *brahmachari*, he should have avoided the experiment like the plague. He said it all in his letter dated 25 February 1947 to Gandhiji.

The entire Gandhian *parivar* was in turmoil. His closest associates like Kishorelal Mashruwala, Vinoba Bhave, Kaka Kalelkar and Narahari Parekh resigned in protest from the editorial board of *Harijan*. Vallabhbhai Patel termed his *brahmacharya mahayajna* as '*adharma*'. Kaka Kalelkar had to rush to Noakhali to dissuade him from proceeding any further in his experiments. Acharya Kriplani, Jayaprakash Narayan, Jivraj Mehta and Nirmal Kumar Bose had also recorded their dissent. His personal secretary, RP Parasuram even quit in protest. Mirabehn, Rajkumari Amrit Kaur, Premabehn Kantak and Chhaganlal Joshi tried to persuade him to abandon his chosen path. The silent majority of dedicated workers were publicly humiliated, while others like Munnalal Shah were stunned into silence. His charisma was no longer working. His only support base was found among young ladies like Lilavati Asar, Sushila Nayyar, Bibi Amutussalaam, Prabhavati and Manu Gandhi, who were already sold on him but the support of the young brigade did not amount to much.

Jawaharlal Nehru was the diplomat of the Gandhian *parivar* who said very little on this subject.

Sabarmati was no longer a home away from home for Gandhiji. The grand experience had virtually collapsed. As early as 1937, he confided in Munnalal Shah that Segaon had become a *dharamshala*. I still hoped to cultivate 'a family spirit in Segaon.'[38] The situation had become anarchic in the meanwhile. His second son Manilal did not find any resemblance whatsoever between the Phoenix and Sevagram experiments. Gandhiji had lost hope in retrieving the situation. He compared his ashram with '*Shamboomela*' (Shiva's Festival) for its anarchic character, being inhabited by "all types of curious and abnormal persons who would ordinarily be regarded as 'cranks' in society."[39] Thus his 'laboratory for *ahimsa*' had turned into a '*dharamshala*', a '*shamboomela*' and 'the home for invalids'.

He wanted to close the shop and run away from Sevagram. After being released from the Aga Palace (Poona) internment camp on 6 May 1944, Gandhiji confided in Mirabehn in utter desperation that he had 'experienced such disappointments regarding the Ashram'[40] and to Kishorelal Mashruwala, he said: "Heaven only knows where I am going to be flung again. No, my safety lies in praying and waiting 'Lead Thou me.'"[41] He must have been reminded of his balmy days at Tolstoy, Phoenix and Sabarmati Ashrams.* He requested Kishorelal to work out plans of setting up a 'brotherhood' as a substitute for Sevagram.

Destroying History

Gandhiji bemoaned the decline in standards maintained by the ashramites at Sevagram, but he refused to introspect his own actions.

---

*Tolstoy settlement (1910–13) located in his friend Kallenbach's estate was his pioneering effort, followed by the establishment of Phoenix Farm (1910-14) and was the hub of his activities until his departure for India in 1914. It faded away gradually until it was forcibly taken over by the marauding African mobs during 1985. The Satyagraha Ashram (1915–33) was established by him in Kochrab village near Ahmedabad after his return to India. He subsequently moved to Sabarmati Ashram (1917–33) established on the banks of Sabarmati river again near Ahmedabad. He was not to settle down at Sabarmati Ashram after 1930. His last ashram was established at Seagaon village near Wardha (Maharasthara) and came to be known as Sevagram Ashram.

The trouble at Sevagram was largely attributed to public dissonance expressed by ashramites on account of his *brahmacharya* experiments. Professor Nirmal Kumar Bose discovered the truth about developments two years after Gandhiji passed away. He raised a query on the subject in his letter dated 20 March 1950 to Kishorelal G Mashruwala. The questions were direct and brutal: "Would you kindly enlighten me on the following questions: (1) Is it a fact that [sometime] back, there was an apprehended breach of peace in the Sevagram Ashram because some members objected to a practice of Gandhiji which he described as an experiment in *brahmacharya*? Is it also a fact that the breach was tidied over when Gandhiji, in deference to the opinion of the inmates, agreed no longer to allow any of the women members to sleep in his bed? What was the approximate data of this crisis in Sevagram? (2) Is it a fact that you objected to his allowing Manu Gandhi to sleep in his bed, as it was a breach of what he had agreed in Sevagram". Relentless in his attempt to corner Mashruwala, Professor Bose was ready with another query: "Do you remember that in one of your Gujarati letters to Gandhiji, you expressed the opinion that the practice of leaning upon girls while walking or the giving of permission to them to use the same bed with him, sprang from a residuum sensuality which lay unborn in the depth of Gandhiji's being?"[42]

Mashruwala in his reply denied any knowledge whatsoever. Professor Bose was not convinced. It disturbed him that valuable documentation had been destroyed, thus denying accurate knowledge to contemporary and future students of historical research. In another epistle on this subject to Mashruwala on 31 March 1951, Professor Bose persisted: "But can you enlighten me on the reason why some of Gandhiji's letters or writings have been actually destroyed [at Sevagram]... I had that from Kaka Kalelkar when he came to Calcutta."[43]

Gandhian-Style Censorship

The war Professor Bose had waged against the Gandhian establishment passed through a series of skirmishes and mock battles without achieving any results. Professor Bose made life miserable for the likes of Mashruwala. Professor Bose and Mashruwala were friends of long standing but now they were combatants confronting each other. Mashruwala made lame excuses. On 3 April 1951, he wrote to Professor Bose: "What I must have send [to Kaka Kalelkar] is the papers belonging to Gandhiji have not been destroyed with or to my knowledge. What I must have said that the correspondence between Gandhiji and me on a particular subject referred to by you, I had no intention of being made available to the public and I had decided to destroy. I might have also said that my colleagues in that particular matter were also of the same opinion and they had, according to my information, destroyed their copies of such correspondence."[44]

Among all his political colleagues, Jawaharlal Nehru was his closest. He had kept himself clear from controversies arising out of *brahmacharya* experiments. Not a word has been breathed by him about the Noakhali controversies in his voluminous writings. He remained the master of generalities. There was, however, a gem of statement made by him on 30 April 1935 in his *Prison Diary* from jail which hit the bird's eye and characterised Bapu sharply: "Even Bapu, he is either a non-corporator or a full-blood corporator… He can think only in extremes-either extreme eroticism or asceticism. Was it not Aldous Huxley who said that the ascetic was the counterpart of Don Juan."[45]

Jawaharlal Nehru quotes Aldous Huxley approvingly in the footnote: "The professional Don Juan destroys his spirit as fatally as does the professional ascetic, whose looking image he is"[46] (*Essays on One and Many: Do what you will*). Jawaharlal seems to have said a great deal while saying so little about his mentor's practice of *brahmacharya*.

SECTION II

Mother Courage

CHAPTER 4

Ba

Contrary to the popular perception of an idyllic, out-of-ordinary couple, the Gandhis were like any other middle-class married unit in India. Their 62 years together witnessed the usual ups and downs. The early years were full of tension, conflict, misunderstanding and near break-ups. Their public persona as a loving couple was certainly true but only towards the last leg of their married life.

From the very beginning of their marriage, Ba realised the futility of confronting her irascible husband. This was the harsh reality of living under the shadow of a charismatic leader. Little Moniya* developed from young Mohandas into Gandhiji and then finally into Mahatma. Kasturbai Kapadia also experienced similar tribulations to become Ba from Kasturba.

This remarkable relationship began with priests and astrologers. These agents of the divine came calling to the sumptuous abode of her grandfather Gokuldas Nanakji at Porbander. The visitors were from Rajkot and their mission was to negotiate the engagement of seven-year-old Mohandas Karamchand Gandhi with Gopaldas Nanakji's daughter, Kasturbai, also, then, all of seven. The two children were completely unaware of the momentous event. Mohandas, as western superstition would have had it, was due to be third-time lucky. Two earlier engagements had fallen through; the putative child brides had died. He

*The pet name of M K Gandhi.

**Her maiden name was Kasturbai Kapadia and not Kasturbai Nanakji as popularly ascribed to her.

had just a vague notion about the earlier engagements because he came to know of them afterwards only.

The Gandhis (for three generations Gandhi's had been chief ministers of the royal Porbander state) and the Kapadias had known each other for long. The understanding was reached in no time and it was decided that the two would be married off after six years of engagement. The two 13-year-olds getting married, as Gandhiji described it himself, were 'two innocent children' being thrust into 'the ocean of life.'

Kasturbai was bold, unafraid and too dynamic for a young girl of her times. Eleanor Morton watched her from close quarters, and remarked: "She was vividly, and buoyantly alive; she was swift and sturdy as a boy,"[1] "but with instinctive reticence." Several others including her grandson Arun Gandhi describe her as 'fearless', 'free', 'proud', 'defiant' and somewhat 'self-willed'.[2] She was more comfortable with other female members of the Gandhian household than her newly-wed husband. Her subtle resistance to what she considered inappropriate was reflected during the six decades she spent with the Mahatma. He could bend her but never break her.

Beautiful Kasturbai

Kasturba's attributes of heart and mind were complemented by her physical charm and dignity. Even though she was small in stature, she possessed the delicate features of a classic Indian beauty: "satiny black hair, delicately featured framed nose and immense eyes in a quiet lovely willful face." Not content with this poetic description, Eleanor Morton added more encomia on the basis of third-party assessments: "Mutual friends could attest to the perfection of Kasturba's little body, to her unblemished flower-like skin, sweet breath, and luxuriant tresses, all obligatory female attributes. It was plain she was destined to grow into a great beauty."[3] The engagement formalised the relation between the power and prestige of the Gandhis and the wealth of the Nanakjis.

Reluctant Moniya was prevailed upon by his father Kaba Gandhi to marry. His marriage was solemnised along with that of his elder brother, Karsandas, 16, and his uncle Tulsidas' 17-year-old son, Motilal. The sister-in-law was assigned the duty of explaining the birds and bees, but the lessons ended in a farce. Gandhiji was listening but not comprehending, and, finally, in desperation, the poor sister-in-law left little Moniya to his own resources. When confronting his bride,* the confidence of the reluctant bridegroom returned and indeed: "all his misgivings about his physical appearance fell away. He saw himself tall, strong and handsome."[4]

Transformation in South Africa

The Gandhis married in 1883. Harilal was born in 1884. Gandhiji set sail for United Kingdom in 1888 and returned as barrister-at-law in 1891. His foreign education was made possible because of Kasturba who sold her dowry assets. In 1892, they had their second son Manilal. The period that lapsed between 30 April 1893, when Gandhiji left for South Africa to practice law, and 9 January 1915, when he landed in Bombay, was the most formative phase of his life. The years in South Africa were crucial for Kasturba as well. They transformed her into the consort of Mahatma. At a farewell function in South Africa, organised in July 1914 in his

---

*The Gandhis were a normal newly-married traditional couple who were trying to come to terms with their lives. Unfortunately, many of their biographers have wrongly juxtaposed them as dialectical beings. The myth of the contrasting couple has been perpetuated by none other than Gandhiji himself. His guilt complex about sex is repeated like a musical refrain in the pages of his *Autobiography*, in expressions such as 'devoted to the passion that flesh is heir to'(p.18), 'centered on one woman' (p. 10), and 'lustful love' (p. 10). Actually it is no big deal. Here is a pure and simple act of post-justification of self-flagellation. Kasturba's grandson Arun Gandhi like many other biographers, the general impression of Gandhiji's highhandedness.

> "By actions and not words, she was making it clear to Mohan how much she objected to his high handedness" (p.18);
>
> "....Mohandas had changed. He had become another person : 'disagreeable and unreasonable'" (p.19);
>
> "How could she make him to understand that she had her own life to live" (p.19);
>
> "a passionate and unbearably possessive young man
>
> " (pp. 67–68).

Source: Gandhi, Arun and S . *The forgotten woman: The untold story of Kasturba; Wife of Mahatma Gandhi.*

honour, he was addressed as Mahatma. Rabindranath Tagore put the stamp of approval on the sobriquet subsequently.

The transformation, however, came with a price. Ba and her four sons became guinea pigs in Mahatma's experiments in communal living. She suffered serious illnesses. She went to jail with him and became the first candidate for his *brahmacharya* experiment. Soon after he settled down in South Africa, Gandhiji made a unilateral decision to mould his family according to his predetermined social theories and practices. He found his wife beyond the pale of intellectual discussion and debate. He often contrasted her with the wives of his European associates. The doors of the exclusive Indo-European 'club', of which Hermann Kallenbach, Henry and Millie Graham Polak, Rev Albert and Ada West and Mrs Joseph Doke were part, were closed to her.*

Kasturba, a 'good Hindu wife' as she proved till the end, was too spirited to give up without a fight. The first major clash of wills was in 1897 when Gandhiji was practising in Durban. His office clerks stayed with him in his house. He treated them as his house guests and members of his family. The resident clerks were expected to clean their chamber pots the first thing in the morning. The chamber pots had to be taken out for cleaning, as there was no running water in the house. The same rule applied to all members of the family: "She could not bear the pots being cleaned by me, neither did she like doing it herself. Even today I can recall the picture of her chiding me, her eyes red with anger, and pearl drops streaming down her cheeks, as she descended the ladder, pot in hand."[5]

Cruelly Kind Husband

Gandhiji commandeered her to carry out the mission without the least whimper. She refused to do so and instead shouted at him and said: "Keep your house to yourself and let me go."[6]

---

*Kallenbach, an architect by profession, owner of Tolstoy Farm, and his financier, was closest to him. Henry Polak helped him in his law practice and lived with him (along with his charming wife Millie) in the same house in Johannesburg and functioned as his deputy for all puposes, Albert West, a theosophist and a vegetarian, was his buddy at the famous onion club. His sister Ada ('Devi Behn'), helped with the teaching. Rev Doke was Baptist Minister of Johannesburg, who wrote his biography.

Ba perhaps got the first taste of the dogged determination that was to become his hallmark. When she had to obey him, she yielded but not without scoring a point: "Have you no sense of shame? Must you forget yourself? Where am I to go? I have no parents or relatives here to harbour me. Being your wife, you think I must put up with your cuffs and kicks."[7] She offered a dignified compromise: "For Heaven's sake, behave yourself and shut the gate. Let us not be found making a scene like that."[8]

The next clash was in 1901. On the eve of their departure to India, Gandhis received gifts from the grateful Indian community in South Africa for the services they had rendered. Those included a gold necklace worth fifty guineas for Mrs Gandhi and some diamond jewellery. Gandhiji agonised over whether he and his family should accept these gifts or not and he finally decided to use these valuables to set up a public trust in South Africa.

But this was without taking Mrs Gandhi into confidence. She had already assumed proprietary rights over the gifts and did not want to return them. She sobbed and remonstrated: "I have toiled and mailed for you day and night. Is that no service? You forced all and sundry on me, making me weep bitter tears and I slaved for them."[9] As was already the pattern, Mahatma won. Gandhis returned the gifts on 15 October 1901 and set sail for India. Gandhiji and Ba returned to South Africa in December 1902, to spend what turned out to be twelve most crucial years of their life.

Ba suddenly matured in her own right. From outside, she appeared peripheral to this irresistible sweep of the Gandhian juggernaut, but if observed from close quarters, her indomitable will power was impossible to miss, even by her husband. He started recognising her contribution to his success. He went to the extent of conceding that had it not been for her, he would not have succeeded in his grand design. She had given him sustained and selfless support and, above all, cheered him in his moments of depression.

By the time she returned to India from South Africa for the second time in 1915, she had carved a niche for herself. Gandhiji, it could be said, had learnt his first lesson in *satyagraha* (passive resistance) from her. She was a passive but an equal partner in his *brahmacharya* vow of 1906. But the husband barely acknowledged his wife's role. She was never an insider.

Father and Son

Gandhiji was jailed on 13 October 1908, for two months. He was confined to his usual haunt of Volksrust prison. Halfway through his term, he received a telegram about the deteriorating health of Ba. The jail authorities were willing to release him, provided he paid the prescribed fine for obtaining premature release. To the consternation of his friends and well-wishers, he refused to oblige. Ba suffered for five long months. She did not mind his long absence as the tension between their elder son Harilal and his father was growing. Gandhiji was unrelenting despite her continuous pleadings on behalf of Harilal. Harilal and his father could barely reconcile their differences during their lifetime.

While Gandhiji was visiting London in 1909, his friend Pranjivan Mehta 'offered Gandhiji a scholarship for one of his sons—Manilal was particularly mentioned.' The recipient was required to take 'the vow of poverty' and serve the cause of Phoenix after completing his education. But according to Nilam Parekh, Harilal's grand daughter, Pranjivandas Mehta told Gandhiji: "Harilal is grown up now. Send him and another meritorious young man to me in London."[10] Chhaganlal Gandhi was chosen for the honour, but he fell ill in early 1911 and returned without completing his education. The next recipient of scholarship was Sorabji Shapurji Adajania* and Harilal was passed over once again and this was the cause of his bitterness which lasted for a lifetime.

The thrust on higher education (and its denial), his marriage (without prior consultation with his father) and his pre-emptory departure from South Africa were, besides other reasons, the cause of conflict between them. In sheer exasperation, she would burst out: "Does he want to keep his sons uneducated? Does he want them to wear a loin cloth? Does he want to make them beggars?"[11]

For a brief while, Harilal became proactive in the movement spear-headed by his father. He courted arrest in November 1910 and was sentenced to six months imprisonment. But it did not improve their relations. A deep rift developed not only between Harilal and Mohandas, but also between Ba and Gandhiji. It was reflected in the letter he addressed to Harilal: "The fact is that Ba does not know her

---

*He was called 'a prince among passive resisters' in South Africa, and was deputed to England in 1912, at Pranjivan Mehta's expense, to qualify as barrister, but died young at thirty-five in 1918.

mind. However, I have nothing to say against your pleading for her."[12] Confrontation between father and son contributed to Ba's deteriorating health. Gandhiji understood it well: "She must have got angry and when I went to see her, she burst into tears and made it appear as if she would die."[13] The inevitable came to pass. Harilal escaped, and shifted to India without Gandhiji's explicit permission or knowledge.

Expiation through Suffering

Ba had serious health problems between 1908 and 1914. Her survival is often described as providential. After a haemorrhage in November 1908, Gandhiji almost wrote an epitaph. He was not able to visit her due to his imprisonment and decided to send a farewell letter through the good offices of his friend A H West. It was more like an epitaph or obituary.[14]

She was operated upon and was seriously ill through the early months of 1909. A distinguished American psychologist and biographer Erik Erikson told Gandhiji: "And, finally, Kasturba's strength of renunciation was, if anything, more consistent than yours."[15]

Faith and a resolute will to survive were two of Ba's greatest strengths. Millie Graham Polak vividly recollected the incident. She was an eye-witness to Ba's illness in 1910. Gandhiji was away in Johannesburg and Ba was only half conscious when he returned to take charge of her. He secured her promise to follow his advice.

An instructive incident in this episode concerns a bowl of beef tea. Gandhiji described it in detail in his autobiography, in a chapter called 'Kasturba's Courage'.[16] The conscientious doctor intended to administer beef tea to his patient and he sought Gandhiji's permission. Despite Gandhiji's refusal, the doctor went ahead as he was under obligation under the code of conduct for medical practitioners.

Gandhiji withdrew the patient from the supervision of the trusted doctor. Ba endorsed the decision, and gave a 'resolute reply' despite her condition: "I will not take beef tea. It is a rare thing in the world to be born as a human being, and I would far rather die in your arms than pollute my body with such abominations."[16] It was a rare sight to see Gandhiji on his knees, pleading with her to decide for herself. Ba needed no prompting: "Nothing will happen to me? Don't worry."[17]

The doctor, exasperated by now, asked Gandhiji to remove the patient from his custody. She was carried in drizzling rain in a rickshaw to Durban railway station for onward journey to the Phoenix settlement. On the platform he carried her in his arms into the compartment. From Phoenix, six men carried her on a hammock. Ba went to the extent of upbraiding a visiting holy monk who quoted from *Manusmriti* for exceptions on consumption of beef that can be made in extraordinary circumstances.

Gandhiji stopped all her medicines and monitored her personally, for two months without stopping. He was Ba's companion, nurse, doctor and maid. The doctor treating her was denied access to his patient. He accused Gandhiji of being callous. But Mahatma had his own way of doing things. He fed Ba lemonade at regular intervals. No other food or drink was served and: "Without a single relapse, Mrs Gandhi stoutly but surely returned to health."[18] Faith had triumphed over science, it seemed.

Family Ties

The period of her failing health was also the happiest period of their association. The conjugal relationship was truly tested. She also passed the test of three serious illnesses. She was always in his thoughts whether he was in or out of jail. The family was more united than ever before. He wrote to Chanchalbehn (wife of Harilal), asking her to look after her sick mother-in-law. He requested her to: "behave as mistress of the house; do not forget that we are very poor."[19] In another letter dated 26 February 1909, he requested her to read 'good writings and poems' to her.

His remaining in and out of jail and her prolonged illness also served his selfish purpose. His *brahmacharya* was tested by default and he came out successful. His enforced separation from her proved to be a blessing in disguise and he admitted this to his daughter-in-law Chanchalbehn without any inhibition: "My separation from Ba [during jail term] was almost involuntary; that is, it was not my choice and yet it proved to be a blessing to us both."[20]

The suffering and physical discomfort that Ba underwent completely transformed her. There was a new discernible energy in her, a newfound confidence. In response to a letter from a Johannesburg woman, she turned poetic while expressing her inability to be with her due to her prolonged illness: "Had she wings, she would fly to the meeting."[21]

Gandhiji was greatly impressed by her courage and bravery. She had refused to be terrorised by death and suffering had become a badge of honour for her. She sought to sustain her husband in moments of crises.

Gandhiji was now confronted with a confident woman. He shared this with Harilal: "So far I can see, she is a new woman altogether."

Jail *Yatra*

Ba still continued to be marginal figure in his political matters. This was ironical because Gandhiji's struggle had brought about a new political awakening among women of Indian origin. They became assertive and volunteered to join the *satyagraha* movement.

Ba was nowhere in the picture. He would not take her into confidence on *satyagraha*. Once she overheard him talking to a group of Indian women in Phoenix about their participation in *satyagraha*. She strongly protested and said: "I am sorry that you are not telling me about this [going to jail]. What defect there is in me which disqualifies me from going to jail? I also wish to take the path to which you are inviting others."[22]

For once Gandhiji was pushed on the back foot. Perhaps, it was male chauvinism that downgraded his *ardhangini* (literally the better half). He mumbled something about her untested potential. He was apprehensive about her determination and scared that she may seek an apology after being jailed. He must have had a macabre sense of humour when he told her: "If you die in jail I shall worship you like a Goddess."[23] She, however, told him with unconcealed glee: "I have nothing to think about, I am fully determined."[24] The job was done and there was no going back. She pleaded: "Could I not then join the struggle and be imprisoned myself?"[25]

Now he was telling Ba that she should go to jail for her 'self-respect', in protest against the draconian Immigration Act of 1913, which threatened to derecognise Hindu marriages. The Phoenix residents including Kasturba, Ramdas Gandhi, Chagganlal, JEKI and twelve others constituted themselves into a band of *satyagrahis* to court arrest. On the eve of departure for Volksrust from Phoenix on 16 September 1913, the departing *satyagrahis* were treated to a gourmet meal cooked by Gandhiji himself. It consisted of chapattis, vegetables, tomato chutney and sweets made of dates and rice.

They were arrested for iilegal entry in the State of Transvaal and sentenced to three months of prison with hard labour on September 23. The *satyagrahis* were consigned to the notorious Martzburg Jail company where they were accompanied by prostitutes, thieves and vagabonds.

The women prisoners were given ill-fitting frocks worn by Zulu women. Food consisted of 'maize grind'. From sixth day onwards, Kasturba was given fruits as an exception on health grounds, after repeated requests by the doctors. She was served a meagre diet of half-a-dozen bananas and a few plums and lemons day-after-day. The *satyagrahis* were hungry all the time. Some of them out of hunger ate banana and lemon skin. The famished Kasturba was a physical wreck and people mistook her for Gandhiji's mother.* Manilal lamented: "She was no longer the Ba we knew."[26] The *satyagrahis* were released on 16 December 1913, after spending three months in jail. Kasturba had a reprieve of another three months before she fell ill in early 1914.

Death Wish

The authorities would not allow Gandhiji to send a letter to her in Gujarati. Ba insisted upon hearing from her husband in their mother tongue. The impasse was hard to be resolved. He consoled her on 4 March 1909 with the following thought: "Happiness depends upon mental state than upon physical surroundings."[27] The above letter was written to her from Pretoria prison.

When Ba was vacillating between life and death during 1908 and 1914, Gandhiji shared his anxiety about her deteriorating health with his close associate, A H West. Death wish was the dominant theme in his letters. He had left her to fate and shared his innermost thoughts with A H West: "If Mrs Gandhi must leave me without even the consolation a devoted husband could afford, so be it."[28]

Earlier, when he was in Volksrust Jail, there was no restriction on the exchange of letters in languages other than English. He wrote a sentimental letter to her on 9 November 1908, assuring her of his eternal loyalty by remaining monogamous in the event of her passing away: "I love you so dearly that even if you are dead, you will be alive to me… I repeat… I will not marry again… It doesn't matter much whether one dies or lives."[29]

He continued in the same vein and talked of her 'deathless soul', thus mentally preparing himself for her death: "It cuts my heart. I am very much grieved but not in a position to go there to nurse you… My coming there is out of question… If you keep courage… If, however,

*"How do you do, Mr. Gandhi? Is she your mother"?

Source : Gandhi, Devdas. *My brother, Hindustan Times*, Feb. 23,1948.

my ill luck so has it that you pass away, I should only say that there would be nothing wrong in your doing so in your separation from me while I am still alive… Your soul is deathless… I will not marry again."[30] This time Gandhiji addressed the letter to 'beloved Kastur' instead of 'Ba'.

He again talked of death and advised Ba: 'You may quietly breathe with your faith in God'. He described her death as a 'sacrifice to the course of *Satyagraha*' and added: "I hope and expect that you will also think likewise and not be unhappy."[31] Obviously Gandhiji had a death wish for her embedded in his subconsciousness. Continuing in the same vein, he showed his abiding affection for his ailing *ardhangini* in his letter to his friend Kallenbach: "Our mutual attachment is the strongest possible testimony of our having lived before in bodies other than the present ones."[32]

Similar sentiments pervaded in his mind during her serious illness in 1914. The death wish surfaced once again in his correspondence: "If anybody should have died it was Mrs Gandhi… And yet the desire in me to die is overpowering."[33]

Evidently, Gandhiji displayed an odd sense of humour when he wrote to his close associate and cousin Maganlal Gandhi about her possible cremation: "Whether she lives or dies, her mind should be pure and tender. I have made all the preparations and inquired about everything in case she dies. There is a cremation ground here equipped with the necessary facility. It is four miles away." After two weeks had passed, she had crossed the hump. He was amazed at her determination to survive and called it 'almost a miracle'.[34]

Raucous Couple

Her illness transformed them into an idyllic couple. Gandhiji was found next to her, day and night for two months, completely dedicated to help her recover from her illness. He would even tease her when she got angry. He made a mock promise and assured her of formal cremation in the event of her demise. He would thus make her blues fly away and half of her pain would be gone. Such closeness of the devoted couple was however, short-lived.

Soon after Ba began to recover, the conjugal ceasefire was the first casualty. Never was Gandhiji so unchivalrous to Ba as in his letter to his friend Kallenbach on 14 April 1914:

"She has both the devil and the divine in her in a most concentrated form. She made yesterday a most venomous remark... And I again gently but rebukingly remarked that she was sinful in her thought and that her disease was largely due to her sins. Immediately she began to howl. I had made her leave all the good food in order to kill her. I was tired of her. I wished her to die. I was a hooded snake... I could not pity her in her sins... I apologised to her... She has a character and she has none. She is the most venomous woman I have ever met. She never forgets, never forgives... All the charges she brought against me she undoubtedly means... She has contrary emotions. I have nursed her as a son would nurse his mother. But my love has not been sufficiently intense and selfless to change her nature... Truly she has so far been my best teacher. She teaches me emptiness of the world, she teaches me patience, forgiveness, greater need for self-sacrifice, for love and charity... On the whole, she has not thwarted me and has been most exemplary. But how can a leopard change its spots... My point is that you cannot attach yourself to a particular woman and yet live for humanity. The two do not harmonise. That is the real cause of the devil waking in her now and again. Otherwise he might have remained in her asleep and unnoticed."[35]

This letter is a psychiatrist's delight and for a layman it is like stepping on a minefield. Here is a clear indication of the asymmetry between Gandhiji and Ba. It is also an indication of the incompatibility between the couple operating at differing intellectual planes. Adjustment is the name of the game in all marriages. It was fine so long as Ba yielded. After all, she was a woman pushed around for too long.

It had been a one-sided contest in the entire thirty-two years of their married life. She was ignored and overlooked for all practical purposes. She saw him totally at ease with the likes of Mrs. Polak, who combined charm and brain power. She must have felt humiliated and there comes a day in the life of all of us when we are expected to stand up and be counted. Such a day arrived for Mrs Gandhi on 12 April 1914, when he wrote the above mentioned letter to Kallenbach. The truth and untruth got intertwined and mixed up in this slanging match. It reads like a confession. Gandhiji had a glimpse of his mother Putlibai in Ba but he could not do without her altogether. His repeated death wish for her falls in its proper place.

Sartorially Yours

All good things of life must come to an end. So was the rich experience for the Gandhis and their associates (except, perhaps, for unfortunate Harilal). He had a long innings to play. Gandhiji arrived in South Africa on 30 April 1893 to practice law. The family finally returned to Bombay on 9 January 1915. Twenty-one years had transformed the Gandhis and their world.

It must have been a sight when the Gandhis landed in South Africa prior to the birth of Ramdas, their third son, in December 1896. Gandhiji had a brainwave before the family left Bombay. He decided that every member of his family, including Ba and children, were to be dressed formally in European clothes. For Ba, he suggested a slight variation. She was to dress herself in a Parsi outfit. Ba protested over the strange prescription. It was of no avail. Once something got into his head, he refused to listen to anyone. The poor lady had never worn European-style shoes. She wept and wailed. So did Harilal, Manilal and the little cousins, for their unfamiliar shoes hurt and stockings bruised the legs. Gandhiji wanted Ba to be dressed as a Parsi since Parsis were 'regarded as the most civilised among the Indians in South Africa.'

The situation completely turned around when the Gandhis landed at Apollo Bunder, Bombay to a tumultuous welcome in January 1915. In his letter to Maganlal Gandhi, Gandhiji was to prescribe pre-emptory rules and regulations of dress for the landing party. He was about to take his first step in the murky waters of Indian politics. He was anxious that the Gandhis must be dressed properly. He expected every child to be attired in Indian-style clothes: "The very young should have a lungi, a shirt and a cap like the round one of velvet we have…I see no need for the boys to have shoes."[36] The toilet paper was also placed on the banned list. The time gap between 1895 and 1915 was not merely chronological but had to be seen in metaphorical terms.

Ba was a lady with a striking personality. Louis Fischer has done justice to this charming lady by drawing her stately portrait upon arrival in South Africa in January 1897. This pen portrait has been drawn on the basis of a period photograph. Kasturba was twenty eight at that time: "[It] shows her a beautiful woman, elegantly dressed in a rich, silk sari. The fine oval face with eyes wide apart, well-formed nose, delicately curved lips and perfectly shaped chin must have made her very attractive indeed"[37] and about him, he said: "[He was photographed] in a European suit, stiff white collar and stiff white shirt, a gay, striped necktie and round button in his lapel buttonhole."[38]

While she looked graceful and charming, and somewhat relaxed, he in his formal dress with stiff upper lip gave the impression of strong willpower, foreshadowing the future yet to be born. Eleanor Morton endorsed the image drawn by Louis Fischer and further noted that two pregnancies had not dimmed her beauty. Yet her delicate frame reached only the shoulders of her husband: "[Kasturba] was perfectly made, faultless as a work of sculpture. Large eyes flashed in their frames of thick lashes, under covered brows."[39] She must have been a sight for 'Gods' with her intrinsic qualities of inner and outer beauty, with her husband looking an insignificant entity in her fleeting moments of glory. The passing years had taken a toll on her body. In a photograph taken by Kanu Gandhi in 1940, she is looking like a frail and emaciated old woman with all the burdens of the world resting on her shoulders. She is seen walking unsteadily, accompanied by Gandhiji with his left hand resting on her frail shoulder.

Guilt Complex

The dialectical relationship that developed between the couple was entirely due to their pursuit of different goals. What he offered her was 'associate commandership'. While Ba was peripheral to Gandhiji in striving for *moksha* or spiritual liberation, Gandhiji and their family were central in her scheme of things. Besides observing *brahmacharya* which was crucial as her *dharma* towards her husband, she was as protective of her sons and her progeny as other *dharma*.

Gandhiji was full of enthusiasm, characterised by restlessness. He was always exploring and experimenting. The sex drive took the centrestage in his early years of adulthood. There is an absorbing but obsessive account of experiments with sex in his autobiography. He considered the sex drive to be an impediment to his involvement with public cause. Life was however, full of coincidences and surprises which proved to be turning points in the life of the Gandhis. Gandhiji fondly called himself 'a lustful man out.' He may have been exaggerating. Most married men are prone to be ecstatic in their newly-married state of bliss. Such a state of being is a passing phase, but not so for Gandhiji.

His obsession with sex was overbearing, followed by his marriage at a young age of thirteen. Kasturba recoiled at his obsession, but could do very little about it. She was to wait and watch until 1906 to be free of the burden, after he took the vow of *brahmacharya*.

The incident that occurred during his father's demise changed his life completely and also liberated Ba from the sexual entanglement. Impelled by the sexual drive, he excused himself from massaging his dying father to be with his wife. He made his intentions clear to Kasturba and woke her up. He meted: "But how could she sleep when I was there? I woke her up."[40] By the time he returned to massage his father, he was already dead.

Practical *Brahmacharya*

This created a sense of guilt in him. He could not forgive himself for this lapse on his part. He would remind himself of 'this shame of my carnal desire even at the critical hour of my father's death'. He talked of 'a blot I have never been able to efface or forget'. His adversity, however, proved to be an opportunity for him. In his own words, he had to "pass through several ordeals before breaking himself 'from the shackles of lust."'[41] Gandhiji also recoiled from the inevitable violence implied in conjugal relations: "Never forgiven myself the violence of which I have been guilty."[42]

He was a votary of non-violence and *satyagraha* and the oppressiveness implied in a conjugal relationship gradually became an anathema to him. He discovered a close affinity between sex, aggressiveness and violence. He agonised over this for many years. The period between his father's death and the vow of a life-long *brahmacharya* did not pass easily. Ba was nowhere in the picture in all this guilt complex that he carried to South Africa also. It was during the Zulu rebellion that the *brahmacharya* inspiration dawned upon him in a flash. The violence during the rebellion and the introspection that followed, persuaded him to make up his mind. Initially, he broached the idea with his associates of the Stretcher-Bearer Corps during the Zulu rebellion. He even organised a volunteer Defence Force to fight the Zulu rebellion on the side of 'the British Empire'. Besides waging a war externally, he was engaged in fighting another war within himself, a war of 'self-realisation', by observing celibacy. Then and there he took the vow to observe *brahmacharya* in thought, word and deed.

After his return from the Zulu front he called his associates, including Maganlal and Chhaganlal Gandhi, to a meeting at Phoenix settlement in 1903. He invited all his associates who stood by him during the days of struggle and fame in South Africa. As usual, his colleagues who had always looked up to him for guidance approved of this decision as well. They, however, gave him a useful piece of advice – to consult Ba. So far, she had been kept out of his initiative. It was Putlibai, his mother, rather than Kasturba who inspired him to take the jump. His mother made him take the vow of celibacy before proceeding for London and Rajchandbhai provided him with the ideological framework for *brahmacharya*. He calculated that this vow was more of a serious business for him than for Kasturba.

He made it appear as *brahmacharya* was the only practical proposition for them. He was already a father of four sons. Gandhiji had been thinking of practising continence for quite sometime. It was practical politics that enabled him to simultaneously unfurl the flags of *brahmacharya* and *satyagraha*.

Ba had no views on the subject. She remained neutral. In any case, she would have fallen in line. Hence, her consent was forthcoming in no time. This would have been to her advantage and spared her further pregnancies. Both of them were thirty seven in 1906 and had been married for twenty three years when he announced his vow of abstinence to the entire world. In any case, they had been practising continence since 1900 (after the birth of Devdas) for all practical purposes.

The decision was not an easy one and took several years of relentless struggle to fructify. Gandhiji adopted all kinds of subterfuge to come to terms with his vow of continence. He recommended cold baths as the ultimate panacea. He exhausted himself with work to kill his normal sex instincts and adopted a number of food fads, one of which was saying goodbye to milk. He experimented by avoiding physical contact and started sleeping in a separate bed. Still there was no reprieve. The conception of his fourth son could not be prevented.

There was, however, a happy sequel to Devadas's birth. There were no nurses on hand to deliver the baby. Ba was stranded due to sudden labour and Gandhiji decided to deliver the baby on his own. And he did a deft job.

He was too worried on the count of his failures whereas Ba was relaxed throughout the years of his trauma. He was troubled in his dreams too: "Gandhiji's vow did not shield him from dreams in which his wife came to him. What she thought and remembered, did not say.

Throughout the marriage she had remained 'reticent'. Very possibly she was grateful to bc spared child-bearing. A different sort of marriage seemed to begin for them both."[43]

The year 1898 was a landmark year for Gandhiji as well as for Ba. After several years of internal struggle to achieve *brahmacharya*, he decided to take the final plunge, driven by practical consideration. He was determined against new additions to his family and decided upon abstinence for at least two years. He was fighting a war within himself. His obsessive physical love for Ba was his constant impediment. She was like a shadow, which would not go away. He was looking for internal peace by physical denial of his wife to himself.

Fighting the Subconscious

He was in regular touch with Rajchandbhai, his inspiration for continence vow. Gandhiji's charisma was so overpowering that it could steamroll all opposition and transform a hostile situation to his advantage. Ba's initial hostility changed to gradual adjustment, acceptance and finally, enthusiastic championship. Later, she became an ardent advocate of his causes, including *brahmacharya*.

Practising *brahmacharya* was particularly galling since Ba did not find its observance too daunting. She would have been the happiest to escape being the beast of burden. However, she complied with his physical demands in pursuit of her *dharma*. He was candid enough to admit that this was the hardest battle fought by him. His enemy was his inner self. It was fascinating in, to watch his conscious-self coming to terms with the subconscious. Gandhiji admitted that his marital status was also creating problems in his way: "Those still in the *brahmacharya* stage and unmarried find it easier than those who had entered into matrimony and had the taste of it, the latter find the process of adjustment very hard. There are several difficult challenges in the world, but observing celibacy on the part of the married is the hardest. It took me several years to observe *brahmacharya* after the birth of Devdas."[44]

Physical separation was his strategy to keep himself on the *brahmacharya* path. He was the happiest man when Ba stayed back in India while he returned to South Africa. He was happy so long as she kept away from him. He wrote to Haridas Venkatchand Vohra from

---

*A close friend of his from Rajkot and a leading lawyer of Kathiawaad. He was also the father-in-law of Harilal Gandhi.

Johannesburg expressing the desire to wriggle out of his promise of her early return. He added, "the question then is as to the fulfillment of my promise to Mrs Gandhi... If however she would allow me to recede from the promise and not insist on coming here [to South Africa], there is a likelihood of my being able to return to India earlier than I otherwise would."[45]

In his correspondence with his daughter-in-law Chanchalbehn, Gandhiji described prison as the safest sanctuary for the practice of involuntary *brahmacharya*. He followed it up with another letter to his nephew Chhaganlal on the same lines. Gandhiji supplicated him to persuade his aunt to stay put in India. If the excuse given out to Vohra was preoccupation with legal work, it was the implausible excuse of expensive life in South Africa that was trotted out to Chhaganlal. Ba was unimpressed and returned to South Africa.

Kasturba the Teacher

With passage of time, he was fulsome in Ba's praise for helping him keep on a straight path: "I had to struggle hard to remain on the straight path," he admitted. His own assertion in his autobiography of Ba's being 'brave' and his being 'nervous' was established in the years of his experimentation with continence as well. Ba turned out to be his first teacher in the practice of non-violence. Her resistance to him was the most incipient form of *satyagraha* which got embedded in his subconscious. Incongruous as it may seem, the disciple ended up as the apt teacher through her intense and devoted *tapasya*. She indeed set him on the path of righteousness without herself being aware of it. Gandhiji told this to Margaret Sanger, an American suffragette, in December 1935: "I became her teacher. I was not an ideal teacher because I was a brute. The animal passion in me was too strong and I could not become the ideal teacher."[46] He further confessed her slavish behaviour in the same interview: "She observes certain decencies which I have not done with her... I have made use of her. She is too much of a Hindu wife."

There were several occasions when he went out of his way to express his gratefulness to her for his deep and abiding love not only for her personal charm, but also for inspiring others. He told his Quaker friend John S Hoyland: "I learnt... the lesson of non-violence from my wife when I tried to bend her to my will. Her determined resistance to my will on the one hand, and her *quiet submission to suffering* my stupidity involved on the other, ultimately made me ashamed of myself and cured me of my stupidity in thinking that I was born to rule over her; and in the end she became my teacher in non-violence."[47]

Ba who was marginalised became crucial to him. The marginal became central in *brahmacharya*: "It was the only time in their long association when she was conceded a status of equality by him. With the practice of *brahmacharya* having yielded dividends after a long struggle, his love for Kasturba multiplied and became deeper and lasting."[48]

Gandhiji gave formal credence to his innermost thoughts on *brahmacharya* positively impacting his relationship with Ba: "In the absence of *brahmacharya*, there is an element of aggression in the man-woman relationship. Our love-tie became stronger, with greater understanding and mutual tendency to be considerate to each other. With *brahmacharya*, I eyed Ba through the practice of *ahimsa*, with the result our love flowered at its best."[49]

Triumph after Death

Ba's death affected Gandhiji deeply. "I cannot imagine life without Ba. I always wished her to go away in my hands so that I would not have to worry as to what will become of her when I am no more. But she was an indivisible part of me. Her passing away has left a vacuum which will never be filled."[50] Her memory would not go away and he confessed: "My mind does not think of anything else but Ba."[51]

He compared her to Goddess Jagdamba. Those were not momentary responses. While reciting from the sacred *Gita* on her first death anniversary, he remembered her affectionately: "I do not know if the departed souls know what is happening here. I do not know, but I believe that in some way this reading [from *Gita*] may be of some good to them. It is, at least, good for our own soul."[52]

Repeated reverential references to Ba were a sign of the insecurity he felt around him. It was only after her death perhaps that Gandhiji understood that Ba was the only homegrown critic who could stand up to him. The rest were either dumb camp followers or his enemies. The four years that Gandhiji lived as a widower were marked by this deep, albeit not fully admitted, loss. He zeroed in on the true essence of Ba by stating categorically: "Ba's chief virtue was her voluntary identification of herself with me... The quality blossomed in Ba on its own when the time came."[53]

The End

She was overburdened because of Gandhiji's public life. She had started feeling disoriented on account of her long incarceration from 1942 to 1944. She was convinced that Quit India Movement would be a failure. The death of Mahadev Desai in the Aga Khan Palace prison unsettled her since she considered him to be her fifth son. The *samadhi* of Mahadev Desai became another shrine for her. She blamed her husband for sending thousands of young men and women to jail for no rhyme or reason. Indeed, she questioned the fundamentals of Gandhiji's political praxis: "Why should Bapu have pitted himself against such a mighty Government? They have unmeasured strength at their disposal and how can Bapu hope to win against such a mighty adversary?" She added: "But even God seems to be against us at present."[54] Gandhiji tried to argue with her but to no avail. Her depression had increased after the death of Mahadev Desai. She also had a premonition of her own impending death. She was more than ever convinced of Gandhiji having led the Indian people to a *cul de sac*. She took up the topic with him once again: "Did I not tell you not to pick a quarrel with this Government? You did not listen to me and now we have all to pay the penalty... There is nothing to do now, but put up with the result of your own doings."[55]

She used to remind Gandhiji that she had tried to dissuade him from picking up the 'quarrel'. The twenty day fast of Gandhiji caused her much agony and she expressed her wish to die before him. May be it was a premonition of her death. She suffered a heart attack in jail on 17 March 1943 and two more attacks followed in January 1944. Harilal, accompanied by his younger brother Ramdas visited her on 16 January 1944, and after that he was nowhere to be found. Police was hunting for him. When her health began to deteriorate fast, she was most anxious for her eldest son Harilal to be near her. She arranged to send a message to Harilal, who was located after an assiduous search by voluntary sleuths. He arrived in Poona on 17 February 1944, to be near his ailing mother. So did Devdas, the youngest. She was greatly pleased to meet Harilal.

While Devdas had been allowed entry into the jail on a daily basis, Harilal was allowed just once. The discriminatory treatment by the jail authorities made her angry. She lamented: "Why this discrimination between two brothers." She said: "They allowed Devadas to come everyday and they tell Harilal that he can come only once! Let [Col. M.G.] Bhandari (Inspector-General of Prison) come to me. I shall ask why a [poor] person cannot come to see his mother as freely as the rich one."[56]

Harilal disappeared once again. She longed to meet him after her health began to deteriorate. Police launched a wide search and traced him to Poona. He made his way to the Aga Khan Palace to meet his mother. He was turned away because he was drunk. He came back on 17 February 1944. He was already afflicted by tuberculosis. Even though he was in a state of inebriation, yet he was allowed entry into the Palace. She was greatly pleased to meet her wayward son. He was allowed to spend half an hour with the ailing Ba on that occasion.[57]

Harilal often went missing. Inebriation was the most common reason for his absence. But his mother was told that his vice was oversleeping. When he turned up on 21 February 1944, he looked dirty, disheveled, reeked of alcohol and was unable to stand upright. Ba knew the truth: "Your mother is dying and you are wasting your time in drinking." She started beating her forehead. She started to wail loudly, and had to be cooled down by Gandhiji. After that encounter, Harilal never saw his mother, Ba died within 48 hours. Gandhiji had reconciled himself to her impending death and accordingly refused Devdas' suggestion that Ba be given penicillin injections. "Why don't you trust God? Why do you wish to drug your mother even on her death bed. An injection repeated every four or six hours would add to her miseries."[58]

She had the premonition that her last moment had arrived. She asked Devdas to take charge of the family after she was no more: "Your father is a sadhu and he has many responsibilities. Harilal is a wastrel."[59] It was the family that was on her mind on the day she passed away. Leaning on Sushila Nayyar as a prop, she asked sweetly of her: "Sushila, where am I going? Will I die."[60] The Mahashivratri day of 22 February 1944 was her day of reckoning. Gandhiji was ready as usual for his morning walk. Ba requested him not to be away from her for even a moment. She sent for her husband when her eyes started to close. As per their mutual wish, she was to die on the lap of Gandhiji: "There were a few hiccups and a gurgling sound from the throat. She opened her mouth, three or four gasps, and all was still."[61]

The last moments arrived as anticipated. Gandhiji expressed the satisfaction that he was near her: "And she passed away in my lap! Could it be better? I am happy beyond measure."

Saubhagyavati

The red-bordered sari made of yarn woven by Gandhiji was brought out. Ba had left this in Manu Gandhi's custody for the occasion: "I wish to be dressed in it when I die."[62] Her bangles and necklace were removed. A necklace made of *Tulsi* leaves was placed around her neck. Her hair was combed after the ritual bath and Gandhiji insisted on it being kept loose. The yarn woven by him was dyed and wrapped around her body. Ba had retrieved the sari in time for Bapu's birthday on 2 October 1943, and it came in very handy to drape her dead body.

Manu (Gandhi) Mashruwala (Harilal's daughter) put sandalwood paste on her forehead and a red vermilion dot in the middle as a symbol of dying married (*saubhagyavati*): "Ba looked beautiful and appeared to be asleep. Red bangles were placed on her sleeves."[63]

Harilal was absent from the scene and Devdas lit the pyre. Gandhiji refused to stir and kept a vigil. He was deep in his thoughts and reverie. He was reminiscing over sixty two years of life they had spent together. It took almost six long hours for the pyre to turn to ashes. Gandhiji leaned on his staff, standing under the shade of a tree. Everything was over by 4:30 pm. The ashes were consigned to Triveni at Allahabad.

The next day Harilal appeared. On 24 February, the three brothers, Harilal, Ramdas and Devdas (Manilal was in South Africa) and their father dined together as per the ritual. Gandhiji did not talk to Harilal about anything in particular. Harilal disappeared as suddenly as he had turned up. He resurfaced at Devdas's residence on the day Gandhiji passed away. He didn't join the general procession, nor did he light the pyre at Rajghat by the banks of the Yamuna.

The best came out of her during her last moments. Everyone around her except for Ba was inconsolable. She was sitting upright in bed, gasping for breath, but she put a brave front by dismissing any show of demonstrative mourning. She murmured a prayer beseeching God's benediction. She consoled Gandhiji by placing her hand on his shoulder.

In response he stroked her head gently, as if assuring the dutiful *ardhangini* of their eternal love.

Ba is Mahatma

In a reminiscent mood long after Ba was dead, he owed his achievement to the principle of *brahmacharya*. Perhaps, Ba single-handedly put him on the 'straight path'. He told Manu Gandhi that Ba alone deserved the title of the Mahatma. While responding to Lord Wavell over the demise of Ba, he admitted that they were a couple out of the ordinary. The thread of *brahmacharya* united them irrevocably and they ceased to be two different entities: "The result was that she became truly my better half. She was a woman always of very strong will which, in our early days, I used to mistake for obstinacy."[64]

A strong-willed woman herself, she discovered during the early days that Gandhiji was a man of steely determination. She had reconciled to losing her individual identity for the larger Gandhian cause. At times, her scepticism found expression and disturbed the surface equanimity. The last imprisonment in the Aga Khan Palace during 1942–44 depressed her as she bemoaned the Gandhian proclivity to sacrifice individuals at the altar of public cause. It was too late, though, to turn her back. And she helped him in all his endeavours.

While Ba was a perfect foil to her husband as his consort, her heart was in the family, which formed the centre of her universe. Those living in the ashrams, whether in South Africa or India, constituted her larger extended family. Gandhis always maintained an open house, with the result that the nuclear Gandhi family constituted a sub-unit within the larger context. While Ba maintained a public posture of contentment with her living environment, there was a part of her existence which she kept to herself. Her four sons lived away from her but they still constituted her real world. She felt at ease with them and derived genuine pleasure from her grandchildren. She also felt very relaxed while pottering about the kitchen. Living on communal food, which consisted entirely of pumpkin, she dreamt of the pleasures of partaking good food. In spite of constant opposition from her husband, she continued to drink tea and coffee for long.

There is a story about Gandhis chancing upon ginger roots and devouring them with relish. The subconscious has its own way of making us let down our guards on occasions essentially it was a life of unending struggle for her. It took a certain heavy toll of her–physically as well as mentally. She aged much before her time. She breathed her last in the Aga Khan Palace internment camp. The eighteen months she spent in jail were a fitting finale to her life of dedication and sacrifice. Never had Gandhiji and Ba been so much in love with each other as in those eighteen months.

CHAPTER 5

Ba, Bapu and Family

When Gandhiji landed in Bombay on 9 January 1915, he was welcomed as a National hero. His mind was working feverishly to replicate the models of Tolstoy and Phoenix farms in India. He was inspired by the Trappist monastery near Pinetown in Natal with its motto of communal living rooted on the principles of 'simplicity, industry and equality'. The Trappist monks were a self-sufficient community practicing asceticism, continence and vegetarianism. They farmed, employed spinning wheels (almost a prototype of *charkha*), manufactured bricks and maintained a tannery for supplying local needs. They were a role model for Gandhiji.

Dudhabhai Lakshmi

Gandhiji was soon to lay the foundation of Kochrab Ashram in Ahmedabad in 1915. He was not looking for trouble but he simply walked into it without realising it. He had no daughter of his own. He decided to adopt, in the words of Romain Rolland, "a small girl belonging to the untouchable class, and he speaks with exceeding tenderness of this pretty little seven-year old creature which makes in his home the rain and the sunshine."[1]

Gandhiji was anxious to set an example by recruiting an untouchable family as inmates of Satyagraha Ashram. Finally, an untouchable family was located in September 1915. Dudhabhai Dafda (a school teacher) accompanied by his wife Danibehn and his one-year-old daughter Laskhmi ('a mere toddling babe') arrived from Bombay to join the Kochrab Ashram on 26 September, to be welcomed by Gandhiji, sitting unrecognised in his cottage in a loin cloth. When queried about the whereabouts of the host, prompt came the reply with a smile: "Right here, of course".[2] He patted little Lakshmi. The arrival created a virtual revolt in the entire ashram. In fact, the whole of Ahmedabad seemed to be on a boil.

On his part, Gandhiji was ready to battle the entire world. The first banner of revolt against him was raised single-handedly by Kasturba. She was not prepared to reconcile to the presence of Dafda family in the ashram. Gandhiji had no choice but to retaliate. Kasturba was asked to leave the ashram. He gallantly offered her to "part [as] good friends".[3] To him, Lakshmi was 'like a daughter' and it did not matter if she was not 'well bred'. Rhetorically speaking, it actually didn't matter to him if she turned out to be "a Mirabai", or indeed, "a prostitute".[4]

Ashram Storm

The storm subsided temporarily, because 'the Pariah family' (to employ his own expression) had temporarily left the ashram. His sister-in-law placed an embargo on their young sons to visit the ashram. Maganlal, his wife Santok and their children left for Bombay two days prior to the arrival of the Dafda family. His loyal lieutenant, Maganlal, lost his verve. He was no longer "the Maganlal of olden days—robust, social, quickhanded and quick-witted". Indeed "He [has] aged.... He is absentminded."[5]

As the turmoil spread its tentacles outside the ashram, 'the people of Ahmedabad decided to boycott him'. Funds inflow to the ashram dried up until an anonymous donor came to their rescue. Gandhiji held Ba responsible for his troubles. While many others including Maganlal left the ashram, Kasturba stuck to him like an unwelcome companion, even as she suffered physically and mentally and became temperamental. Gradually, the storm passed and things returned to normal. Dafda family was adopted but only partially. Kasturba compensated for the past by showering affection on Lakshmi, who was adopted by the Gandhis when she fell sick in 1920. The fact, however, remained that Lakshmi was an outsider and was marginal to the existence of the Gandhis.

There was an occasional word of praise for Laskhmi for being a good girl, coupled with implied threats. Lakshmi was nineteen and had come of marriageable age. Gandhiji started looking for a groom for her. He was in a hurry to give Lakshmi in marriage to a non-Antyaga Hindu, that is, to "a Brahmin (not a *Bhangi*) brought up in Gujarat".[6]

Finally, Lakshmi was engaged to a Brahmin boy named Maruti Sharma, a South African brought up by Laxmidas Asar. As Gandhiji and Ba were serving sentence in prison, the marriage ceremony was performed by Narandas Gandhi in 1933. Her biological father Dudhabhai was not invited. Gandhiji later admitted to Premabehn Kantak: "I now feel that I should not have accepted Lakshmi."[7]

Gandhiji wasted little time on Lakshmi. He claimed to be a dutiful father but not much of a 'mother' to her. She continued to be a ward of her biological parents. She was 'full of shortcomings' and an 'indolent', Gandhiji confided in Premabehn Kantak. No wonder, not many people know of Lakshmi, who passed away on 31 January 1984. She lived in obscurity in a two-room tenement in Ahmedabad, a couple of flights up a dark stairway, 'smelling of urine'. She fondly remembered her return 'to her parents', "wherever he was, and I went home to him for my annual visit just like a daughter."[8]

The Gentle Lamb

Gandhiji's third son, Ramdas Gandhi was the humblest of the lot. An American Biographer Robert Payne described Ramdas as: "a shy and retiring man, so dominated by his father that he seemed not to possess a will of his own".[9] He was modest, humble and lacked confidence by instinct. While making a self-assessment, he confessed his lacuna to Gandhiji's closest friend Kallenbach: "I have not that confidence in me of a young man. I always hesitate and feel that I am not only incompetent but unworthy of anything. There is no ability. I feel I have not been made what could have been if I should have the literary training so necessary."[10]

Ramdas spent all his life as a minor functionary. He was so self-effacing that his youngest son, Devdas, took the centre stage on public occasions such as the funerals of Ba and Gandhiji. Ramdas' wife Nirmalbehn ('Nimmubehn') continued to be associated with the Sevagram Ashram until her death on 21 August 2000. She, like her husband, participated in all the *satyagrahas* launched by Mahatma and was jailed on many occasions.

This gentle soul rarely stirred in public. Surprisingly, he invited an argument with Nathuram Godse, the assassin of Gandhiji. He

---

*According to Gandhiji, "a non-Antyaga Hindu does not mean a Bhangi, it means a Hindu who is not 'an (lower caste) Antayaga.

described Godse as a man of 'reason and logic' in his letter to him. He was prepared for a dialogue, provided he would 'stick to the truth alone'. He also sought God's mercy for the murderer of his father: "He prayed that after their conversation they would be able to chant together the last words of Arjuna in the *Bhagvad Gita*, as he submits himself to the will of Vishnu."[11] Godse was as good in his repartee. After all Arjuna had been inspired by Krishna only to kill his near and dear ones in his cause: "And Arjuna actually performed what Krishna commended."[12]

Ramdas was deeply associated with the Gandhian movement. He spent his entire life in social service. Gandhiji paid him the ultimate tribute when he said: "Ramdas is my best son."

Devdas—The Youngest

While Ramdas and Nimmubehn were true Gandhians, Devdas was his parents' favourite. Since he was delivered by Gandhiji himself, an umbilical connection appeared to exist between the two. Devdas, the introvert, thus came to shoulder the responsibilities that the eldest son Harilal, the extrovert, should have shouldered.

He was also the one to perform the last rites of both his parents even when Harilal, the eldest was around. When Harilal turned up at the residence of Devdas after Gandhiji died, Devdas' daughter Tara queried: "Harilal *Kaka*, aren't you going to the cremation?" He gave a laconic reply. He visited the *samadhi* the next day like any other ordinary citizen. Similarly, he was found missing on the day Ba was cremated, only to join his father and brothers subsequently on the family meal ritual.

One of the few occasions when he got worked up was during Gandhiji's 'laboratory experiments' at the time of Noakhali sojourn, involving Manu Gandhi. He packed off Manu Gandhi and Abha Gandhi soon after Gandhiji's demise, with a stern piece of advice to Manu to maintain stoic silence and not reveal the contents of the diary maintained by her during the Noakhali sojourn at the instance of Gandhiji. Manu has gone on record and confessed about this matter.

While Devdas was extremely gentle and lovable, he also had an iron will like a true Gandhian. His courting of Lakshmi, daughter of C Rajagopalachari, was not to the liking of either Gandhiji or the prospective father-in-law, who mutually agreed to keep politics and personal relations in two separate compartments. Gandhiji argued that how could his son dare court his 'cousin', daughter of his adopted uncle?

Gandhiji used all his tricks to keep Devdas off Lakshmi's shadow, but the determined son persisted and wooed her for six long years. Gandhiji tried to wash his hands off the affair by making Rajaji the front man. This is how he described the situation in a letter to his close associate Surendra: "Devdas's state is extremely pitiable. Rajaji is not likely to let him marry Lakshmi, and rightly so… She is happy and cheerful, whereas Devdas has gone mad after her and is pining for her and suffering… He wishes to obey me, but his soul rebels against him. He seems to believe that I stand in the way of his marriage with Lakshmi and so feels angry with me… Devdas is right in believing that he is pleasure-loving, but pleasure-loving is rather a mild word. His thoughts run after sex pleasure."[13]

Whether it was his relations with Harilal, Sushila Nayyar and Manu Gandhi or with mother Ba, Devdas used to convey his opposition to his father as gently as possible. He was also the only one who would get away unscathed.

Manilal

Born in 1892, Manilal was neither subtle nor diplomatic like Devdas, nor was he self-effacing like Ramdas. He applied cold-blooded logic in his dealings with his father. Perhaps, distance from Gandhiji gave him some degree of objectivity. After Harilal, he was the main source of distress to his father. Manilal settled down in South Africa and edited the *Indian Opinion* that Gandhiji had founded. He managed the Phoenix farm, rather unsuccessfully, after his father moved to India.

Manilal was merely ten in 1902 when he fell sick. At a great risk to his life, he opted for his father's hydropathic treatment. Believing in nature cure and having much faith in Kunhe Treatment, especially 'Kunhe bath', involving use of large quantities of water, both internally and externally, Gandhiji gave Manilal hip baths for his cure. Thus, there grew a deep bond between the two. Again in 1909, Gandhiji was in the best of his moods and wrote to Manilal: "Though you are but a child, I have a high opinion of your character." He called himself an 'impatient' but 'a fond lover' of Manilal.

JEKI Affair

Manilal kept falling in love with the 'wrong type' of women. In 1914, when he was nearing the age of twenty-two, he fell in love with

Jayakunwar Mehta, who, according to Louis Fischer: "successfully assaulted Manilal's continence."[14] Gandhiji felt embarrassed because Jayakunwar (identified by her initials JEKI in his correspondence) was the daughter of his close friend and benefactor, Dr Pranjivan Mehta, who was at one time prepared to bear the expenses of two of his sons, Harilal and Manilal, for their education abroad.

In Gandhiji's abounding desire to experiment, he had given a great deal of freedom to the boys and girls living in the Phoenix ashram. They were allowed to interact with each other. JEKI was rated highly as an ashramite; she was one among the first batch of 16 *satyagrahis* in 1913.

Once she fell ill and Manilal was assigned to carry out nature-cure treatment for her. Then, the relationship started. Manilal was banished to Johannesburg after the JEKI incident came to Gandhiji's knowledge in 1913.

Gandhiji agonised over the incident for months together, but there was no end to his plight. He even contemplated suicide and considered fasting for two days. He gave up the idea because it would have certainly meant the death of ailing Ba. His self-created dilemma is reflected in his letter: "Never perhaps have I spent such days of agony as I am doing now… I have often wanted to take out the knife from my pocket and put it through the stomach. Sometimes I have felt like striking my head against the wall opposite, and at other times, I have thought of running away from the world."[15]

All dramas have a beginning and an end. The JEKI chapter came to a close after she joined fasting Gandhi as an act of expiation. She donated her jewellery and cut her long hair with a pair of scissors. She started wearing white clothes. Gandhiji turned out to be the father confessor to the poor girl. Manilal was punished by his delayed marriage. Gandhiji continued to pursue Manilal for months. He wanted the boy to confess to him but with no result.

Fatima Affair

Gandhis were the honoured guests of the Gool family headed by Joosub (Yusuf) Gool at 7, Buitensingel – one of the best-addresses in Cape Town. The family was Westernised with the Gool sisters* completely relaxed in the company of youngmen. Manilal was accompanied by

* Yusuf Gool's daughters

Rev Charles Andrews* and his parents on this trip. All of them felt relaxed. Gandhiji *went barefoot on the streets* of Cape Town in his informal lungi. Happy days were back for Manilal after the unfortunate JEKI incident the year before. Thus 1914 was a lucky year for him.

Manilal had a rollicking time on this occasion. The Gool family of Gujarati origin was rich and well-respected. The girls were outgoing and westernised. The company for Manilal was intellectually stimulating. He befriended Yusuf 's son, Dr A H Gool and particularly his three sisters, Beida, Jane and Fatima (pet name Timmie). Minnie, the youngest of Gool sisters, had a vivid recollection of two weeks spent by Manilal at their residence: "We were outgoing. We will go to the theatre. We would go to the bioscope. We would go to the opera house. We would go for walks… I don't think Manilal had a lot [of money]. He had a lot of good spirits and a lot of niceness about him. So we would go for walks and sing and read poetry."[16]

Charles Andrews was due to sail on 21 February 1914, and it was time for Manilal also to return to Johannesburg because Phoenix was on the banned list due to JEKI's presence. On the eve of his departure from Cape Town, Manilal was denied permission to go up the Table Mountain: "What is there so remarkable to see in Table Mountain? When you go home to India you can go up to the Himalayas which can contain thousands of Table Mountains."[17]

Gandhiji did not like the goings on at the Gool household a bit. Manilal was forced to revolt this time and he decided to defy his recalcitrant father, who was equally unrepentant. He told Manilal in no uncertain terms: "I must make you swallow bitter draughts." There was however, an assuring note in the same letter dated 12 March 1914: "I don't want to make an ascetic of you… I want to see you indifferent to the common pleasures of the world."[18] Truly said by his great granddaughter Uma Dhupelia-Mesthrie, "Manilal was still his father's prisoner."[19]

Romancing Fatima

The Gool family, especially Fatima, developed warm relationship with Manilal, which was equally reciprocated by him. Communication was

---

* A lifelong friend of India, he visited South Africa at the instance of G K Gokhale as a personal guest of Gandhiji.

on and Manilal visited Cape Town regularly. Mrs Yusuf and her daughters too travelled to Natal and Phoenix frequently.

There is a photograph (circa 1920) of Fatima wearing long shirts and western-style headgear, standing cheek by jowl with Ramdas, in front of Sarvodya building complex at Phoenix. There could be no greater proof of warmth than a memento of Shakespeare's collected works with an inscription dated 24 August 1920: "To Timmie with birthday greetings from Manilal", and, when viewed in retrospect: "The book now symbolises a tale of lost love".[20]

Apparently, Manilal and Timmie came closer to each other in course of time without the knowledge of Gandhiji. The romance had the approval of Gool family. Manilal turned thirty in 1922 and was anxious to get married to Timmie. When Gandhiji came to know of the romance, he gave Manilal a lecture and also denied his request point blank: "As long as you did not think of marriage, you stand absolved from your past sins. This atonement of yours keeps you pure… Take it from me that there is no happiness in marriage… Such is the mysterious ways of God."[21]

Mani and Timmie decided to communicate with Gandhiji through Ramdas. His reply followed: "I read your letter to Ramdas, also Fatima's [Timmie's]. And of course I had anticipated this; Jalbhai [Rustomjee, his friend] did give a hint. You are a free man; so I cannot force you to do anything."[22] Come what may, he was determined to stall Manilal and Fatima from carrying forward their relationship.

Mixed Marriages

Gandhiji declared war against his second son. This time he waved the flag of *dharma* in his own support. What about the children of a mixed marriage and what about the different food habits, he asked him. Being a lawyer, he sought to address his son as a concerned friend and well-wisher. Theoretically, he conceded freedom to him but, in practice, he had Manilal and Fatima tied in knots, never to be untangled.

Here was Gandhiji at his best– supplicating, cajoling and browbeating his son: "What you desire is contrary to *dharma*. If you stick to Hinduism and Fatima follows Islam, it will be like putting two swords in one sheath; or you both may lose your faith. And then what should be your children's faith… May not Fatima have meat at her father's? If she does not, she has as good as changed her religion."[23]

Unsure of his arguments, he dropped Ba's name as the last resort. He asked him if he would dare to ask her permission? Wouldn't she have the shock of her life? Gandhiji had his way. The intimate link between two young people was torn asunder. The hapless son was cornered by an argument seemingly fatuous in the very face of it: "Your marriage will have a powerful impact on the Hindu-Muslim question. Inter-communal marriages are no solution to this problem. You cannot forget, neither will society forget that you are my son... If you enter into this relationship, you may not be able to render any service. I fear you may no more be the right person to run the *Indian Opinion*... It will be impossible for you, I think, after this to come and settle in India."[24]

Manilal was reduced to muttering: *Pujya pitha shri ni pavitra sevama* (in my revered father's sublime service).

Mani's Revenge

Devdas added to his father's woes by courting Lakshmi Rajagopalachari the following year. Ramdas brought some relief in this gloomy situation. He married a bride selected by his father in 1928. Sustained psychological pressure by Gandhiji over his second-born turned him into a cipher. Manilal's daughter Sita Dhupelia recalled: "My father didn't make a single decision without referring to Bapu. My mother was no less enslaved."[25] Manilal married Sushila Gandhi (*née* Mashruwala). His marriage resulted from Ba's incessant pleadings with her husband, who finally turned to his associate, Kishorelal Mashruwala, to search for a bride. Kishorelal, in turn, informed him about his niece living in Akola (Maharashtra). There was a slight hitch about the prospective bride since she was stone deaf. Gandhiji, however, approved of the girl.

Fatima never went out of his mind. She gracefully reversed her steps and they continued to be in touch with each other. She would visit Durban regularly to see her sister Gogija and stay at Phoenix for days and have long chats with Manilal. She eventually turned to religion as a substitute for her unfulfilled romance. She remained a spinster all her life.

His father, throughout their long association, subjected Manilal to severe tests. He was to have his revenge when he came to live with his father during 1945–46. Ba was dead by then. He was astonished to find his father too lenient with his associates. They appeared to Manilal as spoilt children. Earlier, Ba used to provide the necessary correctives. Manilal had a score to settle with his father, he said: "Bapu, you have vastly changed from the time we were under you. You never pampered us; I remember how you made us do laundry work and chop wood; how you made us to take the pick and shovel in the bitterly cold mornings and dig in the garden, to cook and to walk miles. And I am surprised how you pamper the people around you."[26] Bapu had no real answer and he responded with 'his usual hearty laughter'. Thus Manilal, whom Bapu used to call his 'sanitary inspector' had his sweet revenge late in the day.

Harilal— The Unfortunate

Harilal, the eldest, was the most unfortunate of all in the Gandhi family. His was a story of the proverbial Greek tragedy in which the participants knew precisely what was going to happen to them, and yet they were helpless in preventing the outcome. Harilal has been painted as a vagabond, debauch, drunkard and a womaniser. But, he was not so bad. He had gone to prison six times (1908–10) at the instance of his father. Even Gandhiji admitted to his potential as the sharpest among his progeny.

His youngest brother Devdas referred to Harilal as "one of Bapu's best subalterns" in his obituary tribute. Gandhiji in the *Indian Opinion* of 8 August 1908 proclaimed, loud and clear: "I want every Indian to do what Harilal has done", by being a model *satyagrahi*. In an unpublished letter, Gandhiji commended Harilal's "ability to remain unattached". He even placed himself in the role of King Dasharath who worshipped his role model son Rama. What went wrong then? Gandhiji believed that Harilal was doing penance for sins committed by him in his former life. Harilal had a rational explanation to offer for his irrational conduct: "Our views about education are the main reason for the difference of opinion of the last ten [1905–15] years."[27]

While Harilal spent his entire adult life in an accusatory frame of mind, he had a sharpness that could cut through the usual rigmarole. He could also mimic his father perfectly. Ba, however, had a soft corner for her eldest son. The tensions between father and son flared up frequently. There came a moment in early 1915 when civilities were set aside and combativeness took over, in full public view. This time Harilal had decided to charge sheet his father.

He wrote a detailed 12-page letter to Gandhiji that was full of bile and bitterness: "All of us brothers have been treated as a ringmaster would treat his trained animals... You have always suppressed us. You have never spoken to us". Gandhiji was charged with employing "humiliating language". The very authority of the father was questioned: "You are ignorant... You lack understanding." He charged Gandhiji with having "a heart of stone. Love I have not seen in you". Harilal had done exhaustive but negative research. He attacked Gandhian practices such as denying milk and *ghee* to himself, all in the cause of true *brahmacharya* and self-control. Harilal argued that virtues such as charity, selflessness, courage and humility were more important than denying salt to oneself. Harilal's chargesheet however made no direct references to Gandhiji's *brahmacharya* practices. Perhaps, this was considered off-limits, even for an angry son.

The biggest charge, however, was on Gandhiji's treatment of his wife: "But the lot of my mother was worse than mine. I saw her insulted and humiliated. Mrs Gandhi takes too much sugar, which has led to too much expenses; Mrs Gandhi has no right to assign work to the employees of the press, and so on and so forth. I have not the words to describe the misery she had gone through."[28] But the foresaid 12-page letter, written on 31 March 1915, had a reconciliatory end: "I have never deliberately defied you, as you will admit. In the innermost recesses of my heart, I do not wish to be anything but your son—only if I could be fit [enough] to be your son."[29]

Father-Son Fixation

Gandhiji had his own charge sheet ready. In 1906, he wrote about Harilal to his brother Laxmidas Gandhi: "For the present at any rate, I have ceased to think of him as a son."[30] Gandhiji traced the chronology of the conflict to around 1910 when 'his ideals and mine' had begun to diverge distinctly before they finally parted around 1915. Harilal was fond of quoting a proverb in Gujarati: "*bar maro, kanya maro, par gor ka tarbano bharo*, or, in other words, whatever be done should be to please Bapu."[31]

Gandhiji had a rationale for his predicament. He was a firm believer in the theory of *karma* (cause and effect syndrome). The *karma* cycle extended not only to the next life but impacted the present as well. Under this theory, he had a 'bad son' on account of sins committed by him either in the present or the previous life. Gandhiji said that Harilal was conceived: "when I was in a state of infatuation [with Kasturba]".[32]

He wrote a letter to Ba in 1934, holding both of them equally guilty: "I think [Harilal] will remain what he is....How sunk in passion I was when he was conceived! You and I must so reap as we sowed."[33] To Manilal and Sushila, he candidly admitted his neglect of Harilal on account of his public preoccupations: "Mine has been a life of wanderings and it has a number of vicissitudes."[34]

There was hope of reconciliation between father and son when Harilal poured out his heart while sharing a room with his long standing associate Balwantsinha, at Sabarmati. The son admitted to his 'mistakes' and promised to abide by his father's wishes. He decided to live in a village to serve for the rest of his life.

When Gandhiji heard of Harilal's latest determination, he was extremely pleased and gave special permission to Harilal to smoke a pack of cigarettes every fortnight. The father was totally impressed and overjoyed when he came to know about Harilal's tentative decision to spend the rest of his life in a village: "In such a case, I would love to die in your lap."[35] Gandhiji's blank refusal to Harilal to engage himself with the German lady Margarete Spiegel set the reverse gear, with Harilal going down the hill for the rest of his life.

Harilal was a footloose and a dreamer for whom promises remained only on paper. His wish to return to a normal life remained a dream too. His wife, late Chanchalbehn and Ba were amongst the few persons he trusted. After he visited Sri Aurobindo in Pondicherry in 1934, he wrote to Ba: "I long to know whether you would pardon me. I am committed to Sri Aurobindo to behave in future. I shall never repeat my mistakes until my dying days."[36]

As on earlier occasions, he did not keep his promise. He did not return but wrote to her from Hyderabad, where he was living in abject penury:

"Hyderabad — May 5, 1934

Respected mother,

When shall I have the opportunity to sit at your feet? I am looking forward to be blessed by you.

Yours affectionately,
Harilal Mohandas Gandhi"[37]

Conversion to Islam

He was now sick in body and mind and a wanderer who would not stick to one place or thing. Nobody wanted him. He was shunned as a vagabond, given to frequent bouts of drunkenness. His sister-in-law Balibehn dared to slap him repeatedly for his rowdy behaviour in 1932. Gandhiji took vicarious pleasure in this act of violence against Harilal, and termed it as 'an act of pure love'.[38] In another version by Manu Gandhi, Balibehn, her aunt "gave three or four slaps to Bhai (Harilal). Bapu wrote: 'She gave slaps, she did a good thing. There was no violence in it but there was pure love.'"[39]

Soon thereafter on 29 May 1936, Harilal converted to Islam—a traumatic event in the Gandhi family. Ba almost went out of her mind and Gandhiji relapsed into deep silence. He refused to discuss another disreputable act of his eldest son. It was too hard for Ba to bear all this. She was particularly disturbed by Gandhiji's silence. She decided to go on the offensive and spoke publicly about Harilal's debauchery and drunkenness. She upbraided him for humiliating his father through his brazen public pronouncements about his ideology, personality and his very person.

A mother's open letter to her son was released on her behalf in September 1936. She was hurt beyond redemption, and reminded him of his unruly behaviour in his drunken state in public on numerous occasions. His conduct had broken "his [father's] heart into pieces".[40] She was unable to sleep because of concern for her wayward son. She chided his 'Muslim brother' by calling him '*Maulvi*'. She asked of him: "Is that reasonable? Does your religion permit to call a drunkard a '*Maulvi*'." She concluded the letter by reminding her son: "What you are doing would not be reasonable in the eyes of God [*Khuda*]."[41]

But her repeated supplications worsened the situation. Harilal took pleasure in his father's predicament. Newspapers were full of stories about '*Maulvi* Abdullah' (Muslim appellation of Harilal). Harilal did not respond directly but took up the cudgel in a public meeting held in Kanpur on 1 October 1936: "I am Abdullah and not Harilal. Therefore, I do not acknowledge this letter. My mother is illiterate. I do not believe that she can write this… I have only one desire, and that is to die as a worker of Islam."[42] At another public meeting, he decided to hurt his parents directly by saying: "My mother Kasturba requests me to stop drinking,… I will give up drinking but when? At the time when

Pitaji (respected father) and she embraced Islam."[43] He elaborated upon the theme in yet another public meeting: "Bapu has been unable to reform me during past fifteen years. How can he do so in four months?"[44]

But the prodigal son returned to his old faith on 12 November 1936. He wrote yet another defiant letter to his father soon after his reconversion to the Hindu faith: "The question whether I am haunting Ba or you are doing it [remains unanswered]. Ba reacts to me on the basis of biased reports fed to her. I refuse to believe of Ba being not understanding of me. She must have been denied accurate information. Hence my hesitation to write to her. She would write to me, only when she is allowed to do so… Presently, I am in Delhi… If the date of marriage of Manu [his daughter] has been fixed, pl. let me know… The other letter is for Ba. Your most obedient son Harilal."[45]

Mata Kasturba Ki Jai

There was one encounter that captured the tension between father, mother and son. On 1 March 1941, when the Jabalpur Mail, by which the Gandhis were travelling, came to a halt at its usual stoppage at the Katni railway station, they heard a resounding voice: '*Mata Kasturba ki Jai*' [Salutation to Ba]. That was Harilal. The following conversation took place:

"Ba, take this orange."

"Where have you brought it from?"

"From nowhere! I have begged it. It is out of my love for you."

Ba accepted the fruit, but Harilal was still not assured. He further told her: "Ba, it is exclusively for you. If you don't eat it give it back to me".

"Fine, I shall partake of it. How are you presently? Have you ever given thought to your illustrious pedigree? Join us."

He was too diplomatic in his response: "Forget about it. I cannot rise above my present situation."[46]

Now it was Gandhiji's turn to converse with his elder son. The piece of fruit had been begged by Harilal from a fruit vendor. He did not have money to afford it. His father solicited a portion of the 'booty' as his patrimony. Harilal brusquely rejected his request: "No. It is exclusively for Ba". He also added an advice to him. "All your greatness is owed to her." Ba shed a tear or two. When the train started moving, she suddenly realised that she had not offered anything to her wayward son. She again heard the distant outcry: "*Mata Kasturba ki jai.*"[47]

Post-Mortem

Harilal Gandhi was nobody's favourite. He died a derelict, in a tuberculosis hospital in Bombay on 19 June 1948. His two daughters, Manu and Romi (and their husbands), were with him at his bedside. His identity was the hospital tag, placed on him by hospital authorities. Rajaji in his 6 June 1949 letter to Kishore lal Mashruwala made a balanced assessment of Harilal: "Harilal was a fine boy. Like all earthy things Bapu's glory cast a shadow which became Harilal's lot, while all others got the advantage and benefited from it."[48]

Devdas, his youngest brother, however, paid him the ultimate tribute in a memorial piece in the *Hindustan Times* dated 24 July 1948, soon after his demise. The obituary tribute to his elder brother brought out true and sterling qualities of Harilal. Thereby Devdas retrieved for Harilal (though belatedly) the honour due to him.

The tribute by the younger brother is with a difference, depicting him as a footloose nomad who "never knew mental or physical peace in his sixty years of life".

He was a perpetual rebel who rebelled against Bapu's life of 'experiments'. Devdas's mind goes back to four decades earlier when Gandhiji's 'subaltern' was a handsome young man with hair parted 'in the middle with beautiful curls over the forehead'. Even though he resembled his father the most, yet he enjoyed being in 'perpetual opposition' to him, and indeed his 'mock conversion to Islam' was a 'stunt', perhaps only to spite his father.

Devdas brought out the essence of his elder brother in the following phrase: "But a remarkable trait in him was his audacious readiness to suffer the consequences of his way and what he called his free thinking." At heart, Harilal was no cynic, but a firm believer in Lokmanya Tilak's commentary of the *Bhagvad Gita*, hence he always carried a copy of *Gita Rahasya*, "even when he did not have even a shirt to wear."[49]

Gandhiji's great granddaughter Uma Dhupelia-Meshrie has painted a glowing picture of Harilal underlining the great potential of the Little Gandhi: "Harilal belonged to an esteemed category of resisters, which included the likes of P K Naidoo, Sorabji Adajania, Thambi Naidoo,

Surendra Medh, Pragji Desai and Parsee Rustomjee, and he had done no less than any of them. From June 1909 to January 1911, his home (apart from a little over two weeks between sentences) had been prisons. This had included the dreaded Diepkloof prison and the Johannesburg Fort. At Tolstoy Farm he settled down to work, learnt to make sandals and joined others in the long walk to Johannesburg and back. But at heart he was unhappy, 'because not once but twice he had opportunities to study abroad, but denied by his upright father swearing at the altar of his 'new ethic of public service.''"[50]

Failed Father

There was a duality in Gandhiji in as much as he wanted to play the loving parent and high-and-mighty charismatic leader simultaneously. He saw in his four sons images of himself, failing to realise that Harilal was a Harilal and Manilal was a Manilal. They could not duplicate Mohandas even if they tried.

There is no doubt that his progeny viewed him as Old Testament's God, spitting brimstone and fire. His granddaughter, Sita Dhupelia, thought of her uncle Harilal as 'a kind and gentle man', who had been 'completely broken' by Bapu. Also, she did not fail to notice that her parents, Mani and Sushila, lived their days in a "captive state."[51] His sons must have been dying to be normal human beings, but Gandhiji wanted them to be minor saints.

Gandhiji realised as early as 1911 that he was more feared than loved. His sons had a feeling of being suppressed. In a remarkable confession, he was to admit as much: "I do not know what evil there is in me. I have a strain of cruelty in me, as others say, such that people force themselves to do things, even to attempt impossible things, in order to please me."[52] His political guru Gopal Krishna Gokhale considered him 'harsh' and totally inconsiderate, bullying others to fall in line with him.

The finest tribute was, however, paid by director-playwright Dr Ajit Dalvi in his controversial Marathi play *Gandhi virudh Gandhi* (Gandhi vs. Gandhi) in which he attempted to "portray the private grudge of a small individual [growing up] under gigantic shadow."

In his determination to pursue the national goal and in dealing with myriads of other things that his calling ordained, Gandhiji did not get much time to understand his children. Did the Father of the Nation falter when measured by his own yardstick in coming to terms with his progeny?

SECTION III

South African Interlude

CHAPTER 6

Millie and Henry Polak

Hermann Kallenbach and Henry Soloman Leon Polak were close associates of Gandhiji in South Africa. Both of them were of Jewish extraction. They were his partners-in-arm in the cause of Indians in South Africa. While Gandhiji was 'Upper House' to Kallenbach, Kallenbach was his 'Lower House', sidekick and financier. Their relations were always sweet and never soured. Kallenbach was also one of the executors of his will and testament signed on 19 June 1909.

Henry Polak was like a *chhota bhai* to Gandhi. He was articled to Mohandas Karamchand of the Inner Temple, who was then practicing as an attorney in Johannesburg. His relations with Polak were further cemented with the arrival of Millie Graham, his fiancée. Gandhiji was so excited about Millie that he established contact with her even before she arrived in South Africa for her marriage.

Welcoming Party

Millie Graham was dissuaded by Henry's father, JHL Polak, in moving to South Africa due to her delicate state of health. Soon, Gandhiji took charge of the situation. He shot off a letter to the senior Polak and employed all the skills of an Inner Temple attorney to persuade him to change his mind: "If the young lady in question was not at that time in robust health in London, all the more reason for her to hasten her departure from it, so that in South Africa, amidst loving care, a beautiful climate and a simple life, she could gain the physical strength she evidently needed."[1]

He also wrote an assuring letter to Millie at the same time. His persuasive skills did the trick. Millie decided to join the 'heterogeneous family' of which Henry was an integral member. Finally, Millie was on her way to South Africa by boat. The welcoming party, at six o'clock in the morning of 30 December 1905 at the Jeppe station, Johannesburg consisted of the two-some of Mr Gandhi and Mr Polak (the nomenclature by which she was to describe both of them). He was totally impressed by her very presence and, reciprocally, Millie was bowled over by him. Gandhiji was 36 at that time. Here was a medium-sized middle-aged person of brown skin, heavy lips and small-dark moustache striding down the railway platform. It was his eyes which overwhelmed Millie: He had "the kindest eyes in the world that seemed to light up from within when he spoke. His eyes were always his most remarkable feature and were in reality the lamps of his soul; one could read so much from them."[2]

It was an eyeball-to-eyeball interaction of a special kind. There are persons who are able to communicate through body language. Gandhiji and Millie started conversing through their eyes. They immediately made a pact between themselves. Poor Henry was left stranded. He did not understand what was happening before his very eyes. He was to content himself with a mere kiss from his beloved fiancée. Millie was ecstatic about Gandhiji. She even found him soft and musical, and 'almost boyishly fresh'. They chatted away all the way from the station to her new home.

Hardship Station

Millie was a Christian and Henry a Jew by faith. He belonged to one of the ancient Judaic families. The marriage was solemnised the very day she arrived from England. Gandhiji acted as the best man and issued the necessary instructions. The job was done. Henry and Millie became husband and wife on 30 December 1905. They were in the thick of public activities from day one. She was to join Kasturba in performing household chores.

Gandhiji was already calling her "a most valuable acquisition of the family at Troyville in Johannesburg." He painted an ideal picture of his 'heterogeneous family' with no jealousies and hence 'no rival rights'. There was no immediate honeymoon for Henry and Millie, but there were troubles ahead of them. Gandhiji was planning a political struggle to strain his financial and mental resources to the utmost. The Johannesburg household was acutely short of money. Furthermore,

Gandhiji was in the process of tailoring the requirements of his household, strictly in the light of Ruskin's teachings of good society and dignity of labour. Baker's bread became taboo in the Gandhian household. Unleavened bread was prepared laboriously by using hand-grounded flour.

Millie helped Kasturba in household work. Life was hard and Gandhiji made it doubly sure that it remained so at all times. It was a miserable and crowded household which Henry and Millie shared with others. There was no proper plumbing and just a makeshift bathroom under the stairs. The walls were damp in perpetuity. The food was bland and constantly in short supply.

Tensions continued to build up on the political front. Millie got just four peaceful months to herself before the storm broke. There were shoutings, agitations, negotiations and finally arrests during 1908. Gandhiji was burdened with too many things at the same time. He worked from morning till night and returned home after midnight: "[He] was weary and thirsty… He trod on a fat slimy slug, of course, in bare feet, this seemed just more than he could bear, and in a quiet but penetrative voice exclaimed, 'Thank God I will be in a jail tomorrow' and he was. It was a rest and refuge, a time of comparative gratitude, a blessing for him."[3]

Phoenix Farm

His being forced into prison was a blessing in disguise for Kasturba and Millie for whom it was grind and more grind day after day. Further miseries were in store for Millie when they decided to move to Phoenix near Durban, a 400-acre farm he adopted to experiment with his esoteric ideal of simple living and high thinking. His experiments in dietics, nature cure and *brahmacharya*, besides education for young children, owed a great deal to Phoenix Farm started in 1904.

Though the Polak family went along with Gandhiji, but they found it difficult to cope with the adverse conditions prevailing at the experimental farm. Millie gave a graphic picture of the conditions prevailing at the farm to Henry's two sisters, Maud and Sally. At his satirical best, Gandhiji simulated Millie for their mutual titillation: "[There was] not a retrieving feature -beetles everywhere, spiders, ants in the milk, no baths, water bed, people half naked, filth too,… you have not only to tolerate this but love the insect life, you may not destroy any life, I (Millie) could not do it, my idea of simplicity different from G's, I would not therefore live in Phoenix, etc."[4]

Phoenix symbolised the triumph of the spirit of man over unfriendly, inhospitable and mean Nature. Henry and Millie stuck to Gandhiji through thick and thin even though he was too demanding of his associates. Never was Gandhiji so much at peace with himself as in his South African days. He was in the company of Polaks, Wests and Kallenbach. They would communicate on an equal intellectual plane. After all, they had sacrificed their professional careers to fight the causes dear to him. All of them were helping to lay the foundations of an exciting new world. They had only the haziest idea of a new society yet to be born.

The Polaks were the closest to Gandhiji. Millie, of course, was the cementing factor. Henry was Gandhiji's deputy in legal practice and partner in devising strategies on the political and ideological front. Millie provided a pleasant interlude for both of them. Kasturba was so taken up with Henry that she was ever ready to adopt him as her first born. Gandhiji would have none of it because he had accepted him as his younger brother. He was, however, prepared to adopt Maud Polak (Henry's sister) as his 'first born daughter'. He was simply charmed by her spontaneity. Thus, Gandhis became heads of a joint family of brown, white and black and had persons of European, Indian and African extraction on its roll.

Cow Milk Ban

Gandhiji continually experimented in dietetics. There was hardly any rationale for it. He worked by intuition. Rightly so, he has been named a 'legendary eccentric' in dietetics. Even Millie joined him in this fun. He experimented with all kinds of permutations and combinations inflicting the results on his unsuspecting guests. At one time he experimented with a dish of raw onions as a blood-purifier. He and his associates became so fond of Spanish onions in salad that a restaurant in Johannesburg serving them became their special haunt. This group came to be known as 'The Amalgamated Society of Onion Eaters'. It did not take him long to forsake his favourite dish and eventually, he turned his back on onions. They were taboo for being too good for passion. Milk had already been declared a taboo by him for the very same reason.

Millie took the milk taboo rather seriously. Going by his argument, babies and young children should be the champion brutes in matters of sex. He tried to wriggle out of the trap by making a fine distinction between adults and children. She mocked him thus: "A milk-fed child would be a most unnatural little brute. Think of a little child obsessed with sex-passion because it had a diet of milk. It is not reasonable."[5] He was a difficult man, impervious to any rational argument. He would make up his mind on certain matters and turned stupidly mulish on occasions. For him, milk was the Viagra of his times. He was obsessed with food as much as he was with sex. Sometimes, Millie thought that Gandhiji would be much better off if he accepted food and sex as given and then forgot about them.

To Millie, the *brahmacharya* practice adopted by Gandhiji was not her cup of tea. She was sceptical about his attributing all kinds of virtues to *brahmacharya*. Denial of onions, salt, sugar and milk in the name of *brahmacharya* exasperated her. To her, all this experimentation seemed unreal. More so, because it put others to so much inconvenience. His word was law. Whatever he dictated became the gospel truth for others.

She was convinced about Gandhiji playing games with the lives of others. She had begun to drift away from his murky world. Her mind was elsewhere, even though she had committed herself to the Gandhian cause. Intellectually, she refused to accept his outlandish commandments and decided to confront her mentor by employing British undertones that came naturally to her: "Well, I do not want to pay the price I pay for love to be that I am ignored. It seems to me that because I love another I should show the best part of me to that one, and look for chances to give the little acts of courtesy that I believe love and friendship are entitled to."[6]

In other words, she was warning him that he was getting too big for her shoes. For him, love and affection were secondary to his cause. In her view, he maintained the form but missed the content. Millie very much hated his 'love of the uncomfortable'. To her discomfiture, he always tread a circuitous route rather than a straight path. Was he a masochist who liked to torture himself and torture others? Millie was exasperated, but she was yet to reach the point of no return. He was engaged in a bigger game. The whole world was a stage for him. Yet, Millie and Gandhiji remained close to each other at the personal level. It was a beautiful relationship. The trio was deeply involved with each other.

Lovable Gandhi

Gandhiji irritated Millie to no end. Yet, she loved him for his eccentricities and irrationalities. To her, he was a lovable but incorrigibly impossible human being. They used to argue back and forth about the practice of *brahmacharya* which was his latest fad. It took him several decades of struggle to conquer passion. Now he wanted to impose his *brahmacharya* regime over others under the specious logic of what was denied to him must be denied to others. She put the issue frontally before him: "Only that you are still making me feel that you think of it to be a higher condition of life to be celibate rather than to be a parent."'[7]

According to her, Gandhiji was reaching the stage of logical absurdity in arguing that the highest stage of *brahmacharya* would be reached only when mankind decimated itself voluntarily in order to achieve universal *moksha*. She was horrified at this logical absurdity: "There came a time when I felt that if one were going to have a child, it would seem as though it were 'conceived in sin and carried in wickedness.'"[8]

The light comes out of darkness. Henry and Millie had moved out of Phoenix to Durban. She had come to Phoenix to call upon him. In the meanwhile, a new baby had arrived at Phoenix. Gandhiji chided her for not conveying the good news to him. His eyes brightened up and his face was wreathed with smiles after he spotted the mother and the child. Millie was totally impressed with his spontaneous expression for the baby. It dawned upon Millie that not all was lost: "[and] realised that even Mr Gandhi distinguished between abstract truth and human love, and mother-love was always of great beauty and joy to him."[9] On another occasion when Millie was proving to be unsuccessful in weaning away her first-born, he came to her rescue. He simply loved young children. He took charge of the situation by having the little one sleep in his bed and thus assisted in the weaning process rather successfully. Millie was totally impressed on these occasions.

Millie's Psyche

Millie remained on his mind for many many years. What made her so lovable to him? The secret emerges in one of his letters to her: "Though we differ somewhat as to the view of life, there is still a subtle sameness running through our thought which makes you most lovable to me."[10] Gandhiji would go out of his way during his early years of association with the Polaks to identify himself with Millie. It helped him get closer to her. He found elements in Millie that were missing from his life with Kasturba. Millie filled a gaping hole in his conjugal existence.

He tended to be hyperbolic at times but his intensity of love for Millie could hardly be missed. Here goes the circular argument in which he mentions Henry, at least for the sake of form and propriety: "So we are, apart from your being Henry's wife, sister and brother .... But then I am an exacting brother... I do not want the obedience of a daughter that only a daughter can give and should give."[11]

As if such fulsome expressions were not enough, he expressed the pangs of separation openly: "Now, O God, when shall we who have so much in common meet again!'[12] There were also wheels within wheels. While Gandhiji found himself besotted with Millie, her sister-in-law Maud Polak found Gandhiji just irresistible. Henry Polak did not understand what was going on in his backyard. At one time he got so exasperated that he did not see the virtues that Gandhiji had discovered in Millie.

All the probings Gandhiji carried out in the psyche of Millie did not help him very much. She was still an enigma to him. They discussed and debated for long hours. The arguments resulted in bitterness and resentment against each other. He knew for certain that she resented his domineering nature. She also knew that he could twist and turn around an argument to his advantage. It was pathetic to find him supplicating to win her assent. The argument got confused at times but, never mind, the message was clear: "Will you not, for my sake, shake yourself from that little morbidity of your nature? It will become a character like yours. I want a perfect sister."[13]

'Henry's better half' became a 'tender flame' by 14 April 1910. Gandhiji was turning poetic. His platonic sentiments made it so crystal clear: "You and I divide [Polak] .... But alas! he can just now have neither you or me."[14] Jealousy had by now entered Henry's bloodstream. He resented Gandhiji's deliberate and calculated intrusions in his personal and private life.

Millie was not entirely blameless. She too was charmed by Mahatma, who had, by 1910, made a name for himself in South Africa. Henry was Gandhiji's favourite lieutenant but had grown feathers enabling him to take fancy flights on his own. This was also the beginning of the ideological rift that lasted a lifetime. There were differences of perspective cropping up between Gandhiji, the mentor and Henry, the loyal deputy. In all probability Millie was the root cause of this incipient trouble.

Gandhiji recalled his association with Henry and Millie with great nostalgia after he was back in India. He told Mahadev Desai: "I used to tell Polak that he had two wives, Mrs Polak and I, for he would pour himself only before us two and likewise be angry with us."[15]

Henry was in India at that moment of time. He sent a twelve-page rejoinder to Gandhiji showing his puckish sense of humour. He told him that he was on his way to Malabar: "in order to see the Nair women, who, I am told, take one husband after another. That beats you all, who take one wife after another! I think the women are right!"[16]

Millie in London

Gandhiji led a delegation to London to negotiate with the British Government in 1909. Millie was back in London for an extended visit to her family. Gandhiji was very pleased at the coincidence. He would take her on his rounds of visits to his friends and public men. He enjoyed being in England for the sheer presence of Millie. He loved to offer hospitality to his young visitors. It was a treat to watch young people 'eating, drinking, talking and laughing'. Gandhiji would be at his informal best. They would spread newspapers on the table of his hotel room and pile it with "oranges, apples, bananas, perhaps grapes, and a big bag of unshelled monkey or pea-nuts."[17]

He was so excited about the presence of Millie in London that his letter of 30 July 1909 to Henry was full of it. Gandhiji was making the best use of the opportunity of having Millie entirely to himself, especially because she planned to be away from South Africa for about a year.

He had arrived in London by July 1909 and he was still there after four months. He would have her stay at the hotel overnight for long chats. He was ecstatic in informing Henry about the convenient arrangement: "Millie will sleep at the Hotel so I am looking forward to a long and quiet chat with her. Naturally, we are much nearer each other now than we were ever before, having seen more of each other than in Johannesburg, where I rarely met her."[18]

A bit of comic relief was provided when not only his letters to Henry but also Millie's letters to her husband were 'deliberately opened' in Gandhiji's office. Gandhiji was amused and wrote to Henry on the subject. The humourless Henry wrote a stinker to Gandhiji: "You take the opening of Millie's letters more philosophically than she and I do. I see that your days of writing love-letters are over. I am sorry for you! I haven't yet authorised Millie to start a class in marital devotion!"[19] The undertones of irritation with Gandhiji could not be overlooked.

More Irritation

By 14 November 1909, he was on his way back to South Africa. His weeks in the lovely company of Millie on an extended holiday in London haunted him. He admired her for her womanly quality of judging things by intuition, which made her so 'lovable' to him. His obsession with brother-sister relationship would not go away. He would recite it as a mantra time and again without number. He indulged in meaningless talks of his being 'an exacting brother' and both of them being 'mad after truth'. He looked forward to 'a sister's full trust and confidence'. He was literally talking sweet nothings to her.

Was he in competition with Henry for the attention of Millie? Was he looking forward to an assurance of her fidelity to him? He talked endlessly about her, now that he was back in South Africa. He, perhaps, wanted reciprocity from her: "I want your confidence because I hastened your legal marriage and I have been instrumental in keeping you physically apart."[20] Gandhiji was forty by then but he behaved like a teenager. On the very next day he shot off a letter to Henry in which he talked about his sisters, Maud and Sally. There was a brief mention of Millie in the same letter.

Gandhiji did not like Millie addressing him as her brother in inverted commas in her reply to him. Worst still, the word had been underlined three times: "I see you address me Brother in inverted commas and underlined thrice… but will you give me a sister's confidence? If you say 'Yes', I should like to be 'brother' to you." He, however, went on harping on this brotherly syndrome: "Though a brother could never replace a husband, I tried during my stay in London to replace Henry so far as I could. It was no more a wrench to you to separate from me than it was to me to separate from you. We certainly came nearer each other in London than ever before. It was natural."[21] Henry had a reason to be jealous of him. Gandhiji was not beyond attempting to create a rift between the couple.

Persistent Gandhi

As if all this was not enough, Gandhiji assured Millie again and again of his faith in her (when no assurance was required): "You are dearer because there is so much in common between us and because I have entered so much into your and Henry's lives."[22]

By this time, Millie must have been bored stiff by his repeated supplications. She had other things on mind. Her separation from Henry had lasted for about six months. She was feeling the wifely pangs. In her reply to Gandhiji, she would talk more about Henry than about him. He was, however, persistent. He would read more meaning in her letters than warranted by its contents: "Your letter haunts me. It fills me with sorrow and admiration for you. You have written it in love, grief and resignation."[23]

He was curious about everything concerning Millie. He had inflicted her with a detailed letter requesting her to share the contents of her letter to Henry. He even went to the extent of requesting Millie to make available to him, 'the other letter that you wrote'. He did not mince words and told her: "I wish you had sent his [Henry's] letter to me".

By December 1909, he realised that Henry alone was in her mind. After having reduced herself to writing brief notes in response to his detailed letters, she stopped writing to him. Probably she had had enough of Gandhiji by this time. There was, however, no stopping him. What was better in the circumstances than to sow the seeds of doubt in the mind of 'Henry's better half': "Will you not have sufficient faith in him to know for certain that he is incapable of creating a gulf between you and himself." His blabbering continued endlessly boring Millie stiff: "I ask you to trust me *never* to carry Henry along any route without your approval… You have often given me the privilege of analysing you to yourself. You have heroically sacrificed yourself on the altar of duty. But you have done so in bitterness not always free from resentment."[24]

Millie was still in London. Her long absence from South Africa had ruffled his feathers. Millie was also upset because of what she considered his boorishness in emphasising the syndrome of 'perfect sister' and 'perfect brother' repeatedly. Henry was also annoyed with him on that account. Millie was aware of the resentment of Henry. There was no putting off Gandhiji. He merrily went on the same way as before. He persisted with his onslaught. Suddenly there was a gap of four months in letters from him. Admittedly, the discouragement of Millie had begun to have its subtle effect on him. There was hardly any mention of brother-and-sister syndrome. Now he was reduced to a few-liner letters.

The reason was the presence of Henry in London along with Millie: "Now that you are there, I shall not write to Millie except when some special occasion demands it."[25] Now, there was a flood of letters addressed to Henry on 7 May, 15 May, 22 May, 28 May, 11 June, 23 June, 2 July, 23 July and 27 July 1911, indicating their clockwise regularity. Millie emerged briefly in his letter of 2 July, when he reminded Henry of his delayed honeymoon of six years. The ebullience and sparkle in his letters was entirely missing.

Maud Polak

If it was not Millie, then it had to be Maud Polak for Gandhiji. Leaving the field clear for Henry in his dealings with Millie, he turned his attention to Henry's sister Maud. She must have reminded him of Millie, who was not out of his orbit entirely. She haunted him for many years. In 1932, he again wrote to Henry Polak: "What could be more auspicious than I should execute God's will on Millie's birthday."[26]

The first real mention of Maud and Sally was during 1906. Gandhiji had met the Polak sisters for the first time and was charmed by their vivacity. He recalled his first meeting with them vividly in his letter to Henry: "Both the sisters are really most lovable and if I was unmarried, or young, or believed in mixed marriages, you know what I would have done? As it is, I told them that if I had made their acquaintance in 1888 (for not doing which they took me severely to task), I should adopt [them] as daughters."[27]

Maud Polak responded to him spontaneously. She was keen to work with him at Phoenix Farm without the reservations of Millie. He found her of sweet temperament. She was prepared to make sacrifices for his cause. The other sister Sally was not as amenable to him. Maud was a suffragette with a mind of her own. In his letters to Henry, he started singing paeans of Maud Polak. As Millie began to maintain a distance from him, Maud came into the picture. She was ready to fill the gap. He decided to adopt her as 'his first-born'. During his stay in London, Maud was never away from him. Yet, Gandhiji took some time to guess 'the intensity of affection' for her, occupied as he was with the thoughts of Millie. She was, however, keen to join him in South Africa. He shared his thoughts with Mille: "But is all this real or is it the glamour of my presence? If it is the latter, it is too terrible. Anyhow I look to you to observe Maud, analyse her, cross-examine her and find out where she is."[28]

Millie gave a very dismal picture of Phoenix Farm to the Polak sisters. Sally backed off immediately. Maud was, however, made of sterner stuff. She was not to be put off. He felt gratified by her spontaneous response. Now that Gandhiji was on his way to South Africa from London, the real Maud came out publicly indicating the intensity of her affection for him. He said in his letter to Henry: "She cannot tear herself from me. I was watching her at the station. She was on the point of breaking down. She would not shake hands with me. She wanted a kiss. That she would not have at the station, not that she or I was afraid but it should be misunderstood, so she stood rigid on the platform. We have not shaken hands for months. But the night scene I have already described to you has transformed her and with her me."[29]

There was never a sweeter description of a woman's unrequited love for a man. Maud was to land in South Africa and work closely with Gandhiji as his secretary. The romance gradually weaned off by about 1913. It was clear in his apology tendered to Gopal Krishna Gokhale during his visit to South Africa: "I wrote to her [Maud] saying that she had misled me and that you too had been misled."[30]

Suffering Couple

Suffering was the badge of honour for Millie and her husband. It was written in the stars for the ethical couple to suffer for others. Eventually, they were to return home unsung and unknown. During a free-wheeling discussion, Gandhiji had made a self-fulfilling prophecy for Millie: "And you will never find peace," Mr Gandhi said, almost sadly.[31]

To the Polaks, life was a battle in the cause of *dharma*. Sacrifice and scepticism were their life-long companions. The Rev C F Andrews had greater appreciation for Millie than Gandhiji, for sacrifices made by her.

"It was clear to me how greatly Mrs. Polak had suffered. Yet there was a brightness in her face as she welcomed me to her [in England] which told of radiant happiness within."[32]

Millie was a proud woman. She told Gandhiji once that she would kneel before none, not even Gandhiji. She had reservations about him as a private person and public figure from day one. The differences were accentuated with the passage of time. The cooling of relations was essentially ideological and marginally personal.

Millie was a person with a mind of her own and she made this clear at the very outset. She had developed a platonic relationship with her mentor, but she was not prepared to pay the price of the unstinted obedience that he expected from his band of loyal associates. This made her suffer in silence. Gandhiji's letter to Polak emphasised these qualities in the character of Millie: "Now Chhaganlal [Gandhi] like Millie has a habit of suffering mutely."[33]

Gandhiji admired her and loved her deeply. He was glad to concede that she followed her own inclinations: "She is a different type. She knows or thinks of what she is doing. She is a superior woman."[34]

Gandhiji wrote correct but matter of fact and readable prose. He rarely resorted to poetic imagination except when he felt too excited and could no longer contain himself. Millie could have been a prompter for him and, indeed, he kidded her for her innate qualities: "I cannot undertake to answer your prose poem. You have at times flights which baffle me. I shall not comment. Let our hearts speak to each other."[35]

He was inspired to quote from a popular poetic metaphor adopted by Thomas Gray in his *Elegy Written in a Country Churchyard*. On another occasion, he presented Henry and Millie a sumptuously lithographed copy of *Omar Khayyam*. He went lyrical about the ornamental Arabic calligraphy illustrating the volume.

Separation

The 'romance' of Gandhiji and Millie Graham Polak was a brief interlude in her life. Long after, it reminded Gandhiji of sweet bitter memories of 1909. Henry and Millie, on their part, decided to forget the bitter memories of 1909 and came closer. In 1916, they were separated again when Henry was away in India. Her letters to Henry showed deep affection. In just three weeks she felt the pangs of separation acutely. She wailed in desperation: "I think of all the widowed wives, and feel wicked that I am *not content*, but I am sad without you. Life loses its savour, and the day just goes by, but brings little cheer or no joy with them..."[36]

She was so absorbed in Henry that she was prepared to reveal her innermost thoughts to public. She termed them her 'innermost mysteries'. Her letter to Henry was a definitive statement on the chemistry of love: "Do you know, I believe I should be capable of hurting you, making you suffer, if because I had let myself, my whole self cling to you: you loved me less. It gives me a Christian, kind feeling, and I see I possess depths of beauty and ugliness hitherto unknown. But perhaps I would do nothing, neither hate nor desire to hurt but be just above you, untouched by your love or lack of it."[37]

Remember Radha in *Gita-Govind* and physical hurt in the love play in this connection. Millie wanted to be a shining star in the firmament, pure as a virgin: "untouched by passion either human or divine". Here she was talking the language of Gandhiji of passionless love and *brahmacharya*.*

She became indifferent to developments around her. She got into a negative frame of mind but quickly got back to her normal self. At last, she learnt to be happy with the things as they were. But when the eleventh anniversary of their marriage was approaching, she found the separation from her husband unbearable. She was expressing her innermost feelings: "I was not built to live without being loved. I blossom best in sunshine, and not in shadow."[38]

She had the sudden realisation about how little things mattered. Life comprised of little things with occasional big bangs. Here she was: "sleepy, and there was no one to say 'go to bed.'" Probably she had Gandhiji in her mind. If Henry was Little Moments, then Gandhiji was undoubtedly Big Moments for her. In a flash she understood the meaning of life: "Don't you realise how it is the little daily events in life that stand out so clearly, big moments are nearly always met by big emotions and these belong to the heights that we only at times visit never, live on. It is probably for that reason the idealist is so often deceived in his followers,

---

*The pangs of separation were equally felt by Henry earlier in 1909, when travelling throughout the length and breadth of India, he expressed the following ringing words in his letter of 9 October 1909, Madras, to his friend and mentor M K Gandhi: "Don't you find Mille more loveable as time passes? *I do*!!! (amazing discovery, isn't it)?"

he only sees their big moments not their real lives and the moments are rare, the daily round the solid material."[39]

This allegory falls neatly in its place as illustrated by the life of Millie. The year 1909 was the Big Moment when Gandhiji came to be fascinated with Millie. Little Moments constituted the rest of the life that she had to live with Henry. The Big Moment is indeed a passing show in life. Her separation from Henry made her understand herself better. She was also able to place Henry and Gandhi in proper perspective in her life. Both of them had got so entangled in her life that at times it became difficult to separate one from the other.

Another Gandhi

Though Millie viewed things subjectively, she was capable of being objective. She admired the womanly qualities of Gandhiji. She was the earliest to note his proclivities in the matter: "Most women love men for such attributes as are usually considered masculine. Yet, Mohandas Gandhi has been given the love of many women for his womanliness. They found in him a fellow traveller."[40]

Gandhiji was always searching for love and affection to which he responded in full measure. He also adored young children. He was often seen holding a child in his arms, while engaged in discussion. The first child of Millie gave him the greatest joy. In the words of Millie: "the baby became the centre of a new relationship." There was no single detail of the baby's life which did not interest him: "Its weight at birth, its feeding and development, its first signs of intelligence, and its very apparent determination to have its own way—every phase of its physical and emotional mental life was of intense pleasure [to him]." The baby brought Millie closer to Gandhiji. Probably he was reliving his childhood through the baby. He was most impressed with the baby's 'apparent determination to have its own way'.

She also noted that the jail terms transformed the man immensely. He had newer visions everytime he came from prison, which was indeed like a holiday camp for him. He felt relaxed and reviewed his tactics and strategies. The prison terms renewed the man as never before: "Each time he returned to the world one felt that some almost indefinable growth had taken place during his absence."[41]

The South African experience in which Henry and Millie had actively participated was the real foundation of his concept of *satyagraha*. When he was back in India, he joyfully wrote to Millie about the transformation in him: "I am undergoing a revolution in my outlook upon life. As it seems to me so old cobwebs are falling away. But more of this when I have more time."[42]

He no longer addressed her as 'My dear Millie' but more formally as 'Dear Mrs Polak'. India had transformed him. Was the Mahatma in him trying to distance his past and the diplomat in him trying to maintain his old links? During her enforced stay in India, she was to note that Gandhiji had turned more Indian than Universal. He was no longer Mr Gandhi but Gandhiji and Mahatma Gandhi in the eyes of millions. Millie did not matter to him much. She was a small speck in this unfathomable ocean of the Indian multitude.

There is a typescript deposited in the National Archives of India, forming part of its Gandhi-Polak archives entitled *The Why and How of Gandhi* by 'One who knew him'. Henry, who, considered Gandhiji a religious person falling among politicians, and viewed him as 'perhaps the most dangerous and aggressive man alive today', compared him to a lotus floating in the muddy waters. Another pen portrait described him as one who 'thrives on anxiety': "He deals with tremendous issues every minute of his life, yet you find him unperturbed, alert, serene, and attentive in small matters, without the slightest trace of vexation. Worshippers engross him more and more, but his soul dwells apart and is its own company. He can argue and wrestle with himself, and the result is as though he had been communicating with his own peers. I marvel at his self-discipline and his complete superiority to all environment. I seem to see in him something of the ancient virtue of '*tapas*', the potency of will, which could master the forces of nature and force the sun, the moon, and stars to shift from the course."[43]

Millie in India

Times change and men change with time. Millie landed in India in the third year of the First World War. Henry was also in India but left for home, leaving her to her own resources for the next two years. Henry fell sick and nearly died. Gandhiji came to Bombay to see him off. After Henry left for England, Millie too fell sick. Gandhiji was at his chivalrous best. He refused to leave Bombay until she recovered. He would visit her everyday and sit by her bed talking to her for long hours. She felt most dissolute. Tears would roll down her eyes frequently. He was kind to her and: "He would be just there telling me little interesting scraps of gossip or news and occasionally try to make me smile by some whimsicality."

He returned to Sabarmati Ashram after she was on the road to recovery. Soon, he too fell sick and lay almost dying. He remembered Millie and dictated 'a little note of farewell' to an amanuensis. She prayed for him and refused to believe that it was his goodbye. She wrote a note of sympathy to him on 31 August 1938: "So keep hold of your body, please, there is lots for it to do." The brother-sisterly relation had been restored. She signed a letter to him with a flourish: "With sisterly love, Yours, Millie."[44] He was equally poetic in his reply and talked of 'glorious rain descending in torrent' on the parched plains of India.

Millie spent two years in India. She and her two children stayed with her sister at Conoor during their enforced stay in India. She fell victim to an attack of influenza epidemic along with her children. Death, indeed, haunted her during her entire stay in India. Eventually, she moved out of the Nilgiris to Bombay on her way to England. She had to wait for her turn to book her journey back home towards the end of the World War. Gandhiji advised her to stay put at the Matheran Hill Station near Bombay.

She was penniless. He felt 'grieved and distressed' after having forgotten her for all practical purposes. He promised to help. He managed to send her back to 'her dearest Henry'. Thus ended the sad chapter of Millie's life in which she was practically ignored by Gandhiji. Her stay in India was not a pleasant one. She had no place in the Gandhian scheme of things during her stay in India and no money also. She fell ill with clockwise regularity and almost died. She was homesick. She had seen the face of Kali during her stay in India. She felt bored and frightened. The European community in the Nilgiris was hostile to her.

In the end, she went with her children to bid him goodbye. For a brief moment they found themselves on the same wavelength: "The thought, I believe, was in both of our minds: 'Shall we ever meet again in the flesh?'"[45]

Chhota Bhai

Henry was the joker in the pack. In retrospect, he turned out to be a seer predicting the future correctly. Initially, Gandhiji, Kallenbach and he were on the same wavelength. In his autobiography, Gandhiji called him his 'blood brother'. He associated with Gandhiji when the Europeans in South Africa shunned him. He was a scholar who knew Ruskin by heart. He not only knew Ruskin, but also practised him in real life. His religion was the religion of ethics. Gandhiji called him 'a flower teacher'. His looks were deceptive. There was iron in his soul. They began to differ soon after they started working together. Varying outlooks on life came out very clearly in the letter Gandhiji wrote to Henry Polak on 17 August 1911: "My dear *Bhai*, You have a most delightful habit of directing at my devoted head bolts from the blue, and then imagining that things will proceed as before." He angrily responded:

"Apparently you ask for martyrdom quite regardless of the fact that you may be conferring martyrdom upon others [like Henry] who are not willing to receive it."[46]

They clashed soon thereafter over Khilafat Movement. Once again, they fought over the communal question and his fasts during 1932. He responded to Henry indirectly: "I derive however the richer pleasure that our love can persist even in spite of political and spirited differences."[47]

Millie and Henry were his shields to protect him from criticism. He was reduced to supplicating God and his own ego. He claimed his decision to go on fast to be 'firm and so was the declaration'. The gulf between him and Henry kept widening. The contact with Gandhiji had been reduced to a trickle. The differences between them cropped up from time to time. After the Khilafat Movement and his fasts of 1932, new differences flared up over their respective attitudes towards the Second World War.

Henry Polak wrote a detailed letter of five printed pages to him. He had continued to take active interest in Indian affairs. Henry was Jawaharlal Nehru's *bete noire*. He accused Gandhiji of being unduly influenced by Jawaharlal: "However much you are prepared to stand alone in affirmation of what you hold to be true, your loyalty (it appears to me from what I have long assumed) often betrays you into contrary and contradictory courses." He accused Jawaharlal of: "… ineradicable passion for Leftist ideological phraseology and his blindness to facts that did not square with his intellectual prepossessions."[48] Thus soured the deep relations that had lasted for over three decades.

For years, Millie was forgotten. There is no record of any exchange of letters between them for several decades. The relationship with *chhota bhai* also ended. Gandhiji had other worlds to conquer. Time is said to be the best healer. It did not happen in this instance. Only the sweet, sour and bitter memories remained of the days gone by.

Male Bonding

Gandhiji's relationship with Kallenbach was a male-bonding of a special kind. Even the pledge to abjure milk was taken jointly by Kallenbach and him at Tolstoy Farm in the year 1912. The physical and spiritual yearning expressed in their correspondence has not been repeated by Gandhiji ever again. The relationship was everlasting. They were ideological twins and equally inseparable intellectual companions. The deep bonding between them, one a German-Jewish sophisticate and the other a Gujarati Bania, was truly reflected in the message sent by Gandhiji on the eve of Kallenbach's death in 1945: "He [Kallenbach] used to say to me often that when I was deserted by the whole world, I would find him to be a true friend going with me, if need be, to the ends of the… earth in search of Truth."[49]

The 'pact-unto-death' was sealed between them during Gandhiji's stay in South Africa. Here was a formal agreement signed between Lower House and Upper House on 29 July 1911, on the eve of Kallenbach's departure to Europe: "The consideration for all the above tasks imposed by Lower House on himself is more love and yet more love between the two Houses-such love as, they hope, the world has not seen. In witness thereof the parties hereto solemnly affirm their signatures in the presence of the Maker of all."[50] Kallenbach was not to fall in love or marry during his sojourn in Europe.

Kallenbach–Gandhiji correspondence makes the most fascinating reading. Gandhiji goes the farthest in surrendering his soul and body to his soulmate Kallenbach. His sentiments are almost a repeat of expressions found in Bhakti and Sufi poetry: "The point to illustrate is to show to you and me how completely you have taken possession of my body. That is slavery with a vengeance. But then the reward, what is it to be? 'The unwritten contract is you take the body and give the mind by way of study. You cannot take 'no' an answer from yourself.'"

The bond between them remained unshakable even after Gandhiji shifted his locale from South Africa to India. He dreamt of eternal relationship with Kallenbach cutting across time and space. The testament amounts to sharing of little secrets between two adolescents: "I shall put up with you and love you just the same notwithstanding what you may call your limitations, even as you have to do likewise to me. We can therefore go forward—as forward as our legs will carry us and no farther—and still be together, one soul and two bodies."[51]

CHAPTER 7

Dictator Sonja

The years spent by Gandhiji in South Africa were the happiest years of his life. He earned best of his friends and loyalists there. Sonja Schlesin was one of them. Sonja began as his secretary and ended up as the leader of Indian community in South Africa. If she was not a close friend, she could be considered a close comrade-in-arms of Gandhiji. It was a coincidence that his closest associates—Hermann Kallenbach, Henry Polak and Sonja Schlesin— were all of Jewish extraction. Hermann was from Germany, Henry came from Great Britain and Sonja was a Russian. There appeared a deep connection between Jews and Gandhiji during his days in South Africa.

It was Hermann Kallenbach who introduced Sonja Schlesin to him. She was his secretary, who, in course of time took complete charge of Gandhiji, his office and his movement in South Africa. She was a no nonsense person who ran his office like a machine. Her role in making a success of Gandhiji was crucial in the early days. She was not only his governor-general but also his viceroy. She drafted letters for him that he merely signed.

Alter Ego

She came to be his alter ego. She had the longest contact with him extending over four decades. Unfortunately, little is known about her. She has left no reminiscences of her close association with Gandhiji, or of her espousal of the political movement of Indians in South Africa. Most of the correspondence between her and Gandhiji has been lost except for a few letters he wrote to her and a brief mention of her in his autobiography. She was both loved and feared at the same time.

Gandhiji's legal practice had begun to sparkle. He was also deeply involved in the political movement of Indians in South Africa. His circle of friends and well-wishers had expanded. He was in close touch with the Government of South Africa. He had to cope with a mountain of correspondence. He employed four Indian clerks to help him with his work. They were more like his 'sons than clerks'. Neither by training nor by aptitude were they equipped to cope with his stamina.

He was in a state of dilemma. No one was available from Natal where he lived. He could not bring help from Transvaal without a permit. That would have gone against his conscience. The other alternative was to employ a European secretary, but that was unthinkable in those days of apartheid.

The rescue came in the form of a Scottish girl named Miss Dick who did not mind working for a person of Indian origin. She was offered seventeen and a half pounds per month. She took charge of his office and managed it so well that she was 'more of a daughter or a sister' than a mere employee. Unfortunately for him, she married too soon for his comfort. She became Mrs Macdonald from Miss Dick and left him high and dry. He had to start a fresh search for a suitable incumbent.

Independent Spirit

He turned to his friend Hermann Kallenbach in desperation, who recommended a sprightly young girl of 16 years. She was none other than Sonja Schlesin, his ideal secretary. Kallenbach had acquaintance with her uncle who came from the same town as his in Germany. She had come to him to gain practical experience but stayed back of her own volition.

Sonja left a mark on Gandhiji and his work from day one. She was dedicated. She became a schoolteacher in Transvaal after Gandhiji left South Africa. She, however, continued taking interest in Indian affairs in South Africa. Her correspondence with Gandhiji lasted as long as November 1947. She wrote two letters reminding him most affectionately about his determination to live for 125 years. His letter of 1 November 1947 was in response to her letters. By then, he had lost the will to live long.

Sonja was domineering, opinionated and too sure of herself, but she delivered on time. She had a no-nonsense approach to work. She worked day and night for Gandhiji. She came to work for a salary of 10 pounds but would draw no more than six pounds, necessary for her bare existence. She refused, even on insistence to draw the total amount of salary due to her. She would not even hesitate to scold Gandhiji in her usual imperious style: "I do not need more, and if I take anything in excess of my necessities, I will have betrayed the principle which attracted me to you."[1]

Her real character was reflected in a group photograph hanging in Gandhiji's law office. Sonja had short hair. She wore spectacles suspended precariously over her nose. She was used to wearing dark skirts with a tie and a plain white shirt that contrasted with her dark hair and skin. There was an aggressive look about her, as if she was ready to pounce upon the next person. She had a short stocky figure and looked older than her years. She had the perpetual look of a boy scout.

Substituting the Boss

She was a suffragette and practised aggressive feminism within the Gandhian space. In a message she sent to the *satyagrahis* in South Africa, she compared them to 'my sisters in England'—the suffragettes. She did not have children, but her maternal instincts came forth in all she did. No wonder, Robert Payne called her a Russian anarchist and believed that: "Sonja Schlesin was one of those women destined to command and Gandhi became her willing victim."[2] He employed all kinds of epithets like 'difficult', 'impetuous', 'violently opionated', 'masculine-looking', 'foolhardy', and 'silly'. Payne was equally harsh on Gandhiji of South African days comparing him to 'a baronial lord'.

Sonja must have reminded him of his strong-willed mother Putlibai. She not only functioned as a secretary to Gandhiji but also took the entire burden of his responsibilities on her shoulders. She would draft his letters and he would merely sign them. Gandhiji admitted that her English was better than his. She would not hesitate to correct his English. She had her idiosyncrasies that irritated Kallenbach and baffled Gandhiji. He would not dare cross her path. Gradually, she began to take charge of his visitors. She would cross-examine them, admonish them and take delight in irritating them. She was almost always right.

Her aggressiveness was meant for the person of Gandhiji and the cause he represented. Both of them were identical in her mind. Her age and status were no bar in admonishing those who came into contact with her. She was brave and knew no fear.

She would undertake assignments in the dead of night and scoffed at any suggestion for her to be escorted for her protection. She would not hesitate even to the point of insulting a man and telling him on his face as to what she thought of him. She was impetuous enough to land him in difficulties, but her 'open and guileless temperament' helped to cool the temperature in no time. Gandhiji had no hesitation in paying her the finest tribute: "I have often signed without revision letters typed by her, as I considered her English to be better than mine, and had the fullest confidence in her loyalty."[3]

Gandhiji was most effusive in attributing to her 'the courage that would shame a warrior'. When the whole Gandhian entourage was in jail, she took upon herself the entire burden of the political struggle waged by Indians in South Africa. She led from the flanks, front and from the rear. Her example was an inspiration to others. She won the adulation and devotion of thousands of *satyagrahis*. She also carried the entire burden of correspondence on behalf of the movement by herself. She ran the newspaper *Indian Opinion* under her tutelage. She was indefatigable and was here, there and everywhere.

She was *shakti* incarnate. To her, Gandhiji was the ideal *purusa*, an inert being then in jail and thus helpless as a child. A new phase of campaign began with the involvement of Kasturba in the *satyagraha* movement. For the first time women had offered to go to jail for the cause and Kasturba led the campaign which began in April 1913. The women of Indian origin were unhappy over the stipulation that marriages contracted without registration in South Africa were declared illegal.

Woman of the Times

Sonja Schlesin did not offer herself for *satyagraha* for obvious reasons. She was to mobilise *satyagrahis* and guide them from outside in her capacity as secretary of the Transvaal Indian Women's Association. To her, this was another chapter in her suffragette cause. Sonja had come far since her early days with Gandhiji.

She must have been amused when recollecting her early days in the company of Attorney and Bar-at-law Mohandas Karamchand Gandhi. There was also a time when she was slapped for smoking in his office with her legs dangling from his work table. Sonja Schlesin had kept her cool. She had indeed arrived in the very first few weeks in 1909, and: "For the first time she cried before me and apologised and wrote to me afterwards saying that she would never do such a thing and that she had recognised my love."[4]

She had scores to settle with the menfolk. Her application for being articled to him was rejected by the Law Society because of her being a woman: "The articling of women is entirely without precedent in South Africa and was never contemplated by the law."[5] She used Gandhiji as her protective cover for her firing practice against men.

He was never to find a replacement for her after his return to India. It took him a desperate search of two years to discover Mahadev Desai, who evidently measured up to his standards. He was to share his thoughts with Mahadev Desai (circa 1917): "I have got in you the man… I can entrust all my work some day and be at ease."[6]

Mahadev was calm, cool, industrious, loyal, unassuming and intellectually inclined, but he was no Sonja Schlesin. The times had changed. Mahadev was gentle as a lamb who would not hurt a fly. He was also a man of his times, as was Sonja the woman of her times. Gandhiji was nostalgic about his days in South Africa. His only regret was not being able to duplicate his South African team of associates in India.

While Gandhiji was grateful to Kallenbach for introducing Sonja to him, Kallenbach resented her provoking intrusion between him and his friend. Kallenbach was no Kallenbach if he were not to look for an opportunity to spite her. The manoeuvre did not work in his favour. He tried to attack her mercilessly, but Gandhiji gallantly came to her rescue. The incident provoked by Kallenbach was not due to any fault of hers. There was no doubt of his being jealous of her.

The opportunity for him came when she sent a letter to Kallenbach under her signature but at the specific instance of Gandhiji. Kallenbach did not take kindly to this 'affront'. The chivalrous Gandhiji came to her rescue to upbraid Kallenbach. Sonja reacted by raising hell with Gandhiji and there is a hint of it in the letter Gandhiji addressed to his friend Kallenbach accusing him of being petty, touchy, and spiteful.

A beleaguered Kallenbach was speaking on behalf of all those who had been subjected to rough treatment by Sonja times and again without number. However, Gandhiji's loyalty to his colleagues was phenomenal. No wonder, he came to the defence of the stressed lady.

In fact, Sonja was not under attack because she had cornered Kallenbach and turned him into a beleaguered non-person. The prosecutor had been reduced to a defendant, asking for mercy where none was due to him. This was not the case earlier. Kallenbach had introduced her to Gandhiji and she had come under his custody at the instance of her mother. At that time she was just sixteen. Kallenbach was to compliment her, but his compliments were laced with several critical but sympathetic references: "She is clever and honest, but she is very mischievous and impetuous. Perhaps she is insolent. You keep her if [you] can manage her."[7]

Who managed whom was the question that lay in the womb of the future?

Captivating Sixteen

Gandhiji was impressed by her commanding personality and her prodigious capacity for work: "She was then only sixteen years of age but she captivated my clients as well as my fellow-*satyagrahis* by her frankness and readiness to save. This girl soon constituted herself the watchman and warden of the morality not only of my office but of the whole movement."[8]

Apparently, Gandhiji learnt much from Sonja. The ashrams at Sabarmati and Segaon were completely anarchical compared to the ordered existence of Gandhiji under the able guidance of Sonja Schlesin during his days in South Africa. Sonja was at her best behaviour with Gandhiji perhaps because he bent backwards to fall in line with her. She made a success of his professional and political career through personal grit of the highest order. The initial success achieved by Gandhiji may partially be credited to the managerial abilities of Sonja. She was a perfect manager. She worked with clockwork efficiency and would not even spare Gandhiji. She was a bully and Gandhiji was well aware of it. She built a wall between him and others. Gandhiji was the focus of her attention. She performed all kinds of chores for him. She was helpful to him even when he planned to write his autobiography. The tables were completely turned when the autobiography was actually published. She was greatly put off by the remarks contained in it:

"She seemed to mind neither age nor experience. She would not hesitate even to the point of insulting a man and telling him to his face what she thought of him. Her impetuosity often landed me in difficulties, but her open and guileless temperament removed them as soon as they were created. I have often signed letters without revision."[9]

This public expression by him was not to her liking. She blasted him left right and centre. She used strong epithets in several letters addressed to him. She spoke of his 'wretched autobiography', as an instance of his 'caddishness'. Very few persons would have dared to confront Gandhiji in this manner. He took the criticism in his stride and ignored it. All this was forgotten and forgiven. They used to write to each other off and on. Probably she had a grudge against him for having deserted her midstream.

It was not too long before Sonja Schlesin started receiving kudos from the Indian community in South Africa. Her name began to be placed along with that of Gandhiji. She was lucky to have arrived so early in her life. On the positive side, she was helpful, decisive and accessible to a large mass of middle-level cadre and individual satyagrahis. She filled up the vacuum during Gandhiji's imprisonment and was ever ready to take up individual causes.

While his other colleagues like Millie Graham Polak worked behind the scenes, she was found in front directing the movement. She was formidable when confronted and was sympathy incarnate when approached individually. The whole Indian community was all praise for her constructive role. By 1908, her name was a household word. Her importance was recognised soon after Gandhiji, Kasturba and the rest were put behind the bars. She took complete charge of the situation and worked wonders. A series of complimentary references by Gandhiji were published crediting her with performing miracles.

Public Service

Barely one year after joining Gandhiji, come day and night, she was here, there and everywhere. The Transvaal Asiatic Registration Law Amendment Act led to mass agitation by Indian settlers in South Africa. Sonja was fully involved in the movement. She hoped to address a mass rally held on the New-Year's Day in 1908. Gandhiji read out the speech on behalf of 'an unmarried girl of twenty' (with the permission of her parents).

Gandhiji complimented her in the *Indian Opinion* of 15 February 1908. It also carried complimentary reference in his *Johannesburg Letter* of 10 January 1908. She was a girl barely twenty years old and yet there was so much to her credit. Gandhiji was pleased that a girl half his age had worked wonders through sheer willpower. Everyone in the Indian community knew her by name by 1913.

A mere interval of five years had transformed Sonja Schlesin beyond recognition. She was the leader of the Indian women's brigade of *satyagrahis* by her own right.

The year 1911 was the halfway mark between 1908 and 1913. She had begun to be known and respected about this time. The Chinese community also honoured her at a public function in Johannesburg.

She was presented with a gold watch costing ten pounds. Here she was being honoured along with Gandhiji. Soon after his release from prison, Gandhiji complimented her along with one Mrs Vogl for sustaining the cause during his 'darkest hour' of the prison term.

Sonja Schlesin marched alongside Gandhiji and his associates from Charles Town and stayed with him right up to the end. At the instance of Gandhiji she moved to Phoenix to teach English at the experimental school. Prabhudas Gandhi, her student who was twelve at that time, vividly remembered the woman with 'bobbed hair wearing 'a white blouse and a black skirt' descending on the Phoenix settlement accompanied by 10 year old Fatima.* He recalled the human side of the cold-blooded suffragette: "When she laughed, which she did often, her cheeks had dimples in them" and, 'she was of jesting nature, amusing, talkative and smart but when she entered the class for teaching, full calm prevailed.'"[10]

Her dominant maternal instincts must have scored over public postures of the formidable Amazon.

Conscience Keeper

Her greatest moment came on the eve of Gandhiji's departure for India. Gandhiji had a special gift for General Smuts. Their political differences did not stand in the way. It was in appreciation of special respect in which General Smuts was held by him. The gift was from one great statesman to another.

Gandhiji had crafted a pair of slippers with his own hands at Phoenix Farm. He commissioned Sonja Schlesin at the specific request of General Smuts to make the presentation on his behalf. The gift to General Smuts was equally a tribute to Sonja Schlesin for the honour done to her. She

---

*She is not to be confused with Fatima Gool of Cape Town. Her father Imam Abdul Qadir Bawazir ('rich as a nawab') had settled down at Phoenix along with his entire family.

appreciated the gesture and accepted the assignment without exchanging a single word with her mentor.

Another great honour came her way unexpectedly. The great Gopal Krishna Gokhale was on a visit to South Africa. He was a special guest of Gandhiji at Phoenix Farm. Gokhale was the only person whom Gandhiji had recognised as his political guru. Millie Graham Polak was assigned to look after his food requirements. Gokhale was a diabetic and very fussy about what he ate and what he did not. Gandhiji himself was in attendance upon him. Sonja was asked to help him in his secretarial work and arrange for his appointments.

Of all the people assigned to look after great Gokhale, Sonja was singled out by him for her efficiency. Gokhale was all praise for her: "I have rarely come across such purity, single-minded devotion to work and great determination as I have seen in Miss Schlesin… I need hardly say it and yet I say that you must cherish her. Gandhi called her 'one of the noblest beings I have known.'"[11]

It was time for Gandhiji to depart from South Africa. He was more than satisfied with his achievements but was going to miss the mighty presence of Sonja Schlesin. She was his conscience-keeper. She protected him from intruders and from himself also. She was the only one among his associates who would not only stand up to him but also guide him in the desired direction. In India, he missed her greatly. He had too many subservients around him but none could replace Sonja Schlesin. Mahadev Desai filled the bill but not entirely.

Missing Her Presence

Gandhiji had begun to have goose pimples. He began to miss Sonja even before he was to depart for India. Gandhiji had the praiseworthy quality of being more loyal than a king to his associates. He would treat them severely in private, but in public he would praise them and help them to think positively.

In one of his earlier communications to Sonja dated 23 February 1914, he noted that Sonja never reciprocated his compliments. She was very parsimonious in praising him. Sonja would not be Sonja if she would not speak out whatever was in her mind. She termed him businesslike in his dealings with others. Indeed, the boot was on the other leg. Sonja was the most businesslike person he ever met. Was she complaining of Gandhiji overlooking the other side of

Sonja, perhaps hidden from the public view? Was she blaming Gandhiji for overlooking the human side of the woman in her?

Sonja had a special place in his scheme of things. It was unusual for Gandhiji if he did not give a tongue lashing to his associates at Phoenix Farm. Kasturba and her children, especially Harilal, gave much cause for complaint and so did Millie, Henry and Hermann, besides his Indian associates. He claimed to have felt exasperated with everyone with one exception of Sonja.

Everybody praised her but it did not astound her. She had reached a stage when praising meant flattering to her. Gandhiji was to pay her an unusual tribute. This is found in a fragment of a letter to Manilal and Jamnadas Gandhi. He praised her for being poised dialectically to him in all kinds of situations. She always stood her ground while confronting him.

To contradict him became a second nature for her but all this came naturally. She had no axe to grind in taking the opposite side. Her contradicting him stimulated him. In a letter to Manilal and Jamnadas, Gandhiji described his relation with Sonja Schlesin thus: "Miss Schlesin takes an opposite course to mine in all matters, but in some ways I place her character very much higher than that of you all."[12]

Manilal vs Sonja

For 33 years after he left South Africa, he corresponded intermittently with her. She was, however, unable to cope with his son Manilal who gradually assumed charge of Phoenix Farm and the Indian Opinion. There was a running battle between Manilal and Sonja after Gandhiji left for India.

Manilal banned the entry of women into Phoenix Farm soon after Gandhiji left for India. Sonja informed Gandhiji about the impromptuous decision. Gandhiji was dismayed and wrote to Manilal: "I am surprised at your remark about Ashrams here prohibiting the entry of women… It will delight your heart to see the transformation that the women undergo here after a few days' stay."[13]

Gandhiji was uncomfortable with his new role of an arbitrator between Sonja and Manilal. He knew Manilal had no love lost for Sonja. She was prone to lose her temper too often. Here Sonja was placed disadvantageously. Manilal was cool tempered, while she was hot tempered. Gandhiji sympathised with Manilal. He would tell him in all confidence that she was a lost case and nothing could be done about it. Hence, he advised his son to make the best of the situation. Manilal, however, kept pouring his heart to his father complaining about her in one letter after another.

Manilal complained about her in 1914 and 1928. He was still at sea in his dealings with her during 1933. The cold war continued for two full decades with no end in sight. Manilal must have hated her guts. His father kept providing solace to his beleaguered son during all these years. However, he did not have the heart to confront her directly. In his letter of 15 July 1938 to Manilal and his wife Sushila Gandhi he was left twiddling his thumbs in a state of total helplessness: "I follow what you say about Miss Schlesin. But isn't she half crazy? She has written a sort of wild letter even to me."[14]

'The wild letter', however, is not traceable. It would have provided a reverse model for Dale Carnegie of ideal public relations. Manilal became insensitive to Sonja by taking over most assignments of his father in South Africa through a cleverly-designed nibbling process.

Gradually, Gandhiji began to see merit in the principled stands taken by Sonja. Ultimately, he came to realise that it was totally unfair to accuse Schlesin of crimes imagined by his calculating son Manilal. For once he ordered his son to listen to her advice carefully: "There is Miss Schlesin entertaining beautiful dreams about you… You must have sufficient pride in you to be determined that, if you cannot bring glory to your father's legacy, you will not at any rate disgrace it."[15]

It took Schlesin two decades to be proved right in the eyes of Gandhiji, who was no longer a mere Gandhi, Mr Gandhi or Gandhiji, but a full-fledged Mahatma. This must have been her ultimate triumph. Her persistence had once again scored over Gandhi.

My Dear Daughter

Gandhiji observed protocol by being affectionate to Sonja in his correspondence with her. He wished to hear more and more from her. He would address her most affectionately as 'My dear daughter'. He expected her to write at least once a week. He would confide his innermost secrets to her. He would also discuss Kasturba in his letter to her: "Mrs Gandhi has developed remarkably. She has beautifully resigned herself to things she used to fight."[16]

His life had become too busy after he returned to India. He had no leisure whatsoever. He must have loved to reminisce about his days in Africa. He was also proud of what he had achieved in India. He would have loved Sonja to see for herself his tremendous achievements including the name and fame earned by him. He was no longer a Mr Gandhi of South Africa but the Mahatma who carried the burden of political India on his strong shoulders.

While he would have been proud to place Sonja on public display over his ultimate triumph in achieving the foremost status in India, he also realised the futility of his hyperactivities. For a moment he would have loved to opt for solitude and obscurity. Such must have been passing thoughts which were best forgotten by him. Those who reach the pinnacle find it virtually impossible to climb down propitiously. Gandhiji was no exception to the general rule. One must, however, sympathise with him when he confessed to Sonja: "Believe me there is nothing spectacular in the loin-cloth."[17]

Reaching the Pinnacle

Gandhiji had been in India for four years by 1919. He was reaching the pinnacle of his achievements but he found himself all alone. There were no equals to him in India. Those who followed him did it sheepishly and were at his beck and call. As his fame spread far and wide, he found himself lonelier.

He had never faced a situation like this in South Africa. He had a battalion of equals to discuss, debate and dispute with him. They were also intellectually inclined. They had simulated another Athens for him in South Africa. Yet he was confronted with another Sparta in India, Sonja Schlesin could have coped with the whole battalion of his associates in Sabarmati Ashram without a whimper.

His associates respected him, responded to him and worshipped him, but they maintained a respectful distance from him in the true *guru–shishya* tradition of India. There was no meeting of minds with them. Here was a crisis in spiritual terms.

He maintained an open house where all were welcome. In the very process of widening the base of his political movement, he diluted its intellectual content. Those of his peers who could look straight into his eyes wisely stayed away from his ashram.

His word had the force of law. He was so nostalgic about his balmier South African days that he could not resist the temptation to beseech Sonja to launch a rescue mission on his behalf: "How I often wish you were here for more reasons than one. But I must plough the lonely furrow… I have no [Rev. J.J.] Doke here. I have no [Hermann] Kallenbach… [Henry] Polak, in England [Ahmed Mohamed] Kachalia, or [Shapurji Adamjania] Sorab. Strange as it may appear, I feel lonelier than in South Africa… I do not enjoy the same sense of security which you all gave me there. I do not know the people here, nor they me. This is all gloomy, if I were to brood over it. But I do not. I have not the time for it. I have a few moments of leisure just now… and I am giving myself the momentary pleasure of sharing my innermost thoughts with you. But no more."[18]

Employment Certificate

While Gandhiji was reaching the pinnacle of his political career in India, Sonja Schlesin was down in the pits all but forgotten. By 1919, she was a student short of money and in dire circumstances, forced to borrow fifty pounds from her mentor. Her wish was granted instantly enabling her to pursue her studies. Shortly afterwards she became a teacher in the high school at Krugersdrop (near Johannesburg). In 1924, she was tempted to change her job. She wrote to Gandhiji to send her a recommendatory letter.

The employment reference by Gandhiji was prosaic as ever and it did not help Sonja to get another job. This occasion was, however, employed by Gandhiji for horseplay. He decided to have swipes at her with his tit-for-tat compliments: "…The same slovenliness, the same smudging. I can almost see your inky fingers in your letter… I must refuse to plead guilty to all the charges you have noted against me. Why should I care about giving you a 'business certificate?'"[19]

Gandhiji had a sharp memory. He must have remembered her playful note of April 1911 to him 'accusing' him of using his typewriter in total disregard of his 'anti-machinery injunction' laid down in his pioneering work *Hind Swaraj*. She mocked at him by using the word 'know' instead of the archaic 'wot'[20] in line with his 'back to the nature' slogan.

She never changed her job and confined herself to teaching Latin. She began dressing in: "severe long black dress which covered her completely from neck to ankles and wrists". Her black dress was like a shroud in remembrance of her past. Her former pupils recall her as 'an outstanding and inspiring teacher', but 'reclusive'[21] and 'eccentric' with flashes of brilliance as a teacher. Her residence was appropriately called 'The Heritage'. Schlesin retired from her teaching job at the age of 55 in June 1933.

Gandhi at 125

The year 1945 was unlike 1947. It was a year of hope and expectations for Mahatma Gandhi in his private and public life. Sonja was bucking him from the sidelines. It was 'springtime of life' for him and her. Gandhiji at 76 was to assure her: "I hope to write the story of 125 years. Hold yourself in patience till I write."[22] Playfully, he was threatening to launch himself in writing his memoirs of subsequent years. Sonja rose to the occasion in her reply. "I have not the slightest doubt that you will live until you are 125, if only you desire it."[23] She was in full flow in her next letter : "In any case your decision [to live 125 years] has now lifted that cloud, for you are once again in the springtime of life, a more wonderful springtime enriched by the experience of the years—why, your very handwriting seems to have taken on new vigour. You speak of writing the experience of those 125 years. I hope I shall be privileged to share in the sub-editing of at least a part of that volume."[24]

That Gandhiji wished to live for 125 years has been a popular perception for long. He, however, denied it vehemently when Sonja Schlesin posed the question to him in late 1947. By that time Gandhiji was a tired old man. India was literally on fire before his very eyes. There were political and communal turbulence all over the land. His dream of a peaceful, progressive, secular and egalitarian India lay shattered in front of him. His Noakhali experience had disillusioned him. It resulted in a rupture with all his closest associates except perhaps for Manu Gandhi.

He was completely barricaded by November 1947 after he came to live in New Delhi. The two months before he was assassinated were not joyful for him. He felt irritated when Sonja Schlesin reminded him about his desire to live for 125 years. He tried to wriggle out of his commitment that he gave to himself.

He was being a clever politician by denying the obvious. He was already 78 and he had lost all verve to live for another 47 years after surveying the state of the nation. His diary and the diary maintained by Manu Gandhi of those crucial few months are a true chronicle of his unending woes.

He never gave a cause for complaint to Sonja after he left South Africa except for not so subtle references to her in his letters to Manilal Gandhi. She was a model of clear thinking for him. Now he felt threatened by her for reminding him about his alleged vow. Sonja could afford to be large-hearted for once. She must have come to know of his serious troubles both at public and private levels. His letter to her reflects the pitiable state of his mind and he deserved pardon on that account alone: "You talk of my decision to live 125 years. I never could make any such foolish and impossible decision. It is beyond the capacity of a human being. He can only wish."

Here the lawyer in him jumped to the fore, anticipating trouble for him. He was fully cognisant of the weak case to be defended by him. He tried to confuse the issue with many 'ifs' and 'buts' in his weak presentation: "Again, I never expressed an unconditional wish... My wish was conditional upon continuous act of service of mankind. If that act fails me, as it seems to be failing in India, I must not only cease to wish to attain that age but wish the contrary as I am doing now."[25] She persisted in reminding him of his undertaking to live for 125 years. She wished him well and on this enthusiastic note she concluded her correspondence in response to his letter of 1 November 1947: "Far from losing your desire to live until you are 125, increasing knowledge of the world's lovelessness and consequent misery should cause you rather to live longer... You said in a letter to me some time ago that everyone ought to wish to attain the age of 125, you can't go back on that."

Unfulfilled Desires

There was an unstated deep bond of unfulfilled desires between Sonja Schlesin and Mahatma Gandhi. They were together for seven years from 1907 to 1914 in South Africa. For the next thirty three years, they were not destined to meet in person, but they were to communicate via telepathy. One of them was a renowned figure and the other a spinster long withdrawn from the public eye. The public figure and private person joined together in a silent bond. Never did Gandhiji count as many blessings with another woman associate. The inner lying strong bond broke the cold barrier of words in correspondence between them as if in a kaleidoscope.

After his return to India in 1914, Gandhiji was keen to hear from her regularly. Sonja was moody, reserved, withdrawn, and very parsimonious in writing to him. He besought her to keep in touch with him regularly. He almost invited her in 1917 to his address to the National School, Ahmedabad to come and teach in India that is: "if only she would come, we could want nothing better."[26] Sonja was hardly forthcoming. Her responses were interspersed with her long silences which unnerved Gandhiji. In September 1921, he complained to his friend Kallenbach about Sonja not caring to respond.

Sonja was a lonely person given to silences. Subconsciously it was hard for her to pardon her mentor, who had left her in the lurch by moving away to India. The depressive moods were interspersed with moments of optimism and then she would reopen her channels of communication with Gandhiji who would momentarily feel assured. He chose to share his inner feelings with Devi West and told her that Sonja had been writing regularly to him: "... and of course she is as mad and as good as ever."[27]

Like the famous theatrical character Godot, Gandhiji kept waiting indefinitely to welcome Schlesin to India. The old flame was rekindled in 1945 after a long wait of thirty-eight years. The interrupted correspondence was resumed after the death of Kallenbach on 25 March 1945. She was expecting Gandhiji to participate in the Peace Conference at San Francisco. Here, she found an opportunity to join him. She was also hoping to come to India after the San Francisco conference. She offered her secretarial services to him. The visit to San Francisco never materialised and hence Gandhiji supplicated her to come to India: "...but you are dropping in one of these days."[28]

Pioneers of Indian Freedom

It would have been great to have a gathering of Hermann Kallenbach, Henry Polak, Millie Graham Polak and Sonja Schlesin in the company of Gandhiji sitting cross-legged on mud-plastered floor at the Sevagram Ashram, reminiscing about the four decades of their association. It was not to be. Kallenbach passed away in 1945. The Polaks had gradually drifted away from their mentor. Gandhiji was assassinated on 30 January 1948. Sonja passed away in Johannesburg on 6 January 1956. Only the memories remain of 'The Gang of Five' who collectively stroked the fires shaking the very foundation of British Empire in South Africa. In Pyarelal's words: "They were all hoping to return to him in the evening of his life and range themselves around a common hearth like children of a family after a long and arduous separation."[29]

Sonja Schlesin may deserve no more than a footnote in works about Gandhiji but she had created a permanent niche in the heart of the Gandhi of South Africa fame. Here was the Jewish contribution to the Gandhian sage. Let the Polaks of Great Britain, the Kallenbachs of Germany and the Schlesins of Russia stand up and be counted. Sushila Nayyar has paid her the finest tribute. For her there were four remarkable women of European extraction who had come in contact with him. Sonja was certainly one of them. Memories flash back about the remarkable woman who along with Kasturba made Gandhiji break his vow by the well-tried feminine stratagem of shedding spontaneous tears.

Schlesin always had her doors open and invited one and all to confabulate with her on all kinds of subjects. She was the Mother Courage of South Africa for the indentured work force from the subcontinent. It did not matter whether they were Chinese, Pathans, Hindus, Muslims, indentures, ex-indentures or *girmitias* (the term of contempt by which Indian immigrants came to be known). They came individually and in droves to seek solace from her in their hour of trial. Like the mother hen she gave them protection, defended them and fought for them. After Gandhiji went away from South Africa, she moved away from the hurly-burly of political struggle in South Africa. She chose to lead a quiet life afterwards. If Sita Dhupelia was to be believed: "Miss Schlesin… had lived in misery and died in misery."[30]

CHAPTER 8

JEKI: 'The Only Adopted Daughter'

Dr Pranjivan Jagjivan Mehta was Gandhiji's closest friend standing as tall as him. A medical doctor and barrister-at-law, he belonged to a rich jeweller family with business interests in India (and Burma). He was a friend of Gandhiji's since his student days in London and related to his spiritual mentor, Rajchandbhai, by marriage. In fact, Gandhiji had his first meeting with Rajchandbhai at Dr Mehta's residence in Bombay. His son-in-law Manilal Doctor and his daughter, Jayakunwar (Mehta) Doctor, were closely associated with Gandhiji for long.

Dr Mehta was Gandhiji's patron in South Africa and Secretary, Transvaal Satyagraha Fund Committee. He encouraged young Indians settled in South Africa to study law in England with his financial backing. Gandhiji's refusal to sponsor his son Harilal's name was the cause of eventual break between father and son. Thus, Dr Mehta was unknowingly the cause of the rupture.

The closest link between Gandhiji and Mehta was his daughter, Jayakunwar, popularly known as JEKI. Gandhiji was fond of calling her as 'my only adopted daughter'. She lived at Tolstoy and Phoenix Farms for several years, and moved to Fiji to be with her barrister husband, Manilal Doctor in 1914. She was back in India after six years. Hers was an unhappy life bordering on tragedy, except for a few years in South Africa while she lived with Gandhiji. At one point of time, she was very close to Gandhiji working along with him at Phoenix as his teaching assistant. Millie Graham Polak described her as 'educated, clever and attractive' and she 'talked high idealism'.[1]

Manilal Doctor

Manilal Doctor, twelve years her senior, was a footloose maverick who came in touch with Gandhiji during his visit to London in 1906. At that time he was studying for a degree in Law. He continued to be in touch with him after his return from England. Imbued with pan-nationalist zeal, he decided to settle down in Mauritius and float a bilingual newspaper to fight for the cause of Indian settlers there. He must have been inspired by the *Indian Opinion*.

JEKI and Manilal met Gandhiji at Tolstoy Farm on 22 October 1911. They were yet to get married. Gandhiji commended Manilal for his work in Mauritius. He found Manilal a 'pleasant and good-natured person' with 'too much fat' on him. Subsequently, they moved to Phoenix Farm. Gandhiji was charmed by the couple and worked for their engagement.

Dr Mehta had reservations but he reluctantly agreed to the arrangement due to sheer persistence of his friend. There was hardly any chemistry between Manilal Doctor and Dr Mehta who found him brash.It was evident to Gandhiji: "[Manilal] finds it a great strain to conform to my way of living, but he approves of it. So if it suits JEKI, he will be glad [to it]... Besides, Manilal has not the least faith in you. He charges you with having changed your views too often and jumped from one extreme position to another. He makes a similar charge against me also, if not so vehemently... He could be fixed up in [his law practice] in partnership with [L W] Ritch any time."[2]

In reality, the pleadings were not in deference to Manilal but in the cause of JEKI. He was simply infatuated by her. JEKI was cognisant of Gandhiji having a soft corner for her. She was not beyond exploiting this weakness of his to her advantage. She was not in the pink of health. There were doubts about her capability to conceive. Gandhiji sought to plead her cause with great fervour. He advised Dr Mehta: "If she is unfit for conception [after marriage], let us hope and expect that they will behave thoughtfully. If they do not, or cannot, there is nothing for it but to leave JEKI to her fate."[3]

Finally by 1912, Manilal and Jayakunwar were husband and wife. JEKI continued to live happily with her husband at Phoenix. She was Gandhiji's favourite lieutenant who participated in teaching a mixed class of young kids and adolescents. By this time Manilal had had enough of Mauritius and Gandhiji in South Africa. It was time to move to new pastures. He decided to settle down in Fiji to fight for the cause of Indian expatriates (mostly indentured labour). JEKI remained in Phoenix in the safe custody of Gandhiji: "She is, for the present, my only adopted daughter. She is mine more than Dr Mehta's so that it seems likely she will remain with me."[4]

Tolstoy Farm

JEKI had her first meeting with Gandhiji at Tolstoy Farm. The 1100 acre farm was made available to him by his friend Hermann Kallenbach on 30 May 1910. Both he and his friend set up an experimental school there for people with no age bar. Records say that Hermann and Mohandas were assisted by a woman. The identity of the teacher is not known, but it could have been JEKI. It was tough living at Tolstoy Farm with residents feeding on fruits grown by them. They would labour from morning till evening and sleep on the floor without exception. A bed had to be hired for Gokhale during his visit there.

The Tolstoy Farm was a co-educational institution where 'some of the boys were wild and mischievious'.[5] The burden of teaching was largely shared by Gandhiji and Kallenbach. The classes were held in the afternoon as the mornings were preoccupied with exhausting labour work by teachers and students alike. Gandhiji has provided a graphic description of the situation: "The teachers would often be dozing. We would sprinkle water on the eyes, and by playing with the children try to pull them up and to pull ourselves, but sometimes in vain."[6] Gandhiji tried to coerce several young men to teach but failed. The only welcome feature of the experiment was the free intermingling of the sexes. He, however, kept a careful watch over his flock. The best part of school activities was the swimming hour for the students.

Swimming Incident

Gandhiji was a romantic at heart. He felt involved with his wards. In his own words, he 'loved them with a mother's love'. He failed to recognise that the boys were boys and they would always remain so. Even though swimming in the local pool took place under his watchful eyes, hiccups in his 'freedom-and-control' experiments were inevitable. Hell broke loose when a young boy tried to flirt with two young ladies at the swimming pool.

Gandhiji was full of contradictions. On one hand, he permitted young boys and girls to join communal swimming and on the other he was a perfect killjoy who cried wolf over little flirtations and innocent play acting between the sexes. When in trouble, he used to internalise the contradictions by going on fast to expiate for himself and others. His handling of the incidents was totally bizarre. In the true spirit of a *satyagrahi*, he prescribed punishment for himself by fasting for seven days and eating one meal a day for four months. Instead of laughing off the incident, or gently punishing the boy, he decided to make the example of girls: "I wished the two girls to have some sign on their person as a warning to every young man that no evil eye might be cast upon them, and as a lesson to every girl that no one dare assail their purity. The passionate Ravana could not so much as touch Sita with evil intent while Ram was thousands of miles away. What mark should the girls bear so as to give them a sense of security and at the same time sterilise the sinner's eye."[7]

The poor girls were most reluctant to 'cut off their fine long hair'. Gandhiji used all kinds of wiles to bring them around. They seemed to have no choice but to succumb to his pressure tactics. Gandhiji had cut the hair himself to make the girls look plain. Does it not prove that even *satyagraha* or passive resistance implies the use of force? On the contrary, bald pate could stimulate sensuality. That is what happened at Tolstoy. Girls became the subject of public notice with their bald pates.
Was Gandhiji engaged in resolving his inner conflicts by this act of expiation? In his own words: "My eye followed the girls as a mother's eye would follow a daughter," while they were engaged in public activities. In reality, it was through the eyes of father that he must have watched them. Erik H Erickson makes a valid point in interpreting the particular incident: "Is it because you feel a father might be aware of a daughter's attractiveness as a female?... Would not the father or teacher who is aware of young curves but devoted to the growth of the person be better equipped to guide and protect his daughter than the one who 'sterilises' his own eyes."[8]

Was Gandhiji reminded of St Francis cutting the hair of St. Claire as a symbolic act? Gandhiji was to repeat the same with JEKI, 'his adopted daughter', on an elaborate scale with devastating effect on her psyche. JEKI carried the burden as the mark of Cain all her life. Of course, the locale for the other incident was Phoenix and not Tolstoy as in the present instance.

Phoenix School

After the release of *satyagrahis* from jail, Gandhiji decided to shift his school from Tolstoy to Phoenix farm and in January 1913 Tolstoy farm was closed down. Gandhiji, who divided his time between Phoenix and Johannesburg, was the motivating spirit behind the new school as well. He took care of every bit of detail. He would spend hours supervising cooking in the kitchen.

There were twenty-five to thirty children between the ages of five to seventeen attending the school. Having learned his lesson from Tolstoy incident, he decided to handle adult students carefully and, in the words of Mrs Polak, he decided 'to study their developing sex-life'.[9] It did not help matters much because a senior boy did manage to misbehave with a young girl.

A year had passed after Manilal Doctor, had moved to Fiji. JEKI continued to stay put at Phoenix. A great deal of her time was taken up in herding the boys and girls at Phoenix. Her duties increased in the absence of Gandhiji. She was much more at home with the students. The 'only adopted daughter' was doing fine with her 'only adopted father'.

Chhaganlal Gandhi was a mathematics teacher. His brother, Maganlal Gandhi and JEKI taught Gujarati and Gandhiji took delight in holding discourses on *Gita*. Maganbhai Patel taught Sanskrit. The school was housed in two huts surrounded by fields. It consisted of a thatched hut and the other was made of corrugated sheets. Prabhudas, Chhaganlal's son and a student at the school vividly recalls the atmosphere: "Very often our teachers would come with their feet covered to the ankles with mud and sleeves turned up to their elbows. After giving us our lesson they would return to the fields to work."[10] Unlike at Tolstoy Farm, class hours at Phoenix were from nine to eleven in the morning. For half an hour after that, the students were made to dig in the fields.

Targetting JEKI

Gandhiji had given a lot of freedom to boys and girls at Tolstoy Farm. He landed himself into trouble on that account. Undeterred, Gandhiji went ahead with his 'freedom first' principle of boys and girls mixing freely at Phoenix. He had always encouraged unorthodox laboratory experiments in his ashrams. When JEKI fell sick, he assigned Manilal, his second son, to look after the patient. Manilal did a perfect job of nursing JEKI back to health. Gandhiji had once thought of Manilal as a perfect *brahmachari* for the youth of entire India but the *balbrahmachari* and the 'grass widow' fell for each other.

This idyllic situation did not last too long. In an earlier incident, boys had divided themselves into two groups, one probably for JEKI and the other against her. It was all about spending one shilling and three pence found on a morning walk. JEKI had turned into a child with gusto. She did not take Gandhiji into confidence about the matter. Her loyalty was found in doubt and it hurt. Gandhiji took the matter so seriously that he slapped himself five times as an act of expiation on behalf of his youngest son Devdas.

This incident became a talk of the town after Gandhiji decided to make a public pronouncement after the daily evening prayer meeting. He had decided to fight his personal battle with JEKI in the open by occupying high moral ground. It was also an act of expiation on his part. He went on fast once again. His public address makes an interesting reading: "I had some food this afternoon but I did not have any supper in the evening. Even the water I drank seemed to taste bitter… Dev[das] has confessed me to his part in the matter… The boys tell one story and X [JEKI] another… I have come to the conclusion that I should not touch food and water." He added: "You should celebrate such a day when body falls for the sake of truth."[11]

The whole onslaught was directed at the hapless young lady; she had started showing signs of defiance by refusing total loyalty to him. Before departing from Phoenix, he wanted JEKI to write to him to square up things. He followed up with a letter to Chhaganlal and Maganlal Gandhi (rated highly by him) by giving a good certificate to JEKI: "Dear X [JEKI] has had to descend from the high place which she had up to now occupied in my mind. Yet, I consider her a good person… Her sin was undoubtedly great, but we must not remind her of it… You must see that none of the boys insult her."[12]

Poor JEKI was truly cornered. Gandhiji had begun to marshal his forces against her. He had been away to Johannesburg for 8-10 days. Soon after his return to Phoenix the action had begun. Gandhiji and Kallenbach had a grave expression on their faces. There was more trouble in store for JEKI because he had come to know about her affair with Manilal Gandhi. He had been forewarned by Kasturba about it and would not listen to her.

Scandal

The 'bad turnings' always unnerved Gandhiji throughout his life. News had reached him about 'the moral fall of two of the inmates of the ashram' at Johannesburg. He decided to return to Phoenix immediately. His friend Kallenbach accompanied him. He also spoke to JEKI about the whole thing.

He announced his decision to go on fast for seven days as an act of expiation. Ba, Ramdas, Manilal and JEKI offered to join him. His friend Kallenbach was also joined him in his fast: "Y [Manilal] can only be at peace now if he purifies himself through fasting and repentance. He will, I hope, be able to bear the seven-day fast, but if he dies in the process, it will not be a matter of regret."[13]

This was not the end of the matter. After his seven-day fast Gandhiji decided to go on a partial fast for four months. He would confine himself to taking only one meal a day. He now thundered like an Old Testament prophet forewarning the culprits: "If these very people fail again, I shall undertake 14 days' complete fast and one year's partial one-meal-a-day fast. If I have to undergo a fast for the third time for the same reason, I shall undertake a complete fast for not less than 21 days."[14]

Gandhiji must have had a death wish for Manilal Gandhi in his subconscious. He had turned a married young lady into a subject of public ridicule; he had not bothered to consult his closest friend Dr Mehta, JEKI's father, who had placed her under his wardship. Dr Mehta felt like an aggrieved party, who had been sold short by his long-standing friend. He had been so trusting as to place his married daughter under his wardship. The whole world had come to know of the scandal. Dr Mehta had been blissfully unaware of the developments initially. He had landed in trouble courtesy M K Gandhi.

As soon as the news reached him, he dashed off an angry cable protesting the public breast-beating indulged in by Gandhiji at the cost of his daughter: "I do not agree with you. Terrible outrage has been done, damaging to all. I do not approve of your action."[15]

The sanctimonious Gandhi did not see much merit in the intervention by an agonised father. He defended himself in his letter to Kallenbach: "This has reference probably to hair-cutting or to all the penances and vows. We shall see. He cannot understand. He is too much in the world. Hope the fire generated by the fast continues."[16]

Various Versions

There are various versions of the incident. At Phoenix, everyone except Gandhiji was aware of the budding romance. There are several hieroglyphic versions of the same, entwined with thick cobwebs. When Gandhiji came to know of the incident, he came rushing from Johannesburg with his friend Herman Kallenbach in tow. He decided to go on a fast and affirmed his repeated commitment to truth: "Truth is like food to me." Then he went on to talk in parables. He contented himself in referring to 'X' (Jayakunwar), 'Y' (Manilal) and 'M' (Jamnadas Gandhi).

Prabhudas Gandhi in his book mentions Kallenbach talking to 'Y' and Gandhiji talking to 'X' who was 'also looking unhappy'.[17] For his evening prayer Gandhiji singled out Ba, Ramdas, X, Y and others 'desirous of fasting' with him 'for seven days'.[18] Millie Graham Polak gave a hilarious account of the incident. She again talked in parables by referring to 'Y' (Manilal) and 'N' (Jayakunwar). Another author, J N Uppal, in his secondhand version of dialogue that took place between Gandhiji and Mrs Polak is explicit in giving names:

Gandhi	:	Manilal and JEKI are guilty of adultery…
Gandhi	:	"She has confessed to everything…
Mrs Polak	:	Has it been going for long?
Gandhi	:	Yes, for quite sometime; some weeks at least…
Gandhi	:	Several people already know it. Many others could smell it. I seem to be almost the only one quite ignorant of what was going on around me."[19]

The record has been set somewhere straight by Manilal's son Arun Gandhi in his private communication dated 29 February 1980, which was made public only recently:

"When he was yet a teenager (sic) *Bhai* [Manilal] was made to nurse a young woman living at Phoenix. This was meant to be a lesson both in medical knowledge and the ability to curb one's carnal desires. *Bhai* had to do everything for the woman, including sponge and change her clothes. The woman was not at all ill and to have a young man do such personal things moved her and she made suggestive passes. *Bhai* succumbed to these overtures and they were caught by someone while kissing."[20]

To imply that JEKI was a seducer was not a fair statement. Both of them were in early twenties. They were encouraged to be close to each other. They exercised a prerogative that was handed over to them on a platter. Manilal was asked to practice nature-cure treatment for JEKI which involved touching, feeling and massaging by an unsuspecting father. One thing led to another. There were frequent meetings by the riverside. Scandal reached the ears of Kasturba, who mentioned it to her husband who ignored the gossip until it was too late.

JEKI was no man-eating siren out to seduce unsuspecting Manilal, a charge repeatedly made by Manilal's family. She was a polished and sophisticated young girl belonging to an affluent family who had lived abroad for many years. The family was close to the Gandhis for long years. Her father Pranjivan Mehta was Gandhiji's mentor during his first sojourn in London. Unlike most other Indian women she was outgoing and fluent in English and was fond of horse-riding. She played a useful role both at Tolstoy and Phoenix farms. She was fondly referred by Gandhiji as his adopted daughter. She was, in fact, given in marriage to Manilal doctor by Gandhi himself. Manilal Gandhi's life was severally constricted with no place for confident young women in his life. At heart, Manilal was romantic. JEKI brought a fresh breath of air in his life. Only the blanks remained to be filled and his father provided him the golden opportunity of nursing sick JEKI to health. The rest followed. The incident ought to have been taken in proper stride as a bad dream, but in the strange Gandhian universe, it: "plunged Manilal… into one of the biggest crises he would ever face, three months before his twenty-first birthday."

Mystery

The mystery of who's who in this sexual escapade is hard to decipher. No names had been mentioned in print. Finally, Millie Graham Polak solved the mystery by confronting her friend Gandhi. Like an astute father confessor she let Gandhiji do the talking. This confession was with a difference. Gandhiji had been cornered while defending his undefendable position.

This time Millie proved to be too astute for him. Her step-by-step ruthless questioning flabbergasted him. Her narration makes a very interesting reading in character study. Gandhiji appears credulous. JEKI was found to be too clever for her mentor. She never meant what she told Gandhiji. Millie was sceptical from the beginning and applied her British sense of understatement to devastating effects. She did not believe a word of either Gandhiji or JEKI. Perhaps Gandhiji knew the reality but placed blinkers over his eyes to pretend everything was alright with the world.

The dramatic incident is narrated in conversational style. Gandhiji set the ball rolling uninhibitedly: "Lila [JEKI] has been guilty of destroying her chastity. She has had physical relationship with N—[Manilal Gandhi], said Mr Gandhi."

He further added nonchalantly:

"She has confessed all to me."[21]

All along, Gandhiji was under the impression that JEKI took leisurely walks with a book in hand. This was her clever ploy for her regular trysts with Manilal Gandhi. Rumours were freely floating in the ashram about the budding romance. Gandhiji came to know about it when he was away to Johannesburg. The news was shocking, so he came rushing to Phoenix, escorted by Kallenbach. He did not dare to communicate the news to Dr Mehta. He was thankful to God for little mercies. He had made sure of JEKI not being pregnant. Millie could afford to mock at Gandhiji: "Well, that is something to be thankful for! It is indeed, dreadful enough for you without that..."[22]

JEKI the Actor

What was to be done next? Gandhiji was used to taking unilateral decisions. He prescribed expiation for JEKI, Manilal and himself. JEKI was the queen of the show. She made a great show of the event to impress no less than her mentor. However, she had no intention of rendering any expiation. She had no sense of guilt. She did a great deal of breastbeating in public without feeling the least remorse about the incident. She acted her part superbly. She wept and wept for one-twenty-four hours and went on a fast as an act of master showmanship. Gandhiji was solicitous about the delicate state of her health.

The Polaks no longer lived in Phoenix. When, after a fortnight, Millie came to see Gandhiji, he was full of JEKI. He was ebullience personified when he informed Millie in no uncertain terms: "She has acknowledged her sin before us all; she has fasted with me, taken off all her jewellery, put on the garb of mourning and had her hair cropped short as a sign of guilt and remorse. I have great hopes of her again."[23] Very confidently he went on to add: "Perhaps this acknowledgement of her sin will purge her soul of much that was dross in it, and she will, in fact, be the finer for it, when she has fully expiated the harm done."[24]

Mrs Polak was sceptical. She decided to confront JEKI directly. Millie did not find the least indication of embarrassment in JEKI. She suffered no sense of guilt. The boot was on the other leg: "Mr Gandhi was immeasurably more conscious of her guilt than she was herself."[25]

JEKI was highly impressed with the public attention she had received. She was enjoying every minute of undue attention given to her by Gandhiji. The very fact that she had put on a mourning dress and had her hair cropped had turned her into a mannequin on display at the Phoenix stage. Her confession to Gandhiji was not voluntary, but it had been forced out of her. JEKI was no role model, but having placed her on a high pedestal, he had to persist by propping her up for public consumption.

Manilal in Doghouse

In those troubled times for Gandhiji, Ba proved to be of great help. She took his mind off personal worries. She persuaded him to allow her and other women to participate in the passive resistance movement shoulder-to-shoulder with men. On 19 April 1913, he allowed Ba to participate in the movement. Gandhiji was happy. He wrote to G K Gokhale on 7 June 1913 about Ba participating in the struggle and Mrs Jayakunwar Doctor joining her.

The first batch of passive resisters comprised of 16 persons (12 men and 4 women). The female contingent consisted of Ba, JEKI and wives of Maganlal and Chhaganlal Gandhi. The *satyagrahis* courted arrest on 16 September 1913, and were sentenced to rigorous imprisonment for three months. They were released from prison on 22 December and taken in a big procession for their public reception. The decision of JEKI to participate in passive-resistance movement was god sent. She had once again been restored in the confidence of her mentor. He wrote to Harilal Gandhi about her approvingly: "JEKI has accompanied Ba to get arrested. She has changed her way of life altogether."[26]

Short of sentencing Manilal Gandhi to the gallows, Gandhiji decided to place Manilal in an isolation ward in faraway Johannesburg, away from JEKI who stayed put at Phoenix. He made him take a vow of abstinence. He was to remain a practicing *brahamachari* for twelve years. The treatment was reflected in his letter to Harilal Gandhi: "Manilal is in Johannesburg. He has now subjected himself to strict vows and is going through a course of penitence. He will court arrest in Johannesburg."[27]

Gandhiji had a soft corner for his second son. He was convinced that JEKI had actually seduced him. Gandhi's sons, except for Harilal were used to being ordered. Now that Manilal had been cornered, he decided to be defiant of his father to his own surprise and astonishment. Gandhiji was hurt by resistance coming from an unexpected quarter.

His associate Raojibhai Patel wrote two letters intended for JEKI and Manilal. He took care to send the letters to Gandhiji for his approval. Gandhiji destroyed the letter intended for Manilal and forwarded the letter for JEKI to her father Dr Pranjivan Mehta. This was his clever ploy of putting Dr Mehta on notice. The letter intended for Manilal was a tinderbox: "Your letter about M [Manilal], I destroyed after reading, putting that letter in his hand might, I thought, have the wrong effect on him. Now I feel, however, that you should communicate these views to him direct. I have formed a very bad impression about him. It seemed to me that, if he were to read your letter, he would be angry with you and would run into sin, and that would have been a state worse than you have described."[28]

Manilal Counters

Gandhiji had admonished Manilal during their visit to Cape Town. The sulking son charged him with cruelty. Gandhiji was in a rage. He marshalled a range of arguments in establishing his credibility with his son: "You have sinned without knowing it, in charging me with cruelty… I have grown very tender to Ba, as she has observed… This love appears cruel to you for the time being… I am but a fond lover. I have fondness enough in me to make me attached to you for being my son."[29]

When cornered, Gandhiji threw himself back on the support of his *ardhangini*. This new-found love for Kasturba had to do with him nursing her during her illness. In a couple of months, however, he was to charge Kasturba with cruelty and much more in his obnoxious letter of 14 April 1913, to Kallenbach. To his credit, Manilal had forced his father to rare expressions of love and affection for him.

Manilal had another accomplice in crime in Jamnadas Gandhi, the youngest brother of Chhaganlal and Maganlal. He was three years younger to Manilal but a close buddy. Jamnadas and Manilal coordinated their onslaught on Gandhiji. Jamnadas charged Gandhiji with arguing like a lawyer. He had the alacrity to repeat the charge. It hurt Gandhiji to no end, and like a clever lawyer, he sought to rebut the charge by painting himself larger than life in his riposte: "I find from experience that I possess in an especial degree the gift of analysis and of discriminating right from wrong and, in the result, my nice arguments sound like special pleading to others."[30]

The experiment of sending away Manilal and Jamnadas from Phoenix did not work. Since Manilal was twenty two and Jamandas nineteen in 1914, it was but natural for their thoughts to turn to girls. Both felt relaxed as they were no longer being tracked by the watchful eyes of Gandhiji. The result was predictable and worried Gandhiji to no end: "He [Manilal] and Jamnadas appeared to be unbalanced... In spite of Manilal's sad experience, both took the greatest freedom with the girls [at Phoenix]... Their talk seemed to be unnatural."[31]

Jamnadas Gandhi

Gandhiji had to recall Jamnadas. Manilal was asked to stay back so long as JEKI was at Phoenix and Gandhiji away at Johannesburg. Gandhiji did not forget to give him a piece of advice about his food habits: "I have advised Manilal that he ought to religiously avoid baker's bread, tea and coffee and that he should rarely go to Town, never eat the Town food and never sleep in Town."[32] These were stimulants to be avoided by a practicing *brahmachari*. The letter closes on the amusing note of Gandhiji letting his son know that he was still a free agent to decide for himself.

Now that Jamnadas had been recalled to Phoenix, Manilal was all by himself. Gandhiji wrote an affectionate letter to him: "It is my desire to see you esteemed in India as a *brahmachari* of a high order, your conduct so naturally well-disciplined that it cannot but produce an impression on others."[33] Gandhiji's thoughts were now turning to India. He also hinted in the same letter that JEKI was expected to eventually say goodbye to him soon after his return to India.

Talking of *brahmacharya*, Gandhiji had a piece of advice for Jamnadas also. It was soon after the Phoenix sex scandal: "I advise you to marry because I do not credit you with spiritual strength of a high order... I have told you that you will have to marry. All the same, if you have no sexual union with your wife, this cannot but be conduce to the welfare of both of you."[34] As a parting kick Gandhiji advised Jamnadas to avoid sharing bed with his future wife. Thus his ideas about physical *brahmacharya* had begun to take shape in South Africa.

Malevolent Thoughts

The JEKI-Manilal affair unnerved Gandhiji endlessly. His ego had been hurt beyond redemption. He had placed Jayakunwar (Mehta) Doctor on the highest pedestal, but she had a great Humpty Dumpty style fall in his estimation. He tried to repair the damage, but realised the futility of it. JEKI's decision to court arrest along with Ba did not help. She was in jail for a period of three months and even before her release from prison, Gandhi had begun to have doubts about her. He shared his scepticism with Ms Devi West in his letter of 14 December 1913, from Bloemfontein goal: "JEKI behn should adhere to promises made by her to me. Pl. tell [her] that a day hardly passes when I do not give much thought to her... She must grow her hair unless she has definitely heard otherwise from [her father] Dr Mehta."[35]

Apparently, JEKI had decided to be difficult with Gandhiji for the public humiliation she had suffered because of him. Gandhiji shared his thoughts in a series of letters to Raojibhai Patel during February–March 1914. Obviously, he was a worried man on her account. Initially, Gandhiji had assumed that JEKI was coming around. He called her 'a blessed soul' in his letter of 15 February 1914. This letter was a high-watermark of praise for her: "Chi... [JEKI] had to come down from the heights where I had imagined her to be. Still my mind tells me that she is a blessed soul. Her virtues are many. It is our duty to develop them. Her action and guilt were serious indeed. We should act so as not to remind her of them."[36]

But this did not last long. Soon afterwards, JEKI found him a changed man. He saw red after Raojibhai Patel prepared a detailed indictment of JEKI and showed it to him for approval. The letter intended for JEKI was instead forwarded to her father, Dr Mehta, at the instance of Gandhiji. The indictment read as follows: "... And so J's [JEKI's] and ...'s [Mani's] sins have been regarded as heinous. It is because of their extreme hypocrisy that they could be guilty of such [sins]. If they had no mind to deceive, they would, after they had turned into beasts under the urge of passion, have soon become human beings again and stopped pursuing pleasure."[37]

The injured party, in fact, was Manilal Doctor, JEKI's husband, who was blissfully unaware of the unfortunate happening. It was for Gandhiji to heal the wounds, but, instead, he chose to denounce JEKI from the pulpit. He was all fire and brimstone against her by underlining that she was 'still caught in the tools of desire and given to hypocrisy'.

However, he saw some hope for his son. Manilal confessed after receiving a letter from his father which concluded with 'Blessings from your father in agony'. Something unstated must have cropped up to turn him against JEKI 180 degrees sharp. About a year had passed and there was no peace for Gandhiji. His mind was full of malevolent thoughts. He dreamt of exemplary punishment for enforcing *brahmacharya*: "We have heard of men who, passionate in their convictions, cut off their organs when they find it impossible to control their mind. It may possibly be one's duty to do so in such circumstances. One seems now to be back on the right path and the other caught in the toils of desire and given over to hypocrisy."[38]

Love Song

In one of his letters to Kallenbach, Gandhiji called Manilal 'an infatuated lad'. In other words, Manilal was still possessed with JEKI, who, in turn, must have responded to his overtures favourably. Gandhiji talked of Manilal Doctor as an 'injured husband' and 'an honest man'.

Surprisingly, a *brahamcharya*-prone Gandhiji, could not help but sing paeans to forbidden love between Manilal Gandhi and Jayakunwar (Mehta) Doctor: "Love is mute, it does not complain. Love is blind, it sees no fault. Love is deaf, it hears no tales. Love ever gives never demands. Love is constant, never varying whether in adversity, or prosperity. Love is never hurt. Love never tires."[39]

The brave posture adopted by Gandhiji gave a false impression of his invincibility in his large circle of friends. His carefully built ramparts began to crumble under sustained pressure. Kallenbach was his father confessor, to whom he confessed his real state of mind. The JEKI affair had begun to strain everyone around him. Ba was equally concerned as her husband and son were caught in the JEKI syndrome. She did not approve of her being saddled with the responsibility of looking after JEKI. The mother in her resented the exile prescribed for her son. The eternal morose look of her husband added to her woes.

It was a matter of time before she decided to settle scores with JEKI and her own husband. Ba was looking for an opportunity, but even an excuse would have done the job. She accused JEKI of tampering with

Devdas's drawer. Gandhiji decided to come to the gallant defence of the beleaguered young lady by taking responsibility upon himself. Ba suspected her husband of 'telling a fib to shield JEKI'. Gandhiji saw in her 'most venomous remarks', 'both the devil and the divine in most concentrated form'. She was disturbed when she came to know of the letter Gandhiji wrote to Kallenbach: "And I again gently but rebukingly remarked that she was sinful in her thought and her disease was largely due to her sins."[40] Thus started the stream of letters over a period of five weeks to his 'agony aunt' Hermann Kallenbach.

By May 1914, Dr Mehta had been appraised of the unfortunate developments concerning his daughter. Gandhiji had already forwarded Raojibhai Patel's letter intended for JEKI to her father.

He was also able to persuade JEKI to be deported to Fiji to join her husband. Gandhi had the authority of Dr Mehta to do so. He was not only reconciled to her departure but viewed her departure from Phoenix as good riddance. He called JEKI all sorts of names in his letter full of woes to Kallenbach: "JEKI has been found lying more than once… Indeed she is inferior to her husband. The latter is no hypocrite. But JEKI is a finished hypocrite. You must understand what all these discoveries must have cost me."[41]

This must have been an unusual benediction for his adopted daughter on the eve of her departure to Fiji. Another week was to pass before there were additions to the 'muster-roll' of benediction. In fact, those were ramblings of an uninhibited mind: "[JEKI] is inferior. She is a liar, a wretched hypocrite, without pity, without remorse, full of evil passions. Could I ever keep her from her husband? Why, she would soon be as bad as he is and take part in all his enjoyments. Why should she not?"[42]

Threatening Suicide

As if the JEKI affair was not enough, Ba added her bit to the worsening of the situation. Never had Gandhiji agonised so much in life as he was doing now. All kinds of ill thoughts were travelling through his mind. He felt like striking his head against a blank wall. He even thought of committing suicide by putting a knife through his stomach. The other alternative before him was to run away from the world as recorded in *Fragment of letter* by him: "I talk and I smile, I walk and eat and work, all mechanically these days… The heart seems to have gone dry."[43] Gandhiji had genuine reasons to be worried. Mani and JEKI were so infatuated with each other that they had dared to defy him by continuing their secret trysts.

His worries and repeated fasts strained him so much that he became listless and thus declined to do anything but while away his time. He began to tire in no time. He stopped getting up early in the morning which upset his entire routine. Things didn't improve with time. He had only Kallenbach to share his innermost thoughts with: "… lately I have gone through mental shocks and agonies I have never gone through before … I do not talk to anybody. I want to live in solitude."[44] The fast had undone him. He called it a 'very bitter and painful experience'.he also noted: "This fast has brought me as near death's door as possible. I can still hardly crawl, can eat very little, restless nights, mouth bad."[45]

He had not lost hope entirely. He considered fasting by him a necessity. After all, he owed a debt to Dr Mehta, Manilal Doctor and his own conscience. In the same letter, he exhorted: "Mrs Gandhi [is the] most divine". The poor JEKI lost out in the process. JEKI was now out of the Gandhian circuit for the time being. She had reached Fiji to join her husband. Gandhiji had such a big relief.

On 26 November 1915, Gandhiji was delighted to inform Kallenbach that JEKI had given birth to a son in Fiji. Manilal Doctor was a doughty fighter in the cause of the Indian expatriates in Fiji. She was briefly back in India and spent some time with Gandhiji at his *Satyagraha* Ashram. In April 1920, Gandhiji complimented JEKI for being a 'brave and cultured wife'. The couple returned to India where Manilal discovered another cause. He decided to fight the cause of peasantry in Faizabad (Uttar Pradesh).

Manilal Doctor was a footloose soldier who could not stay put at one place. He found himself in strained financial circumstances. The relation between Dr Mehta, his daughter and his son-in-law continued to be strained. Gandhiji intervened in the matter without much success. Finally, Manilal moved to Aden in 1926. JEKI (a mother of two children) was back in Sabarmati Ashram and stayed there for two years. She was no longer a star, but Gandhiji remained loyal to her. She refused to join her husband in Aden and was commended by Gandhiji for her decision: "Chi.[JEKI] is not all keen on going to Aden… If I were free to decide myself, I would certainly support JEKI in her desire not to go… I would, if I could, save every woman from the burden which her husband in his sexuality puts on her."[46]

SECTION IV

Early Years: Foreign Associates

CHAPTER 9

Esther Faering: The Danish Missionary

Mohandas Karamchand Gandhi enjoyed a connection with Denmark through his association with two 'school missionaries', Esther Faering and Anne Marie Petersen, both engaged by the Danish Missionary Society (DMS) to promote the cause of education of girls in South India. Esther Faering arrived in India in 1915 and came in contact with Anne Marie Petersen while sharing accommodation with her in Madras. Miss Petersen was assigned by Danish Missionary Society the duty of visiting schools all over India and preparing reports for them. She decided to take Esther Faering along with her as junior partner.

One of the calls was at Gandhiji's Satyagraha Ashram at Kochrab (near Ahmedabad). The two young women arrived at ashram on 6 January 1917 and spent three days there. They were highly impressed. Esther Faering, in particular, discovered herself completely hooked. She recorded her impression of Gandhiji and his ashram as follows: "Anne Marie Petersen selected me to join her in visiting the schools around India, although I was the youngest. It was then we met Gandhi. My discontent and uneasiness about being part of an organised society, originates from this meeting. He utterly fascinated me and his ideal was mine too from my very youth."[1]

Instant chemistry developed between Gandhiji and the two women. This lasted for over three decades. Esther Faering and Anne Márie Petersen came to be known as 'the children of India' and 'Danish daughters of India' and Gandhiji called them 'the blessed group of foreign friends'. He also made them 'as Indians as [they] became'. He addressed Esther as 'My dear child' and 'Yours Bapu' and Miss Petersen as 'My Dear Annie' in his communication with them. To them, he was the 'living ideal—the incarnation of God in man', 'Mahatma—one of the world's mightiest and most spiritual man' and 'a man, faithful to God and his conscience'. Dealing with him was viewed as a spiritual experience by them, and they saw the hand of God in all his actions.

Flow of Correspondence

Soon after their return from Kochrab, correspondence flourished between Esther and him. Gandhiji wrote to her on 11 January 1917 : "I assure you that we miss you both very much. You were hardly guests to us; you had become members of the family."[2] Another letter followed four days later: "I am glad you found place in the ashram. Yes, both of you we regard as members of the family."[3] Intimacy grew with the passage of time as Gandhiji stressed his very special relationship in his letter of 15 April 1917, to her: "You may address me as Bapu if you like. It means father, in the ashram it has become a term of endearment. I value your affection very much indeed."[4]

Going by the contemporary portraits of Esther, she was possibly one of the prettiest young women ever, to have entered the portals of Gandhian ashram. She has been described thus: "Young, golden-haired, blue-eyed Danish beauty, who was enthralled by his innovative teaching methods and disciplined living and, above all by him personally. Gandhiji also 'experienced an intensely personal [spiritual] passion for Esther'. He loved to cuddle her as a child. He was not beyond scolding the child-woman in her. He would tease her with abundant love and affection: "You are young, you are inexperienced. You have a golden heart… My heart weeps for you", and, who equally: "fell in love with Mahatma Gandhi's spiritual commitment to selfless service".[5]

Her visit was an intense personal experience for her. She had discovered a role model in Gandhi to be emulated. After returning to her school at Tirukoilur, she started wearing *khadi* and turned to vegetarianism. She identified herself totally with his political struggles in Champaran and subsequently against the Rowlatt Bill. Indeed, she began to think and breathe Indian. She began counting days when she would be able to identify herself with him completely, by residing at the ashram.

Danish Mission

The chemistry on both sides worked. Esther was adopted in Gandhiji's enlarged family. She was treated like his favoured daughter. It must have left her wondering as to why he preferred her over the rest of them. This special consideration was the root cause of her trouble during her early stay in India. Esther returned to her mission school, but Gandhiji haunted her like Banquo's ghost. Satyagraha Ashram was on her mind constantly. Mission authorities had begun to show concern over her extra-curricular activities. In their eyes, she was an undesirable rebel spreading dissatisfaction. Her troubles were compounded on account of Miss Petersen's absence from Denmark from 1917 to 1919.

She was a determined young lady in defiant mood. She decided to spend Christmas of 1917 at the ashram with Gandhiji. The missionary conference turned down her request. The chairman of the missionary conference was sympathetic to her, but was isolated, and hence unable to help her. Gandhiji wrote to her on 30 June 1917: "The very change of surroundings is likely to do you good. If you still fail, you have to accept their opposition with resignation."[6] Gandhiji reasoned with her as far as he could. He even comforted her from distant Motihari in Champaran District by telling her: "Not to fret and fume. You are just now passing through fire. It is your clear duty just now to obey those to whom you have given the right to control your movements... They receive the benefit of any doubt."[7]

She was infuriated beyond measure, especially because the mission authorities had refused her the permission to correspond with her mentor. This precipitated the matter further. Gandhiji tried to cool her, especially after he came to know in July 1918 about her intention to quit the Danish Missionary. Gandhiji advised her to stay put: "I am quite sure that you must quietly go through your contract even though you may be prohibited from coming to the Ashram or writing to me."[8]

Indefinable Chemistry

She was totally sold on Gandhiji and did not realise the predicament in which Danish Missionary authorities were placed due to war conditions. She merrily went on her own way. The difference in age between them did not matter. There was an indefinite chemistry between them. She had already donated money and clothes to his cause. Even little gestures meant a great deal to her. Esther thought of tailoring vests for his personal use. Those were ill-fitting and not made of *swadeshi* cloth. She transfixed Gandhiji with her simple but complex queries, like being confused by the definition. To a Dane, by the very logic of things, everything Danish was *swadeshi*. She was however prepared to turn native by eschewing her Danish brand. But her doubts remained on the score.

The authorities were constrained to take note of foreigners associating themselves with Gandhiji and his political movement. Esther was on top of the suspect list. Several new memoranda were in place for restricting political activities by 'school missionaries' by the middle of 1919. The DMS released its own directive *inter alia* emphasising: "We must realise that we are in straitened circumstances, if we chose to work in India." She was persuaded to teach English in Shantiniketan for some time to keep her away from the firing line. There was, however, nothing that could prevent her (DMS or no DMS) active involvement with Gandhiji. She had already begun to identify herself with India and its cause more openly than ever before. Gandhiji was worried about her more than she was herself.

Deportation Threat

She was in trouble with the mission authorities. Her movements were being closely scrutinised by the government. She remained undaunted because she was totally obsessed with Gandhiji. It comes out clearly in her letter of 24 March 1919 to Mahadev Desai: "When I came to India, I felt at once at home; and here I have found my living ideal, the incarnation of God in man. So next to the great experience when Christ became a living reality in my life, I have no other event for which I am so happy and thankful on the day when I first met Bapu; here I found the divine love shining forth clearer than the brightest star… Bapu became for me the manifestation of the love of God… so he came into my life as the living ideal, far which I have been seeking for years."[9] Her God incarnate also reciprocated with equal enthusiasm. He wrote a pulsating letter to her on 10 April 1919 while he was on his way to Bombay by train under arrest.

Esther was now afraid of being deported to Denmark. She shared her fears with Mahadev Desai in another letter dated 4 May 1919: "The CID [police] has inquired in Tirukoilur if I had anything to do with Sgu [*satyagraha* movement]… For me they can do as they like, only as I said often before, I should rather stay several years in prison than leave

India."[10] She was also directed by the DMS authorities in June 1919 to cease correspondence with those involved in political activity.

There was double trouble waiting for her; she had fallen in love with E Kunhi Menon, a young medical student from Kerala and announced her engagement with him in the same month.

Resignation Letter

She was now in direct contention with the Board of Directors, Danish Missionary Society (DMS). She submitted her formal resignation to the business committee of the missionary conference in the following ringing words on 6 August 1919: "and furthermore due to my pronounced sympathy for M K Gandhi and his work, I have been subject to much well deserved criticism from several missionaries; and since I, by various impudent pronouncements have suspected the DMS as a whole, would hereby like to resign from the DMS. Besides, I have given rise to a great deal of criticism by becoming engaged to a Hindu in June 1919, and unfortunately this has caused indignation too. Therefore, this step in connection with the above mentioned has led me to completely lose all right of being in the service of the DMS."[11] Her resignation as superintendent of the boarding school in Siloam became effective from 1 September 1919. The DMS was aware of the fact that Gandhiji had done his best to cool her down and hence he had received a backhanded compliment from the DMS: "He is probably a fine man in many respects, but he is not a Christian."[12]

Gandhiji's mental antenna was alerted to the danger of Esther being deported from India. He started pulling wires right and left, especially after she was no longer associated with the Danish Mission. It was a distress call from him to his friend Charles F Andrews at Shantiniketan pleading with him to personally go and see the Governor of Madras Presidency without any further delay, because Esther was: "in distress less she might have to leave India. It would be almost death to her if she is forced to do so."[13]

Simultaneously, on the same day (22 August 1919) he sent a formal request to Lord Wellingdon, Governor, Bombay Presidency, recommending her naturalisation as British India citizen, and in the meanwhile to grant her a residence permit to join his ashram. In this letter he talked of Esther being 'attached to [him] like a child to its father' and, furthermore, 'she loves India as her own motherland', and was keen to pass [the rest of] her life mostly in the midst of the people'.[14]

Implied Threat

The humility shown by Gandhiji in this petition was simulated, because under it lay the threat of political agitation. The implied threat worked and Esther was allowed to stay in India. He saw the Rowlatt Act and his involvement with the Esther Faering issue as the links in the same chain. He made his intentions abundantly clear in his letter dated 24 August 1919, to his close friend Charles Andrews: "Today our Government stop at nothing. It does not require a philosopher to understand the utter futility of physical force. But you may not agree with my conclusions or inferences. I do want you to agree with me that it is just important to do our best to protect Miss Faering from harm as it is for me to resist the Rowlatt Act with my life and for you to be at Shantiniketan."[15]

After months of sustained tension, relief came her way, when thanks to Gandhiji, she was allowed to stay in India and travel freely in Bombay Presidency. This enabled her to arrive at the ashram in October 1919. His departure from the ashram coincided with her arrival in Ahmedabad. Thus he was nowhere to be found to give her company and guide her. In December, she decided to spend Christmas in Madras in the company of Miss Petersen, who had returned to India after a prolonged absence of two years. She returned to the ashram in January 1920, but Gandhiji was again on the move. His burdening political agitations and the company of Saraladevi Chowdharani kept him away until June 1920. Esther had no choice but to live a lonesome existence at the ashram. They had frequent exchange of letters, but it was no substitute for his physical presence. Here he was providing solace to her from Lahore on 7 December 1919: "I am glad… [You] have enabled me to enter more fully into your heart. Your coming is a joy to me."[16]

Ashram Stay

Esther was truly passionate about Gandhiji and India. She had fallen in love with Kodaikanal and its hilly surroundings (where her true love for her husband blossomed), 'to drink and take all perfect beauty' of 'India's beautiful, glorious hills'. It did not help matters very much. She was in deep trouble. The ashramites were indifferent to her. So was Ba due to the ongoing cold war with her husband.

At heart, Esther was a sensitised European who found it hard to adjust to her native environment. Her woes compounded as she could make no friends and did not participate in public functions such as morning and evening prayer meetings. Gandhiji gave her *carte blanche* permission to pray in her private chamber. He also advised her to help Ba in her kitchen routine. Herein lay the root of a numbing trouble for her. Gandhiji added to her problems by instigating her against Ba all the time.

Initially, things between Ba and Esther worked fine. Ba was pleased to tell her husband about Esther taking care of her. However, the peace did not last long. Ba was already under pressure on account of Saraladevi Chowdharani. Now it was the turn of *malecha* intruders. Ba had virtually thrown Esther out of the kitchen. She was waging a war against her husband by proxy.

The innocent Esther was employed for mere target practice. Things turned too messy for her comfort. Gandhiji could do precious little from distant Lahore except bucking up Esther from the sidelines. She was left with no alternative but to complain about Ba. The fusillade had started in the right earnest. Esther had to run for cover. Gandhiji started complaining bitterly about the conduct of his beloved wife.

He targetted Ba in a series of letters to Esther Faering on 16, 24 and 25 January 1920. He relentlessly made fun of Ba. It all started over Esther offering a helping hand to Ba in her kitchen, an offer which had taxed the patience of Ba. She needed no interference, much less any assistance in her exclusive kitchen domain.

Kitchen War

Ba had no patience with others and was rarely sweet. Her current ill health added to her woes. What should have been the nature of response by a practising Christian like Esther Faering? He provided the answer himself: "You will therefore summon to your aid all your Christian charity to be able to return largesse against pettiness." He also assured Esther from distant Delhi that "You... were [in my thought] the whole of yesterday and during the night."

In another letter battle lines were drawn with Gandhiji and Esther confronting Ba in an unequal context: "I had no notion that you have already observed Mrs Gandhi's pettiness. I simply warned you, as I ask you to come in closer touch with her. As it is, my warning reached you just in time." She was advised not to overtax her "spirit in trying to win over Mrs Gandhi or anybody else... You could still serve her but not be so intimate with her."[17]

He minced no words in denouncing Ba in the final letter in the series: "The evil in Ba, for instance, must not be resisted, i.e., you or for that matter I must not fret over it or be impatient and say to ourselves, 'When will not this woman see the truth or return the love I give her'. She can no more go against her nature than a leopard can change his spots... If she does not respond, she acts according to hers [nature]. And if we worry, we 'resist evil'. Do you agree?"[18] It is to be remembered that he had performed a similar unchivalrous act once earlier on 12 April, 1914 in his venomous letter to his friend Kallenbach.

Bouquet of Letters

Gandhiji began writing to Esther almost on a daily basis. Things would have been better for sure, if he were to confront Esther personally. This was out of the question. He was stationed at Lahore during her entire stay at the ashram. He discouraged Esther from travelling to Lahore. The next six weeks were spent by him travelling throughout the length and breadth of the country along with Saraladevi Chowdharani. His letters to Esther reflected the state of his mind during the entire period.

Here is the day-to-day chronology of developments as seen through the plethora of letters to Esther over the extended period of three months. What had prompted him to do so? Esther must have stirred the serpent resting uncoiled in his *kundalini*. Indeed, the poet in him had been alerted for once. The intensity in his correspondence with Esther was of the same degree as found in Bhakti and Sufi writings. Gandhiji must have felt insecure and in danger of losing Esther for good. He decided to fight all the way. Human beings are at their best when their ego is in danger of being hurt.

Soon after coming to know about Esther's decision to go away from his ashram, the torrent of communications began with a bang on 1 February 1920. In fact, there are two letters addressed to her on the same date. He thus marshalled his entire resources to employ Christian hymns to fight his cause like a clever lawyer that he was. He was to assure her in another letter that she was constantly in his mind and hence, he would miss her 'at the time of retiring' at night. He had felt humbled by his dealings with the young lady, who, in return, must have been overwhelmed by the attention she had received: "To express purest love is like walking on the edge of a sword."[19]

Suspecting that the young Danish dame was like a bird in the bush and not the one in safe hands, he continued with his poetic dirge in a series of letters spanning more than two months almost uninterruptedly. Never had he done so before. After he was through with his poetic addresses to Esther, Saraladevi was given a similar treatment. The poems and hymns with Biblical citations read like the unwinding epitaph of his close association with Esther. Indeed, she must have felt overwhelmed by this versification. It had all begun on 5 February, when he referred to Toplady's hymn *Rock of Ages**[20] to make his point. Gandhiji was unhappy with Esther and accordingly he accused her of making 'experiments in dark'. He must have found the accusation too much and hence retracted

---

**Rock of Ages*

Rock of Ages, cleft for me,
Let me hide myself in Thee!
Let the water and the blood,
From thy river side which flow'd,
Be of sin the double cure –
Save me from its guilt and power.
Not the labour of my hands
Can fulfil Thy law's demands;
Could my zeal no respite know,
Could my tears for ever flow,
All for sin could not atone,
Thou must save, and thou alone.
Nothing in my hand I bring;
Simply to thy Cross I cling!
Naked, come to Thee for dress:
Helpless, look to Thee for grace:
Foul, I to the fountain fly;
Wash me , Saviour, or I die!
While I draw this fleeting breath,
When mine eyes shall close in death,
When I soar to world's unknown,
See Thee on Thy Judgment throne;
Rock of Ages, cleft for me,
Let me hide myself in Thee.

and came up with a supplication with Biblical allusions to Jesus Christ: "But you give me the privilege of calling you my child, *Rock of Ages*, cleft for me and let me hide myself in thee.'[21]

After Esther had made up her mind to say goodbye to the ashram, he expressed his innermost thoughts by quoting from *The Inner Shrine* with 'happy grief ' and 'mournful joy' in equal measure. He had Saraladevi with him throughout the period of his versification, but he was unable to blot the memories of Miss Faering from his mind.

The real avalanche of poetic verses started during the month of March 1920. Verses took over from prose momentarily. He must have felt overwhelmed to express himself in day-to-day language. He had come to know by this time about her decision to migrate to her native Denmark on health grounds. To add to Gandhiji's discomfit, her beau was to accompany her on this trip. On 3 March, Gandhiji admitted to Esther that she was constantly in his mind and disturbed him in his sleep. Admittedly, she was so marginal to his larger scheme of things, yet she loomed so large momentarily as to overshadow all consequential developments in his life.

Versification Through Letters

He was like a magician who produced a poem by Lovell and addressed it to her on 14 March. He threatened to overwhelm her with an avalanche of verses: "I hope to pick up something like his, if I can, everyday."[22] After Lovell, it was Tennyson who turned up on the stage to perform on 16 March with his famous stanza:

> "More things are sought by prayer
> Than this world dreams of. "[23]

The redoubtable Gandhi was reduced to praying for a miracle, so that Esther would come back to his protective cover. If Tennyson didn't continue to hold the fort, it was George Herbert on 17 March. Did it help to soften the grief by repeating the same line, same word and same thought? Thus, he fully recognised that logic didn't work in matters of heart. The next day, on 18 March, he quoted from verses of Richard Baxter: "Another evening has come to fill me with thoughts of you."[24]

By this time he was ensconced in Bombay in the pleasant company of Saraladevi. He had dominated the political scenario with his triumph after stirring the Jallianwala Bagh agitation. But Esther's absence from the scene hurt his inflated ego. He dispatched yet another poem to her: "Oh I could go through all life's troubles singing turning each night to day." On the sly, he could not resist the temptation but to add a postscript: "Do not keep me without anything from you for so many days."[25] Two more poems followed on 21–22 March by Trench and J Bunyan entitled 'I our father's name' and 'Humility', respectively.

Gandhiji decided to placate her with an unending flow of epistles raising her sky high. Esther was no longer amused. She had seen through the hollowness of his promises. He was nowhere to be found during the entire period of her stay at the ashram. She had got into an avoidable spat with Ba. The other residents of the ashram cold-shouldered her and her health deteriorated. She developed liver problem. She decided to move out of the ashram before his return. He made a last ditch appeal to have her to stay at the ashram.

Marrying Menon

What was it that was bothering them after all? Esther Faering and Dr E K Menon had fought against all odds. Finally, they were able to announce their engagement. The Church had looked down upon their union. The local Europeans scowled at the possible 'mongrelisation'. The orthodox Hindus showed concern over the possibility of Dr Menon's conversion. Gandhiji actively campaigned against the liaison. In his eyes, Esther was refusing to perform her *dharma* of service to the ashram.

Gradually, he came to terms with the situation. In the past also, he had reconciled himself to the inevitable. He began to admire Esther for her sheer grit. Finally, he approved of the engagement in his letter of 25 March to her. His benediction came only with a lefthanded compliment: "I am quite resigned to your marriage."[26] His versification campaign had almost come to a stop. His bouquet of poems (and hymns) had suddenly dried up: "I felt I had sent you enough verses to last you for some time."[27]

Now he was engaged in trotting up excuses about delayed correspondence. His span of interest in any person was short. Gandhiji had a tight schedule during October 1919–April 1920, besides coping with Saraladevi. He was away from the ashram most of the time. His health gave away and he was required to take rest. From Bombay he moved to Sinhgadh without Sarala.

At Sinhgadh (of Shivaji fame) fort, he was relaxed, being all by himself. He found time to savour luscious mangoes (possibly the Alphanso variety). He had time to watch glorious sun rise high up in the hills. He was left dreaming of Saraladevi in her absence. Playfully he sought her benediction. Naughty Gandhi! He was behaving like a spoilt child.

Esther Faering was ready to depart for Denmark. She was to embark her ship from Bombay. Her mentor was beckoning her for the last tryst: "...do come up to Sinhgadh. It is a beautiful place. It is reached from Poona by a tonga [with hire charges at Rs 5].[28] Esther spent two days with him at Sinhgadh going over the pleasant memories of her past association with him. As if in anticipation, he had wished her bon voyage:

> "And we on diverse shores now aft, shall meet,
> our perilous voyage past,
> All in our Father's house at last."[29]

Now Heaven seemed to be the destined meeting point for them in their future.

Au Revoir

There was no peace for her. She was physically dilapidated. She missed Gandhiji during the few months she was at the ashram. The DMS people were after her blood. Her engagement to E Kunhi Menon created more bad blood against her. Her only solace was the company of her close friend Miss Petersen. She departed for Denmark in May 1920. The actual reason why she was forced to leave India came out in her confessions published in 1940: "In 1920, I went to Denmark under pressure from the DMS, my father and my sister, had got my dismissal... branded as a heretic and perhaps as something even worse. When the Grundvigians at the request of Annie Marie [Petersen], let me speak in the Youth Societies, I was called a renegade. In 1920, I was engaged by my former committee to depart for India in order to help Annie Marie—regardless of my marriage to a Hindu."[30]

Dr Menon joined her in Denmark in 1921 and both of them solemnised their marriage on 1 July 1921. The cause of India remarried

---

*Seva Mandir was described as the precursor of a chain of 'National Girls' school' to cultivate 'national pride' and values of Christianity.

uppermost with her and had Gandhiji's approval: "I know you are there spreading love for India." The couple returned to India in December 1921. Esther began to assist Miss Petersen at the girl's model school 'Seva Mandir'* at Porto Novo Chidambram District, Tamil Nadu.

Dr Menon was baptised on 6 June 1924. The couple continued to be associated with the activities of Porto Novo school and ashram from 1921 to 1927. Esther and her two daughters contracted malaria and she also suffered from rheumatism. She was back in Europe from 1927 to 1933 and published a biography of Gandhi in Danish in 1930. After spending seventeen years in India from 1934 to 1950, she was finally back in Denmark for good in 1950. She was to pass away in 1962, unnoticed and unknown, spreading love for India.

Esther Faering came to India to proselytise but she was converted to its cause making this her life's mission. She spent her entire lifetime discovering her Indian identity. The best never came out as Miss Danish Daughter of India, because she was, in the words of Gandhiji: "Weary with fatigue, both in body and mind", but who had been "spreading love for India"[31] so long she was alive.

Love Refrain

Gandhiji was a romantic at heart. He had a soft corner for women. Esther Faering was overwhelmed with his 'purest love' when Saraladevi Chowdharani was the subject of his intense attention. His letters to Esther were his 'love letters' and 'long love letters'. How many times would he assure himself of 'I Love You', in response to 'Your wonderful love'. Thus both of them were quits in having 'fallen in love with each other'.

Love never treads a straight path. For him the 'purest love' was 'like walking on the edge of a sword', but, undeterred Gandhiji soldiered on, for him 'love is not afraid', ever patient, ever suffering and hence, 'love will not be denied'.[32] Here was the affirmation of love, because 'true love grows silently but steadily', and, indeed, 'true love is when it must'. Last but not the least, 'love is the epitome of strength' for him. It was always business as usual with Gandhiji. The lawyer in him was impatient to discover 'the law of love'. His love was asexual but full of implied 'sensuality' as reflected in his correspondence with Esther Faering.

CHAPTER 10

Euphoric Mirabehn

Madeleine Slade, with a distinguished British pedigree, was born in 1892. She was destined to cross the path of Mohandas Karamchand Gandhi. She was a great devotee of Beethoven and returned to his fold a decade after Gandhiji was assassinated. She was a great admirer of Romain Rolland, an authority on Beethoven. Thus, three great geniuses of contemporary times, Beethoven, Romain Rolland and Gandhiji, were her inspiration. Gandhiji named her Mirabehn.

She came in contact with Romain Rolland when he visited London in October 1923. She listened to his public lecture with rapt attention. One thing led to another and she soon came to be acquainted with Gandhiji through his biography that Romain Rolland was writing. She was greatly fascinated by the Mahatma after reading the book a year later. Awe struck, she decided to follow his footsteps. Perhaps, her destiny beckoned her to India.

Brooding Girl

Earlier, she lived in India from 1909 to 1911 when her father Sir Edmund Slade was in Bombay as Commander-in-Chief of the East Indian Station of the Royal Navy. The debutante Miss Madeleine Slade was the toast of the town. It is doubtful, if she came to know about Mohandas Karamchand Gandhi then.

She was brought up in great luxury. The Slade House spread over twenty acres of farmland on high ground with well-laid gardens, cow paddocks and rich flora and fauna. She was a brooding child who loved solitude. She used to roam around the vast acres of her grandmother's estate all alone. She loved to interact with Nature and wondered at the unknowable infinite universe. Brooding, withdrawn, philosophical and nature-loving are the characteristics that sum up Miss Slade who later became Mirabehn in Mahatma's company.

This is how she described her surroundings: "Out of doors the twenty acres were a whole world for adventurous exploitation. I got to know every nook and corner, and from the very beginning I had a feeling of fellowship with the trees and plants... Later on, as a young girl, I can remember throwing my arms around trees and embracing them, and to this day that feeling remains."[1]

The tall strapping girl with handsome visage and profuse dark hair was six-feet and could be singled out in any crowd or company due to her striking personality. It was believed that gypsy blood flew in her veins through a remote Russian connection. She was an island to herself and awaited an opportunity to break away from her moorings.

Beethoven beckoned her to Romain Rolland who in turn introduced her to Gandhiji. Initially she was drawn to Romain Rolland: "[He] became an objective which drew me with such force and urgency that at this moment I began trembling all over."[2]

They talked about Gandhiji and the biography* that was still in the press. Her curiosity was multiplied a thousand-times over when Rolland

---

*Romain Rolland's *Mahatma Gandhi* made Gandhiji the darling of the literati, drawing-room intellectuals and the salon women all over Europe. Gandhiji became the fashion of the day.

The French Antoinette Mirabel was all set for a sojourn in India in the same year as Mirabehn. In this task, she was supported by her husband who was; almost 'like a brother to her'. Thus the cult of *brahmacharya* had travelled all the way to France.

Then there was Francisca Handenath of Austria, another enthusiastic neo-convert to abstinence. She felt pity for her husband who found it hard to practice *brahmacharya*. Eventually he had to fall in line for the greater cause of his Darwinian 'evolution'. Thus there was Helene Hanssding (Gandhi's *My Liitle Sparrow*) who pined for him. She compared herself to 'the bird in cage', awaiting to soar high in the sky breaking 'the bars of conventionalities'.

Like Mirabehn, Antoinette, Helene and Francisca belonged to the upper crust of European society. They had money and leisure. They conversed endlessly. They talked of Beethoven, Wagner, Verdi and Romain Rolland in their salons. They took to reading Indian scriptures including *Bhagvat Gita*. They wrote interminably long described him as the second Christ. She could hardly wait to read the book. She read the book soon after it became available to her the very next year.[3]

She started correspondence with Gandhiji and threatened to settle down at the Sabarmati Ashram for life, to be near him, serve him and the cause of humanity at his bidding. Gandhiji discouraged her but she persisted and he gave in. He advised her to stay put at home for one year and duplicate the ashram routine. Following this, she adopted simple living, eschewed meat and stopped drinking. Her family was flabbergasted and tried their best to persuade her to change her mind but she refused. She demonstrated her seriousness by spending some time in a lonely Swiss cottage, practicing austerity as was done by medieval monks. This was her preparation for the life in the ashram.

Beckoning Destiny

After the year of penance was over, she could hardly wait to turn up at the Sabarmati Ashram at Ahmedabad. She wrote the most reverential letter to her newly-adopted guru:

"Most dear Master,

I have eagerly taken to heart all you said, and I now venture to write to you again [after] my year of self-imposed trial being more than over…

I may be able to give expression to my love in work—in acts…

The more I enter into Indian thought, the more I feel as if I were reaching at last, a long lost home… I have given up the drinking of all wines, beers or spirits and I no longer eat meat of any kind.

My being is filled with a great joy and a great anguish: the joy of giving all—I leave to you and to your people—and the anguish of being able to give so little. Dear Master, may I come? Madeleine Slade."[4]

His reply followed on 24 July 1925 in which he welcomed her but also warned her of the hardships: "…The life at the Ashram is not all rosy… I mention these things not to frighten but merely to warn you."[5]

---

letters to Gandhiji, their father-confessor. They took note of Gandhiji because thereby they came to be noticed by others. Mercifully such affairs never last long, or one must be prepared for the fate of long-suffering Mira.

She was not deterred and without awaiting the final instructions from Gandhiji, she decided to set sail for Bombay.

Mystic Joy

Mirabehn reached Bombay on 6 November 1925. The very next day she arrived at the Ahmedabad railway station. Vallabhbhai Patel was a member of the welcoming party at the station. Soon she was on the way to the Sabarmati Ashram in a *tonga,* escorted by the future Iron Man of India and two other companions. She was totally impressed by Patel's persona—the patrician Roman face, the toga (*dhoti*) that he wore and his clean-shaven head. His visage emphasised "power curiously intermingled with a kindly and humorous expression".[6]

By now she had transformed herself into a starry-eyed girl who had lost all sense of space and time. She had also lost her sense of physical being, anticipating her meeting with the Little Master. The state of being starry-eyed remained from her first meeting with him in 1925 to the day of his assassination in 1948.

Romain Rolland had excited her curiosity about India. Encouraged, she showered letters full of mystic joy to Romain Rolland. She had mentally prepared herself to discover a prophet, but instead 'found an angel' confronting her. She had seen the second coming of Christ in him. Gandhiji was equally bowled over by her. He was so enthusiastic that he wrote in the *Young India*: "Do you know that Miss Slade has come here, having burnt all her boats? Do you know that her sacrifice for our cause is greater than that of any of us?"[7]

He wrote to Romain Rolland about Mirabehn on 13 November 1925, "What a treasure you have sent to me." A day earlier Mirabehn had confided to Romain Rolland, "I could never imagine how divine he is." She was gushing with his 'divine love'. Romain Rolland knew his pupil better than Gandhiji. While Romain Rolland talked of her 'passionate' and 'unquenchable ardour', 'admirable energy, and ardent devotion' for Gandhiji, he also noted that "her mind was prey to violent and passionate disturbance."[8]

Soon after she landed at the ashram, she became the centre of Gandhiji's attention. Mira was Saraladevi Chowdharani all over again. By December 1925 he was already full of her. Otherwise, how would one explain his writing to her: "I have your loving present... You have been constantly in my thought. This three days separation is good discipline."[9] No wonder, gossip had crossed the seas and Mira was much talked about in London. He has himself mentioned 'the libel on Mira', published in the *Sunday Chronicle* of London.

Ideal Worker

He went away to Deolali for only a few days, but he could divine her feelings of separation from him. He proposed an eternal bond to her, extending beyond life to death: "Death brings us nearer. Is not the body a bar—if it is also an introduction?"[10]

He announced to the whole world, through a circular of 20 December 1926 meant for the ashram women, of Mira being 'the ideal worker'. On 27 December, he informed her of having received all her 'love letters'. His letters were not without a touch of unintended humour. His obsession with the functioning of the bowels has been termed legendary. It is not surprising to note that he made enquiries about this natural (but personal) bodily function from Mirabehn. In his letters of 2 September, 8 and 13 December 1930 and 23 August 1932, he went lyrical over his and her constipation troubles. He also mentions sweet potatoes being responsible for his constipation woes.

She went out of her way to forget her past. She read the *Bhagvad Gita* before she arrived in India and also burnt her dresses from Paris, aboard the ship. Her London dressmaker had designed a shapeless *khadi* gown for her. She thus disowned her upper-class upbringing and forsook her family. Her family, friends and acquaintances took pity on her: "Every one is sorry for me; people say to me: How lonely you be, lost among all those Indians."[11]

Miss Slade was 33 when she arrived at the Sabarmati Ashram. She towered one foot above diminutive Gandhiji, but looked puny in his august presence. His penetrating eyes dazzled her. He held her by her hands and proclaimed: "You shall be my daughter." This is how he used to address all young girls and women. Romain Rolland had also adopted her as his daughter. The adopted daughter of Gandhiji (and Romain Rolland) felt gratified at the attention she received.

Mirabehn was a determined woman who wanted to possess him, own him, cuddle him like a child and worship him as the Holy Father. Ultimately her obsession became her undoing. Others at the Ashram were cold and cautious with her and considered her to be an intruder. Very soon she realised that the ashram was neither a monastery nor a heaven of peace. It was a place of humdrum existence and routine happenings. Gandhiji's physical presence made all the difference. He was full of enthusiasm and joy all the time. He was extremely delighted to display Mirabehn as his most-favoured exhibit.

He took her along wherever he went. She accompanied him on the inspection tour of trench latrines put up for the annual session of the Indian National Congress. It was a test for her. Her presence was equally put to practical use. He did not possess an olfactory sense. She was to inspect the toilets and report on their condition to him directly. Now the toilets had the stamp of approval of no less a person than Mira.

By definition, honeymoon does not last long. Gandhiji had a fill of her rather too soon. She was sent out of the Sabarmati Ashram to Kanya Gurukul (Daryaganj), New Delhi, and subsequently to Bhagirabhakti Ashram, Poona. Then onwards, she did not return to the ashram except for her brief visits. Subsequently Gandhiji managed to keep her off his track by sending her in exile to distant places, for establishing and maintaining new ashrams. She was back with him from time to time, but never for too long.

Separation

Mirabehn found the pangs of separation too much to bear. She was inconsolable. Initially he promised to write 'love letters' on weekly basis. He tried to give her solace: "The Ashram is not finally at Sabaramati but in yourself."[12]

While holidaying at Nandi Hill near Mysore, he enticed her to visit him but also added: "If you cannot contain yourself, you must come and not feel that I shall be displeased."[13] Her anxiety was somewhat assuaged when she received an assuring reply from him. His sympathetic letter had acted as a balm. He knew how to placate and flatter sensitive human beings of the feline kind. He could turn philosophical if it was required of him. He now talked of 'sorrow over separation and death' as the greatest delusion.

Mirabehn was frank enough to confess that her mind was in the right place and that it was her heart which impelled her to be near him. She could not live away from him. He also liked to have her within his consciousness but from a respectable distance. Her obsession frightened him. It came in the way of his public sensibilities. At the same time, he admired her intellectual capabilities and aesthetic qualities. She towered over the rest of the crowd around him. The state of quasi-stalemate between them must have been written in their stars.

Mirabehn was forthcoming in her emotions but not Gandhiji. In his letter of 28-29 April 1927, he advised her to come to terms with her own psyche. Patience was a virtue to be cultivated. It was, however, easier said than done in actual situation.

She sent two letters to him dated 27 April and 7 May. In the first letter, she confessed her failure to come to grips with her sensitivities: "I have grasped the truth with intellect, but the heart lagged behind for many years."[14] She repeated her predicament in the other letter: "In spite of the intellectual realisation the heart has failed me."[15] She called it her 'spiritual agony'. While Mira had recognised the shadow-boxing by him (like Saraladevi Chowdharani), Gandhiji would admit none of it. Probably he loved no one except himself.

Gandhiji was a compulsive letter-writer. His women associates were expected to write to him on a regular basis. Mirabehn was one of those fortunate ones whom he requested to write to him regularly. There was an avalanche of letters flowing between them. On 2 May 1927, he compared her to a pendulum with an inherent capability to wildly swing back and forth. Indeed Mira had been reduced to a mere pendulum, which is by nature inherently unstable. What could Mira do? She was a victim of unrequited love for the Little Master. Her state of being irritated Gandhiji to no end. He resorted to admonishing her in one letter after another.

It was on 8 May that he administered a severe reprimand to her saying that it was not him personally but his ideals which should have been her focus. He was wrong because she had fallen at his feet not for his ideals but for Mohandas Karamchand Gandhi in flesh and bones. If she fell in love with his ideals also, then it was not as an end but as a means to be near him.

Mirabehn was like a child who could be satisfied easily. A letter or two from him would do the trick for the time being. On 9 May, he was satisfied because he had been successful in assuaging her feeling. There was, however, a turn for worse, after three days. She had once again entered the realm of melancholia. By 12 May, he realised that the panacea suggested to her had proved to be illusory. He was anxiously advising her: "You should not appear to be what you are not."[16]

But Mirabehn was not play-acting and only playing her part in real life. It was he, who was play-acting and not prepared to play his part in real-life drama. Understandably, Mira proved to be a handful for him. What else could he do except offering sops to her? Now he claimed the additional privilege of being not only her father but also her mother. The honour done to Mirabehn was illusory. She was looking for companionship from Gandhiji which continued to elude her. She began to feel disillusioned slowly and steadily, but that was still in the future.

He snubbed her from time to time and also scolded her for not being able to 'resist going over to see Bapu' when separated from him. Once she was packed off to Sabarmati, halfway from Poona, on her way to South to have *darshans* of her *ishtadeva*. Immediately, he felt guilty and used all his wiles by flooding her with a series of placatory epistles. On 29 September 1929, he assured her that "I can't dismiss you from my mind."[17] He charged her of having 'haunted' him in his sleep the previous night. He woke up with a start and 'prayed' for her to be 'free from all harm'.[18] In expiation, he wrote 16 letters to her in the next 34 days.

Intensity of Relationship

The relationship between Mirabehn and Gandhiji became intense during post-Saraladevi period. It picked up momentum in the second half of the 1920s and peaked during the late 1930s. There were all kinds of rumours floating about their relationship, which was at best indefinable. It was widely rumoured that Mira had forsaken her home and hearth, her family and her associations with upper-class stiff-necked British society for half-naked Gandhiji.

He was 60 in 1929 and here is a contemporary portrait of the man based on close personal observations: "...he had become a withered little man, scraggy gray moustache emphasising his all but toothless mouth, and the inevitable loin cloth exposing skinny legs and thighs that supported a shell of skin above a meagre skeleton."[19]

But he was a remarkably charismatic personality with most powerful magnetic eyes. The reason why Mira was obsessed with Gandhiji has a very simple explanation. To shine in Gandhiji's reflected glory was an attractive proposition for several of his associates who joined his bandwagon. Platonic love could be another factor in the situation. Physical or sensual love could be the least consideration. Emotional love for a charismatic personality has worked wonders. Here was a guru-*shishya* relation that lasted quite long. The Freudian explanation would have a father lurking behind the woman in love. Gandhiji was certainly a father-figure to many of his women associates. The emotional attachment of Mirabehn, thus, could be attributed to a multi-faceted personality.

Poetic Expressions

The intensity of her attachment to Gandhiji was shown in her letters during the early 1930s. In the archives of Sabarmati Ashram, there is a letter from Mirabehn addressed to Gandhiji dated 7 June 1931. She composed two ditties (she calls them "little verses") based on old German and Scotish melodies. She dedicated these poems to 'Beloved Bapu'. These faithfully reflect her genuine feelings for the Little Master. One of the poems reads as follows:

> "Tune: Old Scottish folk melody :—"A fond kiss".
> "From the darkness thou
> have led me,
> Earthly possessions now have fled me;
>
> Since the blessed day I
> found thee,
> Thou in holy love hast bound me."[20]

Mirabehn was given to deep and instantaneous emotions. It was no surprise. Suppressing oneself for too long results in dire stress. Mirabehn was no exception. All the same, it was a relation based on mutual consent. She had indicated motherly instincts for Gandhiji in response to his fatherly concerns. She was also protective of him in times of crises. Gandhiji was never too short of such situations in his personal life. Indeed, he lived from one crisis to another.

It was a two-way traffic between them. Gandhiji was no less taken up with her. After a fortnight he responded to her in an equally emotional fashion: "You are on the brain.... All the time you were squandering your love on me personally.... And I exploded on the slightest pretext.... But I was on a bed of hot ashes all the while.... 'Cheer boys cheer, no more of idle sorrow.'"[21]

Mirabehn also rose to the occasion: "The struggle was terrible. I too was on a bed of hot ashes because I could feel that." The chemistry between the two of them was perfect on such occasions. After all, it was "no joke to be [his] daughter."[22]

Bhakti Spirit

Gandhiji was in Yeravda jail in Poona from 4 January 1932 to 8 May 1933. He decided to undertake a fast unto death in protest against the communal award. Mirabehn, Vallabbhai Patel and Manibehn Patel sought appointments with him in jail. Mirabehn was refused permission to meet him. She wrote a record 32-page letter to him pouring out her innermost tensions and thoughts.

The spirit of *bhakti* was the dominant theme of the letter. Each word of the letter sparkled with the spirit, which, in other words, involved selfless service with no thought of reward. She had been on the verge of a breakdown soon after she was refused the interview with him. She came back to her normal self soon. Indeed there was hardly any line of demarcation between the states of normalcy and breakdown in her case. She seemed to transit from one state to another with ease. Her devotion to work was her *dharma* which helped her to maintain her equilibrium. It was the best way to fight depression. Rhetorically, she enquired of Gandhiji: "Who knows if it is all delusion!"[23]

She was a wise woman. She recognised the realities very early in her life. She knew that any amount of reasoning with Gandhiji would not help matters. Finally, she was reduced to dealing with him through instinct, indeed the strongest weapon in the armoury of a women. She was reduced to supplicating Gandhiji in the following words: "I have no thought, no care, no longing in all the world except for you—*you the cause, you the ideal.* To serve that cause in this life and to reach that ideal." She thanked the merciful God who had "brought [her] from utter darkness to life in after life."[24]

In fact, her God was none other than Gandhiji. Here were her raw instincts confronting his cold logic.

Mystic Love

Gandhiji was totally floored by her instinctive responses to crises. He was impressed by her devotion to him and on such occasions he was a perfect gentleman to Lady Mirabehn. He kept assuring her during his fast unto death in Yeravda jail: "Let me put you at ease. When I come out [of jail] you shall certainly be with me and resume your original work of personal service. I quite clearly see that it is the only way for your self-expression... And who can give me more loving service than you?"[25]

Gandhiji was too much taken up with Mira but at the same time he managed to keep her at an arm's length. She was too emotional for his comfort. So she would be on and off in the ashram. At that moment, she was being viewed favourably by him. When he was released from jail, he acknowledged her recent role. His letter applauded her for her 'leading service'. It was also an acknowledgement of Bapu's defeat at the hands of love. It was literally true that no one could give Bapu more loving service than Mirabehn. Valji Desai should know because he was an insider and privy to the thoughts of Gandhi. His reference to 'Bapu's defeat' was the spontaneous concern expressed by Mirabehn when he was in Yeravda jail.

When Gandhiji undertook the fast, his condition deteriorated rapidly by the third day. Mirabehn was unduly alarmed and almost collapsed. When Gandhiji came to know about this, he managed to send a note of comfort to her. He was at his loving best to assure her of his concern: "The thought of you corrodes me."[26] He begged her to write to him immediately. He also promised to send a daily report to her through Mahadev Desai. The very next day he managed to send her a two-liner: "You are not to break. You must be seeing God's grace pouring in abundance as perhaps never before."[27]

Now the roles had been reversed. By this time, she found herself in Yeravda jail and Gandhiji was back in the normal haunts of his ashram after his release from prison. He wrote a note to her on the very next day and cautioned her to avoid being 'overexcited' after the interview with him. This must have been an understatement of the year. She was in the seventh heaven and wrote back to him: "God gave me the light to recognise His messenger and servant in you. He will therefore give me the strength to go through anything and everything for the fulfillment of His word through you... My love would be a poor thing, if it failed at this supreme movement and gave way to misery and desperation. And that is my cry, borne on the wings of a love which knows no bounds."[28]

This statement of Mira goes to prove that mystic love could have as much intensity as physical love.

Habitual Fasting

Gandhiji was in the habit of going on fasts in and out of season. He was on a fast unto death in September 1932 against the communal award, and the result was the loving exchange of letters between them. While in jail, he once again went on a 21 day fast. He was released and broke his fast on 29 May 1933, with the following hyperbolic announcement: "I have just broken the fast. The next task commences. He will find the ways and means."[29] He was on yet another fast on 16 August 1933. He was unconditionally released from jail and announced the suspension of the civil disobedience movement on 23 September 1933.

Thus he went on a spree of three fasts during just one year. He was guided by his conscience and no one else. Mirabehn's condition could be imagined as she lived from one crisis to another. She was inconsolable because he was in and out of jail. On the top of it, she was imprisoned along with Ba for a long duration during 1933. Her condition was indescribable because both of them were in and out of jail at different times during 1932 and 1933. Gandhiji was then 64 and Mirabehn 41. The whole of 1932 and 1933 were years of political turmoil. Mirabehn admitted to her nerves getting 'a little bit outstretched'.

By 1933, Mirabehn was in the Sabarmati Central Prison for nearly eight months for offering *satyagraha*. Though Ba was with her in prison, they could hardly discuss anything. At the most, they could exchange pleasantries or add to their worries by exchanging notes about the unpredictable Mahatma. Intellectual discussions or emotional meetings with Gandhiji were out of question for Mirabehn. And so were the pleasantries with the genteel Mahadev Desai and other associates. Her lovable fauna and flora were missed too. She was reduced to a vegetable for all practical purposes. But she assured Gandhiji: "Don't think, that I am going to have a nervous breakdown or anything like that!"[30]

Her letter was reassuring, but Gandhi was unlikely to buy her argument. He knew her well enough to find her assurance meaningless. Her real state of mind was confirmed in her next letter of 4 May 1933. She found it impossible to live without him. She was full of supplications: "If only I would see you once more in your bodily form, once more hear your voice—somehow, without that human mercy. I feel as if the mind will crack... I have nobody and nothing, else in the world but you—no thought no care but you."[31]

Mental Carbuncles

When Gandhiji decided to undertake a 21 day fast on 8 May 1933, Mirabehn had premonitions of his death. But she assured him "that you will be ever with her dead or alive," and undertook to serve his cause throughout his living days. Yet the agony of separation haunted her. The letter went on in the same vein with depression writ large in it. Her words were deceptive and hardly reassuring. Her agony was equally reflected in her six letters to Gandhiji during just one week.

Surprisingly, she was calm and collected on the day he actually commenced his fast. She talked of her flora and fauna. She was at her romantic best and the Sabarmati jail bloomed with her love of Gandhiji and the natural phenomenon: "Last evening as I watched the golden sunset and listened to the rejoicing birds and the soft voice of the wind in the trees, I felt that the whole of the Nature was filled with the glow of your love—Then the silver moon rose high in the sky and a gentle whisper passed from tree to tree."[32]

The early years were golden years for Gandhiji and Mirabehn when only a few things went wrong. This reminded one of the romantic interludes between Gandhiji and Saraladevi Chowdharani. Gradually, there was a loosening of bonds that had brought them together. Both Mirabehn and Saraladevi made too many demands upon him. They wanted to have exclusive rights over him. Gandhiji was public property and hence not subject to any exclusive copyright prerogative by anyone. But Mirabehn had a diametrically opposite perspective. She was looking forward to a one-to-one personal relationship with him. At the bottom of her heart, she was an insecure being. Very soon he realised that she was a burdensome baggage.

Only a few years back, life looked rosy for her. By October 1929, Jawaharlal Nehru and his brother-in-law, R S Pandit, concluded that the arrival of Madeleine Slade at the ashram had done immense good to Gandhiji's health. In 1932, Gandhiji started taking pity on her. He confided to Premabehn Kantak (his 'father-confessor'): "I may have spoken to you vehemently in defence of Mirabehn, but I have not made any man or woman weep as bitterly as I have made her. My hardness of heart, impatience and ignorant attachment were responsible for such conduct."[33] There must have been a streak of cruelty in him, which made him rebuff Mirabehn time and again. This made him treat those close to him with the disdain usually reserved for his worst enemies.

Reasons of State

Gandhiji had reasons of state to keep Mirabehn at a distance. For this he used subterfuge and kept advising her to keep her emotions under control. In his words, it was to wean herself away from 'this longing for physical meeting'. The struggle to rein in her emotions proved too much for her. There were occasions when she 'managed to tear herself' from him. He advised Mirabehn to psychoanalyse herself and conduct studies in diagnosing the cause of apparent 'conflict' between the heart and the reason in every case you can recall" for reconciling apparent incompatibles.[34]

The situation was hilarious from one angle but it was tragic from Mirabehn's perspective. Was she a victim of her doings? Could she have been a victim of circumstances beyond her control? Gandhiji kept sending her off on missions to establish and run ashrams all over the country. She found the separation unbearable and her health kept failing as well. Her psychological crisis were reflected in her frequent physical breakdowns. It was at the instance of Munnalal G Shah that Gandhiji agreed to recall her at the time Sevagram Ashram was being set up. Here was the fulfillment of her heart-felt desire. She was finally back to Gandhiji.

However, Gandhiji managed to keep her at a distance by persuading her to reside in a nearby village. Her world came crashing around her. 'Perpetual separation from Bapu' was an antidote for pure disaster for Mirabehn, which in turn meant that "Bapu's blood pressure would get worse."[35] Thus the nerves were frayed all round with no solution in sight.

Meanwhile, Gandhiji had a problem with his blood pressure. He was ordered by doctors to be kept in an isolation ward. Literally, blood pressure of Mira also went up. She insisted on seeing him but was denied the permission. She found that her way to Gandhiji's room was barred by Jamnalal Bajaj.

Things never returned to normal between the two. He had become too big for her shoes. There were other worlds for Gandhiji that were equally important. This Wardha incident was a warning signal for her. The end of the 1930s was symbolic. Her contacts with him became fewer and tension free. Emotions were suppressed as she had assumed philosophical overtones. The exchange of letters too came to a trickle.

In 1941, Gandhiji assured her of never having her out of his mind. She did not take the bait and responded as coldly as possible. The warmth was out. She told him of her new interests and did not whisper a word about her longing for him. She was engaged in rendering selected Vedic hymns. Seemingly, Gandhi did not interest her as much as rodents and other creatures did.

Spiked Body

Mirabehn was of the same intellectual calibre as Gandhiji. As emotions waned and time passed by, she viewed him more objectively. He sought her advice on matters that worried him. His troubles during his last years were unending because he did not have the benefit of advice from Ba, Mirabehn or Mahadev Desai. Ba and Mahadev had already passed away and Mirabehn had decided to stay away from him. Gandhiji must have derived genuine pleasure from his communication with Mirabehn which is confirmed by reviewing his correspondence with her.

Gandhiji felt exasperated and angry with himself for having treated her harshly. He pretended to be the guilty party. He had quick change of moods. Mirabehn was equal to the task and responded in similar fashion: "The struggle was terrible. I too was on a bed of hot ashes, because I could feel that Bapu was. This was one of the occasions when, somehow or the other, I managed to tear myself away."[36]

Distance adds charm to any piquant situation. Mirabehn had her revenge by making him worry over her. That "the thought of you corrodes me" was his favourite phrase for her. Physical separation was sought to be compensated for by letters reciting sweet nothings. This was like a struggle for life and death for her. Her periodic but extended returns to his ashram revived her. Gandhiji had to arrange for her departures very delicately. Her departure for Bombay prompted him to put her in proper frame of mind: "You haunted me in my sleep last night and were reported by friends to whom you had been sent to be delirious… And with this I woke up troubled in my mind and prayed you may be free from all harm."[37]

Doubts arise about Gandhiji's real intentions about Mirabehn. Why did he take so much vicarious pleasure in troubling her? Was Mirabehn a guinea pig? Was he trying to simulate the real world under laboratory conditions? He has been accused of being narcissist in his outlook on life. He loved himself so much that he found it too much to develop stable relationships. Mirabehn comprehended this truth very late. It was too late for her to get her revenge on him. She had to await his death in 1948 to say goodbye to him, his country and his cause. Actually she left India to get back to her first love Beethoven. Gandhiji paid her the best tribute when he truthfully wrote to Romain Rolland: "Hers has been an agony with joy. But she has chosen the spiked body and she is bravely lying on it."[38]

Character Assessment

Sarojini Naidu called Mirabehn 'the flower of the ashram'. Nilla Cram Cook drew a picture of the British Admiral's daughter pretending to be a St Catherine: "[Mira] was the admirals and St Catherine. I saw her in the early mornings [in 1933] walking back and on across the terrace as though she were on watch on shipboard. As St Catherine she soothed Amala [Margarete Spiegel], washed clothes, visited the sick, smiled at her work, and was a most loveable personality. Her life was *Bhakti* [incarnate], she had given herself up to devotion and service, and at hours when she sat smiling at her spinning [wheel] in her fresh smelling clothes it was evident that she could have gotten much more out of it than she would have gotten out of a round of British parties."[39]

During her last years of stay in India, she credited Gandhiji with inculcating the virtue of 'disciplining' in her. She forgot that she had inherited this virtue from her Admiral father. This comes out in a conversation she had with Nilla Cram Cook in 1933. Miss Slade reminded Miss Cook about her aristocratic pedigree. After all "that aristocracy had rules… to do things at certain hours, not to talk at the table, not [to] make a noise." She could easily fit into the ashram's rigorous life because "[she] was ready for Bapu's discipline."[40]

She spent most of her remaining years in Pashulok Ashram near Rishikesh. Snakes, lizards and mice were her company during this time. On 2 December 1940, she gave a graphic description to her mentor and talked of coming to terms with an army of mice invading her hut at night, clambering into her bed, nibbling at her feet, slithering up and down her bed and messing up her hair. She was grateful to them for giving her company while messing up with her at the same time. A grateful Mirabehn made sure that none of them were crushed under the weight of her body. Were they good enough substitutes for the company of Gandhiji?"[41]

CHAPTER 11

Mirabehn in Low Tides

There were many ups and downs in Mirabehn's relationship with Gandhiji during her seven years stay since arrival in 1925. He talked of these seven years having passed like a 'dream'. He felt guilty about the love and hate relationship in which she was often subjected to impetuous scolding and complaints. With the anniversary of her arrival coming nearer, he decided to play a true gentleman. He paid handsome compliments to her: "And derive such comfort as is possible from the fact that it was love that was scolding; but I know there was a better way. As I look back upon the past, I realise that my love was impatient. To that extent it was ignorant. Enlightened love is ever patient. Ignorant love is a crude translation of the word *moha* in Sanskrit. I shall learn to be patient. As I watch myself in little things, I know that I have not yet acquired that measure of patience which true love demands. That patience shall come."[1]

Déja vu

Mirabehn realised that the sentiments expressed by him read like an epitaph for the living. This was an expression of unrequited love destined to remain unfulfilled. In any case, the sentiments were not an expression of a father's love for his daughter. The fact remained that Gandhiji had decimated the line of demarcation between mother, daughter, sister, wife and lover with a stroke of his pen. His whole premise was based on the assumption that sexual love had to be exiled permanently. In his revolutionary scheme of things, it was difficult to judge where one relation began and the other ended.

After a while, such sentiments had a *déja vu* air about them. For a few years such phrases as 'a cart load of love', 'my personal love', 'my heart is with you though my body is here' and nothing but 'transparent love' continued to be bandied about. Eventually such expressions went out of fashion as Mirabehn lost his special attention. In 1938, he got involved in controversies about whether 'to touch or not to touch' his women associates: "Should I refuse to have *malish* by Lilavati or Amutussalaam, for instance?"

On her rare visits to the ashram, Mirabehn would get embroiled with his current favourites Pyarelal, Sushila Nayyar and Bibi Amutussalaam. Contact became rarer and the correspondence trailed off. His assurances of continued affection had a stale air about them.

Painful Situation

Mirabehn was too domineering and aggressive with her emphasis on exclusivity. She had strong views about everything and she had not learnt to compromise. Gandhiji was a star and she was just one of his numerous intimate admirers. It was her destiny to be sent away to distant lands, away from her beloved Master.

Mahadev Desai has given a graphic description of elaborate preparations leading to her departure to distant lands for establishing a new ashram from scratch, in the *Harijan* of 25 October 1935.

She willingly volunteered to establish a new ashram on an uninhabited piece of land. She was thus prepared to 'burn her boats' to settle down 'in the inhospitable village of sorrow'.

The tall Mirabehn resembled the perfect image of a *sadhvini* with her kit comprising of a little satchel, with her bedding and a lantern to sustain her in an inhospitable land full of snakes and scorpions. 'The modern *sadhvini*' readily accepted such assignments out of a sense of duty though she had no heart in such challenges. In her own words: "A tremendous struggle was going on within myself. I had always been torn between the longing for the countryside and the longing to be with Bapu."[2]

Her joy knew no bounds when she was given the responsibility of supervising work of the new ashram being set up at Segaon near Wardha. Gandhiji put a spanner by insisting that she live at a distance from him. What could she do except twiddling her thumbs in these circumstances: "The situation became very painful. If living in Segaon was to mean perpetual separation from my Bapu, my health and nerves would not be able to endure it." She got into a vicious circle: "Already my health was giving way under the strain which was seriously aggravated by other people telling me that if I did not stay permanently in Segaon, Bapu's blood pressure would get worse. When Bapu became aware of the fact that my nerves were giving out, he said, if I could not live in Segaon he would himself go there."[3]

Unethical Conduct

Gandhiji recognised the problem but refused to deal with it frontally. He confided to Premabehn Kantak: "What you write about Mirabehn is also correct. She cannot just live away from me. Let us see what happens."[4]
While Gandhiji would pack her to distant places she would often return to him on one pretext or the other. He resorted to flattery when other tricks did not work. He assured her: "My heart and spirit are with you. The spirit is hovering around you. You must not accept defeat… I am prepared to risk your death rather than you should return to Segaon to live."[5]
Being away from Gandhiji compelled her to write a series of letters to him. Amidst his busy schedule he found the stream of letters burdensome. He pleaded with her to restrict herself to one letter a day. Of course, he was expansive enough to assure her: "Anything beyond a week will be too long for me."[6] She continued to be withdrawn. She was asked to be cheerful: "I want you to feel inner joy and strength. God be with you."[7]
The almighty God did not matter as much in her scheme of things as Gandhiji. During the 19 years she spent in India she had become broken in body and possessed no more than a battered and wounded soul. Gandhiji took pity and beckoned her to return to Segaon. He kept assuring her that he was a changed man: "Your body has become dilapidated. I fear I have to take the blame for it in part, if not wholly. How I wish I could also take credit for repairing it."[8]
One of the major point of difference between Gandhiji and Mirabehn was the disorderly character of the ashram. She never came to terms with it. At one stage he threatened to close it down. But his ashram was his first love. It was also a repository of practices inherited from Tolstoy and Phoenix Farms. It was his military academy for training his volunteers, who were to be the torchbearers of his *satyagraha* and *brahmacharya* traditions.

Friendly Nature

There came a time in her life (though at a very late stage), when she longed to get away from Sevagram. It was during the monsoon season that she happened to be there. She was restless and unable to adjust to the atmosphere then prevailing in the Sevagram Ashram. She had a mystic experience all of a sudden: "A terrible anguish took possession of me, and out of its depths came the decision to take silence and devote myself entirely to meditation and prayer, till God gave me light. I felt I wanted to go and live all alone in some forest where I would read only the *Vedas*."[9]

She decided to go to live at Palampur immediately after rains. Prithvi Singh Azad had entered her life and he had indeed occupied the space usually reserved for Gandhiji. He was also embroiled in controversies and the ashram was full of unsavoury rumours and scandals.

She went back to her first love–Nature, which beckoned her from her adolescent days. She rediscovered Nature with greater impetuosity than ever before. Her Nature was benign and welcomed her with open arms. Her flora and fauna were Mira-friendly. In her own words: "As the days went by, my surroundings began to ease and open my heart. The trees and bushes befriended me, the great boulders of grey rock, covered with lichen, were a perpetual joy, and the sound of the stream in the ravine made sweet and gentle music. As for the birds, they rapidly became companions."[10]

Birds, animals and rodents were her best friends because they could not talk back to her. The spirit that suffused her with the beauty and bounties of Nature helped her to discover the sound of music in swinging trees, rustle of the rodents and noise made by birds.

She even discovered the beauties of Nature in the compound of Arthur Road Prison at Bombay. Her imprisonment gave her an opportunity to bring out the poet in her. The spirit of spring had invaded her being. Even crows had been infused with the spirit of *vasant ritu*. She watched closely a crow in the prison courtyard which 'utters soft croaks and would be sweet warbles'. Then there were singing birds descending on the prison courtyard confirming the arrival of spring.

Now her imagination was running riot and thereby she gave free rein to her observations of the scene at the river bank of the ashram: "How the little birds and squirrels must be busy all day in the grass and trees—how the water birds, must be calling as they fly home in the evening to their roosting place by the well—and there, when the night has enclosed all in sable stillness, how the glorious full moon will rise over the river spreading a path of gold across the water to the Ashram bank."[11]

Mirabehn was a romantic with the immortal spirits of Beethoven and Romain Rolland. She made a powerful impact on Gandhiji through this letter. He was sufficiently inspired to reply to her in the same vein. He advised her to sleep in the open and thus maintain a direct contact with stars. He further advised her to escape dew by covering the body: "from toe to neck and the head also if necessary and so long as your lips are totally closed and you are sure that you are only breathing through the nose—to ensure this at the time of retiring you should take a few deep breaths through the nose whilst you are lying flat on your back with legs fully stretched."[12] The set of instructions reads like a lesson in yoga.

Spiritual Contentment

She lost contact with Gandhiji in his last few years and begun to withdraw into her inner shell. In the meanwhile she had come to terms with life. Her experiences had left a bitter taste and she was determined to turn away from them. She had already done so when she'd said goodbye to her family, her beloved estate and her beloved country.

Finally, she had come to live in her Pashulok Ashram nestling in the valleys of the Himalayas. She was at peace with the peasant folk in her neighbourhood. Their poetic folk songs reminded her of ancient ballads. The best part was her coexistence with ants, spiders, lizards and snakes that crisscrossed the floors of her living room or climbed up and down the walls and ceiling. She forgot Gandhiji and watched them with sheer wonder at Nature's enterprise: "But there seems to be a secret pact between animals and men; the former recognise that the latter are doing them no harm, and they return the compliment."[13]

How Nature scored over Gandhiji was proved after his death. She went to New Delhi to mourn him, but was dismayed to find Delhi soulless and 'a city of dead'. She gave out an instantaneous cry: "Back to the life and light of the fields and forests, where Nature knows no such thing as mourning for the dead, because there is no death. For me Bapu is there and not here."[14] Thus, she was back to the friendly environment of Pashulok near Rishikesh.

How could Mirabehn forget Gandhiji. He was a part of her history. Besides they had an indefinable, long-standing relationship. The whole of their mutual existence was in fact an exercise in coming to terms with each other.

Romain Rolland had commended her to Gandhiji as 'my daughter'. She met Gandhiji for the first time on 7 November 1925 and kneeled before him in great reverence. His first benediction to her was: "You shall be my daughter." She addressed him as 'Bapu' (my father). Mentally, a pact was signed and sealed by them in perpetuity. The relations were further strengthened when he told her: "That is why I told you once I wanted to be not merely in the place of father but mother also to you."[15] He had also told her: "I want you to be a perfect woman."

Here was the Indian version of Prof Higgins, educating and training Miss Dolittle. His search was for a 'perfect woman' who practised *brahmacharya*. Mirabehn had a peculiar understanding of *brahmacharya*. Her interpretation was contrary to how Gandhiji viewed it. She defined *brahmacharis* as those who have an 'inborn aversion' to sexual life.

Defining Woman Power

She had another thesis to offer on the practice of brahmacharya. She sang paeans to the innate capability of female species to practice *brahmacharya* with ease. She believed that male species possessed a 'devouring passion' for sex. She took the example of 'birds and animals' to prove her thesis: "They have passion for breeding… only once in a year. For the rest of the time, male and female, young and old, all live a life of natural celibacy."[16] Here she aligned herself with Gandhiji bemoaning the fate of human beings: "With what fine conditions and instincts God has provided the animals—He must have given us the same in the beginning. Yet now men and women have got into such a mess sexually!"[17]

She talked of a fluttering hen 'running for dear life' troubling and crying 'piteously', 'the cow weak and patient' and 'the peahen quiet and retarding', contrasted with the aggressive cock, bull and peacock full of 'domineering passion' forgetting that underneath the female of the species could only be coquettish, inviting and fetching.

It was a battle cry advocating a return to nature, in line with 'pre-logical thinking' of primitive man, who had a limited vision, with his thought processes circumscribed by sheer instinct. Mira had conveniently forgotten that the contemporary sexual excesses were a reflection of man's cultural progression rather than his regression.

Margaret Sanger was the only woman to corner Gandhiji on celibacy. Premabehn Kantak had asked intelligent questions of him on brahmacharya. No other female in his entourage including Mirabehn had ever thrown any light on celibacy as practised by Gandhiji and themselves. Her letter on *brahmacharya* consisted of her meandering thoughts gone wild. The significance of the letter lies in the fact that it was 36 pages long and intended to hold the attention of her mentor for as long as possible.

Whatever rises up must come down is the basic law of human nature. This is what precisely happened in the relations between Gandhiji and Mirabehn. Their relationship was at the lowest in 1934 by which time she knew she was unwanted and therefore decided to go away from the ashram. Gandhiji was perhaps waiting for this and was happy to let her go. He freely talked of 'her personality having been suppressed' under him and he hoped: "She will gain her former independence of character."[18]

She returned to him temporarily to supervise the establishment of the Sevagram Ashram. However, he was unhappy with the progress of the project and held her responsible for the delays. He was determined to get rid of her and made up his mind to settle in Segaon without her. Hence he ordered her to stay put in Maganwadi village to be away from him. In the meanwhile Gandhi fell ill and on the advice of doctors, he was moved to Ahmedabad. She was permitted to see him before he was moved out of Segaon to Ahmedabad.

It, however, did not escape her attention: "[A] strange artificiality had suddenly been raised [between] Bapu and me, which haunted [me] like a nightmare."[19] By denying free access to her, she was once again brought to the state of a nervous breakdown. She was refused permission to see him and forcibly sent back to Maganwadi. For the first time she had been forced to realise that she was totally unwanted.

All sorts of rumours floated around about the break between her and her mentor. In her *Daily Notes,* deposited in the Nehru Memorial Museum and Library, she gave credence to such rumours. In her *Notes* of 11 September 1938, she said:

"The day began with my writing out an answer to Mill's article in the American Press in which he had said that Bapu is now being attended on by a beautiful young lady doctor [Sushila Nayyar] with raven locks and that the faithful daughter of a British Admiral had been relegated to village uplift work."[20]

Enter Prithvi Singh

The relationship between Gandhiji and Mirabehn is better understood through her involvement with Prithvi Singh Azad whose arrival on the scene changed it completely. Gandhiji announced Prithvi Singh's arrival through a press note on 20 May 1938. Prithvi Singh, born on 15 September 1892, was a colourful personality with a revolutionary past. He was a Bhatti Rajput from Lalru in Haryana. He was sentenced to life imprisonment for participating in the Lahore Conspiracy Case (1915). A part of his imprisonment was spent in the Andamans after which he was transferred to Madras and then to Rajahmundhry jail, from where he made his escape in 1922. He eluded the police for 16 long years by escaping to Canada. He was released from jail on 22 September 1939 after 25 years of adventurous existence. Gandhiji called him 'a cent per cent model prisoner'. Ultimately he sought Gandhiji's protection , who was totally impressed by his reforming zeal.

Prithvi Singh considered his life to be 'a thrilling romance'. Gandhiji hoped to reach out to other revolutionaries through this 'powerfully built' Rajput who had "decided in consultations with his friends to surrender himself to me and be guided by me."[20] While Gandhiji saw a true disciple in Prithvi Singh: "completely non-violent in thought, word and deed," Mirabehn saw in him a soul mate for life. Prithvi charmed her as no one else before, with the exception of Gandhiji.

Prithvi Singh gradually replaced Gandhiji in her affections. The years between 1939 and 1943 were the years of romance between them. While Prithvi was quite flattered by her attention, he felt uncomfortable when she became obsessed with him.

From day one, her excessive concern for him made him uncomfortable. But he did not have the heart to discourage her. She continued to live in a dreamland of illusions. He admitted to this incongruity in his autobiography: "There is however a revelation of how she had to undergo a transformation through my coldness and hard-heartedness on account of which I had to bid good-bye to the Ashram [during 1939]."[21]

He found himself in a dilemma without any possible escape: "I could not surrender to her love. I did not know how to escape it… I could not… say [to Gandhi] that Mira loved me and that I could not reciprocate her love… At last, like a coward I sneaked out of the Ashram."[22] The great revolutionary who had dared to confront the might of the redoubtable British Empire had turned tails when confronted with the willpower of an intractable and obsessive woman.

Headlong in Love

The romance began with a flurry of letters from Mirabehn to Baba Prithvi Singh Azad in October 1939. The first few letters were addressed to 'My dear brother'. Subsequently she shifted to 'Dearest Prithvi' and changed to 'My dear comrade' and 'Dearest friend'. But she always ended her letters with 'yours ever Mira' or 'Your ever loving sister'. She constructed an entirely new edifice around him. She termed him a messiah come to transform Segaon Ashram by turning it into 'the nerve centre of India' and 'if Sewagram would be made sound, Bapu would die in peace".[23]

She was over joyed at his decision to be at "Bapu's feet" at Segaon: "God will surely bless you for this decision—and if a sister's prayers are any use, you have them to the full!"[24] She found herself drawn towards him. She found virtues in him which others could not find: "God has changed the vague pain of all these years into a burning fire. But the grand difference is that now… I have found you at last!"[25]

Only a day had passed when on 11 November 1939 she started to count her blessings and thanked God almighty for turning her deeply-felt pain into "joy - deep joy". She quoted Gandhiji of having "understood" and "appreciated" her feeling. She was also thankful to her 'dear' brother Prithvi' for awakening her *kundalini* and thus making her realise: "Yet my capacity has never yet been used fully."[26]

She promised to write on a clean slate for him. By now Prithvi had replaced Gandhiji in her affections. History was being repeated once again in Mirabehn's emotional life. When Prithvi was to go away from the ashram for a short while, she felt pain: "Yesterday I was overwhelmed because you were to go away." As with Gandhiji, she clung to him for a moment: "It was because the pain was unbearable."

She decided to share her 'deep joy' with Gandhiji: "When I said [to Bapu]—'But I shall want your blessings'—he said, …I should now like you to be guided entirely by Prithvi Singh. You have understood one another… I suppose nothing in the world would show more fully his trust in you!"[27]

At one time Gandhiji flattered Mirabehn by advising her to conduct herself like 'a true Hindu wife' by following Prithvi's footsteps in 'everything', over to the extent of joining the Communist Party of India. She didn't like the advice a bit and accused Gandhiji of attempting to throttle her in practicing her long-cherished ideals.

Full Independence

Gandhiji was not reconciled to Mirabehn's romantic interlude. He fought rear guard skirmishes with her and Prithvi for five long years from 1939 to 1944. His tenacity in this connection began to pay dividend. She had no compunction in confessing to him that her 'capacity has never yet been used fully', thereby blaming Gandhiji without naming him for allegedly suppressing her potential which had thus far 'remained unusable'.[28] Prithvi was embarrassed when she told him in her next letter: "I have been but half a being. You have made me whole."[29]

She begged Gandhiji to grant her a charter of freedom: "Bapu [had] given me full liberty to lead my own life my own way", in order to "become free according to my nature." She recalled wistfully: "Seventeen years ago, when I came to Bapu, I put myself in his hand and he, with the fullness of his love, took complete possession" of me. Prithvi Singh Azad was unmoved although he gave her some hope for 'the next birth'.

Instead of blaming Prithvi for rejecting her, she began to find faults in her long association of seventeen years with her mentor. She admired him for inculcating in her 'self-reliance and self-expression', but to the extent of undermining her capacity for 'any sustained or independent work'. She considered herself to be 'a person of free energy, enterprise and self-reliance', who had lost her capacity for initiative during her long association with him. It was through her hard *tapasya* involving 'silent prayers and reading' [of sacred text] over a long and sustained period of fifteen months that she had become conscious of 'her real self', thus assuming 'new strength and freedom'; and, thereby, coming into her own after a long stay of fifteen years in India. She took courage and asked him to grant her full freedom. She was granted her wish, but Gandhiji told her with tongue in his cheek: "but you realise don't you, that 'you cannot have your cake and eat it'".[30]

Indeed Prithvi had taken just a few weeks to transform her through his magic wand. At the same time she must have felt embarrassed by her girlish outpourings. She requested Prithvi to destroy the letters after reading it. She is on record to have addressed 36 letters to Prithvi, of which 12 letters were addressed to him in November 1939 alone. Such was her intensity.

Depressed Mood

Unfortunately for Mirabehn, her expectations were never met. This made her sink deeper in depression. Prithvi Singh was never forthcoming because he liked to hedge his bets with great care. All this marked the advent of her usual depression. She had realised this much earlier when she had confessed to Gandhiji in 1927: "In spite of the intellectual realisation the heart has already failed me."[31] Mirabehn built castles in the air by considering Prithvi her husband and traced her love for him to her previous life. She was keen on being a mother and would have loved to have a child by her reluctant lover. All these gossips were shared by Gandhiji with N K Bhat in his letter of 19 August 1940. Hers was a triumph of heart over mind, again and again.

She repeated the same mistake in her dealings with Prithvi and she rued the day for her error of judgement. Never mind that the later half of 1939 proved to be the best period for her. It was too short, but it was welcome so long as it lasted. Suddenly in 1940, she realised that all was not well with her. The result was depression followed by days of silence and seclusion.

This lasted for fifteen months during which she would speak just once a day for just half an hour, or twice a week to Bapu, whenever she went to see him. She would spend the rest of the time reading the *Vedas* and *Puranas*. She believed there would be a turn in future, after proper propitiation of her gods (on earth). Before Bapu was to leave Sevagram, she went to see him and touched his feet on the spur of a moment at the time of departing. She had not done this before. By now she had a full measure of Prithvi and was gratified to her mentor for having opened her eyes to the realities of the situation.

Reviving the Past

Prithvi was still irresistible. She gave a new twist to the relationship by extending an invitation to him for comradeship. She wanted to forget the past and revive old bonds. He replied: "Your wishes will be sacred."

By March 1942, her condition was the most pitiable as she was prepared to yield completely. She had told Prithvi in no uncertain terms of her *dharma*—surrendering to him and praying to God to give Prithvi as 'my husband'. This privilege was denied to her by fate. After being thwarted, she decided to extend her hand of comradeship to Prithvi. She was battered in body and soul, but never gave up hope. She even looked forward to joining him in her next birth.

This was the inane talk of a woman who had been betrayed not only once but twice in spite of her total commitment and devotion to the objects of her worship. Hardly anybody cared to place faith in her words about 'the zest to live and strive returning to it'. She pursued Prithvi endlessly and expressed anguish at her unrequited love in her letter of 23 March 1942. To her, love could be a one-way traffic and thereby an exclusive prerogative of Mirabehn. How could she be denied the privilege of falling in love because of absence of response from the other side? To marry or not to marry was a bilateral decision: To love or not to love was not.

The letter which followed after about an year, on 23 March 1943, revealed this state: "You ask me to renounce my love, as if it were some sort of self-indulgence… You do not realise that *real love*, love that arises from the depths of the soul, increases the power of service and is as sacred as religion. In a woman love and faith become one… A woman's fullest strength comes to her only after she has found her beloved."[32]

In another letter, which was undated, she hoped to meet her unwilling lover 'in the next birth'. Prithvi Singh Azad rose to the occasion by asking her to 'renounce [her] love' for the cause. Mirabehn was holding on the last straw as Prithvi was not available to her at any price. He knew she was too domineering for his taste and on a rebound from Gandhiji. She had only two gods to propitiate. He was neither Gandhiji nor Beethoven. Eventually, Prithvi married a Gujarati brahmin, Prabhavati Dave.

Hurt Gandhi

Gandhiji was greatly hurt by the Prithvi Mirabehn incident. He could not forget that she opted for Prithvi Singh Azad but kept his counsel to himself. He considered himself an injured party. For the first time he decided to address her formally as 'Dear Miss Slade' in his letters of 6, 12 and 14 June 1944. He was annoyed and spiteful: "I like the English coolness and correctness [in her]."[33] After a day or two he felt guilty about his obvious lack of manners and decided to come a notch or two down from his high pedestal by assuring her: "Of course, you are to me what you have been always."

At the subconscious level he was compelled to treat her shabbily: "So that [He] may be rid of the fear that has possessed him." He may have been frightened at the prospect of losing her. In an attempt to bring things back to normal, he pleaded with her: "It should be clear to you that I have never doubted your devotion… My love for you remains wholly unaffected."[34]

Having placated Mira, he directed all his ire at Prithvi Singh Azad. After all, it was Prithvi who came between him and Mirabehn. He conveyed malicious gossip about Prithvi and accused him of chasing young women: "It appears that you had spread your net wide beforehand, got Nanabhai to side with you and through him influenced me… You cling to Mirabehn and tried to win me back through her." [Furthermore], "You cast lustful eyes on two [Gujarati] girls but neither of them fell into your hands."[35]

Another month passed before the situation returned to normal. From the heights of Panchgani, where he was on a holiday, he wrote to the remorseful Mira: "Devdas described grief over my reverting to your original name. I have capitulated." He was now a gentleman and confessed to her: "I know you forgave me long ago. But it is good to ask for forgiveness."[36]

Prithvi Singh Azad had walked out of her life and married Prabhavati Dave on 27 November 1943. He was out and Gandhiji was up and in.

Sense of Fulfillment

Mirabehn appeared reconciled. She was back to her chores of looking after cows, birds, rodents and reptiles. She had her brief forays to Sevagram to have the *darshans* of the Mahatma. He was engrossed in his *brahmacharya* experiments and indeed had very little time for her. There was very little in common between them at this stage of life.

Gandhiji's death, however, stirred old memories. Looking back, she was expansive about her close association with the great man. She claimed that: 'the door to the imprisoned soul had suddenly opened after his death', and: "from that moment a new sense of the eternal abides within me." She had a sense of fulfilment: "For [her] there were only two, God and Bapu. And now they had become one."[37]

She went to New Delhi to mourn his death. She felt lost in the crowd. Everything had become unfamiliar and foreign. She immediately returned to her *Pashulok*. She received a portion of his ashes in a little copper urn. She dropped the ashes into the Ganges at Rishikesh. She felt one with Nature and wondered over its majesty. Gandhiji was her first and last link with India. Her life had now become meaningless. She had no one else to communicate with. She was once again gripped with a sense of 'blundering melancholy'.

For several months she could not decide anything about her future. On the spur of a moment she had a sudden inspiration for looking into her long rusting box containing material about her first love Beethoven. She shut her eyes, and discovered for herself: "Yes it was the spirit of [Beethoven] from whose music I had been separated for over thirty years that I heard and felt, but with new vision and inspiration."[38] Her tensions had once again disappeared. A new hope had begun to stir within her. She decided to go to Vienna where Beethoven's music was awaiting her. She also imagined that there were more Gandhians in Europe than in India. So she said goodbye to India on 28 January 1958, exactly ten years after Gandhiji's death.

Back to Beethoven

Mirabehn came to India in 1925 and lived the next thirty-one years trailing Mahatma in spirit and person. She lived like a vagabond throughout her stay in India. Her partial gypsy blood must have prompted her to do so. Gandhiji was her entire world but while pursuing him all she got was nervousness, tensions, depressions and breakdowns. By 1948, she had reached the end of her tether but somehow managed to carry on for another decade.

At last, Beethoven was more on her mind than Gandhiji. Only one of them was expected to come out victorious. She had the forests outside Vienna beckoning her in the sub-conscious. Above all, Beethoven, like Gandhiji, was a mystic who inspired her to strive for the ultimate. She was at last at peace with God and the world. She had come to terms with herself at the fag end of her living days: "The Almighty in the forest! I am blessed, happy in the forest: even trees speak through Thee. Oh God! What glory! In such woodlands there is peace to serve Him."[39]

She left India on 28 January 1958, to be near Beethoven. She confessed that India or Gandhiji no longer interested her. She lived for another quarter of a century. In her will made on 29 September 1983, she desired her body be cremated and her ashes buried in the forest that inspired the best of music in Beethoven.

She had written to Bapu on 15 December 1932: "What is it that prevents the heart from following or co-operating with reason?"[40] It did not happen when she lived in Sabarmati and Sevagram ashrams, or in the little cottage with full view of the Great Himalayan Range. This miracle had come to pass in the forest above the Beethovenstein near Vienna. In the end, Mira was reconciled to life and corrected the imbalances in her life.

Gandhiji (her 'Oriental Father'), Romain Rolland (her *mon père*), and Beethoven (her role model) were eternally united in her mind. This comes out in Romain Rolland's letter of 25 December 1931, to Luciene Price written soon after Gandhiji's visit to Romain Rolland in Switzerland: "On the last evening, after the prayers, Gandhi asked, me to play him a little Beethoven. (He doesn't know Beethoven, but he knew that Beethoven was the link between Mira and him; thus in the end all our gratitude goes back to Beethoven).[41]

CHAPTER 12

Cook and Spiegel: The Mad Duo

Gandhiji referred to Nilla Cram Cook as the 'Fallen Woman' and Margarete Spiegel, whom he renamed Amala, as the 'Mad Woman'. Both of them, full of eccentricities, kept him preoccupied and worried. He often found it irritating and unbalancing. However, it provided him comic relief from his public preoccupations and refreshed him.

Both Nilla and Amala were of Jewish origin. Gandhiji was never comfortable with Amala, the German, who tarried with him for a year or two longer than Nilla, but eventually moved out of his orbit to Tagore's Shantiniketan. Both of them discovered a father figure in Gandhiji. Nilla Cram Cook, an American seeped in Greek culture and civilisation, had converted to Hinduism. She would be the happiest in the *tantra* environment of India. Gandhiji had a love-hate relationship with her, but she never uttered a word against him. Amala was a victim of Nazi persecution in her homeland Germany and had decided to move to India. She was a timid and idiosyncratic person with weird responses. Gandhiji managed to keep her at a distance. Indeed, her stupidities were her strongest point. Cook said it all when she described Amala as 'everyone in exaggerated form'. Perhaps that was precisely the reason why she appealed to Gandhiji in spite of her oddities.

Vivacious Female

Nilla Cram Cook, who had a distinguished pedigree, was the most vivacious woman who crossed his path. Her father, George Cram Cook, was founder of the Province Town Players. He was a friend of Eugene O'Neill and Edmund Wilson. He moved to Greece and his daughter followed him. She married a Greek and had a son by him. She had been compared by her peers to Isadora Duncan. For her, dance, drama and sex were the right concoction for ideal living. Above all, she was bohemian by upbringing.

From Greece to India was a short haul for her. She used to claim that Buddha, Christ and Allah were the names of the Greek God Dionysus. She was an accomplished linguist who knew French, Greek (both modern and ancient), Hindustani, Persian, Arabic and some Turkish. She had studied Sanskrit and was familiar with India even before she came here. She had been inspired by Ananda Coomaraswamy's *Dance of Shiva*. She visited Kashmir soon after she landed in India.

Cook converted to Hinduism during her stay in Kashmir, but in essence she represented the bohemian spirit of Greenwich Village. Even though she engaged herself in social work involving the abolition of untouchability in Bangalore, she remained a bird of passage who loved to dance her way through life. She had peculiar ideas about human existence. For instance, she would have loved to introduce the *Kamasutra* as a compulsory subject in school curriculum. In nutshell, eroticism motivated and inspired her. Such was the maverick who crossed the path of the Mahatma. He welcomed her with open arms and had to pay a heavy price for his unintended folly.

Yeravda Meeting

From Kashmir she moved to the princely state of Mysore. She came to be widely known after she gave a performance of the *Nataraja* dance. She joined in the protest against the ban over entry of harijans into temples. She also delivered a lecture on the subject to the Untouchables' League in Bangalore. She was a big hit. She made friends with several young men and there was a hint of scandal about her.

Here was a young vivacious American woman so well informed about the Hindu religion and traditions, going places in India. Her fame reached Gandhiji while he was in the Yeravda Jail. He was keen to meet this American woman who had converted to Hinduism. He invited her to visit him in jail. As indicated in his very first letter to her: "It is very great work you are doing… I am therefore surprised that anybody should cavil at the work itself or take exception to the fact that you, who have become Indian by adoption and by right of love, should have taken the lead."[1]

Cook was excited upon receiving his complimentary letter. This was in response to her letters describing in detail how she was faithfully following his guidance to the last detail. She was engaged in street cleaning and followed his dietary instructions regarding living on fruits and vegetables. She also refused to take milk, for which she was complimented by him. Here was a soul mate for him who was 'interested in the question of scientific or hygenic and spiritual dietary'. That she could perform physical labour was another feather in her cap. It made him gush with pride whenever he talked about her: "As you seem to have read practically everything I have ever written, perhaps you are aware that I have lived on fruits and nuts for over six years, that I have gone without milk for over nine years, and it has been the most disappointing thing for me to have been obliged to take even goat's milk. I know of no one of my acquaintance who has been able to do hard physical work as also hard mental work, as you seem to be doing, [living] merely on fruits and vegetables, that means, no proteins and no fat of any kind."[2]

Gandhiji had gone overboard in his enthusiasm for her. In fact, he had sent seven letters to her before her arrival in Poona. The very next moment she was on a train to Poona to have her first *darshan* at the Yeravda Temple. Yeravda was then a village on the other side of the river that flowed through Poona. The Central Jail of Bombay Presidency was located there. It was popularly known as Yeravda Temple because Gandhiji was imprisoned there for several years.

She was looking forward to meeting an outstanding charismatic personality, presumably of great physical charm and beauty. She arrived there with great expectations but was disappointed. The first impression belied her hopes of him: "[He] was the ugliest-looking human being I had ever seen.* I had heard that Gandhiji was not very beautiful

---

*Yet another American woman, Gertrude Emerson, who spent several months visiting India in the early twenties noted:

"But the text of Gandhi's face was what chiefly interested me. I am almost tempted to call him ugly. To begin with, his head is small, even for his short stature, though possibly the proportionately broad Indian shoulders make it seem more so. Close-cropped iron-grey hair with the long wisp generally worn by Hindus—I never saw Gandhi himself wearing the cap his followers have adopted—a forehead with very deep horizontal lines, a long nose shadowing a distinctly Oriental mouth with a clipped moustache, thin cheeks, dark eyes rather far apart with indefinite eyebrows and heavy eyelids—such

to look at, but had not expected anything like this. My instinct was to turn and run."[3] But she heard the voice say: "So you came."

When he conversed, it made him look even uglier. His toothless smile repulsed her and she wanted to run away from him. Without any ceremony, he launched a direct assault on her personal character, enquiring whether she had 'carryings-on with the Crown Prince of Mysore'. She gasped for breath and told him tongue in cheek that the Crown Prince was only thirteen. Then it must be the *Yuvaraja*, he shot back at her. He further queered the pitch for her by raising such outlandish queries as if: "this defiant attitude to sin were peculiar to me or characteristic of all self-respecting American girls."[4]

All the same, Gandhiji made a great impression on her at the first meeting. Her ugly-duckling image of him was only a passing phase. She had never known a person of such high calibre. He had indeed upset her equilibrium.

Romantic Interlude

She lived in style in a nearby mansion (owned by Lady Premlila Thakersay) for her meeting with him at the Yeravda Jail. The romantic in her impelled her to get up at three o'clock in the morning and slip past the night watchman and go straight to the nearby village. She splashed in the dark waters of river *Mukti* to wash her sins, as a good Hindu would do, and to seek her *mukti* (spiritual liberation). She thought

---

is his general appearance as well as I can describe it. Perhaps it is the effect of sharp features too much crowded into the lower half of the face that is its most distinctive characteristic. Perhaps it is the troubled forehead and the deep-set lines running from nose to chin. The lines are those of suffering and old age, now not very far away, although in years Mr Gandhi is only just fifty-two. When he smiles, one notes with a shock how the lines in his face deepen and how the absence of two or three teeth in the lower jaw accentuates the impression of advancing age. There was something inappropriate about that smile. Gandhi once remarked to me that it was his sense of humor which kept him going sometimes. But I have heard many people lay claim to a sense of humour".

Source : Gertrude Emerson. *Gandhi religious politician,* Asia, May 1922, p. 391

of herself as *nagin* of Kashmir, as the 'Fallen Woman' and a persistent sinner or Demetrakis (of Greek mythology). There was a waterfall formed by the river and she decribed the vision thus: "and I danced across it, laughing and throwing water across to the stars."[5]

She managed to get into all kinds of situations. She viewed herself as the *nagin* of Kashmir. She saw herself as a fallen woman, the nomenclature by which Gandhiji was to describe her. She had even tried to identify herself with Gandhiji. She imagined that she was performing *tapas* (penance). She went back to Bangalore mighty pleased with herself. Gandhiji had tried to inculcate a sense of guilt in her sinful soul. She decided to discard her saris and jewels, which she gave to others, and furthermore: "she shaved her head, wore a monk's robes, and wrote Gandhi a letter everyday."[6] She became an ascetic and went on to live in a village temple near Mysore. She tortured her body. Her menstruation stopped and she thought she had achieved piety through this act. She had helped Gandhiji in establishing a close relation between observing *brahmacharya* and stoppage of periods.

She had become a true Gandhian. Her health had begun to deteriorate following the vigorous routine. This, however, helped her to cement her relations with her mentor. She would write a letter to him daily to keep him informed of her day-to-day routine. However, this relationship did not last long. She was a bohemian and not a Gandhian by any standard. Her flirtation with Gandhian practice was only a part of her bohemian existence. She wanted to experiment with esoteric ideas of all sorts, but shied away after the novelty had worn out.

Just three weeks after she had received kudos from him in his first letter, she decided to reverse gears. He was nonplussed by her addressing him as her son. He twitted her: "I am fast making daughters and sisters. But mother I have not found… [your letter] smells of the hysteric."[7] Numerous complaints against her were brought to his attention. His unimpeachable sources warned him about her character. He was now on his guard. He wrote to her soon after he had been briefed about her past. He was a worried man on her account.

Christ in Gandhi

Relations between Cook and Gandhiji were the cosiest in spite of his doubts about her character. In any case, she continued to be in the seventh heaven. The ugliness that she had seen in Gandhiji on her very first impression was no longer there. Cook had carried two books, Richard Gregg's *Economics of Khadi* (1928) and Arthur Avlon's *Tantra of the Great Liberation* (1913) with her. He seemed to agree with her on practically all issues raised by her. He smiled benignly as soon as he spotted her. Immediately thereafter she felt at home.

After she got to know Gandhiji closely, through correspondence and visits, the fickle woman was completely transformed for the time being. He was an icon to her and she must have been dazzled into total submission. She saw herself in the role of Sita and Parvati combined, and she was the godly consort of the heavenly Gandhiji. The two most powerful Gods of the Hindu trinity, namely, Vishnu and Shiva, were conjoined in her. She was no longer an 'erring child' talked to by her stern father. She was the spirit incarnate to Gandhi and thought him to be beautiful: "For the first time, we talked as spirit to spirit without the complication of father talking to erring child."[8]

To show her total loyalty to the Gandhian cause, she decided to shave her head. He called her a *sanyasin* for 'all intents and purposes'. This exclamation by him came with a price. He demanded the gift of a bald pate from her: "Therefore you have to remove hair from your head and have a close crop almost amounting to a shave."[9] As a sidelight to this incident, he advised her to tie a wet rag around her shaven head to escape the sun. Her shaving of hair was evidently an offering to the gods as recompense for all the sins she had committed. And, in the process, she had managed to merge her identity with that of Gandhiji. Now for Gandhiji, Cook had come to belong to the fraternity of the unisex.

When she was shaving her head in the bathhouse at the prompting of Gandhiji, there came a flash in her mind. She began to see visions while shaving her head. She saw the image of Christ in her mentor. She also had a role demarcated for herself in the second coming of Christ. She was another 'Mary Magdalene, wiping the feet of Christ with her hair'.[10] Actually, there were several Mary Magdalenes in Gandhi's real life. There was a lady saint by that name. There was also a fallen woman by the same name. Cook must have been all these combined into one. Even though she had shaved her head under orders from Gandhiji, she had felt transformed on account of her own volition. In her own words: "The Bapu-fixation came out of the primeval world I had lived back through [in the Ashram]... What had happened to me in my shaving my hair and changing my sex was the final outcome, the attempt to be Bapu."[11]

She was in love with Bapu, the father-figure who was so near yet so distant. The other choice for her was to identify herself with him. For her, there were only two choices between Gandhiji and God. Now they had become one. It was, however, not one-way traffic. Gandhiji had been deeply affected by her spontaneity, or to put it in his own words, 'her proclivity to dance for joy'. He was no less effusive in complimenting her. He told her in no uncertain terms: "My spirit hovers about you as a mother's about her child." He added in the same letter: "I would love to own you as a child."[12] Being on the cautious side, he had laid down a precondition for her. She was expected to be prim as a virgin. She would, however, apply no breaks in expressing spontaneous joy over his being so considerate to her: "I began to love him intensely and felt his spirit hovering around me, particularly at three-thirty in the morning when I bathed and picked up my rosary."[13]

Another Radha

The shaving of the head proved to be a traumatic experience for her. To her it was symbolic of change in sex. Indeed, the sexes had got mixed up in her mind. Women had been transformed into men and men had begun to behave like women. It was a mixed up situation, and, according to her: "The world was lost in the labyrinth" and, indeed her world was entirely limited to the Gandhian ashram. It was a small topsy-turvy world. She had no hesitation in comparing the ashram to a 'psychological laboratory'.[14]

It is a well-known fact that *Gita* was his *Bible*. He always went back to *Gita* for spiritual sustenance. With all her regard for Gandhiji, she found it impossible to be reconciled to his ideological framework. She told Gandhiji that his Krishna of *Gita* did not appeal to her. Her favourite Krishna was to be found in the Krishna of the *Bhagvat Purana* engaged in perpetual *rasa lila* by the banks of the Yamuna. She would rather be a Radha collecting *kadamba* flowers and dancing on the banks of the Yamuna. It was all Greek to Gandhiji. He felt uncomfortable with her. Her letters were too poetic for him. He refused to comprehend the subtle difference between the two Krishnas. After all, he was not a man of poetry by conviction.

What could she do if he felt uncomfortable with her. While recognising that she was full of poetry, he advised her to sublimate the art for service to humanity. Here Cook was on a stronger wicket and she knew it. She knew her mind and decided to perform what came best to her. She said to herself and to all the women in the world: "May you be Radha."[15]

Acting the Part

She was a great actress. There is no doubt about that. She wanted to play Parvati, Sita and Radha to Gandhiji. She also wanted to play mother to him, but to him she was simply a daughter. How do we reconcile the contradictory stands? Let the matter rest with the dialecticians for finding a solution. For women like Cook, all that was *lila* and a part of the great design to assume an 'immeasurable bliss and beauty'.

Gandhiji was her convenient instrument. She would rather forget his philosophy of *brahmacharya* which he continued to preach to her. She was garrulous and liked to talk to him 'spirit to spirit'. She would rather like to remember him lying flat on his sick bed in Bombay with high blood pressure and welcoming her with open arms: "I don't bite! Come here, come near me," he had said to her.

"How beautiful he was... For the first time we talked as spirit to spirit, without the competition of father talking to erring child." And he was no longer 'Bapu' but the 'third party', arbitrating between them. He completely won her over when he ordained her: "A white sari," he said softly: "you should have a white sari."[16] That white saris are usually worn by widows in India as a sign of lifelong mourning must not have been lost on her.

Now that she had shaved off her hair and had a bald pate, she hated to look at herself. She had turned ugly in her quest for spiritual beauty. Gandhiji was joyful at having accomplished his bald-pate project successfully. He said 'bravo' to her. The exact words uttered by him were: "I said you'd do it." The worst was yet to come. He had demanded of her to wear a half *dhoti*. She did not like it, but fell in line readily to comply with his draconian order. It gave him much satisfaction to find her a spit image of how he must have viewed her: ugly, funny-looking and outlandish changed-sex woman. The *dhoti* did not give proper protection to her thighs. He suggested to her, "You must be wearing something underneath, [and added], some extra ones I can give you."[17]

Margarete Spiegel got one as a gift from Cook. She got into trouble on that account. Now that Gandhiji had enforced physical discipline on her, he must have felt triumphant. She did not like it, but felt flattered at the same time for the special attention being paid to her by him. She was the talk of the town as the 'current favourite' of the old man. The news travelled to the United States, her home country, about her new *avatar*. An American publication named Sarojini Naidu, Mirabehn and Nilla as his 'Three Graces.

Dogged *Karma*

It was her *karma* which dogged her everywhere. Her past adventures would make Gandhiji anxious. Even her young son who had accompanied her to India looked 'unnatural and theatrical' to him. He told her to stop being hysterical. He accepted her as his 'daughter' but kept reminding her of her past 'sins'.

He would say: "if therefore ...you will not travel from error to error, as you seem to be doing just now."[18] He promised to own her up as his child, provided she behaved and not 'travelled from error to error'. He ordained her to stop her 'exclusive or secret or private liaisons'. He never trusted her and believed that she was in a trap and needed to be rescued: "You have a fearful struggle in front of you to overcome the wretched past. But if truth really possesses you, there is nothing to fear... I want you therefore to be on the watch-tower."[19]

By April 1933, there was a turnabout in their relation. She had assured him that her past was definitely behind her. Gandhiji wasn't sure if she would reform. His fears came to be true. On 9 October 1933, after prayers Cook disappeared. He was distraught and made a public statement on 17 October denouncing her. He called her a perpetual liar and thief. She borrowed money left and right. She never cared to return her loans. He also warned people to keep away from her sexual escapades.

It was a pathetic sight to see Gandhiji making such a brazen statement about his adopted 'daughter' and still hoping to reform her. It was a vain hope as Gandhiji and Cook happened to operate at different wavelengths. Intellectually, they were a world apart. Emotions held them together. It was a thin wedge that united them.

Menstrual Cycle

Gandhiji had sincerely come to believe that there was a direct relation between the menstrual cycle and *brahmacharya* for women. However, there is no medical evidence to support his thesis which he flaunted so fondly. He had assured all true *brahmacharis* of liberation from the menstrual cycle. At one time Cook convinced herself of establishing her credentials as a practising *brahmacharini*: "The only thing that remained now was to get rid of the menstrual function. I decided I would have no more of it, and from the time I decided it stopped! Month after month I henceforth had the satisfaction of seeing it did not dare defy me."[20]

Cook seemed to possess Alladin's magic *chirag* that enabled her to defy biological process. Gandhiji, however, never believed her. He refused to give any credence to her assertion. She wrote a long letter to him on 13 June 1933, crediting the menstrual miracle to her self-abnegation. He called her too poetic and imaginative. He chided her for her child-like conduct. In brief, he disbelieved her innocence: "We cannot become children because that is impossible."

He rejected her construction 'upon the scarcity of the monthly flow'. He feared the worst. He suspected her to be pregnant. He was graphic in depicting his predicament: "My fear is that the decrease is not, in you, a healthy sign. You are not free from the sex emotion... and on scarcity and irregularity in your monthly condition must be regarded as a sign of some internal derangement… unless you and I [and the Ashram] are so blessed that you suddenly reach the requisite condition of natural purity that would stop the monthly flow and be a sign of perfect health." Apparently, Cook was not telling the truth and Gandhiji was definitely off the mark to discover situations where none existed. He was crossing into the spiritual territory when he advised her: "When you reach that state you will have no boils etc., and no other bodily or mental ailment."[21]

Now that he was almost sure of her pregnancy, he advised her to avoid abortion at all cost. He stressed 'the moral necessity' of avoiding abortion. Cook did not care. She was more than a match for him. Cook was a child of passion. Love was her entire existence. She found sanction for sexual love in her very nature, her biological needs and her intellectual necessity. Sex for her, was an exploration into the uncharted seas. She found sanction for her conduct in the Krishna of *Bhagvat Purana*.

Fallen Woman

Gandhiji addressed Cook as 'N' in many letters that he wrote to her. He also called her Nilla Nagini from Kashmir. The trouble lay with her personality. She was a delectable person, spontaneous in her expression, friendly and sympathetic to people around her. She had a perpetual smile on her faceand was a total contrast to other faceless ashramites. She was able to get together a circle of young men wherever she went in India. Gandhiji did not welcome her as she disturbed the equanimity of the community and upset the equilibrium of Gandhiji himself. Nonetheless, her laughter resounded through the corridors of the staid ashram long after she left.

Her intimate friendships caused her much troubles. One of her closest friends was 'R' as identified by Gandhiji. Cook and 'R' had advanced from friendship to intimacy. She had shown one of his letters to Gandhiji to tease him. She told him about 'R's intention to contract 'spiritual marriage' with her. Gandhiji defined it as 'spiritual friendship bordering on marital relations'.[22] After about ten days he was a worried man. The explanation offered by 'R' did not satisfy him. He took the poor man to task because he was found lurking behind his responses: "A subtle emotional love which is undesirable and which borders on the impure."[23]

'The man of restraint' as Gandhiji called 'R' was being belaboured for his natural response to his healthy and proper instincts. Gandhiji wrote a separate letter to Cook on the same date. He expressed his fear of 'the old infatuation lurking' in 'R'. In the same letter he called her 'a fallen woman'. Cook resented his belabouring 'R' for no fault of his. In the meanwhile Cook got involved with 'S' as if she intended to flirt with all the letters of the Roman alphabet. He felt irritated when she pleaded on behalf of 'S' to be given another chance. He forced Cook to write to 'S' over his 'unwarrantable familiarity' with her. Besides 'N' and 'R', there was another character called 'B' who was equally belaboured by Gandhiji: "For I gather from your letter that all the time you were with N. [Nilla], you were unmoved by animal passion. This is impossible." During 1933, he was convinced of the reign of sexual passion, in intimate relations between two sexes: "[except] for any person who is not utterly impotent or who is not a God, and I suppose you are neither the one or the other".[24]

Negative Approach

Cook was in Gandhiji's direct firing line and he took pot shots at her, in and out of season. He seemed to have been running a psychological laboratory at the ashram in order to ferret out all the details of the working of minds of his whole range of associates. Better he should have been a father confessor for ferreting out the last ounce of sinful details from the sinning faithful. He applied the usual techniques to Nilla with deadly effect. Bit by bit he made her confess her past life. He termed it a "ghastly story". In his own words: "She seems to have led a most extravagant and immoral life, even from tender years. She was open to the advances of practically any person, and she was no better after her acceptance of Hindu religion."[25] The 'Fallen Angel' had finally turned into a 'Fallen Woman'.

It was possible to view her relationship with Gandhiji from the perspective of other associates of the old man. They were employed as his intermediaries or messengers in his dealings with Cook. Narandas Gandhi was on the top of the list, especially because he looked after the day to day management of the ashram. Cook was introduced to Narandas on the eve of her joining the ashram. She was like a daughter to him for three to four months she stayed at the ashram. She had impressed Narandas by performing incredible acts of asceticism. She tortured herself bodily in all possible manners.

She was, however, too clever for the whole tribe of Narandases. The alarm bells began ringing much too soon. Gandhiji had suddenly realised the meaning of one of her letters to him. She had talked of 'having fallen in Bangalore'. Gandhiji realised the full purport of her confession to him only when he came to know that she was 'really pregnant'. However, he reconciled himself to the situation. What must be, must come to pass. Cook had a hearty laugh when he disclosed her secret to Narandas: "I will welcome that. That will test us too. If her heart has become pure, it is our duty to shelter her."[26]

Despite odds Gandhiji was obsessive about Cook. He was also possessive about her, so much so that he kept a watch on her every step. And, for that, the task was assigned to Narandas Gandhi. He directed him to read the contents of letters to her. He again talked of her having 'little control over mind'. In other words, he had diagnosed her malady correctly. Essentially, she was governed by sentiment and passion rather than logic and reason.

Obsessive Gandhiji

Gandhiji was possessive about Cook. He admired her acumen in persuading him to go on fast. That she was the embodiment of sexual passion was his favourite topic. He once wrote to Narandas: "I think it will save many young men. If she is pregnant, the cause is one harijan named... It is difficult to judge as to who tempted whom... Show her as much love as you can and rear the plant."[27] If the harijan boy from Mysore was the cause of her pregnancy, then the conception must have taken place, it was speculated, when she was involved in her street-cleaning and temple-entry *abhyans* in Mysore. It contradicted the earlier assumption of Gandhiji about the Prince or the Yuvraj of Mysore being the cause of it all.

Finally, he turned to warhorse Premabehn Kantak for advice. He had discovered three faults in her: leading an immoral life, borrowing money (and not returning it), and telling lies. At the same time he praised her sky high. He particularly singled her out for her knowledge of the *Mahabharata*. He requested Premabehn to cultivate her after she joined the ashram, but soon after he dissuaded her from asking Cook about her past or reminding her about 'her memories of sinful pleasures'. If Cook were to talk to her about her past, then she too would be a sinner. Premabehn confronted the *Nagin* with great compassion.

In the next letter he requested Prema to act as the moral police over her. He considered Cook to be trustworthy and expected disciplinarian Prema not to be anything less than stern with her. It is more out of pity than consideration that he viewed his volatile ward: "There was no limit to her sins. Likewise there is no limit to her good aspirations." Gandhiji saw the devil and angel in her in equal measure. However, pity rather than sympathy and understanding continued to be his battle cry: "But she has lost everything as a result of immorality. She lost control over her mind."[28]

Mirabehn on War

Cook was 24 in 1933. She was not particularly fond of Mirabehn but since the latter had been assigned by Gandhiji to educate Cook about the culture of the ashram, she could not do anything against her openly. Though Gandhiji had a feeling that Cook was incorrigible, yet he did not lose hope and very cleverly operated from behind the scenes to reform Cook. Mirabehn was his handy instrument. Cook was put off by Mirabehn pretending to act naturally, knowing fully well that she was a mere marionette in the hands of Gandhiji. She knew it and so did Cook. Mirabehn invited Cook for a walk to have a heart-to-heart talk. Cook described the conversation that took place between the two of them: "You see," she surprised me by exclaiming, "how impulsive you are? Impulses should be controlled. We should never give in to them".[29]

The admiral's daughter was underlying her superiority by birth over a theatre director's daughter. It struck Cook that she was the 'fallen woman' being addressed by an 'unfallen woman'. The vacuum in Mira's life came out in a flash before her eyes. Mira, the insecure, had the cheek to advise Cook to be preoccupied every minute of the day. Upon further query from her whether there was anything more to life than being busy like bees in a beehive burdened by the queen bee [Gandhi], to the last detail, sharp came the response from Mira: "What else? Be of service, follow the rules, control impulse, discipline yourself."[30]

It was Mira who was summing up her own autobiography in just one sentence. Everything fell in its proper place soon after she talked to Cook, who was not sure if Mira was actually mocking Gandhiji; perhaps not because Mira's senses had been deadened but due to her long association with him. Unfortunately, Cook was not reconciled to the system. She did not take too much time in deciding to quit. She fled from the 'prison-house' of Sabarmati Ashram without even saying adieu to Gandhiji. She had not reconciled to anyone except Kasturba for whom she had the softest corner. Cook found Kasturba 'an immaculately-groomed lady'. She remembered the neat border of red embroidery on her *khadi* sleeves. For Kasturba: "*Khadi* was only *khadi*, but she remained a lady."[31]

Special Relation

Never had anyone so closely associated with Gandhiji been subjected to a barrage of accusations on personal character as Cook. She had been so absorbed in him that she did not react to any of the charges. She could afford to forgive him because in him she saw her father. He provided her security which her own father had failed to do, despite the fact that she was a fallen woman for him.

There came a time when he burdened her with his enormous unreasonable demands. She was subjected to sustained pressures by him. He was most unreasonable in treating her like a doormat. She became a puritan to please him but it did not work. This went against the very grain of her nature. In the end she fled from him. She had had enough of him. Intellectually, she could never come to terms with him. Her relationship with him was essentially emotional in character. There were, however, many occasions when he would be most considerate to her.

When he was at his genial best he would shower all his love on her. He would confess that he could not keep her away from him. He would even convey his 'love' and 'kisses' to her. He expressed such fine sentiments in his letter of 8 May 1933. He followed with another letter on the very next day: "But you must write a detailed letter daily giving your bodily and mental condition, your food and S's [Her young son] food."[32]

In yet another letter on 17 May, Gandhiji assured Cook that his spirit hovered over her 'as a mother's about child'. This blessing, however, was extended on one day and withdrawn the very next day. He would listen to all kinds of gossips about her and react instantaneously. Cook was a subject of too frequent gossip, part true, part exaggerated and most of it without foundation. He never reposed confidence in her for any sustained length of time.

Romantic Figure

In the given circumstances, a proper assessment was not possible. He was a father figure who expected to be obeyed without question. She was expected to operate within his personal orbit. It was thus not possible to establish credulous relations between them. It was not written in her stars. But not all was lost as evidenced by his own deep yearning for her: "For the last three or four days I have not heard from you. I have developed regarding you a mother's anxiety."[33]

Here was a complex relationship which could not be explained rationally. Logic no longer worked in this case. He had assumed the role of both mother and father to her. She was also greatly to be blamed for the muddle. There should have developed an intellectual partnership between them. Instead she saw a traditional Indian guru in him. This was a relationship that needed to be evolved by unwinding the psychological compulsions underlying the conscious and subconscious layers of the mind.

All said and done, Cook remained the most romantic figure that crossed Gandhiji's path. He stayed under his shadow for barely an year or so. The relationship was sustained as long as it lasted because he acted like an engineer of soul to her. The best in her did not necessarily come out by confronting her mentor. Indeed, she avoided confronting him. She let him speak his mind and did not grudge tolerating him for the rough treatment meted out to her. Here she proved to be a dutiful traditional Indian daughter to him. She tortured her body to live a bare existence to please her icon. And indeed icons are only worshipped and not subjected to dialogue, discussion or dispute.

The real face of Nilla Cram Cook cannot be known only through the letters written to her by Gandhiji as these present a unilinear view of the relationship. It is her letters to Gandhiji that should be placed side by side to grasp the actual situation. The letters of the Mahatma are matronly in their tone whereas letters written by her, as Gandhiji described them, were poetic and imaginative. She was a romantic who bared her soul in her letters to him. She was simply bowled over by him.

Gandhian Legacy

She had never seen the like of him. In the Indian tradition *Shakti* (the female aspect) is proactive and *Purusha* (the male aspect) is shown as inert and inactive. Cook was the active agent when compared to Gandhiji who merely reacted to her. Unfortunately, there is no trace of her letters. What we have is her book *My Road to India* (1939). It is a remarkable work but it remains silent about her relation with him, except for a brief mention of their first meeting at the Yeravda Jail. There is not a word of complaint about the treatment meted out to her by Gandhiji. This was, indeed, the best tribute by Cook to her benefactor.

Nilla Cram Cook finally left the ashram in the first week of October 1933 without informing anyone. His public appeal for her to return to him proved to be of no use. According to an Associated Press dispatch published in the *New York Times* of 29 November 1933, Nilla had decided to disavow 'Gandhi's way of Life'. She was forcibly deported from India on 14 February 1934. She was to file a libel suit against a New York newspaper for insinuating that her 'train ride with Gandhiji from Bombay to Wardha was a romantic escapade in which the two of us eloped for a joy ride', after her return to New York.

The Gandhian legacy inherited by her during her four-month association with him did not leave her throughout her life. Gandhiji presented her with a copy of *Koran* in 1933. She decided to translate the Holy Book in English along with a detailed commentary by her. She carried the copy with her during her travels to Greece, Afghanistan and Turkey. She finally settled in Iran. Her labour for twelve long years bore fruit and her English version of the *Koran* was published in 1945. According to her, the then Minister of Education of Turkey, Hasan Ali Yujel called her 'the Luther of Islam' due to her liberal interpretation of the religion.

Thus in this remarkable woman the best of Greek, Indian and Islamic culture and civilisations.

The Wandering Jew

Margarete Spiegel (1897–1968) whom Gandhiji had named Amala was a total contrast to Cook. She was dull, boring and slow-witted, but totally sold out on Mahatama. He compared her to Max Mueller for her ability to master thirteen languages. However, he was too impatient with her. Once he called her 'as mad as a mad hatter'. If Cook was like a rampaging bull, Amala was a picture-post gentle cow munching grass on the rolling hills of the Deutschland Alps. She was a German Jew teaching at a government school. She was a pacifist completely floored by his writings and soft corner for womanhood: "No man has even shown more understanding of women than ascetic Mahatma Gandhi. To him all women are sisters. As he is free from all passions, he is able to discover the soul of a woman, as no other man can."[34]

She was about thirty when she visited India in 1932. She stayed at Sabarmati Ashram for three days. Like Cook, she also met him at the Yeravda Jail: "He was sitting in the court[yard] of jail under a mango tree, surrounded by a group of women and men. I was thinking of Jesus or Socrates. The first meeting of him was the most impressive experience I have ever had in my life. I felt the magical fascination, which emanates from a truly great man. He, the prisoner, was the real master, the Jail Warden bowing towards him in reverence."[35] She was converted to the thought of Gandhiji even before she decided to settle in India. By 1933, the Nazi tide was at its height in Europe. It did not deter her from talking about Gandhiji and India to her pupils.

His description of cow in his writings was one of her favourite topics. Her pupils would laugh at her in describing the cow as a sacred animal. She dared to prescribe selections from Gandhiji's writings in the *Young India* (1919–22), for her course in early 1933. It was beyond the comprehension of beef-eating children of Germany. It was like giving pearls to a pig, as they would say in German. To Amala, it was nothing short of 'sacrilege' and it forced her to discontinue lessons. She also held a grudge against her students because none of them agreed to convert to the Gandhian thought. She was already feeling the heat of racial prejudices pervading Germany. They would call her 'Asiatic' and she would feel honoured by the description. It placed her at par with Gandhiji. She wrote to him about the treatment she was being given in Germany usually reserved for harijans in India.

Margarete was forgetful, fat and clumsy in her habits but a simple hearted and naive person. She had read Gandhiji's two works, *Self-restraint versus Self-indulgence* and *Key to Health*. Gandhiji regarded eating as a necessary evil. She, on the contrary, had a weakness for food. She bombarded Gandhiji and Mahadev Desai with her inquisitive letters. She sent over twenty letters to both of them for which she was awaiting their replies. She also sent Gandhiji a series of cables. He admonished her for spending money on 'love cables'. He suggested that she content herself with mere 'love letters'. Gandhiji was fond of sprinkling his correspondence with affectionate words like 'love'.

She was already in awe of him. She viewed him as her super-God. He asked her to calm down and be a real daughter to him, that is: "if you would be a real daughter to me". The letter-writing continued for quite some time: "I had your beautiful letter. I prize your letter."[36]

In the meanwhile, the persecution of Jews had intensified. She was upset and shared her thoughts with him. He advised her to remain calm, even though she may be thrown out of Germany. She had made up her mind to settle in India. He welcomed her, provided she was prepared to adjust herself to the rigorous life of the ashram. She was a gourmet and a glutton. It was very difficult for her to survive on the bland food of ashram's communal kitchen.

German Cow

She was in two minds. The choice was between Rabindranath Tagore's Shantiniketan and Gandhiji's Sabarmati Ashram. Her predicament was shared by Gandhiji: "Why was there a struggle to choose between Gurudev and myself? We are no competitors… No more therefore of choice making, if you would be a real daughter like Mira."[37]

Initially he was most considerate towards her: "It is a matter of joy that I have friends to whom I can write without reserve and without any fear of being misunderstood."[38] These were sweet nothings reserved for Margarete. However, such expressions were never repeated after she settled down in India. She proved to be a pest who attempted to involve him in every little thing she did. He began to be exasperated with her. He had too many things to do and had no time to listen to her inanities. By 23

June 1933, he began to show his resentment openly: "I have your two stupid and silly letters… I never knew that you were so unbalanced, suspicious and hypersensitive… Or that you were less than a daughter to me…? Love."[39] Two days after her arrival in the ashram, she was complaining to Narandas and kept complaining so long she lived there. Gandhiji thought her to be "obstinate but her motives are pure… but she has no sense of proportion when she speaks."

Soon after Amala landed in India Gandhiji went on fast. She was worried to no end. She was excessively concerned about him and blamed God for his pain. She also went on fast in sympathy with him. She decided to work for the cause of the harijans. She was so sure of her consequential demise that she drew up her testament on 2 May 1933: "In order to save the money for my burial, I leave my dead body for dissection to the Sasoon Hospital in Poona."

She thus made a dramatic entry into India. Her obsessive behaviour made Gandhiji feel uncomfortable. He decided to keep her at a respectable distance. He chided her for declaring him a super-God. She would worship every stone that Gandhiji walked on. She looked out-of-place in a colourful Rajasthani *ghagara.* She did her best to look like Mirabai, who she believed was the favourite of Gandhiji. She looked so awkward in Indian outfits that Gandhiji had to order her to stop wearing them. It was followed by Amala going hysteric for several days.

Margerete had an incidental sense of humour. She wanted to marry and have about a dozen children, even though: "no one ever kissed me. Isn't it wonderful to have found a father".[40] She confided to Nilla Cram Cook: "Bapu says I'm so stupid because I have studied so much child psychology."

Gandhiji had favoured Cook with a gift of two short *dhotis*. Amala was not so lucky. So she bothered Cook endlessly. In exasperation, she gave one of the *dhotis* to Amala, expecting her to wear it. Amala would not dare think of wearing it. It would be an act of sacrilege, she thought. For her, the *dhoti* was a sacred relic to be preserved. However, she was so forgetful that she misplaced it. She was hysterical again and subjected the ashram girls to close scrutiny. Her battle cry was *Bapu ka dhoti kahan hai?* ('Where is Bapu's *dhoti*') She cursed the thief who had dared to steal it. The *dhoti* was still nowhere to be found.

Morbid Margarete

Margarete Spiegel was a fit case for being investigated by the Society for the Prevention of Cruelty to Animals (SPCA) for psychological enormities committed over her person during her stay at the ashram. To F Mary Barr, Gandhiji described her as a difficult case. In his letter, he again complained of Mirabehn wasting four hours everyday over Margarete. He was equally spiteful of her: "Did I say I would write twice a week? I thought I had said you could write twice a week."[41] The deepest instinct of a normal woman is to be a mother. Amala was no exception to the rule. Gandhi tried to probe her mind: "I have your letter. I call it good because it is truthful. I know you were deceiving yourself and me. Will you tell me what your nature demands."[42]

The peace between them could not last too long. Gandhiji went after her with a vengeance. He mocked her for her 'unbalanced letter' and called her a morbid person. All these imputations were on account of her inability to withstand the rigorous lifestyle of the ashram. In his letter of 2 February 1934, he called her 'idiotic' for her complaints against the ashram managers. This would upset her and Gandhiji again would be all sugar to her: "I shall love you in spite of your faults. You have no cause to fear me. You must dismiss from your mind the thought that I hate you… On the contrary you have given me many reasons for loving you."[43] He assured Amala that Mirabehn was no match for her: "She is not perfect." About the same time he made a different presentation to Puratin J Ruth: "She is foolish, of course. If she was not, she would not cling to me, for she had to bear many hard blows from me."

Indeed it was her misfortune to be treated roughly by Gandhiji. But still she did not complain about him. Finally, in his letter of 14 July 1934, he asked her to get lost. He encouraged her to stay away from him. By now she had realised that she was not in the same class as Mira, the Admiral's daughter, or Rajkumari Amrit Kaur, the Princess from Kapurthala. He, however, discovered that Amala was a hard nut to crack. She insisted on staying with him. She did not mind the insults. He told Mirabehn: "Amala is as mad as ever. But she is better with me than elsewhere."[44] He began to be concerned about her. He shared his fears with Narandas: "But I am really afraid that she will go off her head. She is hardly in her senses… And now she had become impatient to marry."[45]

What bugged Gandhiji the most was her persistence to marry immediately. Her latest obsession was not Gandhiji but her preoccupation to be a mother of twelve kids. Marriage had become a priority with her. He was sure that she was going off her head. She was also growing thinner day by day. He confabulated with Narandas Gandhi to find ways and means of coping with her: "She is hardly in her senses. I observe that she is not free from passion. In consequence of her trying to suppress it, it has become uncontrollable."[46]

Amala, 'the pure one', was heard by the Almighty. Her wish was almost granted. There came Harilal Gandhi on one of his rare visits to the ashram. He seemed to be the most eligible widower for her. They clicked with each other. All this made Gandhiji a worried man as he was aware of the dissolute ways of his son.

Marrying Harilal

Harilal had come to stay at the ashram and had successfully shed off his old bad habits. He was even committed to spending the rest of his life in doing constructive work in a village. In his enthusiasm, Harilal started to learn charkha weaving from Manu, thus drawing 'father's love': "Now regard me as your only friend."[47] Gandhiji was mighty pleased with his wayward son. The process of reformation in Harilal coincided with the arrival of Margarete Spiegel at the ashram.

There was only one flaw in the ointment. He was feeling intensely lonely. It had been more than a decade since his wife Gulabehn passed away. In his letter to his father he supplicated: "I am tired of my lonely life. I wish to have a life partner. I wish to marry, that is remarry". His father, who was by now in a generous frame of mind towards Harilal, consented provided he found 'a suitable widow'.[48] Earlier, Harilal was not squeamish in conveying similar request in a somewhat threatening tone to his sister-in-law Balibehn (real name: Jivibehn): "I want to have a life partner. I am thinking of remarriage. If all of you keep resisting, I will get married on my own."[49] He compounded this wish with threat to disown his young daughter Manu.

Gandhiji placed a number of preconditions before his eldest son could marry Amala: "There is no need at all to be in a hurry to come to a decision about Amala's letter. I think you will have to drop the idea. You should write and tell her plainly that any children that may be born will have to be brought up in a simple manner. And whatever means of livelihood the Lord provides will probably be in Wardha. If you start going to women or drinking, she should be free to leave you immediately. And you may write this only if you are sure that you wish to marry her. Amala's letter seems a good one to me, but I didn't know her as she reveals herself in it. I am, therefore, of the view that you will not be happy unless she comes to feel strongly that she cannot live without you."[50]

Gandhiji proved to be a killjoy. He wanted to kill two birds with one stone. He knew for certain that Harilal would not live at Wardha under the same roof as him under any circumstances. Harilal had revolted all his life to keep away from his father. Gandhiji didn't want the marriage to take place. He manoeuvred to stall it. He had done this on other occasions also. Pyarelal had also been cornered by him. The near certainty of marriage between Amala and Harilal Gandhi turned into an uncertainty due to games played by Gandhiji.*

Failed Romance

He was not only trying to cope up with Amala but also with Harilal simultaneously, because they seemed to be co-conspirators against Gandhiji, who had smelled the romance in the air. Perforce he went on the defensive and became ready to build ramparts to defend his shaky position. While appreciating Harilal's dilemma on one side, he began to attack him relentlessly on the other. He accused his son of craving for 'sex pleasure' and told him to go ahead to 'satisfy [his] craving' in defiance of his father, who had all along 'advocated renunciation' of sex. How could he: "tolerate [his] remarrying in the circumstances? He

---

*There is a feeling of intense loneliness to be discovered in Harilal's letter of 17 April 1933, to his sister-in-law Balibehn. There is not only supplication but also a threat implied in his letter:

> "In particular, I am tired of lonely life. I want to have a life partner. I am thinking of remarriage. If all you keep resisiting, I shall get remarried on my own, and withdraw from the responsibility regarding Manu. [(Gandhi) Mashruwala]
>
> Ironically this letter by Harilal was all about advising his sister-in-law regarding the arrangement proposal for his sixteen-year old daughter Manu.

Source: Nilam Parikh. *Gandhiji's lost jewel: Harilal Gandhi.* National Gandhi Museum, New Delhi, 2001, pp. 63-64.

offered to invite Harilal to quit and 'carry on [his] search for a wife' and '*to remarry*'. He told him to take the help of Mahadev in this connection, or sort out the problem with Amala directly, but on one condition alone of disclosing 'your previous life.'"[51] Neither his name, nor that of Mahadev Desai was to be mentioned to win favour of Amala. Gandhiji was being cruel as a father.

Harilal had taken the initiative of establishing direct contact with Amala, but apparently nothing had come out of his efforts to persuade her to marry him. Harilal conveyed this latest information to his father, who was thereby emboldened to place further restrictions on his elder son's path. Having succeeded in dismantling all the bridges, lonely Harilal attempted to unite with an equally lonely and insecure Amala, Gandhiji scored once again through his well-crafted but negative diplomacy. Harilal who was desperate to get married, left the ashram in utter disgust and moved to Rajkot and subsequently shifted to Junagadh. Soon, he resumed drinking and converted to Islam. Thus Gandhi's 'jewel' which he had 'got back' after so much effort was 'lost [once] again' entirely due to faults of his own. Eventually, he was left twiddling his thumbs and contended himself by confiding to his third son Ramdas: "You have a right to make effort, never to know your destiny."[52]

Move to Santiniketan

Gandhiji did not have a very good opinion about Margarete Spiegel. While recommending her case to Narandas Gandhi for her admission to the ashram fraternity, he said: "[she] is quick in learning things by heart, but she is not very intelligent." "She is obstinate but her motives are pure… But she has no sense of proportion when she speaks."[53] However, he was sending contradictory signals to Narandas.

Gandhiji had belatedly come to realise that he and his associates at the ashram had gone too far in denigrating her. The Harilal incident had disheartened her very much. She had come to the Gandhian ashram to discover peace of mind. However, her mental condition had deteriorated. Sabarmati Ashram proved to be a whirlpool in which she was in danger of being mired. She decided to go out and try her luck afresh. She was lucky to get a job of a French teacher at Santiniketan. She began to look cheerful once again. She said goodbye to the ashram and moved out to Santiniketan. Gandhiji wrote to her: "I am glad you like Santiniketan so well and the people in it."[54] A lot more must have remained unsaid between the two.

She confessed in her letter of 18 May 1933, on being a humble 'Jewess' who was 'only vain' for Gandhiji. Here was her cry in the wilderness: "Bapu, if you really knew how I loved you."[55]

She was so much charmed by Gandhiji that she loved him even for his faults. Finally, she returned to Germany and started writing her memoirs but passed away on 13 June, 1968 before she could complete the book.

SECTION V

Early Years: Indian Associates

CHAPTER 13

Saraladevi: The Romantic

Saraladevi Chowdharani came very close to Mohandas Karamchand Gandhi. Their whirlwind romance lasted barely two years but it succeeded in upsetting the balance of the Gandhian establishment and shook its very roots. However, now she is a part of history and a mere footnote in contemporary Gandhian literature. She, however, left scars in the mind of Gandhiji for the rest of his life. Mahadev Desai was to recall in his address to the Gujarat Vidyapeeth that Saraladevi had dazzled everybody like a flash of lightning. Indeed, she was a meteor that arose from nowhere and disappeared like a flash.

Lonely Child

Saraladevi Chowdharani was born to Janakinath Ghoshal and Swarankumari Devi on 8 September 1872. Both the parents were model *bhadralok* of Bengal. Janakinath was one of the two secretaries and the spirit behind the 1901 annual session of the Indian National Congress held in Calcutta. Swarankumari Devi was the elder sister of Rabindranath Tagore (Rabimama to Saraladevi). Interested in literature and theosophy, she actively participated in the nationalist movement. Saraladevi lived her early years in Tagore House in Jorosoko in Calcutta. Her mother, elder to Rabindranath by five years, is believed to have pioneered the literary genre in Bengali that is now associated with the name of Rabindranath Tagore.

Swarankumari had little time for her daughter who was brought up by stern nannies and an even sterner tutor. She had a grudge against the whole world. Her mother had left her totally helpless to fend for herself in the unmanageable ruckus world of the large Tagore household. She also nursed resentment against Rabimama who had stolen the literary thunder from her mother.

Saraladevi was a woman of many moods, very high strung and given to quick responses. She was too conscious of being a Tagore, hypersensitive and equally hyperactive. Her interests ranged from composing music and singing to organising social and revolutionary activities. Sister Nivedita, Swami Vivekananda and Bankim Chandra Chatterji were her role models. She was the spirit behind Anushilan Samiti, an organisation for training revolutionaries.

She was also the spirit behind 'The Worship of the Brave' movement. She edited *Bharati* from Calcutta in pursuance of her revolutionary ideals. For her the road from Saraswati (the Goddess of learning) to Shiva (the God of destruction) was a short one. She also became the militant face of the Bengali renaissance and came to be popularly known as Bengal's Joan of Arc. In her own words: "My pen reverberated with the power of Shiva's trumpet and invited Bengalis to cultivate death."[1] *Bangabashi* compared her to Durga with some exaggeration. She was also described as the manifestation of *Shakti*. Even Gandhiji had referred to her prowess as *Shakti* incarnate. Admittedly, she had charmed herself into wide public attention in Bengal.

Meeting Gandhiji

Her first meeting with Gandhiji was purely coincidental. He had arrived from South Africa on a visit to India and had taken the opportunity to attend the annual session of the Indian National Congress in Calcutta, during 1901. Sarala's father was in charge of the session. Thus, there was a tailor-made role for her to be on display. The session opened with a song composed by her. She had composed the music and conducted the orchestra of 58 persons and a chorus of four hundred persons selected from different parts of the country. They sang in unison to the theme of 'Hail to India'. She had a meeting with Gandhiji to persuade him to contribute to *Bharati*. His fame had preceded him from South Africa and she looked forward to sharing his experiences of the political struggle in South Africa with her readers.

Saraladevi was courted by the whole tribe of *bhadralok* eligibles. The granddaughter of Maharishi Devendra Nath Tagore, a niece of Rabindranath Tagore and daughter of Swarankumari was the toast of the town. She had decided to remain a spinster. She was forced into marriage with a two-timer widower, Rambhuj Dutt Chowdhary from Lahore. He was a *theth* Punjabi (deep-rooted native) of *zamindari* background. He also composed patriotic songs in his native Punjabi. He swept her off her feet. She adapted herself to the Punjabi milieu with rare verve. She and her husband met Gandhi at the *Kumbh Mela* in Hardwar during 1915, but actually came closer during 1918. Both of them joined the Indian National Congress in the year of the Jallianwala Bagh massacre. By then, she was forty-seven and Gandhiji nearly fifty.

Punjab was in ferment by this time. The Jallianwala Bagh massacre had taken place around this time only. He was to visit Punjab and tour the province extensively, with Saraladevi as his accompanying baggage to public meetings in and outside Lahore. He made the residence of the Dutts at Lahore his headquarters. He submitted a formal report on Jallianwala Bagh to the Congress Party. His '*Punjab Letter*' published regularly in *Young India* and *Navjivan* is an official record of his hectic days in the province. His autobiography has a vivid description of his triumphant entry into Lahore: "The entire populace had turned up out of doors in eager expectation, as if to meet a dear relation after a long separation, and was delirious with joy. I was put up at the late Pandit Rambhuj Dutt's bungalow, and the burden of entertaining me fell on the shoulders of Shrimati Saraladevi. A burden truly it was, for even then, as now, the place where I was accommodated became a venerable caravanserai."[2]

Lahore Welcome

Gandhiji had arrived to a tremendous public reception at Lahore. He was received in style by Saraladevi at her residence. He had been invited by the Rambhujs to stay with them during his tour of Punjab. In the meanwhile, Rambhuj found himself in jail. Gandhiji hesitated to accept the invitation, but he was prevailed upon by Sarala not to refuse it. The Rambhuj residence became the Mecca of political activities. Saraladevi was a perfect hostess. She travelled with him extensively. She occupied the stage with him and freely mixed with the crowds as a *prima donna*. In his *Punjab Letter*, he was to give a vivid impression of their growing intimacy: "In Lahore I am the guest of Smt Saraladevi Chowdharani and have been bathing in her deep affection. I first met Saraladevi in 1901 [in Calcutta]. She comes from the famous Tagore family. On her learning and sincerity, too, I get evidence in ever so many ways."[3]

This was the public face of Gandhiji. Fate had decided otherwise for him, because Saraladevi was waiting to welcome him with open arms for personal reasons. In his early *Punjab Letter*, he publicly made an announcement of his first impressions of his hostess. He was still settled comfortably at the Rambhuj's by the end of January 1920. So here was gleeful Gandhiji who informed his crony, Maganlal Gandhi, also his major-domo at Sabarmati Ashram: "Saraladevi has been showering her love on me in every possible way."[4]

Maganlal was, however, not amused. He knew about Rambhuj being in jail. Was Gandhiji intentionally prolonging his stay at Lahore? But Maganlal did not complain. Saraladevi was a perfect hostess. She had shadowed him all the time in and out of Lahore. She was the shadow that haunted him during his sleep. He had her all to himself. Rambhuj came out of the jail by the end of January 1920. She had a 'new glow on [her] face' and, indeed, she had 'the image of a lioness'.[5]

Ba did not fit the bill in this respect. She had no intellectual pretensions of any kind. She was no charming company. She was only a faithful traditional wife and mostly a silent spectator to what was happening around her. It was around 1906 that her husband had begun to see virtues in her. Gandhiji found companionship in myriad young women with intellectual pretensions. Anasuyabehn Sarabhai was one of them.

Saraladevi Chowdharani was different from the rest of them. She was aristocratic, gorgeously dressed, sensuously beautiful and imperious. In short, she had everything that Ba lacked. He was now peaking in his political career and this was precisely the opportunity he was looking for to have a companion fitting his contemporary status in the public eye.

Past Memories

The several months he spent perambulating to and fro from the residence of the Rambhujs, cemented his relations with Saraladevi. They travelled throughout the length and breadth of Punjab. They got to know each other well. Anasuyabehn Sarabhai was a common friend. He informed Anasuya on 9 February 1920, that 'Sarala's company' was 'endearing'. The first impressions had been lasting. A year hence, he recalled his visit to Punjab in his public speech at Ahmedabad. He had a vivid recollection of the first meeting: "In Punjab, I found Saraladevi. I first came to know her in [1901] and then I saw the husband and wife in Hardwar. Saraladevi invited me to Punjab. I accepted the invitation but felt nervous. At the time she extended it, she was separated from her husband. That made me wonder whether it would be proper for me to accept her hospitality… I had from her as much service as from one's own sister and thus became her debtor."[6] Be it noted that he described her adopted sister in the Ahmedabad address. The drama was yet to unfold itself in full.

Next he planned to take Saraladevi along with him during his travels throughout the length and breadth of the country. He dedicated the year 1920 to her as indicated by his itinerary. While proceeding from Kashi to Delhi during the last month of February, he was accompanied by her. Immediately thereafter, she was in Ahmedabad joining him once again. He formally reported her arrival in Ahmedabad. He provided his hosts with her brief bio-data. He informed them of her 'poetic power' and her popular song 'I bow to India' which had come to be known all over the country. He also informed his readers of *Navjivan*: "Her musical talent perhaps exceeds her gift for poetry and she is, therefore, in demand at every Congress."[7]

When the Ides of March were followed by the April spring, he informed his youngest son, Devdas, about his landing in Bombay accompanied by who else but Saraladevi? They spent about two months in Bombay. In his opening ceremony speech on *swadeshi* at Bombay on 4 June 1920, he proudly told the whole world of his joy at escorting Saraladevi on that particular occasion, "[She] was dressed in *khaddar* sari and blouse."[8]

He wanted to be doubly sure about his friends getting to know about his latest discovery. He wrote to Abbas Tyabji with tongue in cheek: "I pleaded with Saraladevi to write to you on my behalf but she said nothing but a letter in my own writing would do."[9]

Swadeshi and *Khaddar*

Swadeshi and Saraladevi Chowdharani proved to be a lethal combination which egged on Gandhiji and took him all over the country. Romance was in the air. He was now complaining about Ba refusing to take to *khadi*. She continued to stick to mill-manufactured textiles and here he was telling everyone within his listening distance in his public address that: "He was taking Saraladevi all over India with him as she had better understood his *swadeshi* principles than his wife, though he complained that she did not practice the use of *swadeshi* cloth to his entire satisfaction."[10]

No wonder the *Bombay Secret Abstract* of 25 July 1920, quoted him saying in one of his whirlwind public addresses: "In which he said that he took Saraladevi, rather than his literal wife, all over India, because she understood the principles of *swadeshi* better."[11]

In absolute terms, Saraladevi had scored over Ba. She wore *khadi* dresses. She gave enthusiastic talks on *swadeshi*, *swaraj* and *khilafat*. She was exhilarating company for him in his *parikarma* throughout the length and breadth of the country. Last, but not the least, she was a museum piece on public display for the titillation of others.

Time flies but memories leave their mark on the sands of time. Now that he had completed the mission of introducing her to the country, he took the task upon himself of informing his friends abroad. Here he was informing his good friend Kallenbach about his perambulations accompanied by Saraladevi and his son Devdas: "…and another faithful companion on whom you would dote. I have come in closest touch with a lady who often travels with me. Our relationship is indefinable. I call her my spiritual wife. A friend has called it an intellectual wedding. I want you to see her. It was under her roof that I passed several months at Lahore in Punjab." Inevitably, references to Ba were also there in the same letter: "Mrs Gandhi is at Ashram. She has aged considerably, but she is as brave as ever. She is the same woman you know her with her faults and virtues."[12]

Saraladevi was the topic of discussion in undertones and overtones amongst his friends, associates and family members. How could Ba not be affected? The years 1919 and 1920 were years of mental torture and agony for her. Tension was palpable in their day to day relations. He let the strong-willed wife go her own way. Rambhuj was no Henry Polak and Sarala too was not much of a Millie Graham Polak. Still things continued to turn in favour of Sarala for the time being.

Khadi Mannequin

The romance between Gandhiji and Sarala was cemented during 1920. It took concrete manifestation by this time. She was effectively sold on his mission in the cause of *khadi*, a role she performed to perfection for him. *Khadi* became the dearest link between them. While *swadeshi* was an important plank of his concept of *swaraj*, *khadi* was the concrete physical manifestation of the *swadeshi* movement. It provided a distinct identity to those participating in the national movement as an act of defiance of imperial hegemony. The fact that Saraladevi took the lead in this matter was widely appreciated.

By April 1920, Gandhiji was singing paeans to Saraladevi for having provided 'the finest impetus' to the *swadeshi* movement. She had come forward with the idea of wearing sari and blouse made of hand-spun *khadi*. Gandhiji found that it was difficult for women to take to wearing *khadi*. It was as yet too rough for a wear. Here was Saraladevi who was willing to perform to his bidding. He got a sari and blouse especially made for her. Even her Rabimama (Rabindranath Tagore) approved of her initiative: "If you do not feel awkward in that sari of yours, you may go anywhere and to any party you would find it would be well with you."[13]

She still felt embarrassed to wear the new dress. She decided to test herself by wearing her *khadi* sari and blouse to a high class society reception. It so happened that Rabimama was in Bombay, and the socialite Lady Dinshaw Petit (Jinnah's mother-in-law) threw a party in honour of the poet. Rabindranath Tagore dared her to wear the *khadi* dress to the party. She felt hesitant as she made the entry, but felt relaxed immediately thereafter.

She was the cynosure of all eyes. Encouraged, she began to wear *khadi* to all public meetings and functions. Being accompanied by adoring Gandhi and because of her *khadi* wear, she began to be noticed widely. She was to be credited for introducing *khadi* as the socialite staple. She was equally responsible for breaking the resistance of common men and women to *khadi*. Truly, Saraladevi has been designated as the first and foremost Gandhian fashion model.

Indeed, Saraladevi scored over Gandhiji hands down on this score. While Gandhi persisted in telling everyone within hearing distance that 'this type of cloth' was known as *khaddar* in North India, and it was called *khadi* in Bombay Presidency, he found no takers for *khadi*. Kasturba had put her foot down. He was reduced to supplicating Sarala on this score. There were doubts about Saraladevi also. His associates thought differently: "[the] woman who had never worn anything but the finest Dacca muslin could not possibly bear the weight of heavy *khaddar*".[14]

Love conquered all. Sarala had a personal statement to make. *Khaddar* cemented the bond between Sarala and Gandhiji. He now had something to crow about, thanks to Sarala and her uncle Rabimama (Rabindranath Tagore): "Thus, the uncle and the niece who have acquired a reputation in this country for their artistic sense, did not reject *khadi* from that point of view at any rate. On the contrary, they introduced *khadi* as a dress for women in gatherings of such people."[15]

Khadi provided the rationale for Gandhi to tow her along with him all over the country. The caravan rolled on to its predestination with hurried relentlessness. Love is not only blind but inexorable in its pursuit. The *khadi* sari was no longer a mere symbol of *swadeshi*, it had turned into a fashion statement.

Women were attracted to *khadi* saris worn by Saraladevi, in large numbers. Its novelty was its greatest virtue. They would touch her and feel the new dress material. She was a mannequin on display. Their curiosity was indeed limited to her physical presence rather than her public addresses. Nobody took her political discourses on the public platform seriously. Saraladevi also took the whole thing in her stride. This is amply proved by her performance on the eve of the *Khilafat* conference held at Bareily, the heartland of Indian conservatism.

Gandhiji was invited as the chief guest. He decided to take Saraladevi along with him as an advertisement for *khadi*. All that Saraladevi could think of was what would come naturally to the mind of professional fashion models on road show. The underlying spirit that motivated Saraladevi was reflected in the letter she wrote to Gandhiji on the subject.He reproduced it faithfully in his *Young India*: "I have done my packing racked with conflicts as to what to take and what not to take with me—whether to wear *khaddar* dress while addressing the audience or *swadeshi* silk, the point of which will not be so well understood—Whether to take up the trunk or to wrap the holdall with clothes inside the bedding—Whether to be smart and fashionable as of old or to be simple and common only. I have at last chosen to be the latter. But it is taking time and trouble to assimilate the new method."[16]

It would have been expected of the Gandhi-Saraladevi duo to discuss strategy and tactics of reaching out to the *burka*-clad women, but instead the discussion was confined to inane matters like choosing between a trunk and a holdall for packing dresses for Bareilly. He would have been expected to snub his heart-throb straightway. Nothing of the kind happened. Instead, he reproduced her letter in the *Young India*.

Truth has a way of coming out in the end. Gandhiji admitted by July 1920 that his strategy of building her as a political figure in her own right had not worked. Her political discourses went awash with the audience, who turned up to have a look at the lady caught in the Gandhian whirlwind. She attracted the female of the species to her meetings in droves. Some of them admired her for wearing 'coarse but beautiful white sari'. Others took pity on her for changing from *bhadralok* wear of costly silk saris to the common-man dress of *khadi*. The imperious Sarala needed no pity, but she was frank enough to tell Gandhiji: "Her *khaddar* sari impressed her audience more than her speeches and her songs came out next, her speeches last."[17]

Passion and *Swadeshi*

Swadeshi was his ideal and Saraladevi his role model. He seemed to have exhausted the romantic vocabulary in singing paeans to her. He always talked of her distinguished *bhadralok* background, her sensitivity to the arts and her total commitment to *swadeshi* movement. In his eyes, *swadeshi* was her passion, little did he realise that her passion was much less for his cause than his person.

She was also anxious to look her very best in his eyes. Actually it was mutual admiration of two individuals. They behaved like lovelorn teenagers with stars in their eyes. Having stopped wearing Dacca muslin saris, she resorted to wearing rough *khaddar* saris in the hottest of seasons. He was no less gallant in singing hallelujahs to her: "Her *khaddar* saris continue to preach true *swadeshi* more eloquently than her tongue."[18]

If Gandhiji had any poetic sense, he would have her *khadi* sari theme set to music. It was now time to come out in the open for the whole world to relish the romantic sideshow going on in political India. Passion makes the ordinary-looking extraordinary. This is what happened to Gandhiji in 1920. His thesis ran something like this: Saraladevi was a paragon of all virtues. She could commit no mistake. After all, she was a woman of consequence belonging to the famous Tagore family.

To him, Rabimama and his niece were the most artistic persons in India. He had also termed her 'an erudite lady', doing public service. The power of her pen had been proved during her editorship of *Bharati*. He also sang paeans to her musical and poetic genius. He testified joyously to her recitation of a popular Punjabi patriotic song at the 1919 Congress session. The litany of praise was fulsome and somewhat jaded for the rest of his associates.

Gandhiji played his romantic drama on the public stage. He had viewed 'the image of lioness' in her. Her husband Rambhuj and Gandhiji saw the manifestation of *Shakti* in her. In fact both of them were equally infatuated with her. The intensity of the relationship of Gandhiji with her was of a special order. He would hate to be separated from her. She had perforce to go away to Lahore to solemnise the marriage of Rambhuj's elder son Jagdish. The marriage was solemnised on 19 May 1920. In his letter to her dated 1 May 1920, he was beseeching her to get back to him. He even sought a 'boon' from her.

Gandhiji used to enforce strict discipline in the ashram expecting the ashramites to perform all household chores including cooking and cleansing in the kitchen. The residents were expected to clean up communal toilets. However, he made an unstated exemption in her case. She was the reigning queen and, thus, above the law. This was the talk of the town. Eventually, it reached his ears. Gandhiji never dared to dictate his terms to her. He also lacked the courage to tell her to her face. The imperious Tagore had turned the icon in Gandhiji into a cowering mouse.

He resorted to the subterfuge of telling but also not telling the truth: "Great and good though you are, you are not a complete woman without achieving the ability to do household work. You have preached it to others. Your preaching will be more effective when people know that even at your time of life and in your station you do not mind doing it."[19]

His strategy did not work in actual practice. She refused to change her old bad habits. Gandhiji was a lame duck reformer, because he was himself being threatened to be reformed. Love is not only blind, but it is doubly so. Instead of a reformer reforming the recalcitrant object, he gets reformed for the worst.

Possessive Lady

Gandhiji was determined to place her on the highest pedestal. It was uncharitable of Sushila Nayyar to accuse Saraladevi of being possessive of Gandhiji. In fact, it was he who went out of his way to protect her. Normally, women are prone to be sentimental in man-woman relationship. The reverse was the case in this instance. Saraladevi maintained her sangfroid in her pulsating relationship with him. She was a very ambitious person. At worst, she could be accused of being a social climber. Why not? Gandhiji would be her road to public success!

Gandhiji found himself at a disadvantage in this relationship. In the course of his deeply-felt involvement with this Bengali-born lady, he found practically everyone in his entourage ranged on the opposite side. At one time he was prepared to risk his public career in her cause. The propagation of *swadeshi* including *khaddar* was his subterfuge to take her along with him. Yet, it would be unfair to impute any sexual impropriety to him. He was attracted to her because she compensated for all that he had missed in Ba. Even as late as 1 February 1945 (soon after Ba passed away), he wrote to Munnalal Shah: "Perhaps you do not know how many of my plans came to nothing because of Ba's limitations."[20]

One finds oneself in entire agreement with one of his more sympathetic critics: "Her relationship with Gandhi is worth studying because it was personal to a more striking degree than his other relationships. It was erratic, in the sense that word carries when applied to novels. The letters between them that survive do not express the alliance of comrades— though that must have been a large part of what passed between them—but a love relationship."[21] Probably, the relationship was entirely platonic. Admittedly, platonic relationships have a large component of eroticism. The fact, however, remained that the line of demarcation between sexual, sensuous, erotic and platonic was only of degree and not of kind.

The momentum of sentiments (or sweet nothings) never lessened as long as the relationship lasted. It continued to be upgraded with the passage of time. He wrote to her from Calcutta in high-flown language: "My love for you is not a task. It is one of the keenest pleasures of my life." He combined his little wooing with his self-appointed role of her teacher: "And you must bear with me if in the process of helping sometimes I seem to be rubbing you up the wrong way."[22]

He had fallen ill. He stayed in the salubrious environment of Sinhgadh in hilly Maharashtra. He had leisure and hence his imagination began to run riot. He missed Saraladevi and expressed his intense feelings of separation by quoting one of lovelorn Mira's *bhajans* in praise of Krishna, underlying her unrequited love:

"Mira says, O Lord Girdhar Nagar,
My eyes see all things in a new light."[23]

On the following day, he shared his dream with her: "To my great joy, you returned within two days. I asked 'How so quickly' you returned within two days. You replied, 'Oh it was Panditji's [her husband's] trick to have me by him… I discovered it was a dream."[24] He was pining for her. She had actually stayed back at Lahore to arrange the marriage of Rambhuj's son (through his previous marriage). Now he was supplicating her to come to where she rightly belonged.

Intellectual Companionship

Gandhiji also interacted on an intellectual plane with Saraladevi. He attempted to upgrade her knowledge by educating her. He would send her translations of the poems of lovelorn Mira. He also attempted to educate her in the intricacies of *Ashtavakra Gita* (containing the dialogue between King Janaka, and the low-born and ugly-looking philosopher Raikva). Such dialogues were interspersed with love talk. He encouraged her to publish a pamphlet, "*At the point of the spindle*" preaching *swadeshi* to young people. He started giving her publicity in the columns of *Young India* and *Navjivan*. He published her essay-poem entitled *Bandhu* (Brother). Since the 'profound' contents of the essay fell flat on the readers, he offered to interpret the essay for them. "Thereupon, some of them write to me to say that they had gone through the article and reflected over it, but had failed to make its meaning."[25] He was so blinded by love that he discovered meanings in her discourse where none existed. It should, however, not be forgotten that his fascination for Saraladevi was owing to his thirst for intellectual companionship. Saraladevi fitted the bill to perfection.

The year 1920 was the year of expressions like 'bathing in her affection', 'showering her love on me' and the woman who 'cast that spell' are scattered throughout his letters to her. The intensity increased so much so that the phrases like, 'my love', 'the keenest pleasures of my life' began to be employed by him. Thenceforth, she began 'to haunt me in my sleep' and he dared to write to her, 'I love you more for loving you less'. He called her his 'spiritual wife', the statement being on record twice in his letters.

Her responses must have been equally intense, but those are unknown because most of her letters to him are not accessible. She could have been more circumspect in her replies because to her the relationship was the key to her political ambitions. He, however, mentioned in his letter of 16 September 1932 (long after the chapter was closed), that her latest communication to him had been 'flowing with love'. Too much should not be read in his use of 'love' because he had the tendency to use it rather too freely.

Gandhian Vitality

If Saraladevi is merely a point of reference and a peg to hang something on, then his intense relationship with Saraladevi is to be viewed in an entirely different perspective. The relationship could not be reduced to a middle aged fifty year old man chasing a forty something old woman. There were impulses embedded in his subconscious which impelled him to idolise Saraladevi, the beautiful aesthete from the Tagore family.

It is no longer amusing to find his love letters interspersed with religious discourses: "Just as the pot disappears into the earth, the waves subside into water and the bracelet dissolves into gold, so this universe, projected out of me, is reabsorbed into me."(*Ashtavakra Gita*, II, I)

This obtuse observation is followed by down-to-earth sentiments as found in his letter of 2 May 1920: "You still continue to haunt me even in my sleep." He employed the art of flattery to win over his lady love: "No wonder Panditji [Rambhuj] calls you the greatest *shakti* [embodiment of life force] of India. You may have cast that spell over him. You are performing the trick over me." In the end, he commits the unpardonable sacrilege of comparing her with *Bharatmata* [Mother India]: "If you are the greatest *shakti*, you will enslave India by becoming her slave in thought, word and deed."[26]

Saraladevi was an abstract concept for him. She was an ideal of the unattainable woman of his dreams. If one were to close one's eyes for a moment and go over the exchange of letters between Gandhiji and Saraladevi, one would find it hard to believe that such a development did come to pass in the life of an ascetic Gandhi. Such letters are usually exchanged between lovelorn and immature boys and girls in their early teens.

In reality, it is a great tribute to the vitality of Gandhiji who avowed to practice *brahmacharya* in 1906 against his normal instincts, which were not only alive and kicking but also continued to torture him constantly. They not only tormented him but also mocked at him and disturbed him in his dreams. In fact, *kama* was never subdued by him entirely. It went underground in his subconscious by successfully employed hit and run tactics against him. Kama continued to remind him of his existence by knocking at his door constantly. Gandhiji took due note of the God of desire (and sex) without necessarily acknowledging his debt to his robust adversary. It is an occasion for celebration, because Gandhiji has proved to be one of us by joining in tribute to sensuality through his abiding love of womanhood as represented by the delectable Saraladevi Ghoshal—Tagore Chowdharani.

It would be unfair to consider Saraladevi as a decorative doll in the Gandhian pantheon. She was a remarkable person in her own right. In many ways, she was a true daughter of her mother, Swarankumari. If her mother was a novelist, poet, song-writer and editor, so was her daughter Saraladevi a singer (of repute), composer, editor and practitioner of martial arts. If Swarankumari maintained a salon by attracting the intellectual elite of Calcutta, so did her daughter Saraladevi in Lahore, by gathering together the political elite of Punjab. Saraladevi was a woman of her times as the vanguard of women's liberation.

CHAPTER 14

Saraladevi in Limbo

Saraladevi Chowdharani was a creation of overheated imagination of Mohandas Karamchand Gandhi. The close relation lasted only during the heat of the moment. Differences cropped up between the two soon and made them look incompatible human beings. A quirk of fate had brought them together.

Gandhiji, the politician, was a public property but Saraladevi sought to monopolise his private life. He could have continued the sideshow, but his associates became too diffident for his comfort. They strongly resented her intrusion. Finally, compelled by circumstances, Gandhiji found himself on the side of his recalcitrant associates.

Cold War

Gandhiji could not confront her directly but conveyed the message that he wanted her to follow other ashramites in performing the daily chores: "You should be proud of their jealousy and watchfulness. They want to run no risk and they are right. You and I are duty bound to satisfy every lawful requirement." Having made his point rather hesitantly, it was business as usual between them. He concluded the letter on a romantic note: "You ask for a reward of your great surrender. Well, it is its own reward."[1]

Humility and surrender were words missing from her vocabulary. Gandhiji realised this too soon. The very next day she resented his changing attitude to her. He was forced to respond to her with two of his distressful letters. She counter attacked by asking him to stop sermonising. Now it was his turn to defend himself: "If my love is true it must express itself in sermons so long as you do not realise the ideal accepted by you as worthy."[2]

Obviously this was a hard sell by him. It did not go well with the imperious lady. He was shaken by 'nasty things' conveyed to him. Coldness was definitely creeping into their relations. The words were left unsaid but the message was clear. He had laid claims to being a lover and a law giver in equal-measure. Gradually the law-giver began to assert over pliant lover. Infact, in his letters to her, he began to sign as Law Giver to emphasise his changed stance towards her.

It was not possible for him to sacrifice his public career for her sake. Saraladevi could turn out to be a public liability. She also realised that there was a *lakshman rekha* drawn by him which she was forbidden to transgress. The ashram discipline was too much for her aristocratic tastes. She had little faith in the ideology of *satyagraha* and non-violence and much less in *brahmacharya* which he espoused and practiced.

She was a devotee of *Shakti* and did not rule out the use of violence in human existence. She had expressed loss of faith in the efficacy of *satyagraha* as a political instrument. She was imperiously opposed to the concept of non-cooperation, which in her prophetic view was based upon hatred of others; and activity, moreover, like non co-operation could be taken up by others also. She told Gandhi plainly: "She would love Bapu more if he was free of hatred; an activity, moreover, like non-co-operation could be taken up by others also."[3] At one stage she was certain that he could leave this 'dirty' work to others.

Platonic Love

Gandhiji made a last-minute attempt to square up the simmering differences that were taking an ideological turn, although they were purely personal. He tried to patch up but realised the futility of his efforts. His lengthy letter of 17 December 1920, was more to keep the record straight. It makes the most interesting reading not only for stating a few facts, but also for leaving out a great deal unsaid.

Even though he assured her: "your love for me is based on your belief in my purity and gentleness," he clarified to her that political 'non-cooperation' was his *dharma*. He indicated in no uncertain words that given a choice he would opt for his politics rather than his love for her. He had made his choice and it was for her to decide either to bend or to break in his cause.

Dissonance of people close to him had assumed titanic dimensions due to his exclusive preoccupation with Saraladevi. Ba was hurt the most because of his indifference. He mocked her in undertones as well as publicly and this distressed her. Ba was left with a few choices but to fight for her rights. She was aware that Gandhiji had spent nearly three months in Sarala's company and had taken her along to other parts of the country. She found solace in Gandhiji's close associates who sympathised with her.

Gandhiji kept passing snide remarks against her. He complained bitterly to Maganlal Gandhi about her conduct in the ashram. He accused Kasturba of partiality towards the members of her immediate family. She also charged him with display of public hostility towards her elder son, Harilal. He went to the extent of ticking her off completely: "Her staying in the ashram is in vain."[4]

He employed all kinds of negative expressions to malign Ba in his letters of 16 and 24 January 1920. In both these letters he talked of her 'pettiness', of not possessing 'even temper' and not being 'always sweet'.[5]The most serious charge came in his letter to Narahari Parekh in which he accused her of having 'obstructed many plans'[6] due to her difficult nature, negative attitude and intellectual incompatibilities.

It was not only Ba who was resentful of his special (and somewhat excessive) consideration for the legally-wedded wife of another person. The tension was palpable in the letter written to him by Shankarlal G Banker. He was extremely distressed over the brazen conduct of Saraladevi in snubbing him and other associates. Gandhiji was angry beyond words and fended him off with a sense of mockery about his own conduct: "And if you are afraid of Saraladevi, she is not here today and will not be coming here till Tuesday."[7]

There were many others who conveyed their resentment openly to Gandhiji. They included C Rajagopalachari, Devdas, Mahadev Desai, Mathuradas Trikumji (his sister's grandson) and Maganlal Gandhi. Maganlal was cynical even after Gandhiji made a presentation to him: "Saraladevi has been showering her love on me in every possible way."[8]

Dining-room Incident

Maganlal was keen to take on the issue and the opportunity came when she landed at Sabarmati Ashram during May 1920 to stay there. As usual, she was treated as an honoured guest. On that occasion, the time-honoured practice of the ashramites sitting together and sharing their food was violated; Gandhiji and Saraladevi sat on a cushioned bed separately from others while taking their meals. They never bothered to move to the dining hall during the community meal. It had never happened before.

The ashramites were angry beyond measure and conveyed their displeasure to the manager of the ashram, Maganlal Gandhi, who in turn conveyed their collective displeasure to Gandhiji through Mahadev Desai. Gandhiji conveyed back to Maganlal that she was so absorbed in discussion with him (Gandhiji) that both of them forgot everything else. Consequently, they did not visit the dining room and continued the interesting and absorbing conversation. He had a ready excuse as well: that he felt sick and would take his meals at leisure. In any case he took no cereals like others.

It did not take him too long to realise that his explanation was not convincing and that he had made a fool of himself in the process. He wisely decided to make up through due amendments. Gracefully, he offered an unstinted apology to Maganlal for his inexcusable lapse of good manners, grace and, above all, ashram discipline. He took recourse to breast-beating. Here was a confession forthcoming from him:

"5. I am no more as scrupulously firm as I used to be;…

9. The power which was mine, in virtue of which everyone was obliged to listen to me has disappeared."[9]

In the circumstances, he was no model who led by 'example and percept'. All these brave words turned out to be meaningless in the presence of Saraladevi. While he apologised to Maganlal, to Saraladevi he talked of higher things of life by quoting from the scriptures: "Even after that Self (*atman*) is Pure consciousness and Beauty *par excellence*, the man continues to be full of lust is headed towards a morass."[10]

The incident seemed to have been forgotten in twenty-four hours and it was business as usual with him: "My staunchness has not disappeared. My ideas have grown stronger and more piercing. My indifference to world pleasures has increased. What I used to see but dimly has now become clearer to me. I have grown more tolerant, so that I am less particular about others [doing what I want them to do]."[11]

Did he have Saraladevi in mind when he talked of his laxness described as tolerance by him? It might have crossed his mind by this time that she could turn out to be a liability for him. He was too sharp to ignore the danger signals. As a person who knew human nature, he recognised that for a break to be successful, it should be gradual and not abrupt to absorb the shock.

In December 1920, Gandhiji was still engaged in rescuing the situation. He talked of the need to 'cultivate patience and trust', because 'among lovers and friends there is neither sinner nor saint'. He went out of his way to assure her that there would be a permanent niche for her in his scheme of things: "And therefore it is that I ever pray for a humble and contrite heart for you."[12]

By August itself she had begun to apply reverse gear. Gandhiji wrote to her from Bezwada (or Vijayawada): "Your letters have your usual self. Some of them decidedly despondent and sceptical and suspicious." He admonished her for critical references to his associates who were threatening to be rebellious. He advised her to be deserving 'of their love and affection' and also discouraged her from visiting Calcutta during the time he planned to be there. He could, however, not resist the temptation to express his love and affection for her: "I and (if you are mine in the purest sense of the term)" etc.[13]

While he was on his way to Bombay by train, he sent another epistle to her the very next day. Meanwhile, he received a letter that caused him great distress. She did not like to be sermonised, much less treated like a school-going lass. Again and again he asked her to receive satisfaction through his 'complete surrender'. The seeds of discord were already sown.

This line of demarcation did not appeal to her. Sarala wrote two letters to him underlining the ever increasing distance between them. A stage had arrived when she told him openly that she neither understood his language nor his line of thinking. It hurt her very much; he had accused her of a complex nature. He must have found it hard to explain his current status to her: "I have certainly not betrayed any annoyance over your complex nature, but I have remarked upon it."[14]

She had started retaliating and thus contested the very foundations of his ideological thought: "Non-co-operation was based on hatred and she loved Bapu the less therefore. She would love Bapu more if he was free of hatred; an activity, moreover, like non-cooperation could be taken up by others also."[15]

Here was her clever response: "I love you more [for] loving me less for any hate you may see in me… Hatred is essentially the voice of cowards N [on-] O [peration] is self-purification."[16]

Dissonant Fallout

The ground was being prepared for the final break up. Now he was required to explain his past commitments to her. He had called her his 'spiritual wife'. How did he define his special relation? To him the meaning of spiritual wife was clear: "I have been analysing my love for you. I have reached a definition of spiritual wife. [It is] a partnership between two persons of the opposite sex where the physical is wholly absent. It is therefore possible for brother and sister, father and daughter."

He conceded to her the status of 'wife' in recognition of common ideals shared by them. The argument gets complicated by such gratuitous remarks: "While either party is physically married to another, but only if they are living as celibate."[17] It is a complicated argument to explain his platonic love for Saraladevi. He must have been looking upto her for intellectual companionship.

Was Gandhiji's description of Saraladevi as a spiritual wife purposeful? Was he trying to work out a mechanism to reconcile his public activities—come to terms with Ba, fit his relations with his irreconcilable associates and accommodate Saraladevi as well in his scheme of things? It is difficult to conceive Gandhiji ('Law-Giver') with bent knees supplicating Saraladevi for a reprieve.

"[You] Have the exquisite purity, that perfect coincidence, that perfect merging, that identity of ideals, the self-forgetfulness, that fixity of purpose, that truthfulness? I am too physically attached to you [as my spiritual wife] to be worthy of enjoying that sacred association with you. By physical attachment I here mean I am too much affected by your weaknesses. I must not be a teacher to you, if I am your spiritual husband, if coincidence or merging is felt. On the contrary there are sharp differences between you and me so often. So far I can see our relationship, it is one of brother and sister. I must lay down the law for you, and thus ruffle you. I must plead gently like a brother evertaking care to use the right word even as I do to my oldest sister. I must not be father, husband, friend or teacher all rolled in one."[18]

Saraladevi was not amused. She could not make anything of the letter. He was trying to be her lover, husband, brother, father, friend, guide and mentor all at the same time. This was perhaps the last of his substantive letters to her. For sure Gandhiji did not send greetings for the new year in 1921. By the end of 1920, the seemingly irrevocable bond between them was broken.

Did he have a premonition of the break between them? Did he pen his letter of 17 December for posterity to judge him in the right perspective? Wasn't he giving her the same treatment that he had reserved for Mirabehn? The parallel is most striking between the two situations. He began to feel uncomfortable soon after Sarala became obsessive of him and this had begun to interfere with his political functioning.

The women in his life can be compared with the *sutradhar* in traditional Indian drama, who makes a brief appearance and then disappears altogether for the plot to unfold. Till the romance lasted, Saraladevi performed her role to perfection. Once this was over, she moved out of his orbit for good, to be forgotten completely. But she was the one who haunted his thoughts throughout his living days.

The chronology of events can be traced through the correspondence between Gandhiji and Saraladevi. There are sixty letters on record from him to her. Except for two letters, the rest belonged to the period between 1919-1920. The last letter is dated 1947. By then, she was ill and dying. The poignancy of separation comes out in his letter to C Rajagopalachari of 1924: "Yes, your guess is correct. The fair friend is Saraladevi. She wants to bombard me with more stuff but I have refused to give further accommodation."[19]

Supplicant Sarala

Gandhiji's memories of Saraladevi were revived once again in 1932 upon hearing from her. He was delighted to receive her letter 'overflowing with love'. Now she meant nothing to him but he did not have the heart to disappoint her. His replies were mere words. Saraladevi took to spiritualism in 1937.

Now Saraladevi turned into a supplicant. She asked for favours from him from time to time. At one time, she had an eye on Indira (Nehru) Gandhi as the most eligible bride for her son Dipak, who had spent considerable time at the ashram under Gandhiji's personal tutelage. She wrote to Gandhiji to beseech Jawaharlal Nehru on her behalf. Gandhiji could not say no and wrote a letter to Jawaharlal Nehru on the issue without putting his weight behind the request. He was just being sanc-*timonious without meaning a thing*:

"I got today the accompanying [letter] from Saraladevi. I have told her Indu is left free to do so as she chooses and that she is not likely to entertain any marriage as she is still studying. I have told her too that I am forwarding the letter to you. If Indu was at all prepared to consider a marriage proposal, I regard Dipak to be a good match."[20]

Indira was 16 and Nehru's reply was an emphatic 'no'. Gandhiji followed it up with another letter assuring Nehru that he would break the news to Saraladevi in as gentle a manner as possible. One only wonders what the Mahatama would have done if the year had been 1920.

Saraladevi's visits to the ashram had become rare. Her husband had passed away and she shifted from Lahore to Calcutta. She became religious and wandered aimlessly from place to place. She also spent some time in the Himalayas in her state of intense mental distress. She found it difficult to cope with stress. Her health began to deteriorate as she was suffering on account of a swollen spleen.

Gandhiji consulted Dr Dinshaw of the Poona Nature Cure Clinic on her behalf. He advised her either to be treated by a natural therapist or be prepared to be admitted to the civil hospital. She was now like Harilal Gandhi who would suddenly turn up at the ashram and disappear without informing anyone. Gandhiji apparently dissociated himself from his past by pretending that it did not exist. In response to a query from one of his *Navjivan* readers he was to confess: "[At least] on one occasion, when I was about to be lost through placing too much confidence in my own self, I was saved only through God's grace."[21]

Gandhiji was self-righteous to the extent of becoming inconsiderate at times. This happened during his initial years with Saraladevi when he did not care about the feeling of his associates who were exasperated at his public display of affection for her. At the most, he would confess to his unintentional errors of judgement as if those were of little consequence. It was the turn of Saraladevi to be forgotten. Was it that easy?

Perdition for Gandhiji

Fortunately for Gandhiji, Saraladevi did not leave any record for the coming generations to view her case. Gandhiji is the defendant, the respondent and the judge. He must have read his Dante well because he admitted to having taken a free fall and thus reached the periphery of hell in the process of the freewheeling courtship. Fortunately for him, he was saved from 'going to perdition' because of the love and affection of near and dear ones.

In particular, he mentioned the name of his son, Devdas, grand-nephew, Mathuradas, and his Man Friday, Mahadev Desai, as his saviours: "I had, not very many years ago, all but fallen… It was their love which claimed me so tightly and strongly… pulling hard enough to tear the chains to bits and rush into hell-fire."[22] Then he made a categorical statement as if bothered by a guilt complex: "The thought of my wife, kept me from going to perdition."

He had claimed at one time that his relations with Saraladevi were purely platonic. However, he had admitted the intrusion of passion-pure and simple. Unfortunately, his autobiography is completely silent about this relationship. He must have found it 'so personal' and delicate for public consumption.

Polygamous Marriage

His conversation with Margaret Sanger on this issue was very revealing. Perhaps the best came out and he admitted that the subject of polygamy was seriously discussed between Saraladevi and him. Sarala justified polygamy under special circumstances. Gandhiji also hinted at the possibility of 'divorcing' Ba at one time.

Gandhiji was frank enough to admit to Margaret Sanger in viewing the possibility of a polygamous relationship: "Now I don't ask this question to put you in a corner. This is the argument I had with a woman with whom I almost fell. It is so personal that I did not put it into my autobiography. We had considered if there can be this spiritual relationship… I come into contact with an illiterate woman [Kasturba]. Then I met a woman with a broad cultural education. Could we not develop a close contact, I said to myself? This was a plausible argument, and I nearly slipped."[23]

He was too horrified at the consequences of his precipitous action. He must have been concerned about the negative fallout of the publicity in the press. He was saved from purgatory at the last minute: "I don't know how. For a time it seemed I had lost my anchor. I was saved by youngsters who warned me. I saw that I was doomed, they also were doomed. I decided I was not right in my argument."[24]

His memories of Saraladevi were momentarily revived in 1932 when his grandnephew Mathuradas Trikumji wrote a play in which he took a liberal view of divorce. Gandhiji disapproved of the play and reaffirmed the sanctity of marriage in his response. In his letter to Mathuradas, he referred to his spat with Ba in 1915–16 over the admission of the harijan family of Dudabhai Dafda into the ashram and speculated over the implications of divorcing Ba and consequences thereof: "If [I] had divorced Ba on the difference over untouchability, surely we would never have known the beautiful relation between us which suits today." Saraladevi was perhaps uppermost in his mind when he talked of the interesting possibilities: "Who can say in what condition Ba would be living and with whom I would have rushed into marriage? But the idea that there can be no divorce was engrained in us, and so the crisis passed and only its memory is left now."[25]

Gandhiji was all alone in 1945. Kallenbach, Ba and Saraladevi passed away about the same time. Ba was dead by 1944; Kallenbach, his best friend, passed away in 1945 and Saraladevi, who brought out the romance in him to public view, was also dead by 1945. He was thus left to his own resources, to somehow survive for the next three years.

Unspoken Link

His closest associates assiduously tried to forget the Saraladevi episode in his life as a bad dream. But Sushila Nayyar was an exception. She refused to be a party to the conspiracy of silence. She very candidly pointed out the deep underlying love between Saraladevi and Gandhiji. Two three decades that followed 1920, were momentous years of his life. While Gandhiji was adulated day in and day out, she nursed her wounded pride away from him, lost in her thoughts, reminding herself of the missed opportunities.

They made only formal courtesies when in physical proximity but otherwise their mutual chemistry was remarkable and felt by both. The chemistry of joining hearts must have worked with both of them. Truly said, unfulfilled desires are any time more powerful than fulfilled ones, which are easily forgotten. Sushila Nayyar made a note of the subtle link between Gandhiji and Saraladevi: "Saraladevi said goodbye to the centre of events of Gandhi's life. But she was to remain part of the circle of kinship till her death on 19 August 1945."[26]

Her son Dipak was a link between them, long after they had separated. He had been brought up at the ashram under his direct tutelage. So long as she lived, she was not reconciled to Dipak marrying Chhaganlal Gandhi's daughter Radha. Gandhiji was the prompter in this business and the marriage, therefore, took place after Saraladevi's death. He must have done this for maintaining the tenuous link with the lady in distress.

Past Memories

His memories were mixed with his powerful desire to justify himself in the eyes of the world. The urge to reconcile the irreconcilable while exposing his sensual desire and at the same time suppressing it, is a standard practice in his writings. Such thoughts must have been crowding him in 1947. By then he had been politically isolated by his colleagues. He must have ruminated over his past. He was to note in his diary: "I have never sought the company of a woman with a view to satisfying my passions. Of course, I mentioned one exception."[27]

Only two days were to pass when he wrote to Rajkumari Amrit Kaur in the same vein: "With one solitary exception I have never looked up on a woman with lustful eyes." His moral sense of guilt bothered him and he tried to elaborate upon the colourful episode in his life: "Even the one solitary instance referred to by me was never with the intention of despoiling her."

Probably, he remained totally unconvinced of his elaborate explanation. Reference to one solitary instance was enough to put him on the defensive: "Nevertheless my confession stands that in that case my touch had lustfulness about it. I was carried away in spite of myself and but for God's intervention, I might have become a wreck."[28] During 1936, he talked of his irresistible urge to possess a woman in his waking hours. He does not mention names but it is worth speculating about the dame he must have had in his mind.

Hour of Reckoning

She may have been constantly in his thoughts but her presence was unwelcome. There is a passing mention of her physical presence in his correspondence. In his letter of 30 May 1940, to Prabhavati, he informed her that Salaradevi had arrived at the ashram: "I suppose she will be here for a day or two longer. I do not know her movements."[29]

Obviously, he cared for her but could not afford to go back to his 'bad' old days. Sarala had aged by then. She was no longer the same vivacious lady who had welcomed him with open arms in 1919 when he had spent several months in her pleasant company. Her earlier arrogance had disappeared. She sought advice in 1944 as a penitent seeking guidance and solace from her guru. His reply was pre-emptory and must have discouraged her: "I cannot guide you from a sick-bed… All I can say is that you do such national service as comes your way."[30] Sarala had convinced herself by this time that she was nobody in his scheme of things. In any case, it was too late because she was to pass away the very next year.

She was in an extremely bad state of health. Gandhiji made a show of being kind to her. In November 1944, he was solicitous enough to go out of his way to invite her to visit him at her own pleasure. He was looking forward to meeting her. She was getting from bad to worse. He continued to receive reports about her deteriorating health.

It was her son who gave 'a sorrowful account' of her health. Gandhiji could afford to turn generous: "Disease like birth and death is a part of us. May you have the strength to suffer what comes as your lot."[31] Three months passed and her situation further deteriorated. He shot off a letter to her son Dipak advising him to arrange for her proper treatment: "What else can we do? The result is in God's hand, is it not?"[32]

He Remembers Saraladevi

The last time he mentioned her name in public was on 13 June 1947, during his speech at a prayer meeting in New Delhi. He was then at his sentimental best. He remembered her a lot. He referred to her in a prayer meeting after she passed away on 19 August 1945. He was reminded of Sarala and her husband, Rambhuj, who had brought a poem with them when they came to meet him.

The particular poem had been penned by Rambhuj when he was still in prison. Rambhuj could not sing. He requested his wife who had a melodious voice to sing it. Sarala sang as never before. The refrain of the poem consisted of the following words: "Never admit defeat even if you should lose your life. And I told myself that I would never accept defeat."[33]

How would history judge Saraladevi Chowdharani? She was of the *bhadralok* and would have found it virtually impossible to identify herself with her mentor and benefactor for any length of time. Gandhiji had expressed his failure in reforming her. An instance or two would prove the point. Rambhuj wrote to Gandhiji about preparations for the marriage of his elder son: "All marriage clothes have been made of *swadeshi* silk made in Banaras. It is somewhat costly but excellent stuff. We have rigidly excluded all foreign silk."[34]

The great *brahmacharya* experiment of Noakhali (1946–47) was one extreme of the spectrum. His *brahmacharya* vow of 1906 was the other end. His great romance with Saraladevi (circa 1919–1920) lies in the middle. All the three experiments are links in the same chain of Gandhiji exploring sensuality in its three dimensions of denial, romance and *moksha* (achievement). To study the concept of *brahmacharya* without understanding his great romance with Saraladevi is to miss the trees for the wood.

SECTION VI

Married *Brahmacharya*

CHAPTER 15

Prabhavati: The Nun

Prabhavati claimed a distinguished pedigree. Born at Srinagar, district Saran of Bihar, in June 1906, she belonged to one of the most reputable Kayastha families of Bihar. Her father, Braj Kishore Prasad, was a top-notch lawyer and politically very active. He was President of the Bihar Provincial Congress Committee for several years and managed the Champaran campaign of Gandhiji very effectively. He was an ascetic figure given to public causes.

His elder daughter was married to Mrityunjaya, the son of his close friend and comrade, Dr Rajendra Prasad. He married his younger daughter, Prabhavati, to Jayaprakash Narayan. The marriage was solemnised in October 1920. As customary, the newly-wed bride slept in the bedroom of her mother-in-law. Soon she returned to her parents for a prolonged stay with them. Her premature *gauna* (second marriage) ceremony took place in 1921. The marriage was not to be consummated in the beginning and it was not consummated until her dying days. JP made up his mind to go for higher studies abroad. He left Patna for USA on 16 May 1922 and was there for the next seven years. Poor Prabhavati was left to her resources and was forced to fend for herself.

Adopted Daughter

Gandhiji had stayed at the residence of Braj Kishore Babu during his Champaran campaign. He was impressed with the young lady hitherto notorious for throwing pans and saucers at all and sundry during her rages. He requested her father to send Prabhavati to stay at Sabarmati Ashram as the adopted daughter of the Gandhis. Her father agreed and she was to live with her adopted parents till the time JP came. Kasturba passed away in her arms while in detention at Aga Khan Palace in Poona on 22 February 1944.

Gandhiji was her guru, adopted father, teacher, father confessor, physician and psychotherapist all in one. He gave her regular lessons in Sanskrit, Gujarati, English, Mathematics, Health and Food Sciences. While at Sabarmati, she started maintaining her diary and continued with the ritual for the next forty five years. It is a faithful record, reflecting her inner thoughts on her relations with Gandhiji and Jayaprakash.

Prabhavati had so much identified herself with Kasturba and Gandhiji that she became one with them. Gandhiji, to quote Pyarelal, was very much impressed with her 'lack of sexual interest or desire'. She was a practising *brahmacharini* without having taken the vow of *brahmacharya*. Thus she was a nun in the making. On her second visit to Sabarmati, she was anxious to take the vow of *brahmacharya*. Gandhiji dissuaded her from taking the vow without consulting her husband. Actually, there was an epic conflict between JP and Gandhiji over the loyalty of Prabhavati.

She had taken the vow of *brahmacharya* without consulting her husband. He came to know of the decision in November 1929 when he returned to Patna from the United States. It was like a bolt from the blue for him and shock beyond redemption. He tried his best to persuade her to change her mind. She refused to relent. He loved children very much.

He had looked forward to a normal conjugal relationship between the two of them. It was not to be; *Ketu's* shadow had fallen on them.

One month after his return, he called on Gandhiji at Wardha in December 1929. He was accompanied by Prabhavati. Gandhiji welcomed him with open arms and treated him like a long lost son-in-law. However, he refused to give JP a sympathetic hearing on the issue of Prabhavati. He preferred to remain neutral. JP's mission had failed and he felt bitter about it. Ultimately Prabhavati was to choose Gandhiji over JP. All this comes out clearly in the triangular correspondence between JP, Prabhavati and Gandhiji. She was to participate in his wide-ranging *brahmacharya* experiments during 1944–45.

JP was very harsh on Gandhiji as reflected in his correspondence with him from 1929 to 1936. Thereafter, there was hardly any exchange of letters between them. Prabhavati was forced into the unpleasant task of being an interlocutor between the two.

Gandhiji won hands down in his battle for Prabhavati. He was indeed a magician who had cured her of her acute hysteria. She would lose consciousness for hours together while living in Bihar. Soon after she returned to Sabarmati, her hysteria disappeared magically.

Representing Prabhavati

Jayaprakash Narayan belonged to a lower-middle class family of Sitabhadra. Despite class differences, Prabhavati's father chose JP as a bridegroom. JP's father was a petty government official, away on tours most of the time. Braj Kishore Prasad was impressed by JP and had seen the spark of brilliance in him. Prabhavati did not identify with JP's family and preferred to live in the ashram. Her mother-in-law was not reconciled to this and persistently demanded that her daughter-in-law should return to JP's ancestral home. This, therefore was Prabahvati's period of anxiety which she experienced even after JP's return.

Gandhiji spent considerable time in cheering her up, negotiating with her in-laws and husband and in reconciling her to the rest of the world. She always looked forward to him for his guidance and found separation burdensome. She was always worried and had a fear of the unknown. Gandhiji was constantly in touch with her father, partly for political reasons and partly on account of her worries. Prabhavati was left commuting between Sabarmati Ashram, her parental residence and the ancestral home of her husband. Her mother-in-law remained a difficult person to negotiate.

Mahatma spent considerable time and energy in trying to design strategies and tactics to get her back to the ashram and have her stay there for as long as possible. On one hand he would cheer her up and on the other he would try his best to persuade her father-in-law to see reason. He was able to cajole her father-in-law and thus helped JP to fall in line. While he was holidaying at Nandi Hill during April 1927, he assured her that she was always in his thoughts and he expected her to write to him regularly. He was thus operating on several fronts on her behalf.

Negative Fallout

But his magic did not work all the time: "All my efforts to have you in the Ashram have failed so far. I have given up hope." By January 1928, he was back to square one once again while trying to get her back to

Sabarmati Ashram. In the end, he expressed his helplessness in making her in-laws change their mind: "What can I say to you? I am almost helpless."[1] Prabhavati became so obsessed with Gandhiji that she would not tolerate separation from him even for a day. Even Gandhiji felt exacerbated and began to show his irritation. He was a great man but could not see his 'adopted daughter' suffer every minute. He asked her to write a letter to him everyday.

Phrases like 'I haven't given up hope', 'I am still trying', 'you must not be dejected', and 'You have to be brave and firm' recur like a musical theme in his correspondence. She continued to be depressed, worrisome and hysterical. Her hysteria was the highest manifestation of her desperation. She would remain unconscious for hours together. Miraculously, this would get cured the moment she would return to the ashram. Gandhiji and Prabhavati appeared to be co-conspirators who worked in unison to find ways and means of staying together.

Prabhavati had become so devoted to Bapu that her life did not exist beyond him. It came out in the first entry in her diary: "April 29. I woke up at 4 o' clock… I walked a little with Bapu. Then I prepared the water for his bath, cooked the food, ate. Rubbed some oil on Bapu's feet. Slept. Fanned Bapu. Cleaned up. Then sat a while with Bapu. Bapu asked me to translate Gujarati letter into Hindi, which I did… Went walking with Bapu… Massaged Bapu's feet… Went to sleep at 10 o' clock."[2]

Prabhavati was in a triangular interrelationship with Gandhiji, Braj Kishore and JP—a situation in which the husband was at a disadvantage. She drew upon the assistance of Gandhiji to cope with her in-laws. She cajoled JP, when he was in the US, to allow her to take the vow of *brahmacharya*. JP wanted that the decision should await his return from the United States. JP's return to India changed the situation. The distress between the husband and wife turned into confrontation. Gandhiji assumed the role of self-appointed referee with understandable bias. The theme of separation is recurrent in the exchange of letters between them from 1927–28 to 1938.

Consummation of Marriage

JP insisted on the consummation of marriage. Prabhavati had the least interest in the physical side of marriage. She was adamant in refusing JP. Her escape lay in returning to the care of her loving adopted father. So even after JP got back, Prabhavati found solace in Gandhiji and the ashram. Gandhiji was most considerate towards her, assuaging her misery on account of the physical separation between them.

He tried to instill courage in her by asking her to be firm and brave. He advised her to engage in social work to forget her misery. Nothing worked in actual practice, even when he assured her: "Your nervousness caused me pain."[3] Prabhavati was not at all assured because his letter let the cat out of the bag. There was no end to her worries. He posted this letter to her from far off Rangoon: "Why this listlessness? Why the crying? Why the sorrow?"[4]

If this was the situation during 1928 and 1929, it was equally worse two years later during 1931. He advised her repeatedly without being able to relieve her anxiety: "You should stop worrying unnecessarily. God does the worrying for us."[5] He put the finger at the right spot when he warned JP on 27 November 1930, that she was 'ailing' and faced with a moral crisis. He sought the advice of Dr Jivraj Mehta who was of the opinion, that: "if she finds it difficult to keep marital relations she should be able to abstain."[6]

Afraid of Shadows

Prabhavati considered the years from 1934 until the end of World War II as the 'time of loneliness, worry [and] estrangement'. Gandhiji's 'hostage from socialism' was like a wandering minstrel in his years of exile. JP moved from place to place for the cause of socialism. There is no mention if the desire to forget his private woes contributed to the larger public cause. He had developed a haggard look about him. He travelled for months together and would come back to Prabhavati emaciated, slovenly attired and 'looking like a *fakir*'.[7] His wife used to have sleepless nights worrying about him. The magic did not work because her maternal instincts were no substitute for her dormant wifely obligations. She felt exasperated with her husband

and in desperation confided in her mentor: "What would be the use of *my going? Jayaprakash cannot even spare a minute to talk.*"[8]

In late 1930s, Prabhavati and JP stayed in Allahabad. Gandhiji would send her letters on the address of the Searchlight office to escape the hawk eyes of her suspecting husband. About May 1937, when he was to pass through Allahabad on his way to other places, he did not have the courage to send for her to meet him at the railway station.

JP considered him the real spoilsport acting as an impenetrable wall. While Gandhiji was quite capable of provoking JP, Prabhavati too would nag her husband constantly. JP reciprocated in the same measure. Finally, constant nagging would work to her advantage. JP would let Prabhavati visit the ashram to spend some time with Gandhiji. JP would demand her return expeditiously. Gandhiji would try to raise her spirits but to no avail. This cat and mouse game went on endlessly. His real target was JP who would not confront him directly. Thus the play acting between the three of them went on endlessly.

Sandwiched between JP and Gandhiji, Prabhavati ended up as a pathological wreck. Hitherto Gandhiji considered himself qualified to provide therapy to worrisome Prabhavati. It refused to work now. On the contrary, the Prabha effect had begun to work upon him. While helping her to attain peace, he had lost his own peace. And so had JP. The reason for this state of affairs was obvious. JP had started applying pressure and had become impatient. While she dared not throw pots and pans at JP (as she did during her unmarried days) she could cock a snook at him by resisting him through impenetrable silence. She had learned her lessons in *satyagraha* well.

Gandhiji's mind was working feverishly to rescue the damsel in distress. He would have been the happiest if JP were to release Prabhavati from her conjugal responsibility, and further, allowed her to be permanently stationed at the Ashram. JP would have none of it. Gandhiji encouraged Prabhavati to speak her mind to JP. He was cheeky enough to advise Prabhavati: "You should tell Jayaprakash that the only treatment for you is to stay with me."[9]

The above letter was posted by him from distant Utmanzai in the North-West Frontier Province(NWFP).

Little Girl's Secrets

All these made no impact whatsoever. Finally, he appealed to Prabhavati in the name of Ba: "Ba asks: What! Prabha will not come to stay with me or will she never come for my sake? Write to her."[10]

Prabhavati had begun to mark her letters private, secret and confidential. Several times she requested him to tear her letters immediately after reading them. Gandhiji felt uncomfortable with such requests. After all he had always claimed to be a transparent person. But Prabhavati was like a little girl who shared her innermost thoughts with him and wanted that no one else should know of her personal troubles. Whenever Gandhiji received a special request, he complied without quibbling over it. She did not want Jayaprakash or her in-laws to read her mind. After a while, Gandhiji began to feel exasperated with her. He took it upon himself to admonish her.

Prabhavati worried Gandhiji to no end but he felt exhilarated while handling her problems. She inspired him and made him laugh. The national adulations he received did not fill the psychological vacuum. She provided Gandhiji with lighter moments that were otherwise missing in his busy routine.

To talk to her about marriage was like showing a red rag to a bull. Brij Krishna Chandiwala wrote to Prabhavati seeking her advice about marital matters. The letter hurt her to no end even when the request was made in an innocent way. It reminded her of her unhappy and tortuous marriage. Gandhiji gently rebuked Chandiwala for his unintended impropriety.

Gandhiji was, however, proud of her with her warts and all. He was satisfied that she followed him faithfully with no questions asked. It was a true guru–shishya relation based on personal loyalty. Poor JP could not do anything.

'Polygamous' JP

Gandhiji worked feverishly to find a solution to her woes. Like a clever lawyer, he prefaced his case with the following remarks to JP: "Prabha came to me with your consent as well as of Braj Kishore Babu's… True, Prabha does not give you conjugal, because by her very nature, she cannot… Now tell what should I do."[11] He came out with half a solution and recommended that JP should contract another marriage and free Prabhavati of all obligations. He backed his advice with scriptural sanctions: "It was no *adharma* contracting another marriage."[12]

JP recalled Gandhiji's advice as 'ruthless logic'. He ended up observing *brahmacharya* by force of circumstances. Gandhiji was in the seventh heaven because the situation had turned in his favour. It suited him either way: "Therefore, it is my firm [belief]... she should be emancipated. And, you should remarry. I do not find any harm in it... How can your concupiscence be restrained from committing [marital] rape? You consider [it] just essential and beneficial for soul... In my opinion [you will set an example for society] if you [remarry]... Several youths commit rape on their wives."[13]

JP did not trust Gandhiji. He would listen to him patiently. He would not react in his presence but ultimately followed his own way. How helpless Gandhiji felt in such circumstances is indicated in his letter to Vallabhbhai Patel: "I know his charge against me. But I am helpless. He seems to have calmed down a little now."[14] JP happened to be in Bombay and had to see Gandhiji. Prabhavati was in the entourage of Gandhiji.

JP would turn up everyday and talk over his domestic life with his wife and avoid meeting Gandhiji. The fact, however, remained that JP could have burst at any moment. His *ardhangini* (better half) had been taken away from him and his friends made fun of him at the Lahore Congress (1929). Gandhiji added to his woes by suggesting that he contract another marriage and free Prabhavati of marital obligations. Even Prabhavati did not approve of the preposterous proposal and protested.

Exploring Reconciliation

Gandhiji tried to make Prabhavati join hands with her husband in pursuit of her *dharma*. Prabhavati did not like the suggestion but did abide by him. Her bidding goodbye to Gandhiji during the Working Committee meeting made a pathetic sight. There were tears streaming down her face: "Gandhi told her: 'No, go, stay with him, try to understand each other. You must go. Think of Ashram afterwards.'"[15]

Gandhiji's idea was to bring about reconciliation between husband and wife. He had seen enough argumentation between the two of them.

He wanted her to win over JP with love and affection. Gandhiji considered it best to send Prabhavati to JP.

But the gulf between Gandhiji and JP could not be filled. Gandhiji tried to quieten him with his sweet nothings. There were occasions when he talked of the rights of women to their own bodies and their conjugal rights in absolute terms. Those were, however, passing thoughts which were never pushed to their logical end: "I appreciate your pain... your distress thus caused distress to me... your desire to live with Prabhavati is natural. In this connection I don't want to keep her in Wardha. Your life is becoming drab... We shall discuss this matter when we meet."[16]

Prabhavati was very upset because of the tussle going on between the two. She was in Wardha on 26 August 1934, and had received a telegram from JP asking her to return forthwith. She went rushing to Bapu and had a long chat with him. He told her to have faith in him. Her restlessness continued. JP reached Wardha on 8 October. There is a pathetic entry in her diary describing the state of her mind: "Jayaprakashji arrived today. I feel very sad and worried, and for this reason do not write much. I do not understand what is happening. I meditate on God. Give me peace. During the massage, talked to Bapu a little."[17]

As usual she went rushing to Bapu who explained her *dharma* to her. Bapu and JP talked alone keeping Prabhavati out of the reckoning. Gandhiji employed all his skills to read JP. He agreed to a compromise formula. Prabhavati would stay at the ashram for a year after which she would return to her husband.

Gandhiji assumed that things were working out satisfactorily. He was happy and assumed that the couple would live happily thereafter. He shot off a letter to Prabhavati bearing good tidings: "It was also good that you went and stayed with JP for some time. If, similarly, the marriage is also settled, all your problems will have been solved. See that you don't fall ill before that."[18]

The self-appointed nature cure faddist advised Prabhavati to eat *neem* leaves and take hip baths and go on morning walks regularly. It didn't help matters because JP was demanding his conjugal rights. The simmering resentment continued on both sides. The health of her father had deteriorated. It prompted her to move to Bihar and spend a few days with her husband.

JP was irreconcilable. In utter exasperation, Gandhiji wrote to her that he had done his best to placate JP and if he did not respond what could be done except throwing one's hands in despair? Without mentioning JP and Prabhavati by name, he suggested a solution in his letter to Vijaya N Patel: "Even if either husband or wife desires their relations to be like those of a brother and sister but cannot live like that in the same house, it will be their *dharma* to be separate."[19] This advice was in line with the suggestion to JP at Lahore to contract another marriage.

Jayaprakash at Sea

In 1936, Prabhavati tried her best to placate JP during her short stays with him. Prabhavati was expected to stay with her husband permanently as discussed with Gandhiji earlier. The issue at stake was not merely living together but conjugal rights of the husband. JP felt estranged. She was, however, in no position to yield ground to him on that score. He refused to be served by Prabhavati and would not take the food cooked by her. Gandhiji advised her to move out to her parental house and she followed it.

Prabhavati was in a bad shape. She had begun to have fits. Gandhiji tried to lift her spirits. Gandhiji and not JP was the centre of her universe. She was impatient to get back to Wardha. She was anxious to share her secrets with him. In turn, he was anxious to probe into the inner recesses of her mind. He was, afterall, her father-confessor.

Gandhiji in his letter of 24 May 1936,[20] advised Prabhavati to avoid being frank with JP who was impervious to being persuaded. His new strategy was nothing short of confronting JP frontally. He intended to corner him through a sudden panzerian movement.

He had no objection to her return to the ashram provided she had JP's permission. He advised her to deal with her husband with 'firmness and calm mind' and tell him all. In other words, JP had failed to realise the depth of her feelings in choosing ashram life. Gandhiji said: "He will calm down without doubt, if he is convinced that you have in you no such thing as sexual desire. Your freedom from desire should put out the fire of his, just as water puts out any fire. Why should you be afraid and lose peace of mind, when you do have faith in God?"[21]

His strategy failed because Prabhavati lacked the courage to face JP in this context. The situation did not improve even after two years.

Gandhiji told her in 1938: "The only treatment for you is to stay with me."[22]

In the end it was not Prabhavati but Gandhiji who chickened out. Her tension had travelled to him. He was burdened with many things and could not concentrate on improving Prabhavati's relations with her husband. He started persuading her to be a good traditional Hindu wife who was to follow in the footsteps of her husband faithfully.

JP's Mentor

JP had no reservations in accepting Gandhiji as his mentor. He was thus a father figure to both him and Prabhavati. It was a relation of regard, affection and circumspection. JP fought out with him over his conjugal rights, but the skirmishes between them were within the limits of propriety.

Initially, they began on a welcome note. JP was fresh from the US. He had already made an impression on Gandhiji through his 'sincere letter' sent to him in November 1929. Gandhi was particularly enamoured of his unusual frankness. He shot off a welcome letter to Jayaprakash: "I cherish the wish that your marital life may be an ideal one. About Prabhavati's attitude of indifference we shall talk when we meet."[23]

His best wishes for a happy married life proved to be illusory. Confrontation became the order of the day. Prabhavati had begun to have frequent fits of hysteria in which she often lost consciousness for hours together. Gandhiji pleaded with JP to send Prabhavati back to the ashram. That was the shortest road to her recovery, he assured JP.

He also underlined for JP the fact of Prabhavati being confronted with a moral crisis. He reminded JP of the inalienable rights of women: "The difficult question before you is that of freedom of women. If Prabhavati has as much freedom as you, you must concede to her the right to think for herself."[24]

Forgetting Prabhavati

Gandhiji was keen that Prabhavati be released of her familial obligations so that she could assume larger public duties. Gandhiji had an advantage as he knew JP's financial vulnerability. He pestered Gandhiji for financial assistance, who in turn did not hesitate to ask prickly questions: "To what extent it is right for you, considering your communist beliefs, to accept [monetary] help from me. I cannot say." He rendered the final insult to Jayaprakash by reminding him: "It has never seemed to me right for anyone to go begging for loans."[25] Gandhiji reminded JP that his entire expenses had been underwritten by the Birla family. Obviously he was using Prabhavati as the bargaining counter.

JP was a doughty fighter. Come what may, he wanted Prabhavati and therefore he sent off a telegram to Wardha asking her to come back to him. He was furious when Gandhi advised him 'about forgetting Prabhavati'. It was in this context that Gandhiji modified his demand by asking JP "to forget her just for one year". The Mahatma was not keen to keep his promise after one year: "I am in quandary. Prabha does not wish to leave either me or the Ashram. How then can I push her out? I want that Prabha should follow you about and the differences which have cropped up between you two should be patched up. But if Prabha cherishes certain ideals, these ideals are apparently different from yours. For this I am certainly responsible. Having lived with me, my ideas and my conduct have certainly made an impression on her. I do not know what is right to do."[26]

Having declared a state of emergency against Jayaprakash, he turned to Prabhavati: "Why are you frightened? Is Jayaprakash at peace? Is... Jawaharlal? Or Rajendra Babu? We are all dependent on other as much as we are independent."[27] By this time Gandhiji was able to outwit him once again. Poor Prabhavati was transferred, albeit temporarily, to the custody of her husband. Physically she was with Jayaprakash, but her mind was still mortgaged to Gandhiji.

Conjugal Rights

The year 1936 was the most turbulent in the relations between the three of them. The wrangling between husband and wife intensified. JP carried his tale of woes to Jamnalal Bajaj. He talked to Jamnalal about the undue influence exercised by Gandhiji over his wife, which was responsible for the virtual breakdown of their marriage.

To be fair to Gandhi, Prabhavati repeatedly went on record saying she adopted *brahmacharya* as her credo entirely of her own volitions: "I had decided to adopt *brahmacharya* of my own free will entirely uninfluenced by Gandhiji. In fact he had tried to dissuade me. He would repeatedly tell me to go and join Jayaprakash, look after him and serve him. He repeatedly said so in a series of letters to me. I took the vow on my own. I had been inclined in this direction since my childhood. My stay at the Ashram reaffirmed my resolve."[28]

Gandhi felt so anguished that he was prepared to ask Prabhavati to give up visiting rights to him. He decided to be spiteful to Jayaprakash: "True, Prabha did not give you conjugal satisfaction, because by her very nature she cannot. She was free from passion even before she came to me. We can go by what she says. She told me this repeatedly and firmly, and I accepted her word. Now tell me what I should do. If you want that Prabha should give up visiting me or writing to me, for your peace of mind. I will accept this reconstruction."[29]

JP would not reply to his letters and chose to be mum about Prabhavati. The situation came to such a pass that Gandhi lost track of him. While visiting Wardha, JP would avoid meeting Gandhiji. He would reluctantly meet him in the end to complete the formality. On such occasions, Gandhiji would confront him with letters or telegrams from Prabhavati indicating her keenness to get back to Wardha. They found direct communication difficult. Gandhiji informed Prabhavati: "He is not a person whom I or anyone can stop from following his own bent."[30]

This state of affairs continued till 1941. JP had promised to come to see Gandhiji in December 1940 but he did not turn up. Also, he did not offer any explanation as if to snub him. Gandhiji asked Prabhavati about his whereabouts. Finally, JP's letter came, expressing dissatisfaction quite openly. Gandhiji opened his mind to Prabhavati: "He seems to be somewhat dissatisfied with what I am doing. But then was he [ever] satisfied?… Tell him that though he remains dissatisfied [with me], I will be fully satisfied [with him]."[31]

While in detention at Dealali Detention Camp, the acerbic JP had a dig at both Gandhiji and Prabhavati by adding fire to his communication of 28 October 1941, to Gandhiji. "I was surprised as well as pained to know about Prabhavati. Our relationship was never based on harmony of thoughts, then why should she be so disturbed over my ideas. You may kindly make her understand."[32]

Battle of Wits

The battle between them had turned into a battle of wits. There was a merciful intervention of the Quit India movement. Each one of them had separate political paths cut out for them. Prabhavati was in Bombay at the time when Gandhiji was arrested on 9 August 1942. Prabhavati had an inkling of the developments and had conveyed confidential information to him. Gandhiji did not believe her and told her that he was due to return to Wardha soon. She was unlucky as she was not in his company at the time of arrest. Sushila Nayyar, Sarojini Naidu and Mirabehn were with him and were arrested.

They had the rare opportunity of spending about two years in the company of Gandhiji at the Aga Khan Palace internment camp. Prabhavati had to stay out for the next two years. In fact, she returned to Patna while the Bihar police kept on searching for her in Bombay.

After his release from prison, Gandhiji was involved with his *brahmacharya* experiments in which Prabhavati was also involved. The experiments had to be stopped due to public controversies surrounding them. Gradually, Prabhavati lost track of him. There is very little mention of Prabhavati to be found in the post-1945 period. There is hardly any reference to Prabhavati in his subsequent writings. His diary of 16 May 1947 contained the following laconic entry: "From tomorrow Prabha will come for massage."[33]

JP became a prominent political star in independent India. He was no longer a rebel without a cause. He had become a respectable and prominent public figure and a strong voice of the Left. He was the only person who addressed Jawaharlal Nehru as '*bhai*'. Eventually, Prabhavati was reconciled to her husband. Prabhavati was his dedicated companion and his *ardhangini* for 25 years after Gandhiji's assassination.

Epitaph

Her last meeting with Gandhiji took place under the tragic circumstances of JP deciding to leave the Congress and form his own party. It was 29 January 1948, a day before his death. They met him at the Birla House in Delhi. Gandhiji did not approve of his decision but expressed faith in JP's integrity. Prabhavati touched his feet but there was no smile on his face.

Jayaprakash left for Bombay and Prabhavati went on her way to Patna. The husband-wife couple was not present when Gandhiji died. Prabhavati lived for another twenty five years. She was always found in JP's company—whether at public platforms or private meetings. She believed the 'bad part of their life', 'worse than her imprisonment in jail' was over: [In] "recollecting those years, she was so moved as to…[say] in 1969 with tears in her eyes that Gandhiji would be happy today, if he could be alive to see how she and Jayaprakash had come together in later years."[34]

Gandhiji's constant admonition to Prabhavati that 'Jayaprakash isn't married to you', no longer held water. She passed away at 67 on 15 April 1973. Somebody described JP's condition thus: "He felt he had no zest or interest in life, that the very will to live was dead within him. He continued with his political work to the extent that his health permitted, but as a matter of duty, from which he could draw any spiritual satisfaction."[35] At least Prabhavati, JP and Gandhiji had come to terms with each other.

Legacy

Prabhavati's stoic character came out during her last years. Suffering was her badge of honour throughout her life. She fell a victim to cancer during her last years. This did not show on her face and she was at her best during those days. Writhing in pain and completely immobilized, she cheerfully supervised arrangements for his nephew's marriage. The marriage ceremonies were predated, but *Yamaraja* chose to cheat her by a mere whisker. The last famous words articulated by her were "Bapu… Ba".

Her death finally reconciled JP with Gandhiji. He shed many a tear and thought after going through the correspondence between Gandhiji and Prabhavati "Why was I harsh with Gandhi?"[36]

Her legacy to JP consisted of two boxes containing her marriage apparel, *sindoor* box, photographs, her diaries and personal correspondence. The despondent husband went over the lovelorn letters to her from his US days. In utter dismay, he started tearing them off. It was hard to dissuade him from doing so. Sixteen letters of her closest friend Kamala Nehru—each letter no less than four pages—narrating her tale of woes were rescued for posterity. JP handed over those letters to Indira Gandhi who chose to put them under lock and key for good.

CHAPTER 16

Kanchan: The *Duvidha* Shah

Munnalal Shah and his wife Kanchan Shah were part of the *brahmacharya* experiment for married couples. Living in the precincts of the ashram, they were subjected to closest scrutiny.

Gandhiji had worked out a set of detailed guidelines on how to practice celibacy while still in marriage. He regretted that he could not be a life-long *brahmachari* and drew immense pleasure to see Sucheta and Acharya Kripalani, Prabhavati and Jayaprakash Narayan and even Kamala Nehru observing *brahmacharya*. However, there were times when he would fail in his endeavour.

One of his closest associates, Dattatreya Balkrishna Kalelkar, confessed long after Gandhiji was dead that he had failed in his effort to remain a married *brahmachari*: "I continued to sleep with my wife until she died, some years ago. I embraced her, I kissed her, I fondled her, but I had to deny her the ultimate satisfaction of intercourse, 'The greater the temptation, the greater the renunciation', Bapu always said…I have to admit that I myself and others felt torn between my duty to my wife and my duty to my view of *brahmacharya*, because part of me believes that sex is an appetite, like eating, that should not be denied."[1]

Role Models

Munnalal G Shah was a lawyer by profession and an all purpose manager of the ashram. Gandhiji wanted to have Munnalal and Kanchan as his role models. He expected them to set an example for others.

He was most considerate to Kanchan. She and Abha Gandhi refused to be part of his *brahmacharya* experiments during 1945. This is reflected in his letter of 6 March 1945, to Munnalal. It was followed by another letter requesting Munnalal 'not to publicise Kanchan's name'. Consequently, Kanchan's bold refusal created bad blood between him and the couple: "You are not Kanchan's owner, as she is not yours. But all these years I have not been able to make you understand this."[2]

Here was a stream of do's and don'ts flowing endlessly from him for the harassed Shahs. "You should not touch each other. You shall not talk to each other. You shall not work together. You shall not take service from each other." If all this did not work, Munnalal was advised to move out of the ashram. He was also threatened with purgatory for violating his married *brahmacharya* vow. There was, however, a leeway provided for Munnalal before he was to take the final jump: "If you think that the self-control suggested above is beyond your capacity, you should give up the ambition to cultivate it."[3]

Cheating Act

His set of instructions was wearisome. It was only the beginning of the hurdle race that lasted for ten long years. After all, Gandhiji was an indefatigable machine that never stopped working. In his scheme of things, it was best to keep Munnalal and Kanchan away from each other. In a weaker moment, he allowed the pining couple to get away together from his watchful eyes. Normal instincts took over and Munnalal and Kanchan joined and mated as it came naturally to them.

Gandhiji realised rather too late that he was foxed. The knives were sharpened for the poor (and frightened) couple. His cryptic comment was: "I understand about your fall." Lest their example be followed by the rest of the community, he warned Munnalal to desist from broadcasting the violation of his *brahmacharya* vow. His imagery had come to full play: "You were mentally meeting her everyday. It was better that you should meet physically also, if it had to be so."[4]

Having gone so far in his generosity, he withdrew with his left hand what he had offered with his right hand. He put an enabling clause to frustrate rather than facilitate the union: "Surely living together does not necessarily mean sharing the same bed."

In view of the raging controversy within and outside the ashram, he was constrained to take permission of Munnalal for involving Kanchan in his *brahmacharya* experiment: "Should she avoid touching a man even for the sake of serving him? Tell me hesitatingly what you think."[5]

The Shah couple had been singled out for special attention. He found that Munnalal Shah was subservient and prepared to carry out his orders. While Kanchan was not pliant, he expected Munnalal to make her fall in line. Moreover, Munnalal could be conveniently kept under constant surveillance.

It was Kanchan who had resisted the practice of physical *brahmacharya* for married couples. Gandhiji decided to appeal to Kanchan by talking to her directly. At one stage he complimented her by placing all the blame at the doorstep of Munnalal: "My sympathy is always with you. Munnalal has not conquered passion. If he had, yours also would have disappeared."[6]

He also wrote a letter to Munnalal on the same date. He blamed him and doubted if Munnalal had 'become completely passionless like Shiva' and, indeed, "this was beyond [his] capacity."

Physical *Brahmacharya*

His efforts to tame the Munnalal–Kanchan duo had failed but Gandhiji did not lose heart. In the middle of 1946, he once again tutored them to observe married celibacy consisting of three sets of rules: (1) no touch, (2) no physical craving, and (3) no sleeping together. He also tempted them with the offer of staying together in the ashram. He thought his offer was generous because he realised that otherwise: "You will be listless all the time, be unhappy and make others unhappy,"[7]

If this did not work, he was prepared for both of them to live in a separate house away from the ashram. Preach as he might about the virtues of physical *brahmacharya* or display publicly Munnalal-Kanchan duo as his role models, albeit reluctantly, for married couples, he knew that his panacea would not work, more likely than not it was bound to rebound on him.

Munnalal was under so much pressure from the countervailing forces of Gandhiji and Kanchan that he became flustered. He could not cope with his mentor's demands, but, at the same time he was mighty afraid of defying him. Also, he was unable to cope with his demanding wife. She told Gandhiji that she wanted her conjugal rights to be restored.

In the end, the old man was prepared to come down halfway. So he wrote to Munnalal: "I do not say, or wish, that you should go to Kanchan. But if she or you feel such a desire, I would encourage you."[8]

Munnalal at Sea

Munnalal was planning to be away from ashram for two months, hence Gandhiji wanted the answer to his question. Gandhiji was blunt and explicit in his expressions while discussing sexual matters. His expressions were also full of taunts for the comfort of Munnalal: "Kanchan does desire sexual pleasure. You also have the desire. It would not be anything strange if you lived together and satisfied your desire."[9]

Gandhiji had denied the satisfaction of legitimate natural instincts due to a married couple: "Self-suppression is not going to help. Hence do what is natural for you. Thwarting Kanchan's desire will harm her. She is good and has the spirit of service. She will lose these things in the end." His letter of 19 August 1945, to Munnalal, was followed by a long chat with Kanchan Shah. The poor girl was under so much psychological pressure from Gandhiji: "As regards Kanchan, I do believe her complaint to be justified. I clearly see that it is your *dharma* to settle down somewhere with her."[10]

While Munnalal had taken the vow of married celibacy, Gandhiji knew it would be violated soon if Kanchan and Munnalal lived together. He was now advising the couple on do's and don'ts to be observed by them in their present state of married *brahmacharya* bliss: "If your self-control breaks, it will be you who will break it. She will neither resist nor tempt you. Why will it profit you to be afraid of yourself?"

Gandhiji realised that Kanchan and Munnalal were in tandem with each other although they took different positions before him. They also knew he was soft with Kanchan and they exploited this weakness to their advantage. Whenever arguments failed, her tears won the day for her.

Craving for Sex

Gandhiji was very explicit in sexual expressions in his correspondence with both Munnalal and Kanchan Shah. His original expressions have been moderated in English translation. Munnalal had frustrated him by his policy of masterly inactivity: "You will not be able to overcome your love, or attachment, or whatever you call it, for Kanchan." There were strings attached to his generosity: "You crave for the pleasure of the flesh. So does she if she can have them. But she is pining for them."[11]

He concluded on a high note saying that nothing was reprehensible about conjugal relations, as he put it graphically: "in your desire for sexual pleasure." He concentrated all his ire over Munnalal, his convenient scapegoat: "You wish to soar high but that is beyond your capacity."

Nearly five years had passed but there was no improvement in the situation. Munnalal was still indecisive. This added to his frustration with Munnalal-Kanchan duo. The flustered Munnalal had eminently succeeded in confusing Gandhiji in the end. Finally, Munnalal had his revenge. Now Gandhiji was prepared to leave Munnalal to his resources. Kanchan had also begun to be painted in the blackest colour: "Kanchan is on fire. Who else but you can quench this fire?" He could also discern very clearly: "And yet fire is burning her up."

At last, Gandhiji had seen through her game. He felt that this shameful hussy had 'married to gratify her passion'. He decided to conclude this letter to Munnalal with a fatherly piece of advice: "Is it not your *dharma*, now, to satisfy her? If you were completely free from passion, I would have nothing to tell you. After giving Kanchan the gift of children you may observe *brahmacharya*, or you should calm her not with anger but pure love."[12]

Blackmail

Now the question that worried him was not sexual rectitude between married couples but the possibility of couples coming to live together with all kinds of possibilities inherent in the situation. That Munnalal and Kanchan would come to live together disturbed the equanimity of Gandhiji to no end. Now that Kanchan had formally put the suggestion before him, should the permission be granted? Kanchan was anxious to go to Malikananda accompanied by her husband, who was denied permission to accompany her.

Gandhiji kept hammering into Munnalal's head the dangers of accompanying his wife to another place: "Either forget that Kanchan is your wife or start living with her."[13]

The Shah couple was properly policed. Munnalal suspected that his letters to Kanchan were opened. He was even admonished by Gandhiji for marking his letters 'private'. He continued putting hurdles in the way of the Shahs to set up a separate household. He had to give in when Kanchan decided to force the issue. He had no choice but to yield to her: "I accept your notice. I have already told [Munnalal] that you should set up house."

Gandhiji, however, continued to hold the Munnalal–Kanchan duo in a state of suspended animation. He could depend upon the indecisiveness of Munnalal:

"It will be enough if you do not make up your mind that you cannot live with Kanchan."[14]

He would placate Kanchan, but kept Munnalal confused and indecisive. His words of sympathy to Kanchan read so hollow:

"I feel sorry for you; and equally for Munnalal. I have written to him and told in so many words that he should set up house with you and that, if the two of you cannot voluntarily observe self-control, you may have children."[15]

His generosity always came with a price. He never forgot or forgave the Shahs for defying him.

Delivering a Baby

Gandhiji repeatedly told Munnalal that breaking of the vow was nothing short of committing *adharma*. While Munnalal was indecisive, Kanchan placed Gandhiji on the defensive: "One must not be in a hurry to accuse anybody."[16]

She confided in Sushila Nayyar and told her of her intention to live separately and have children. When informed about Kanchan's determination, as usual Gandhiji issued a warning to the vulnerable Munnalal: "It seems to me that a separate establishment for you two and *brahmacharya* go ill together."

The relations between Kanchan and Gandhiji had touched rock bottom: "My own view is that after having [Kanchan] in the same bed with me once it was wrong to discontinue it through ignorance. I do not know who forbade her. I spoke neither to you nor to her about this. I am mentioning to you for the first time. This is all I wish to say. My experiment, as you know, has been suspended."[17]

However, he soon changed and began to feel sorry for Kanchan. Frustration was written all over her face. This time Gandhiji decided to be magnanimous and ordered Munnalal: "You must not have Kanchan living separately."[18]

There was no solution to her predicament, but none was intended by him. Munnalal was like a mechanical toy which could be wound up or unwound to the desired extent. He responded to the myriad moods of Gandhiji in the most predictable manner possible. This time the diktat was intended for the pliant Munnalal: "But one thing is clear, namely, that you should tell Kanchan in plain words that you don't look upon her as your wife and that she also should not look upon him as your husband... Indeed, you two should not live in the same place."[19]

Benign Mood

Within six months Gandhiji was benign again. The bracing air of Mussoorie, where he was stationed during May 1946, was one of the reasons. Meanwhile, he had made up with Kanchan. He had taken her along on his trip to Sodepur (in Bengal).

Gandhiji was in a wonderful mood. He wrote to Munnalal from Guwahati: "She is a simple-hearted but very much of a child also. As she grows up in age, she does not correspondingly grow in understanding."[20]

He could not resist having a dig at Munnalal for thwarting Kanchan's normal development. Happy times were back for her. After reaching Delhi from Simla, he conveyed the happy tidings to Munnalal in allowing the duo to set up a separate household:

"Would you like to start as soon as possible, or are you content that you have the promise."[21]

Gandhiji had taken Kanchan on his travels to Bengal, Assam and Madras. This time he invited her to visit him at Poona. To make sure that everything worked in Kanchan's favour, he wrote to Munnalal: "In short you should know that I have given my word to Kanchan that as long as she is firm in her desire to live separately with you I shall support her in her desire."[22]

He went to the extent of telling Munnalal expansively: "I see your spiritual progress only through her happiness."[23]

Assessing Munnalal

Munnalal G Shah was a young man who joined hands with Gandhiji, assuming that an idyllic atmosphere prevailed in the ashram. Munnalal soon discovered the contrary. Gandhiji himself concurred with Munnalal on this score as early as 16 May 1937: "There is truth in your complaint that Segaon has become a *dharmashala*. But what can I do? I feel helpless."[24]

Munnalal began to feel the heat soon after he joined the ashram. He began to lose his peace of mind. At one time Gandhiji even advised him to get away from the ashram for the time being and to proceed to Aurobindo Ashram in Pondicherry. Munnalal found the atmosphere at the Aurobindo Ashram congenial. He sent for Kanchan to join him there. The peace of mind that he achieved at Aurobindo and Ramana Maharishi ashrams was not adequate to sustain the battering he was to receive from Gandhiji from 1939 to 1947. Yet, Munnalal was an honourable man in the Gandhian entourage.

Munnalal was extremely devoted to Gandhiji and his cause. He was a selfless and self-effacing worker who worked quietly and unobtrusively. He could withstand any punishment. Gandhiji gave a privileged treatment to Kanchan. Kanchan was possessive of Munnalal. Relations between the three went up and down all the time. Munnalal could afford to view everything with equanimity. No-holds barred hostilities were resumed among Munnalal, Kanchan and Gandhiji soon after her pregnancy was announced.

Pregnant Kanchan

Kanchan's pregnancy was a blow to Gandhiji. He realised that he had been fooled by his associates. Munnalal, the proclaimed *brahmachari*, had cheated him over his *brahmacharya* vow. Gandhiji was furious as his idealistic scheme had fallen to the ground.

Was he being impractical? As Indira Gandhi was to point out to him in her own context, he was. She said: "You can ask a couple not to get married that makes sense to me. But when they are just married, to ask them to live a life of celibacy makes no sense. It can result only in bitterness and unhappiness."[25]

His entire ire was directed against Munnalal whom he now called a fake *brahmachari*. Gandhiji expected Kanchan to "overcome… sexual urge for three years at least."[26]

The real bashing was reserved for her husband: "Can the fact of pregnancy be concealed. Surely you have committed no sin."[27] Lest Munnalal should reach a comfortable conclusion from this assertion of Gandhi's, he was left in doubt as to what the old man really thought of him: "And even if you have committed a sin, you should not commit it by hiding the fact of Kanchan's pregnancy."

He spurned Munnalal: "You have committed no sin, but you cherish a great pride." Munnalal had made a laughing stock not only of himself but also of Gandhiji. Thus both the guru and the *chela* (disciple) were in the dock: "Everybody thought that you were a strong-willed *brahmachari*."[28]

As on earlier occasions, Gandhiji's anger died with time. He came to terms with reality. He continued enquiring from Munnalal about Kanchan's enigmatic silence, who would not write to him. By February 1947, his anger had fizzled out. He had decided to convey his blessings to the expectant mother: "May her delivery pass off without difficulty."[29]

He directed Chimanlal N Shah to make special arrangements for pregnant Kanchan. His disenchantment with the Shahs ended at the time of the safe delivery of a baby girl in June 1947. He wrote to Kanchan Shah in his own hand: "I hope you are now content. Munnalal is in your hands, and certainly you are in his. If you understand this, it will be more than enough."

All Victorious

All three of them appeared to have won. Kanchan had the baby, Munnalal had played by the rules of her game and sired his first child and Gandhi had acted as a gentleman in blessing Kanchan. He had also yielded to her in the end. He supplicated her to return Munnalal to his custody. Suddenly Munnalal had become indispensable in his scheme of things. Gandhi expected Munnalal to return to the ashram and take charge of it: "If the ashram does not improve, how can Sevagram improve? If Sevagram does not, how can India."[30]

Kanchan's motherhood and the recognition conceded to Munnalal by Gandhiji came due to the baby. The incident indicated that Gandhi was a gentleman with a big heart and his anger was a mere ruse and charade to hide his immense affection for his associates.

Honeymoons never last too long. It must have been the briefest honeymoon between Gandhiji and Munnalal Shah. Munnalal asked his permission to join him but Gandhiji was not willing:

"Your striving is false. Your attachment to Kanchan will not go by your keeping away from her. Nor even by your living with her."[31]

But there was a happy ending to this letter. He coyly suggested a name for the new-born baby: "What is wrong with the name Jivram?"

After about two months, his letters turned venomous. Not even Kanchan was spared: "You have not fallen with Kanchan. You have both risen and fallen. If anybody is to be blamed, I am ready to take the blame. I understand your attitude of mind. It remains the same as it was. Never mind if you have more children but be calm."[32]

Teacher and his Disciple

Their relations were not necessarily antagonistic. They were like a traditional guru (teacher) and *shishya* (disciple) in which belabouring was considered part of the learning process. The *shishya* would not mind it in the Indian context. On the contrary, he may consider berating an honour and privilege. This was precisely the reason why Munnalal stuck loyally to Gandhiji through thick and thin.

Gradually there emerged a unique portrait of Gandhiji's in his association with the Munnalal–Kanchan duo. Gandhiji was so human and childlike that he responded spontaneously to a situation, reacted uncomfortably and calmed down in no time and reflected a great degree of intimacy rarely displayed outside his intimate circle. His ashram was not only as anarchical as a large joint family in India but also showed remarkable cohesiveness and unity underlying its substratum. The ashram indeed constituted his whole world. It was also a microcosm of the world around it. It was no monastery and it was no patch on his Tolstoy and Phoenix ashrams in South Africa. It was more of a *dharamshala* (caravanserai) with visitors coming and going constantly. The fact, however, remained that the Ashram had a solid core which reflected its *corps d'espirit*. The Munnalals of the world belonged to that core.

Retrospective Gandhi

Gandhiji had become introspective and had mellowed down. He began to see virtues which he had failed to notice earlier. Even Munnalal began to receive kudos. For the first time he talked to Munnalal with all the humility at his command: "If you wish to stay with me, you should bear with me and accept me as I am."

But he found it difficult to come to terms with Munnalal. Too much of Munnalal was upsetting him. He reminded Gandhiji of his own failures and all the pent up feelings of anger, hatred and intense dislike erupted from time to time: "I do not look upon you as a child, but you behave like one."[33]

All that made him ruminative of his past. In his letter of 6 March 1945 to Munnalal, he went over his whole life and mission. He described himself as 'a man of character' who would never compromise and bear the consequences, come what may. He described himself as a man of strict principles: "I am as much against compromise as I am for it."

Gandhi clawed his way through the whole tribe of his friends, associates and well wishers on the *brahmacharya* issue. He continued to be adamant and promised to get back to the practice in future: "If I completely give up sleeping together, my *brahmacharya* will be put to shame."

This happened to be his constant refrain. He also believed whatever he did had God's sanction. So there was a degree of finality about his actions. He was the judge and the prosecutor at the same time.

Munnalal was fortunate to be his medium for passing on his definitive message to the world. He concluded the letter to Munnalal on a defiant note: "Thus, I am what I am... What else may I give up? I cannot give up thinking."[34]

Last Days

Earlier, he had rejected Munnalal's request to visit him at New Delhi, with much disdain. Exactly after a month, Gandhiji wrote to him asking him to visit New Delhi, with great pleasure. He thanked Munnalal for all the sacrifices he had made on his behalf. But while extending the invitation, Gandhiji could not resist the temptation to have a dig at his notorious indecisiveness:

"If living together with Kanchan you cannot free yourselves from passion, you are not likely to do so living apart. You should be able to do so only it requires mental self-control of the highest order."[35] And added: "She is right in believing you to be weak."

This was his way of saying goodbye to the most genial person in the Gandhian entourage. Nobody loved him, not even his wife, but everybody ended up loving him.

SECTION VII

Odyssey of Sushila Nayyar

CHAPTER 17

Triangular Syndrome

Mahadev Desai, Pyarelal and Sushila Nayyar constituted Gandhiji's triumvirate. Mahadev Desai (1892–1942) joined him as his secretary in August 1917. Gandhiji thought highly of Mahadev and often referred to him as his 'heir'. He placed him at par with his former associates like Sonja Schlesin, Henry Polak and Maganlal Gandhi but singled him out for three qualities—'regularity, fidelity and intelligence'.[1] Gandhiji would compare him to 'a poem of justice'.

Pyarelal was the second member of this triumvirate. He left college to join the non-cooperation movement in 1919 and gravitated towards Gandhiji in 1920. He worked closely with Mahadev in 1942. Sushila Nayyar, the third member, was a medical doctor and Pyarelal's younger sister. She came to live permanently at the ashram along with her mother and two other siblings. Sushila was 15 years younger than Pyarelal and functioned as Gandhiji's personal attendant, masseur and medical advisor. She became privy to his innermost thoughts. The brother-sister duo functioned in conflict and in co-operation with Gandhiji and with each other.

First Introduction

Sushila Nayyar came into Gandhiji's life, courtesy her elder brother and stayed with him until his death. Pyarelal had already joined the Gandhian entourage following Gandhiji's call to young students to boycott educational institutions.

Sushila had her first glimpse of Gandhiji when he visited her native Gujarat District (Punjab). She saw him for a second time at a public meeting at Rohtak (Haryana). She clung to her mother as the latter elbowed her way through the vast crowd of women to reach him. Her mother extracted a promise from Gandhiji, that he would see her when he next came to Saraladevi Chowdharani's Lahore residence.

When Gandhiji expressed keenness and said that Sushila should join him, she was only six years old and the youngest of the family of two brothers and one sister. He made Sushila take off her shoes and sit on his lap. She took kindly to the old man. Gandhiji told her mother to gift the girl to him. Sushila had to wait until she completed her schooling for her first visit to the ashram. She was 15.

Pyarelal invited her to spend a two-week vacation with him at the ashram promising that she would be 'with Gods on earth'. His description of ashram children and of the ashram school made her 'see them as illustrious company'. In order to shield her from appearing 'foolish, by not knowing how to pronounce the *shlokas*' at her first prayer meeting, he coached her until he was confident she 'had the lesson by heart'.[2]

Ashram as Magnet

Her vacation turned out to be a great experience, though it started off badly. Pyarelal was called away and left alone, she felt miserable and homesick. Ba came to her rescue. Sushila discovered in Ba a substitute for her mother and began to spend every night in Ba's hut. Sushila also discovered in her an ideal of Indian womanhood. In January 1932, Sushila again spent six weeks in the ashram, and this time she was alone, when her mother and Ba courted prison after Gandhiji's imprisonment. When she returned to New Delhi to study medicine, she found her heart was not in it. She kept on coming back to the ashram. Her process of getting integrated with the ashram had begun in the right earnest.

Sushila met Gandhiji once again in Calcutta when he was under the treatment of Dr B C Roy, who suggested that she should look after Gandhiji for a month during his convalescence. She was to remain with him for good, after Gandhiji requested her to be his personal physician. Slowly, ashram became a part of her consciousness, and gradually she got integrated with the mission and the spirit underlying the Gandhian road to self-liberation. Her whole family was now an integral part of the mission.

The stay at the ashram was, however, not all that pleasant. The Sabarmati Ashram was like a Joint Hindu family with countervailing forces pulling at each other, rather than a prototype of ashrams of antiquity. Also, it was no medieval monastery governed by strict rules and regulations. Gandhiji has variously referred to Sabarmati Ashram and Sevagram Ashram as, 'an ashram without rules', 'a home for invalids', 'a mad house' and 'a *dharmashala*' for one and all.

Romantic Pyarelal

Pyarelal had a rare sensitivity. He carried his emotions on his sleeves. Having spent his entire working career with Gandhiji, he was believed to be a model *brahmachari*. Paradoxically, he craved for the company of women. In 1935, Pyarelal got infatuated with a young lady named Yoga Khare and believed that she was responding positively. Gandhiji came down with a heavy hand to break the relationship. He devised all kinds of charges against Pyarelal.

Consequently, Sushila had begun to feel the heat, simply because she happened to be arraigned on the side of her brother. In Gandhiji's eyes, Pyarelal had done enough damage to the institution of *brahmacharya*. In fact, he had mocked at it. In his letter of 26 March 1935 to his nephew Mathuradas Trikumji, Gandhiji accused Pyarelal of being 'blinded by lust', and: "in such a state he expects to have a vision of God. None but God can rescue him from this situation."[3]

A year had gone by and Pyarelal's love for Yoga Khare was soon the talk of the town. Gandhiji supplicated Pyarelal and also threatened him: "I am extremely pained… What are you doing with whom and for what purpose? Is there any thought behind it? …Have you abandoned everyone? You have brought shame to the training I gave you."[4]

This proved counterproductive as Pyarelal became more adamant than ever. His family members, including Sushila, were worried about him. Pyarelal had become very aggressive and irrational in his responses. Pressure was put on Yoga to ignore his advances. Gandhiji reminded Pyarelal in May 1936 while vacationing at Nandi Durg to forget his infatuation: "I do not think Yoga has gone to the extent you imagine."[5]

But while Yoga gave in to the pressure, Pyarelal continued to raise the level of conflict. Gandhiji was quite unnerved when Pyarelal decided to renounce the world and take to *sanyasa*. It was now the mentor's turn to supplicate Pyarelal in the name of Yoga, who in his view would not have approved of the latest turn of events.

Two years passed by but the problems refused to go. Pyarelal looked like a true pupil of Gandhiji. He must have learnt the techniques of civil disobedience and non-cooperation from his mentor rather too well. The situation threatened to go out of control. Pyarelal decided to go on a fast after he came to know of Yoga's engagement to one Ramchandra. Gandhiji was worried that Pyarelal may follow his example of fast-unto-death as the angry pupil had already extended the duration of his fast to the second day. Thus a note followed from Gandhiji to Pyarelal to lay his doubts at rest.

Yoga's Engagement

The next crisis came with Gandhiji blessing the engaged couple. Pyarelal protested and believed that the engagement was forced.

Gandhiji's was undoubtedly, a fertile mind. He was working with Pyarelal's mother to take Yoga off his mind. They planned to marry off Pyarelal to Sharada, an inmate of the ashram. Here was Gandhiji giving a piece of advice to his mother: "Marry Sharada off to Pyarelal. She will agree if I persuade her. But you must take up the responsibility."[6] Forgotten were the vows that ashramites were expected to observe celibacy. He talked to Sharada who assented to the marriage.

Dejected and forlorn, Pyarelal left the ashram in November 1937, upsetting everyone. Gandhiji was in serious trouble because now he had to cope not only with Pyarelal but also with equally irreconcilable Sushila: "You went away leaving me sick and Sushila in tears! …Right now, my anxiety is increased. And Sushila is absolutely shaken."[7]

Pyarelal was in a rage, unbalanced and losing his equilibrium. He gave a dressing down not only to his mother and his sister Sushila, but also to Ba. He asked Gandhiji to mind his business. This frightened Gandhiji who was now almost on his knees to supplicate him: "My reputation is in your hands, O Lord, protect me."[8]

Those years were years of torture for Gandhiji, Sushila Nayyar and others. Here is a graphic description provided by Gandhiji himself: "You have become part of me… Then I will eat when he eats and starve when he starves, when he fasts I will fast too."

It was unbelievable for Gandhiji to follow the example of unruly Pyarelal. Here was a situation in which contrasting treatment was given to Harilal Gandhi (his eldest son) and Pyarelal. While Harilal was in trouble with his father for defying him, Pyarelal was ultimately treated as a favourite: "My love for you will be as much as for *swaraj*."[9]

The nagging fear of Pyarelal running away returned after a fortnight. Ba informed him on 27 May 1938, about the disciple's plans. Sushila was the other dimension of this complicated situation. She was on the verge of a breakdown. The pressures proved too much for her. They were also proving too much for Gandhiji. He begged of Pyarelal to help him by helping his sister: "But, then, who am I? Do I know her? Or, if I know her, why I am not in a position to explain what I see?"[10]

Pyarelal was still sulking in August 1938, but he was back soon, as Mahadev Desai's deputy, thanks to the persistent efforts of Gandhiji. Sushila followed her brother back to the ashram. Thus it was the end of the first critical scene.

Sushila in Trouble

Sushila Nayyar was about to complete her medical training at Lady Hardinge Medical College, New Delhi. Subsequently, she was to take charge of the ashram on a full-time basis. She had started off as a favourite of both Gandhiji and Ba. Gandhiji claimed to be both father and mother to her, as seen in the letter he wrote to Pyarelal: "I have always tried to draw her to me. As in the case of others, in Sushila's case also, my attempt has been to be a mother and a father. But I was not aware that she had a greater need of a father. In my future efforts I shall remember this."[11]

Sushila Nayyar played the longest innings with him from amongst all his women associates. Gandhiji had a stormy relationship with her. Her relations with Ba proved to be of even keel throughout their association. Even Gandhiji had conceded to Ba in this matter: "Here we have a situation where Ba worships Sushila. What does anything else matter."[12]

While Ba had established her credibility as mother to Sushila, Gandhiji proved to be a mercurial father, totally possessive of her. He found it difficult to establish a stable relationship with either Sushila or Pyarelal. The late thirties were years of Sushila and Pyarelal, as were the early thirties of Mira who dominated the scene.

After Pyarelal, Gandhiji was critical of Sushila Nayyar and Mahadev Desai. Mirabehn proved to be the spoiler. Mahadev Desai had tried to build bridges with Mirabehn soon after she joined the ashram. He took lessons from Mira in French. This led to a close bonding between the two. Gandhiji did not like it and gave him a dressing down. That marked the end of his French lessons.

There developed a special relationship between Sushila and Mahadev Desai. Mirabehn's role changed from a friend to a tormentor. She was accused of turning Gandhiji against them. The presence of young Sushila and her special relations with Gandhiji, Ba and Mahadev apparently threatened Mira. Mirabehn decided to set up a fight and disturb the triangular equilibrium. Jealousy was the prime motive. The main consideration, however, remained the exclusivity with which his woman associates viewed Gandhiji.

Mahadev in Crisis

Mirabehn spread gossip about the special relationship Gandhiji shared with Sushila. When Gandhiji came to know about this, he shared his concerns with Sushila: "I have written [to Mira] a letter saying that she spreads poison by talking to others about you and me. And so, she should not talk about you and me to anyone. She has found this a hard condition."[13]

About this time Pyarelal and Sushila were in New Delhi. Mira continued to be a matter of concern to Gandhiji. He shared his troublesome thoughts with Rajkumari Amrit Kaur. He forwarded three letters received by him from Mirabehn, for her comments. Amrit Kaur was directed to destroy those letters after reading them. Those letters were said to have contained 'poison'. He, however, paid a left-handed compliment to Mira: "Robbed of Mira's hysteria they are sound."[14] Mira had her own reasons to complain. She had been left friendless in a vast unfriendly world.

Simultaneously, three copies of Mira's letters were mailed to Pyarelal and Sushila at their Delhi address. Thus Mira had succeeded in launching a three-pronged attack on Gandhiji, Sushila and Mahadev. Mirabehn depicted the situation in the most colourful imagery. Gandhiji was instantly reminded of incidents in the *Ramayana*. This question must have crossed his mind, if Mira was placing him in the same class as Ravana in his harem. He had a hearty laugh at his own cost:

"Is not Mirabehn's description similar to that of Ravana's palace by Tulsidas? Ravana is lying unconscious and his numerous queens are reclining around him in various states of undress. I laughed and cried when I read it. How could I have been affected in that way? Disregarding Mirabehn's exaggeration, I was affected by what remained in the letter and I wrote that I would change my practice. What if the suffering on the 14th was the result of those physical contacts."[15]

'The suffering' on 14 April, 1938 was considered a great setback for him in his relentless pursuit of *brahmacharya*. In his letter of 14 May 1938 to Pyarelal he refers to the incident of 'the 14th in the daytime and of the 9th instant' with a guilt complex. On May 3, he shared his concern with Mirabehn of "that degrading, torturing experience of 14th April". Following the Dantesque analogy from the *Bible* he felt like being hurled from the heavens by the infuriated God: [I] "had no right to be there in my state of uncleanliness."[16] The incident was made explicit to Amritlal T Nanavati in his letter of 2 May, where he talked of his utter helplessness.[17]

Mirabehn was indeed being too realistic for his comfort. A careful reading of this letter indicated that she was not exaggerating. While her jealousy was one factor in the situation, she was speaking on behalf of the majority of ashramites who were concerned about the series of developments involving Gandhiji's closeness with a group of young girls and women surrounding him.

Dream Land

Sushila specialised in giving a daily body massage to Gandhiji. But by February 1939, he was compelled to stop taking service involving physical contact from girls due to overwhelming public criticism. His confidence had also been shaken by the dream he experienced on 7 April 1938. For the first time, his personal confidence had been shaken to the very roots. He now talked of his 'diseased mind'.

Here Pyarelal factor had once again come into play. He was compelled to supplicate Pyarelal: "If you remain composed then I may regain my self-confidence," and further added: "This means that I have found the guru that I have been looking for."[18] Who would not be flattered by his sweet-nothings reserved for Sushila: "Lately you have been figuring in my dreams. Shall I call it attachment or love?"[19]

She was indeed in trouble on account of her alleged involvement with Mahadev. She wept bitter tears. His feeling sorry for her was laced with a rare sense of subtle humour: "A wicked person sees everyone as wicked. Do I belong to the same category? How very perverted I must be to imagine even for a moment perversity in a pure-hearted like you."[20]

Gandhiji possessed an iron fist hidden in his soft gloves. He was the master of strategy and tactics in all kinds of possible situations. He did not like the close association between Sushila and Mahadev. He also knew that Sushila would not like to go out of his orbit. He decided to apply his carrot and stick policy to break her association with Mahadev by pandering to Pyarelal and subtly placing Mahadev in the doghouse as made apparent by subsequent events. The year 1938 was a year of personal crisis for Mahadev.

Gandhiji knew that his pressure tactics had worked. The break had come to pass. Now the only concern for him was to vindicate himself in his own eyes. He also knew that no one was impressed by his elaborate apologia: "You are not a Goddess, nor is Mahadev a God. The future is bright if this illusion has been dispelled. I consider both of you simple-hearted. The only difference is that you have not experienced lust. Mahadev has to do so in full measure. He is a married man after all. But the God of love is subtle. You were both unaware of his attack. You needlessly blame yourself. Desire had certainly taken possession of you. But you were not aware of it at all. For that matter even Mahadev was not aware of it. Mahadev was not careful. And he was not even aware of that."[21]

Here was an instance of perfect murder in which the accused got away because the accused and judge happened to be the same person. The task of the judge was very much facilitated because he had the confession of the accused as dictated by him to the last comma and full stop. Indeed, the accused Sushila Nayyar and Mahadev must have been ever grateful to their mentor for having rescued them from the purgatory into which they had assumably fallen.

Unfortunately, things don't work out in this fashion in real life. Deep scars are bound to be left and they take a long time to heal. Pyarelal, Sushila Nayyar, Mahadev Desai and even Gandhiji felt the difference. The spontaneity in their relations was gone forever. The age of innocence had been replaced by the age of knowledge and awareness. Now doubts began to be expressed about the very efficacy of *brahmacharya*. Even the move from Sabarmati to Sevagram Ashram helped little. It was just a matter of time before scepticism travelled down to the very bones of Gandhiji himself.

Mahadev Crucified

Gandhiji used Pyarelal to crucify helpless Mahadev who came in the firing line of both. Pyarelal called Mahadev all sorts of names. Mahadev would get so unnerved that he would lose his composure. Gandhiji pretended to be a close observer of the scene, all the time stirring things up: "I have not exonerated Mahadev independently… Right now,

Mahadev has lost the capacity to decide whether or not he has committed a wrong… What can poor Mahadev do? Hence it is useless he considers himself innocent and a thousand times more so if he considers himself guilty."[22]

He supplicated mercy for the beleaguered Mahadev and requested Pyarelal 'to wipe the tears [of Mahadev] if you can'.[23] He also knew that Pyarelal's capacity to recover was in inverse proportion to his congenital tendency for prolonged relapses. Gandhiji thus went out of his way to keep Pyarelal in good humour and Pyarelal was not the one to let an opportunity go away.

Gandhiji was equally guilty. After all it was he who had initially accused Sushila and Mahadev Desai of committing impropriety. Gandhiji was sorry after having made the accusation: "Am I omniscient? My understanding has not always been correct. And on this occasion, I see myself distressed and senile, so what wonder if I act like a jaundiced man who sees everything yellow."[24]

Reconciliation Attempts

There was a torrent of letters flowing from him to the brother-sister duo. He wrote to Pyarelal again on 15 and 16 May, followed by letters to Sushila on the same date. In fact, these letters read like mercy petitions. He began to plead the cause of Mahadev in the court of appeal of irreconcilable Pyarelal. Mahadev decided to go into hibernation. He wrote a letter to Pyarelal which was too humiliating for Mahadev.

Gandhiji stopped the dispatch of the letter and rendered a personal explanation to Pyarelal. Poor Mahadev 'was anguished and given to crying'.[25] Gandhiji had changed his tracks once again. He had assumed the role of defence counsel for Sushila and Mahadev. He transferred the responsibility for the mayhem on to his shoulders: "Where there was no wrong at all, I saw wrong and insisted that all of you should see it."[26] On the very next day, he told Pyareial: "I am now putting out of my mind the distress of Mahadev and Sushila."[27]

However it was not easy. Sushila was a pliant listener and he was comfortable dealing with her. He would call her "stupid girl" or "stupid little daughter" which was also an attempt at reconciliation. The routine usually assigned to attend to him on day-to-day basis was restored to her: "I lie down in the bath-tub. I get sleep. My legs are massaged. My head and feet are massaged with *ghee*."[28]

The message was clear: "Come back soon and take your place in the queue". He was being playful as well: "Can't you understand that there can be stupidity tempered with knowledge?"[29] He beseeched Sushila to share his happiness. He also suggested to her to give a fitting reply to three offensive letters from Mirabehn.

Gandhiji Placates Sulking Sushila

Sushila straight away refused to return to the Gandhian royal court. She conveyed her displeasure to him through Pyarelal: "[Pyarelal] writes that [you think] you have lost for ever the place you had in my heart and that consequently you have lost your lustre."[30] This disturbed Gandhiji to no end. The ground was however being prepared for eventual reconciliation. Gandhiji dispatched a telegraphic message to Pyarelal assuring Sushila: "[Your] right of serving had been specially reserved."[31]

Sushila and Gandhiji kept making their moves cautiously like accomplished chess players. Gandhiji made one compromise after another to win over Sushila to his side and thereby ensured Pyarelal's return along with her. He was now begging her to be forgiven. He instructed Sushila to destroy the letter after reading it as he was afraid its contents may become public. To the credit of Sushila, she did not destroy his letter of 16 May 1938 enclosing copies of Mirabehn's three letters to him referring to flasks of 'Mira's hysteria'.

He kept on telling the brother-sister duo that they should return to him as there was nothing but ruination for both of them. In his impatience, he bombarded her with letters. The fourth and fifth letters were sent by him on 17 and 18 May, preceded by three letters on the previous two days. "I accept your version of what happened on the 9th night [between her and Mahadev]… Believe me, I admit I may have been a prey to illusion."[32]

He became unusually secretive. He destroyed her letters after reading them. While he was making every attempt to placate Sushila and Pyarelal, he let Mahadev fend for himself. Mahadev was a quiet sort who never demanded his rights and privileges. His case was overlooked due to his own fault. It would have been difficult to imagine him to be a part of the shouting brigade of the Pyarelal-Sushila duo. Gandhiji felt he could always admonish him: "Your poetic imagination sometimes blinds you to reality. There is nothing but cowardice in your letters."[33]

Recalcitrant Sushila

Sushila's hide and seek with him exasperated Gandhiji. He finally sought to know if she had abandoned him altogether. He wrote: "Do you or do you not wish to come?"[34] She would not commit. The next twenty four hours were tortuous for him. His limits of patience could no longer be counted in months and days. She went on complaining to him in one letter after another.

He turned to Pyarelal as the last court of appeal. One must sympathise with him for the pathetic situation in which Gandhiji had landed himself: "I cannot even claim purity of mind. I am willing to admit that I might have had a dirty mind. Can it be not that my diseased mind might have aroused me and I might have seen the reflection of my morbidity in that innocent girl and in her actions? ...I have somehow started feeling that in all these incidents I alone played the role of Satan and by imputing guilt to an innocent act have caused untold misery to Sushila, to Mahadev, and even to you."[35]

Why did Gandhiji let them off so easily? Possibly, Pyarelal and Sushila filled a vacuum in his subconscious. The very physical presence was essential to satisfy his unstated longings. He must have been ready to pay any price to have them back. He was prepared to wash his dirty linen in public in order to possess them: "How can filth be removed unless it is brought out through discussion."[36]

Fear psychosis may have overtaken him in the end. A stage came when he was not prepared for any more insults. He decided to stand and be counted. To Pyarelal he wrote: "I shall not write more... All of us cannot be mad at the same time."[37] He was impolitic to Pyarelal in his other letter as well: "You are at present ruling over me. I often feel like complaining but I dare not. How did I come to have so much fear?"[38]

Gandhiji was himself responsible for this odd state of affairs. He encouraged the brother-sister duo to commit acts of defiance and get away scot-free. He encouraged acts of insubordination also. Who would come to his rescue if he were not to rescue himself? When confronted with the irascible duo, his state of mind was clearly reflected in his letter to Pyarelal: "At the moment I am unable to talk. If I try, I am likely to burst into loud wailing."[39]

Mahadev

Of all the main actors Mahadev Desai comes out as the best. There had never been a more loyal and committed secretary to Gandhiji than Mahadev. In fact, the Gandhis had adopted him as their fifth son. He was perhaps the only intellectual besides Vinoba Bhave in the Gandhian entourage. He was devoted to Gandhiji. While Gandhiji went out of his way to placate Sushila, he made an example of Mahadev for others. Poor Mahadev withdrew into his shell and took a long time to come out of it. Ba paid the best posthumous tribute to him by regularly visiting his *samadhi* at Aga Khan Palace. Finally, it must be said to his credit that he did not utter a single word of displeasure either in private or in public about his mentor.

The fact, however, remained that Gandhiji was jealous of his man Friday on several counts. He was as gentle as a lamb and had many admirers within and outside the ashram. Those who hesitated to approach Gandhiji found themselves at ease while interacting with Mahadev. The jealousy was also on the count of the bond he had developed with Sushila.

Although the episode was eventually buried, Gandhiji's doubts on the relations between Mahadev Desai and Sushila returned after he discovered that they had exchanged two letters between themselves. He peeped into the letter to get the content. Curiosity (read jealousy) scored over rectitude. In the first letter from Mahadev to Sushila there was a drawing of the moon in it. Doesn't moon symbolise romantic love? In the next letter there was mention of 'physical passion' in Sushila's letter to Mahadev. That set the alarm bells ringing in his mind. It revived old (unpleasant) memories. He refused to give a clean chit to Sushila and much less to Mahadev. He wrote: "But for me it has become a question of my veracity… We cannot be complacent regarding physical passion in anybody's case."[40]

This extract is from the letter he wrote to Mahadev Desai from distant Mardan in North-West Frontier Province. Gandhi never brooked rivals and trusted no one in such matters. He added a footnote in his letter to Mahadev: "Tell Rajkumari [Amrit Kaur] about physical passion so that I need not write to her separately."[41]

So, at times Gandhiji exonerated Mahadev and at other times he did not. This way Sushila and Mahadev were kept in perpetual suspense. And like a guilty party, he sought to give a clean chit to himself by mumbling: "I think I have not blundered."

CHAPTER 18

Sushila in Trouble

Sushila Nayyar deserved sympathy and not derision for her acts. She was caught up in the *brahmacharya* vortex without realising its full implications. For her, it was enough to receive so much adulation from Mohandas Karamchand Gandhi, the reigning star of Indian politics. She lived on and off in the ashram due to her preoccupation with her MD degree which she completed in 1941.

Gandhiji's concept of *brahmacharya* was constantly evolving and had begun to take concrete shape by the late thirties. Gandhiji was coy in expressing his thoughts in public owing to the controversial nature of his experiments in *brahmacharya*. The participation of young women in his *brahmacharya yajna* was essential to the success of his mission. He felt relaxed in their company. It also gave him an opportunity to have a laugh or two with them. Indeed, he claimed to be one of a kind in female company. Sushila's brother Pyarelal was caught in the vortex for entirely different reasons. Dedicated as he was to the Gandhian cause, he was not able to cope with the demands made upon his person in his experiments with *brahmacharya*.

Hieroglyphic Language

The responses and reactions of Sushila Nayyar to the insistent demands of Gandhiji upon her resources was bewildering. Very few persons would have been equal to the pressures brought to bear upon her. Her predicament rather than that of Gandhiji should arouse a sympathetic chord in the objective observers of the scene.

Gandhiji's pathos after being separated from Sushila during her absences in New Delhi to prepare for her medical examination came out in his letter of July 1940 to her: "Pyarelal does try to make up for your absence, but how can I do it? Where would he find a hand like yours? He sleeps even closer to me than you did. But who would be jealous of him? However, I have not regained that fearlessness that I had with you."[1]

She would have felt sorry for Pyarelal. Though he tried his best he could not earn Gandhiji's approval. Sushila was a shadow that would not go away. The evolution of the concept of *brahmacharya* is best seen in the example of Sushila Nayyar. The year 1938 was the most crucial for him in the sense that he broke and resumed physical contact with women several times under public pressure. He employed specious arguments in making exceptions. These were tactical withdrawals on his part with several ifs and buts and exceptions galore. Ba and Sushila would be his exceptions to exception.

Gandhiji and his associates used hieroglyphic language on the subject of *brahmacharya*. One has to read between the lines before comprehending what was actually happening. However, a pattern began to emerge by the middle of 1938 with climaxes reached once in 1944–45 and then in 1946–47.

It was physical touch of women in the initial years leading to the 1938 complex and novel bathing arrangement followed by his experiments in sleeping with women during 1945–46 with the climax reached in Noakhali during 1945–46 in what he believes to be his climatic *brahmacharya mahayajna*. The person of Sushila recurs in all the stages in what he claimed to be his *brahmacharya mahayajna*.

Sustained Tantrums

There was a phase when Gandhiji wanted to be left alone and when his happiness did not depend on Sushila's presence. In one letter of this period he pleaded: "For God's sake leave me alone to rest in peace. I had enough of you." This did not last long, however, and other epistles show him reversing his position: "Why are you tormenting me?" and "I wanted to sleep, but what can I do when I cannot sleep? I even walked for about half-an-hour." But just like Banquo's ghost thoughts of her would not go away: "If I say that I did not get any sleep last night, you may attribute it to my sinfulness… But I must tell you people about the turmoil I am passing [through]."[2]

Shifting positions, Gandhiji enquired about the state of her disorderliness and asked for ways and means to get rid of it. He seems to have conveniently forgotten that he was the cause and effect of her disorientation. It appeared he was anxious to throw the guilt on her shoulders: "That you would go to the toilet only when I did is also part of your disorderliness is it not?" When his sense of loneliness and feeling of guilt returned to him, he would agonise over her separation, contrary to earlier occasions when Sushila used to agonise over the same: "You were not there and I woke at 2 o'clock last night."[3]

His agony subsided soon after he received her letter and on the very next day he informed Sushila that he had a sound sleep. All was well with his world so long as Sushila was in an amicable mood.

Games with Pyarelal

Pyarelal discerned a one-in-a-million opportunity for which he must have been waiting for many years. Gandhiji had suppressed Pyarelal so much that he had developed acute antipathy towards him, often expressed in defiance. Pyarelal was rude and often threatened to expose him publicly. Gandhiji was scared of Pyarelal. In one of his frankest letters he made no bones about the latter's potential to harm him: "Why am I afraid of you? Why this fear of writing or saying anything? Do you know the reason? I think I know it. Having frightened you many times, I have myself become frightened. Perhaps I have no remedy for this fear. Is it that you do not have the remedy?"[4]

At one time Mahadev Desai, Pyarelal and Sushila Nayyar were in the doghouse, Pyarelal due to Durga Khate and Mahadev because he was guilty in the eyes of Sushila's elder brother and (her guardian angel) Pyarelal; but all of them were close to him and hence indispensable on practical grounds. Mahadev and Pyarelal constituted his secretariat and Sushila besides being his personal physician was his attendant responsible for massaging and bathing him. It was thus essential to break the log-jam. Since Pyarelal was the hardest nut to crack and along with Sushila constituted two sides of the triangle, it was practical politics to come to terms with him at the cost of gentle Mahadev.

Gandhiji worked out a convenient arrangement with Pyarelal favouring him, under which Gandhiji was to be Sushila's guide. She was not consulted and the situation was presented to her as a *fait accompli*: "Pyarelal and I have since come to an agreement that only I should guide you, not he."[5] The hard sell simultaneously scored over Pyarelal: "I have taken your tears in the morning as atonement for the pain you gave me."

Gandhiji started depending on the brother-sister duo heavily to perform his day-to-day routine work. While Pyarelal was to render secretarial assistance, Sushila was to act as his medical attendant in addition to her responsibility of massaging and bathing him. He liked to be mothered by Sushila in his daily routine.

Mahadev Snubbed

Mahadev, who had long memories, was not reconciled to the situation. His relations with all three of them became formal. He was snubbed not just once but twice and he could not take kindly to Pyarelal's imposition on him. He even contemplated breaking off with his mentor. Gandhiji was worried at the chain reaction that would follow Mahadev's resignation and sought to prevent it using a different pretext: "If you decide to leave me, will Pyarelal stay on? And if Pyarelal leaves, will Sushila stay."[6]

Loyal as he was to Gandhiji, Mahadev finally chose not to force his resignation even as it further compromised his position. His situation had become unenviable because Sushila was exonerated but not him. On the contrary, Gandhiji rubbed fresh salt on his wounds by taunting Sushila about Mahadev: "He has no hatred towards you. Only he is not any more under your spell."[7]

To soften the blow, he added, "For this I hold myself responsible." He thus succeeded in creating a wall between Sushila and Mahadev as well as in bringing them down by a notch or two through clever manoeuvring and joining hands with troublesome Pyarelal. Mahadev slaved along with him but was not reconciled either to Gandhiji or to the brother–sister duo.

Gandhiji admitted to the truth in his letter to Sushila on 23 May 1938, where he admitted responsibility for separating her from Mahadev: "Can it not be that my affliction is the result of my latent lust? May be it is not."[8] In his letter of 26 May to Pyarelal, he talked of his 'dirty mind', his 'morbidity' and compared himself to a Satan who acted as a 'killjoy'. He had to remain a killjoy for denying others what he had foresworn in 1906. The vow of *brahmacharya* was a revenge he took upon everyone else.

Towards the end of his life, Mahadev Desai found himself together with Sushila Nayyar. They were quarantined together in the Aga Khan Palace internment camp in Poona where Mahadev breathed his last on 15 August 1942, barely four days after he was interned at Aga Khan Palace at Poona.

Sushila deservedly paid a handsome tribute to Mahadev after he passed away. He was the only genuine conscience keeper of the Gandhian legacy. Soon after, when Ba too passed away on 22 February 1944, two *samadhis* (one for Mahadev and one for Ba) were erected in the jail premises. Ba had considered him her fifth son. While on her death bed, she said: "I am going to sleep by Mahadev's side."

Devdas at War

While Gandhiji could easily have his way with Mahadev, he found it hard to cope with his fourth son Devdas. Devdas could not reconcile himself to the larger-than-life role Sushila played in the Gandhian circle. He was very uncomfortable with the hold Sushila had over his father.

Devdas was gentle but had an iron soul. He did not hesitate to make his displeasure known to both Sushila and his father even though he was a man of few words. He would often talk to Sushila critically. Although it did not change the situation, Sushila began to feel very uncomfortable in his presence. She often had tears streaming down her face, which made Gandhiji equally uncomfortable. He would provide solace to her: "Do you think there was any malice in what Devdas said? If there was any it was directed towards me."[9] He tried to comfort her after she passed on to him two hostile letters she had received from Devdas: "Why are you so much afraid of Devdas and the people here?"[10]

Gandhiji continued to provide a protective cover to Sushila not only against Devdas but also against other hostile elements, particularly the ashramites. Inmates of the Sevagram Ashram repeatedly sparred with Gandhiji over his outlandish practices. His relations with Sushila had come under their special scrutiny. They also disapproved of the brother sister duo monopolising him, throwing tantrums and keeping him on tenterhooks.

Devdas did not change his views about Sushila's association with Gandhiji in spite of his father's persistent efforts. His hostility expressed openly during 1938 remained undiminished even in 1940: "Your impression about Devdas is correct. But if he has contempt it is not for you, but for me."[11] Devdas knew his father too well from a close distance while in South Africa, and from a distance when they both were back in India. He had known Gandhiji as a self-righteous and self-opinionated person from his early days. There was no point in arguing with him, but Devdas had his way of making his point of view known. His silent but stony disapproval was more eloquent than his approval.

The concept of *brahmacharya,* instead of dividing, united the father and son duo. Indeed, the boldest resistance to the Gandhian practice of *brahmacharya* came from within the family. Ba, Harilal and Devdas stood shoulder-to-shoulder, but at different times and on different occasions.

Chinks in *Brahmacharya* Armour

Sushila Nayyar was the only woman associate who emerged as a vital link in all three stages of Gandhi's *brahmacharya*—physical contact with women in the 1930, followed by *brahmacharya prayog* in early 40s that culminated finally into *mahayajna* during the Noakhali sojourn.

Her name does not figure specifically in either the second or the third phase. In fact, she denied her participation during his Noakhali sojourn, when specifically asked by Professor Nirmal Kumar Bose about it. Gandhiji, however, admitted to her participation in the *brahmacharya mahayajna* in response to a query from Professor Bose. Probably this was the reason for her displeasure with Professor Bose. She had accused him of having a dirty mind during the course of her conversation with Ved Mehta.

There was an unpleasant fallout of her close association with Gandhiji. It broke up her engagement to Dattatraya Balkrishna Kelkar's son. In her own words: "[Her fiancee] wanted to marry right away, but I wanted to wait, and first serve Bapu and the country. Then he said something very nasty. He said: All you Gandhiites profess these ideals about service, but you really just can't tear yourselves away from your lord and master. You all bask in his reflected glory. Well, go back in his reflected hell. That was the end of our engagement, and I never wanted to marry anyone else."[12]

Exception to Exceptions

There were repeated occasions when Gandhi foresook any physical contact with women barring the exceptions which he made for Ba, but extended it at times to Sushila too who became indispensable in the performance of his daily rituals. Gradually she took over several functions which Ba performed, besides acting as his medical consultant. Since Pyarelal acted as his secretary, it gave Sushila the key to the innermost Gandhian secrets. At one time Gandhiji compared Sushila with Ba and justified the reasons for treating them as exceptions: "From the beginning I have regarded Sushila Behn in the same way as Ba, as an exception."

Gandhiji had made a case for maintaining parity between Ba and Sushila in undertaking physical service to the exclusion of others. At one time he had declared to the whole world the stoppage of physical contact with women with no exception. He had to go back on his decision within the next twelve hours. He was forced to make an exception in favour of Sushila: "[His soft heartedness had put an end to the intention. I could not bear the tears of Sushila and the fainting of Prabhavati."[13]

He had reserved the finest compliments for Sushila on that occasion: "Sushila has observed *brahmacharya* since childhood." Gandhiji felt that Sushila was eminently qualified to be present during the ablutions in the bathroom: "Sushila has been present in the bathroom while I have bathed in the nude and in her absence Ba or Prabhavati or Lilavati have attended on me."[14]

Those who choose not to tread the straight and narrow path find great satisfaction in travelling unmarked alleys and uncharted bye lanes. Gandhiji was certainly the kind who took delight in traversing twisted paths. Perhaps he had a definite purpose in mind. We are not sure. But was he sure of his destination?

Sushila's absence created a void in Gandhiji's life. She went everywhere with him like his shadow. She was there in the Aga Khan Palace internment camp and also during his Noakhali sojourn. She was a spinster who had decided to devote her entire life to him.

Sushila was extremely upset when Gandhiji allowed Rajkumari Amrit Kaur and Kanchan Shah to serve him. While it was not a fault in others' eyes, for an insecure Sushila it was 'unpardonable' since it sought to displace her from the high pedestal. Gandhiji ran to Pyarelal to seek his assistance. Here was another opportunity to throw tantrums. What was the ultimate outcome? It is best described in Gandhi's own words in his letters to Pyarelal: "Yesterday the turmoil in my mind was beyond endurance… It was untruth to let [Sushila] believe that I am keeping her as my physician. I want to draw her to me. The reasons are many… How can she have the heart to leave me?"

As if this was not enough, he had to give an undertaking to behave according to the ground rules laid down by Sushila. He promised an oath to dissociate himself from taking service from other girls and woman associates in future. He had to beat a hasty retreat and he confessed: "There was untruth in saying 'yes' to Rajkumari [Amrit Kaur]. It was softness on my part to give them the impression of being needed when I actually did not need them."[15]

Bathing Gossip

While Gandhiji was preoccupied in placating both Sushila and Pyarelal throughout 1938, he had thereby exposed the flank to attack from others. Indeed his special treatment of Sushila had created considerable turmoil in the ashram. The words reached Gandhiji's ears. He issued a secret circular with its audience limited to twenty select associates. Those fortunate ones included Ba, Sushila Gandhi (his daughter-in-law), Manu Gandhi (Harilal's daughter), Sushila Nayyar, Mirabehn, Rajkumari Amrit Kaur and Amutussalaam. The circular was to be returned to him after it had been perused.

There were a number of charges he had to confront. They all had to do with special favours shown by him to Sushila. He was further charged with crossing all the limits of propriety in dealing with her. There were specific charges levied against him. One of the charges pertained to resting his hands on her shoulders during his morning and evening walks. Questions were also raised about the denial of similar privileges to young men of the ashram. The most serious charge pertained to his daily bathing ritual: "I let Sushila have her bath just when I am myself having my bath. And I cover myself with her sari."

Gandhiji challenged his critics to come out in the open. Nobody had the courage to come forward. The controversy refused to die down. Was this ritual a part of his *brahmacharya* syndrome? There is no explanation for it in his writings. Sushila, however, told Ved Mehta that his physical contacts were no part of his *brahmacharya* design.

Why did he have to share his bath with Sushila? His apologia for bathing together was saving time. She was required to take her bath in fifteen minutes flat as well as service him within the same period. This was a specious argument, if any. In any case his explanation was too elaborate for words:

"The bathing arrangement is this: She bathes in the space behind the bathtub [in which Gandhi takes his bath] and while she is bathing I keep my eyes tightly shut. I do not know the manner of her bathing—whether she bathes naked or with her underwear on. I can tell from the sound that she used soap. I have seen no part of her body which everybody here will not have seen. What can be terrible is that she massages me while I am lying naked."[15] Here was a 'A Circular Letter' issued by him on September 12 1938, for limited eyes to be read and returned to him after reading it.

Welcome Years

Sushila was special for Gandhiji. The tantrums that characterised the relationship earlier went away. An enthusiastic Mahatama sang paeans to her in his letter to Pyarelal: "She has experienced everything I have in me. Even though Sushila has entered late in my life, she is more absorbed in me. Hence I would even make her sleep by my side without fear."[16] She was, thus, an instrument in perfecting his *brahmacharya* practice. Sushila, though, claimed that there was not much in sleeping next to him. It was like sleeping comfortably next to your mother.

Sushila returned to Delhi to complete her medical education. She obtained her MD by 1941 and by 1942 the political struggle for independence had begun in the right earnest. It had led to long imprisonment of Gandhiji in her company. Sushila arrived in the nick of time in Bombay and ıuckily found herself located in the same prison with Gandhi, Mahadev Desai and Ba. After Ba and Mahadev's demise, their restraining hands were no longer there to hold Gandhiji. He was out in the wilderness entirely by himself. He was entirely on his own to conduct his freewheeling experiments in *brahmacharya*.

Gandhiji handed over a list of people he used to sleep with to Munnalal Shah in his letter of 6 March 1945. Sushila does not figure in this list. This, however, does not settle matters for good. He had made a fine distinction between *brahmacharya* experiments and sleeping together. In fact his *brahmacharya* experiments grew out of his practice of sleeping together with women. Gandhiji used to have frequent shiverings and his body would go cold. This required body-to-body contact to warm him up. Sushila had argued that young girls and women slept with him as grown-up daughters sleep with their mothers or fathers. Not even in India do grown-up daughters sleep with their fathers.

Truthful Account

Abha Gandhi talked freely to Ved Mehta and it seems to be one of the most authentic accounts of the *brahmacharya* experiments available on record. She was supposed to have told him that: "it was common knowledge that Sushila Nayyar slept next to him."[17]

Ved Mehta also talked to Sushila Nayyar on the subject. Her version of the event makes very interesting reading: "But long before Manu [Gandhi] came into the picture I used to sleep with him, just as I would with my mother. He might say, 'My back aches. Put some pressure on it'. So I might put some pressure on it or lie down on his back and he might just go to sleep. In the early days, there was no question of calling this a *brahmacharya* experiment. It was just part of the nature cure. Later on, when people started asking questions about his physical contact with women—with Manu [Gandhi], with Abha [Gandhi], with me, the idea of *brahmacharya* experiments was developed."[18]

The mystery about the role of the *brahmacharya* experiments has further deepened as her brother Pyarelal did not mention her name in his voluminous memoirs of Gandhiji. He, however, devotes considerable space to the role of Manu Gandhi in *brahmacharya* experiments.

The fact remained that no women involved with Gandhiji in *brahmacharya* experiments admitted to their respective involvement. Sushila has not spoken a word. Manu Gandhi has not whispered on the subject in her remarkable records of her days in Noakhali and New Delhi. Other participants too have chosen to remain under wraps.

Abha Gandhi is the only exception. She was sixteen when she was invited to sleep with him. In all her innocence she assumed that he had invited her to join him in his bed to counter his shivering spells. She must have felt gratified at being asked to warm him up. Here was a very revealing conversation that took place between Abha and Ved Mehta:

"Did you still wear your clothes?"

She hesitated and finally blurted out:

"He did ask me to take my clothes off. But, as far as I remember, I usually kept my petticoats and choli on."

"But what about him?"

"I don't remember whether he had any clothes or not". "I don't like to think about it."[19]

Enough was enough. Eventually her husband Kanu Gandhi had to intervene. Kanu Gandhi, Manulal G Shah and others volunteered to warm up his cold body when required.

Vinoba Bhave however made the best comments over the subject: In case Gandhi was a perfect *brahmachari*, he did not require his *brahmacharya* to be tested. And if he was an imperfect *brahmachari*, he should have avoided the experiments on principle.

CHAPTER 19

The Living Hell

Noakhali beckoned Gandhiji. It was his greatest public triumph as well as his biggest personal tragedy. Distant Noakhali, in Bengal, was being ravaged by communal riots. The appalling incidents were the antithesis of what the Mahatma stood for throughout his public life. Noakhali was a vicious challenge to his entire philosophy of life.

Ironically, the sojourn in Noakhali was also Gandhiji's escape from the ugly realities of life, one of which was the creation of Pakistan. Congress leaders, who were virtually his political creation, had started avoiding him. Gandhiji's ashram associates, too, didn't make his life easy. The 'Punjab Ministry' (to employ the colourful phrase of Parasuram)—comprising Pyarelal and Sushila Nayyar—added to his personal problems.

All these touched a chord. Which is why he was ruthless in leaving out practically everyone from his Noakhali entourage. Pyarelal and Sushila Nayyar were with him as essential cartage. Abha Gandhi got in because she was Bengali by origin. Kanu came along to accompany his wife, Abha Gandhi. Others in the contingent included Sushila Pai, Nirmal Kumar Bose, Parasuram and Prabhudas. Professor Bose and Parasuram constituted his personal party. Manu Gandhi joined him midway. The local Bengali contingent was deputed to Noakhali villages for relief work.

Planning the Trip

Gandhiji was determined to turn a new page in his life. He handed over the editorship of the Harijan group of newspapers to its trustees, who included Kishorelal Mashruwala, Kakasaheb Kalelkar, Vinoba Bhave and

Narahari Parekh. This temporary transfer of editorship ended in a disaster, as did the Noakhali sojourn. Except Manu Gandhi, all his associates who accompanied him had turned against him.

His relations with Sushila deteriorated considerably and did not return to normal until his dying days. His personal assistant Parasuram was the first to go. N K Bose followed suit. Even Pyarelal and Manu gave him anxious moments. Sucheta Kriplani highly disapproved of his *brahmacharya* experiments. Amutussalaam would not listen to him. His senior associates, namely, Sardar Vallabhbhai Patel, G D Birla, Swami Anand, Nathji and Thakkar Bapa, remonstrated with him, as did his youngest son Devdas.

So, Gandhiji took a decision. None of his old associates were to keep him company at his temporary headquarters. He scattered them for rehabilitation work in the villages. He himself moved from one village to another during his *yatra* for the cause of victimised Hindu villagers of blighted Noakhali. Only Parasuram and N K Bose were assigned to give him company. Manu Gandhi joined him when he was midway. He had decided to be on his own in his interaction with the Muslim rural peasantry of Bengal. He intended to win them over to his side.

Even Abha Gandhi, who knew Bengali and was fully conversant with his physical requirements and daily needs, was kept out of his chosen circle. Pyarelal and Sushila Nayyar were posted at separate villages. He wanted to be left alone. "[Even if Abha] was not happy to be separated from me, but *dharma* dictated the course and so I sent her away. I had also started regarding her service as a necessity. However, in this difficult sadhana of mine, how can I afford to make a habit of getting service from others?"[1]

While he kept Pyarelal, Sushila and Abha out, he urgently requested Manu Gandhi to join him at a later date. Was this in relentless pursuit of his plans for *brahmacharya yajna* to be performed away from the prying eyes? Parasuram and Professor Bose were asked to oversee his daily rituals, usually performed by young girls and women associates in the past.

Daily Rituals

This time Professor Nirmal Kumar Bose was singled out for special attention. Earlier, Gandhiji had never been associated with him so intimately. He was a reputed anthropologist but new to the intricacies of being a butler and a nurse to Gandhiji. Being an intellectual, he was expected to match Gandhiji's sharp intellect. Being a Bengali, he also acted as his interpreter. Parasuram assisted Professor Bose in his daily chores, but he was expected to perform the work of secretary, typist and also his personal assistant.

Nirmal Bose met Gandhiji for the first time on 18 November 1946. Bose's duties were all encompassing. They included a one hour massage preceding the bath. One ounce of mustard oil mixed with an equal quantity of fresh lime juice was to be used. Gandhiji would lie on a table in the courtyard of his host's residence all naked and shaded from the sun under an umbrella. The additional routines included shaving him on alternate days, and scraping his leather sandals after he returned from walks.

Gandhiji's food habits were not simple. His meal used to be varied and elaborate with quantities specified to the last ounce, temperatures strictly prescribed and cooking methods such as grating, mixing, heating, cooling and sprinkling detailed as in a medical prescription.

He was up by 4.00 am, and by 5.30 am, he was ready to take his 16 oz of fruit juice. This was followed by early morning prayer and brisk morning walk. At 7 am, it was 16 oz of goat's milk and 8 oz of fruit juice. At noon, it was 8 oz of goat's milk mixed with one ounce of fresh lime juice and an equal quantity of vegetables including green leaves, boiled and cooked with no salt. There could also be one grape fruit (sprinkled with glucose) or the milk of a green coconut. His last meal of the day was at 3.30 pm, consisting of: "8 oz of milk, but without any lime juice in it, boiled vegetables, as in his breakfast, and a fair quantity of fruits like papaya and some nuts."[2] He would vary his menu only when he imposed restrictions on himself in penance or when he was indisposed. Thus, his menu, though simple, was elaborate and cost his hosts a great deal of expense.

Gandhiji moved from village to village in order to bring peace to Noakhali and find solace for his turbulent inner-self. His longest stay was at Srirampur, from 20 November 1946 to 1 January 1947. Manu Gandhi arrived from her native town during this time and gave him company from 19 December onwards. He moved to Chandipur on 2 January 1947, where he had his next extended stay. He moved out of Noakhali after nearly four months. He bravely wobbled from one village to another, ravaged both physically and mentally. It was indeed a miracle that he survived the ordeal.

The peace of mind, which he looked forward to, proved to be too illusory. Despite Gandhiji's attempts to avoid the brother-sister duo, Sushila and Pyarelal pursued him. Gandhiji confessed to Nirmal Babu in Srirampur that he had become physically weak and asked him not to tell anyone as it could create panic: "[He requested Nirmal Babu] to refrain from telling anybody about his physical weakness, particularly to Pyarelal and Sushila Nayyar. But he had already written something to this effect in his personal diary, which was in Gujarati, and which his associates were in the habit of reading when they came here."[3]

Brewing Trouble

The Noakhali sojourn marked the beginning of the catastrophic developments in Gandhiji's life. He missed Ba's benign presence. In his diary entry of 22 September 1946, six weeks prior to his arrival in Noakhali, he wrote: "It seems to me so very hard to maintain detachment of mind in the midst of this raging fire. My heart-search continues."[4] After just two days he confessed to a friend: "I am filled with agitation; why could I not suffer this anguish with unruffled calmness of spirit."[5]

What was bothering him so much? There was trouble at the Sevagram Ashram on account of his *brahmacharya* experiments of 1944–45 involving young girls and women of the ashram. In his own words, he had discontinued experimenting because of the persistent requests of his closest associates. The thought of *brahmacharya*, however, was never off his mind. On the contrary, he intended to upgrade the experiments (*prayog*) to *brahmacharya yajna* during his Noakhali sojourn.

He was looking forward to Manu's arrival. While he was determined to involve her in *brahmacharya yajna* as a major player, the game of hide and seek went on between him and Sushila, who had to rest content as a side actor. He sent off a note to Pyarelal reflecting his true state of mind at that particular moment of time: "I am still groping [in the dark]... Here I am out to perform a stupendous *yajna*... There can, however, be no running away. And where can I run away?"[6]

The next letter to Pyarelal followed after three days of informing him about the arrival of Sushila in his temporary headquarters at

Srirampur. The big explosion involving her took place on 17 December. It came to be known as the 17 December incident.

After this episode, his relations with Sushila never returned to normal. Like Mirabehn, she too was banished on missions that kept her away from the path of Gandhiji. From Noakhali she was sent back to Sevagram *Ashram* to look after the affairs of the *ashram* hospital. Even her shadow was not to cross Gandhiji's path during his Bihar visit, which immediately followed Noakhali. She tried to get back in his favour but without success: "A telegram from Sushila came from Delhi offering to help Manudi [Manu Gandhi]. I sent a wire that it was not necessary. No letter from Sushila for many days."[7]

December 17 Incident

Gandhi had the longest stay in Srirampur. He stayed in a house belonging to one of the most respectable families of Noakhali. It consisted of a series of detached huts with a spacious one at the centre. Gandhiji occupied the central hut, which was surrounded on all sides by thick groves of areca and coconut. His associates, including Nirmal Babu and Parasuram, occupied the huts surrounding the central hut.

The bed on which he slept was huge and three people could easily sleep together. This comes out clearly in his letter of 25 December 1946, to Sardar Patel: "And now I am dictating this letter to [Manu], lying with my eyes closed so as to avoid strain. Sucheta [Kripalani] is also in the room. She is still asleep and I am dictating this letter in a low voice, lying on the wooden bedstead. The bedstead is of a size in which three persons can easily sleep."[8]

It was 17 December 1946. Sushila Nayyar was in Srirampur on one of her off-and-on visits. Manu Gandhi was to reach the place after two days. At 3.20 am, his associates heard a cry coming from Gandhiji's hut. It was 40 minutes earlier than the time he would normally get up from the bed. He was agitatedly talking to Sushila in a decibel that was easily cutting through the serene dawn that had not yet fully descended.

Nirmal Babu was greatly worried and rushed to Gandhiji's hut. He was stunned into silence by the scene inside but did not raise an alarm. He found Gandhiji sitting on his bed reclining against the wall. His eyes were closed but tears were streaming down his face. Sushila was standing next to him, also in tears. She was attempting to engage him in a conversation, but he would not listen to her. An angry Mahatma shoved her away with a swift movement of his hand to express his displeasure. He repeated this several times.

Everything passed on as usual during the morning prayers after which Nirmal Babu spoke to a number of persons staying in other cottages. All of them had heard an anguished cry coming from the central hut occupied by Gandhiji: "It was Gandhiji's voice, and then we heard the sound of two loud slaps given on someone's body. The cry then sank down into a heavy sob."[9]

Nirmal Babu thought it would be wise not to intervene in this crisis. He spent the day as if nothing had happened. Gandhiji had enough trouble from the Sushila-Pyarelal duo. He always went out of his way to placate them. Perhaps it was now time to say enough is enough.

Although no one asked him about the incident, Gandhiji had not forgotten it and the pain it was causing him. Perhaps he also understood that his associates must have heard his loud cry. This was reflected in his evening prayer. Local villagers had also come to participate in it. He used the occasion to reflect on his tiff with Sushila without mentioning her or the incident. He also regaled the audience with anecdotes of his childhood days. He talked of a memorable incident in his life when he had gone to watch a play without the permission of his father.

His angry father did not utter a single word after he returned home, but in protest he wept and beat his head. Reminded of the same incident, he performed an encore with Sushila on 17 December. This is how he described the predicament of his father, which may help understand the Srirampur incident: "Similarly, he at the time of his anger that night began to beat his own head. But he did not like to weep like others. Instead he wanted to unburden his heavy heart by placing before the whole world what he had committed by being angry."[10]

Gandhiji considered Sushila his adopted daughter. The act found him emulating his own father subconsciously. It was not only an act of expiation but also a public demonstration of protest against Sushila's unkind behaviour towards him on a continuing basis. The incident forced Gandhiji to give a response that he would not have preferred. During a public speech in Srirampur, to a bewildered audience comprising villagers, he said: "I am not a mahatma; I am an *alpatma*. I am an ordinary mortal like you."[11]

What Exactly Happened?

The 17 December incident turned out to be a repetition of the Roshomon story. There are two versions of the incident. Each version is a variant of the other. Here Nirmal Babu performs the role of *sutradhara* to perfection, a role for which he was eminently suited because of his intellectual background. He was, however, forced to give up the role of *sutradhara.* He fell to the temptation of being an actor in the drama. Thus Nirmal Babu the *sutradhara* ended up as an objective partisan.

The incident on the morning of the 17 December aroused Professor Bose's curiosity enormously: "He wished to learn from me as well as from Parashuram 'if Sushila Nayyar had fallen in our estimation' (*Tumhare nazar me gir gain hai*?), on account of that day's incident."

At that stage Nirmal Babu endorsed the Gandhian version without any second thoughts. The fact, however, remained that Nirmal Babu was not qualified to pass any judgement without knowing both sides of the story. The version preferred by Gandhiji was as follows: "She is against any plan of tour on foot in the present condition of my health. She thinks that, at least, one old companion who knows about my personal needs should accompany me, and she offered her own services. She suggested that it would not be safe to depend on new workers like you and Parasuram, who know so little about my physical requirements."[12]

Sushila was trying to wriggle back into his favour by accompanying him on a repeat of his famous Dandi March. This time he proposed to walk on foot, all alone from one Muslim-dominated area to another. He had succeeded for once in arousing jealousy in the mind of Sushila, by the simple device of keeping her at arm's length during his trip to Noakhali.

Loud Slaps

Encouraged by the opening gambit on the previous day, Nirmal Babu once again explored the incident on the next day (March 20) during the bath. He was completely floored when Gandhiji told him that he had administered a slap to himself. 'The loud sharp sounds' had been reverberating in his mind for three seemingly interminable days. Gandhiji had a sad look on his face. While recalling the incident he had confessed: "No, I did not beat her, I beat my own forehead. When I was twenty-five years old, I once beat my own son, but [it was] the last time."

He, however, did not tell Nirmal Babu that the slaps he administered to himself were an act of expiation for his father beating his forehead for the acts of his itinerant son, and equally an act of expiation for the beating he had administered to Harilal in 1894.

On the morning of 17 December, when Gandhiji was conversing with Sushila regarding his decision on repeating his Dandi March in Noakhali, he had decided upon his barefoot march from one Noakhali village to another accompanied by just one companion. His state of health had worried his associates. His age also went against him. He was, however, undaunted. Sushila found an opportunity for rehabilitation. She offered to accompany him on his second Dandi March as his companion, associate, doctor, cook and messenger. She saw visions of her massaging and bathing him as a loving mother would have done. They started arguing about the matter at 2.30 am, and it was but logical that the argument should turn acrimonious after about an hour.

The two loud slaps that Gandhiji administered to himself were not only his accounting to his father and his elder son Harilal, but also to Sushila for the treatment she had rendered him for a decade and half. Here was the Father of the Nation begging and entreating her day after day but Sushila simply rebuffed him.

Sushila was in a bad shape after the incident because she had been exposed to ridicule and shame. She had lost all courage to speak her mind. She decided to take her other associates into confidence after he had freely talked about her to others. She also decided to record her impressions of the event and bring the same to the attention of Nirmal Babu and Parasuram. Pyarelal took away her notes.

She wrote the account another time and gave it to Gandhiji on 18 March for being passed on to Professor Bose and Parasuram. He tore up the notes to pieces because her notes contradicted the version already provided by him to Professor Bose. She repeated the performance a third time. This note also met the same fate. It was not delivered to the concerned parties. Finally, she decided to narrate the tale of her distress for the fourth time and had it delivered straight to Professor Bose and Parasuram.

Curious Dream

Incidentally, she arrived in Srirampur the previous day at the invitation of her brother. As usual, she was invited to stay with Gandhiji in his room for the night. This was only two days before Manu was to arrive in Srirampur. At night she went through Bapu's diary and found the remarks: "I had a curious dream."

Sushila tried to find out more about the dream out of sheer curiosity but he would not say a word about it. Both of them went to sleep and got up at 2.30 am. He was feeling restless and shivering. At 3 am, Sushila woke up because she got disturbed by the noise of Bapu jumping in his bed. Evidently he was jumping to warm up his body. He began to narrate his 'curious dream' to her. She requested him to go to sleep, but he insisted on narrating his dream. She felt embarrassed on account of the ongoing tension. This was not the end of the matter: "After the dream he started explaining that his present step was a *tapascharya* [penance] for him."[13]

She was being inconvenienced. This was not the end of the matter. After prayers were over at 4 am, she came across his letter, which mentioned his plans to go on a *yatra* to rural Noakhali. Sushila sent a note requesting him to allow her to accompany him. Her persistent requests irritated him to no end. He insisted on his lonely pilgrimage through the villages of Noakhali.

He felt irritated with Sushila as he was unable to convince her. Eventually his irritation turned into anger. He became emotional like a child who has faulted. She picked up her papers and decided to walk away to avoid further acrimony. It irritated him further and the result was that he beat up his forehead so loudly that it was heard by those staying in the adjacent cottages. She rushed and tried to stop him. In her own words, she was 'completely unnerved and stunned'. The 22nd of December, 1946 was Kasturba's death anniversary. It was as usual celebrated in a formal manner. Sushila returned to Srirampur to participate in the ceremony. Prayer time was 4.15 am, Sushila Nayyar, Manu Gandhi and Parasuram read the *Bhagvad Gita*. On meeting her, he again talked about his 'curious dream'. She lost her nerve completely and confessed to Parasuram and Professor Bose with telling effect: "I found that my self-control has not returned as yet. I shall therefore keep away now. If I am needed for anything you will let me know."[14]

Perhaps it was for the first time that Sushila Nayyar was terrified of meeting her mentor. Gandhi had indeed cornered Sushila for once. Now it was Gandhiji's turn to get distracted. He tried to make up with Sushila and chose Professor Bose as his emissary. The next day, that is 23

December 1946, was a Monday, his day of silence. He wrote out a note to Professor Bose in which he confessed:

"I do not know what God is doing to me or through me. If you have the time and inclination I would like you to walk to Sushila [at her village station] at daybreak and return after passing sometime with her and learning about her requirements and her health. You can give the whole of our conversation about her without reserve. The rest you will know from her if she cares to tell you. You can show this [note] to her if you wish."[15]

Trouble with Parasuram

Nirmal Babu came back but there is no record of what transpired between them. Sushila was now a ghost who haunted Gandhiji in his dreams. There was another crisis situation upon him and Parasuram was the author of this new trouble for him. The Tamil Brahmin lad from Kerala was utterly devoted to Gandhi as his man Friday. He was his secretary, cook, valet and messenger boy. Initially Gandhiji was all praise for him. In his letter to Narandas Gandhi he termed Parasuram as a 'silent worker'. In a statement to the press, he described him as his' most devoted, selfless and silent stenographer."[16]

Once Gandhiji took his advice on the 17th December incident. Sushila also took him into confidence by writing a joint letter to him and N K Bose about her troubles with Gandhiji. She thanked Parasuram profusely for his 'brotherly love'. To his credit, Parasuram never hesitated to call a spade a spade. Finally, he broke up with Gandhiji and wrote a ten page letter to him on 1 January 1947. It was both frank and brutal. The sophisticated diplomacy of Professor Bose was not for him.

Gandhiji never employed another secretary during his stay in Noakhali. He repeatedly kept on enquiring about Parasuram, whom he would have welcomed with open arms, if he chose to return. But he was most uncharitable to Parasuram when he wrote to Sardar Patel: "Parasuram the typist has left. His departure had made no difference. He has lost his balance."[17]

Parasuram had talked to Gandhiji about the 17 December incident. For the first time, Gandhiji wanted to know from him, his views about Sushila Nayyar. He had his reservations about her, which he conveyed to him. He talked to Gandhiji on another occasion and he followed it with his long letter to Gandhi, threatening dissociation from him.

The letter had evidently been written in coordination with Nirmal Babu. Both of them were a perfect foil to each other. Nirmal Babu had a clear conscience on this account because Gandhiji himself had advised Parasuram to draft his letter in consultation with Nirmal Babu, who had despatched his letter to Gandhi on 3 January 1947. In between, Gandhiji had shot off his reply to Parasuram on 2 January refuting the charges levied against him. He advised him to talk it over with Sushila and Nirmal Babu. Parasuram had placed Gandhiji in a difficult situation.

Parasuram had a point to make. According to him even his own sons Manilal and Devdas considered her to be a suspect. So did C Rajagopalachari who had complete contempt for the 'Punjab Ministry'. Sardar Patel would have been too glad to get her off Gandhi's back. Rajkumari Amrit Kaur was of the same view. She would know because she was considered very close to Gandhiji and could view things from close quarters during her extended stays at the ashram. Sushila had also picked up a quarrel with Jawaharlal Nehru at Panchgani. In any case, Jawaharlal, with his intellectual hauteur and class consciousness, did not think much of young girls and women crowding around Gandhiji.

Punjab Ministry

Satis Chandra Das Gupta had coordinated the Noakholi sojourn of Gandhi from the beginning to the end. He was thus a close observer of the scene. He was severally critical of Sushila and in his view, Gandhiji's going on a walking tour in order to be free from Pyarelalji and Sushilabehn because they were pestering him beyond his endurance.[18]

Why was nobody telling Gandhiji about this matter directly? In Parasuram's opinion, those who knew were either too polite to speak out or lacked the necessary courage. He claimed to be a seeker of truth who was not afraid to talk. Parasuram had made two demands. His major demand was for Gandhiji to get rid of Sushila. The second demand was for terminating what he had described as 'that Pyarelalji affair.' Obviously he was referring to Pyarelal's single-minded pursuit of Manu Gandhi. He had a simplistic solution for endless troubles from Sushila: "Just marry her off and be done with her."

Parasuram should have known better. She was there because he liked her to be around for his personal reasons. Gandhiji would not have dreamed of getting rid of the 'Punjab Ministry' and hence Parasuram had to go. That Sushila was eventually dispatched to Sevagram constituted an entirely different chapter in his life.

The indictment letter from Parasuram was directed against Sushila Nayyar. To his credit, he viewed her as a normal human being except for her relations with Bapu. In no time would she be transformed into a neurotic, jealous, quarrelsome and arrogant female full of destructive tendencies in the eyes of Parasuram. Her association with Gandhi brought out the best and the worst in her. The battle cry of Parasuram was emblazoned in his letter: "I want Sushilabehn to leave you."

He listed a series of charges. He viewed the 'Punjab Ministry' as a single entity. He would have liked Gandhiji not only to get rid of Sushila, but of her brother Pyarelal also. To him, Pyarelal was a decent human being except when he was placed in the company of his sister, or when he was engaged in wooing Manu Gandhi. In other words, if Sushila was the ignition that lighted Gandhiji, it was Manu who provided the necessary propulsion to Pyarelal.

Parasuram viewed things in black and white. There were no grey shades in his scheme of things. His was a hammer-and-tong view of things. Sushila was his pet obsession. Pyarelal had viewed Gandhi "like wax in her hands". In the process Parasuram had burnt his boat. His letter was a record of his bittersweet memories. The job had been done.

Bapu Responds

Gandhiji started reading Parasuram's letter at 3 a.m. in the morning and took one hour to finish it. He rejected his arguments and chose to fire back at Parasuram: "It contains half truths which are dangerous. You wronged me, the parties you mention yourself and the cause by suppressing from them your opinion about them."[19]

There was some weight in this but on the whole his arguments were essentially aimed at scoring points over Parasuram. The substantive charges about leniency shown to Sushila were unanswerable. His leniency with Pyarelal and Sushila had played havoc with the moral fabric of the Sevagram Ashram. Gandhi rejected his charges outright. He saw a 'conflict of ideals' between the two of them. Parasuram was relieved immediately, because, in his view: "That will be honourable and truthful. I like your frankness and boldness."

Gandhi was in two minds as to whether the letter should be publicised or not. He advocated its restricted circulation. Since Pyarelal was privy to his entire correspondence, he was bound to show Parasuram's letter to him. Parasuram made his task easy. He promised not to disclose the contents of the letter to anyone. That took care of the press attached to the Gandhian entourage. The press would have flashed the contents of the letter to the whole world. A first-class scandal jeopardising his Noakhali *yajna* would have followed. Here Parasuram had chosen to act as a perfect gentleman.

Gandhiji was, however, wary of the news leaking out. In any case he could have been accused of keeping back the truth. That would have gone against his basic tenet of not keeping the truth hidden under several bushels of secrecy. His letter ended with a piece of advice to Parasuram: "Finally let me tell you that you are at liberty to publish whatever wrong you have noticed in me and my surrounding."[20]

Unhappy Nirmal Babu

Now it was Nirmal Babu's turn to go on record. He wisely decided to formally convey his views on the Parasuram incident to Gandhiji. Parasuram had sent his stinging epistle to Gandhi on 1 January 1947. Gandhiji responded the next day, by denying all his allegations. On 3rd of January, Nirmal Babu followed with his version. Besides Gandhiji, Parasuram, Nirmal Babu and Sushila Nayyar conferred with each other and between themselves. That Nirmal Babu had openly sympathised with Parasuram was no secret.

Nirmal Babu's was an intellectual response, in contrast to Parasuram's emotional outpourings. His was an exploration in the theory and practice of Gandhian ideology. The letter struck at the very roots of his *brahmacharya* cult: "Parasuram's complaint against you is that he has observed some elements in your behaviour, both before men and women, which may injure your reputation with the public. He is of the opinion, this will prove detrimental to the cause which you represent."[21]

Prof Bose had even expressed scepticism about the intentions of those who claimed to follow him faithfully. The obvious reference was to his *brahmacharya* practices, rituals and the cult in general. He saw nothing but disaster awaiting those who followed him slavishly.

The scholastic critique provided by Professor Bose reads as follows: "You (Gandhiji) seem to have a love for self-mortification also and a soldier's type of discipline. There is nothing wrong in these by themselves. But people sometime practice these virtues not out of spiritual necessity in the pursuit of a lofty ideal but only to find favour with you."[22]

What he was saying was that Gandhiji's disciples were practicing selflessness for selfish reasons.

Neurotic Mind

Professor Bose elaborated upon his theme in his farewell letter of 5-6 April 1947 to Gandhiji: "But I began to feel uneasy in Srirampur soon after the 17th of December… incident… in which Dr Sushila Nayyar was involved. She used to come frequently, may be generally on account of her patients. But each time she came, we found you no longer in an unruffled happy state, and fits of impatience used to be often in evidence. They might never have reached a high pitch, but they were there all the same."[23]

Nirmal Babu had also decided to confront headlong the issue of *brahmacharya* experiments: "You wanted to find out by means of that experiment whether any lustful feeling evoked either in you or any woman by lying on the same bed with you at night."[24]

Sushila had assured us that no feelings except for the feelings she would have for her mother bothered her. The elaborate explanation of Sushila had few takers as argued by Professor Bose: "But I have noticed for sometime past that [Sushila] has been in terribly unbalanced state of mind. She has been crying and crying and been very touchy about small matters. Manu Gandhi who had come recently was also reported to have spent two hours crying on the day I was at Feni. These two instances have led me to ask myself whether some harm is not done to these girls by their association with you, although there may be no harm for you personally."[25]

Here Nirmal Babu was completely off the track. Gandhiji was in as much terrible state as the two young women. He had shed bitter tears once on 17 December 1946, but his diary reflected it all. His response to the developing situation was totally irrational. Since he hid his true feelings, he suffered more. Sushila gave him no peace of mind because she blamed Manu for usurping her rightful place. Manu, in turn, was irritated by the presence of Pyarelal, who kept chasing her.

No Nirvana

There was unhappiness all around in Noakhali. The poor Hindus were unhappy because they had been victimised. The Muslims were unhappy because they were being sanitised. Gandhi was unhappy with Nirmal Babu, Parasuram, Sushila, Pyarelal and Manu. Each one was qualified to find faults with the others.

Gandhiji did not discover his *nirvana* in Noakhali. He found peace in his relations neither with the external world nor in his interaction with his inner self. Parasuram was indeed most perceptive in describing Gandhi's predicament: "It is like the case of Noakhali Hindu people. They have not the courage to say how they have been wronged and by whom. Like that, most people could say the opposite thing. But if pressed for a fresh opinion they will go on in another way."[26]

It is difficult for ordinary men, much less for men of eminence, to come to terms with the realities of the world. Illusion and imagination clash with reality. In his letter of 3 January 1947, Nirmal Babu had hinted at the imaginary world in which Sushila lived: "[There was] something else in the behaviour of those who try to follow you in Bengal."[27]

He spelt out the psychology of such abnormal persons in great detail in his letter of 18 March 1947 to Gandhiji. Earlier, when Nirmal Babu enquired from Sushila whether she was involved with Gandhiji in *brahmacharya* experiments, she referred to "X" in his letter but denied her involvement with him. Subsequently Nirmal Babu checked up with Gandhiji himself: "It was just because of that last night I first ascertained from you if she had any connection with the experiment and you replied in the affirmative."[28]

Intellectual Indictment

Like a good prosecutor, Nirmal Babu went on to press his own case by hitting where it hurt the most: "But you must not take any of this as an indictment against X [Sushila Nayyar] or A [Pyarelal]. It only means that we poor mortals are often motivated and carried away by unconscious desires in directions other than to which we consciously subscribe."[29] He added: "I had an idea when she told me the information that she had nothing to do with prayog, that she was screening facts, may be even from herself."[30]

After Noakhali it was Bihar's turn to receive the healing touch of Bapu. *Nirmal Babu had enough of him.* He said his final goodbye in his letter of 5-6 April 1947, which he sent to him from Calcutta. He spoke frankly of his failure to achieve what he had set to achieve in the company of Gandhiji: "As soon as my faith in your ability or perhaps desire to shake off the old completely and be true to the bold future was weakened, the scales in my judgement turned in my scientific work in the university."[31]

Now was the time to leave Gandhiji to God, his own resources, Manu Gandhi, Pyarelal and Sushila Nayyar. That Sushila was not restored to her former pre-eminent position she had held before is another story.

SECTION VIII

Manu the Lovable

CHAPTER 20

Noakhali *Yajna*

Manu Gandhi was plump, pale and wore thick glasses and had an ever ready smile. She was barely literate and no authority on the theory and practice of the Gandhian cult. Intellectual discourse was not her cup of tea. Yet she was chosen as Mahatma's closest companion during 1947 and in early 1948. She was the star of the Noakhali show. Gandhiji's hand was resting on her shoulder when he was shot dead by Nathuram Godse. Manu was a lonely child. She lost her mother when she was barely 12. At 14, she came to live with Gandhiji. She was the daughter of Jaisukhlal Gandhi and granddaughter of Amritlal Tulsidas Gandhi, Gandhiji's uncle. Manu participated in the Quit India Movement of 1942. She was arrested and placed in Nagpur Jail. At that time the Gandhis were detained at the Aga Khan Palace detention camp at Poona. Kasturba suffered several heart attacks after her husband decided to go on fast. Manu was transferred to the Poona detention camp to look after the ailing Kasturba.

Kasturba's Wisdom

There was considerable surprise in the Mahatma's inner circle when Ba insisted on having Manu by her side during her last days. Ba is purported to have said: "If Manu is available I want none else."[1] How highly her services were rated by Ba was proved by her inheriting Kasturba's necklace of *tulsi*, the string with which she tied her hair, her saffron box and sandals. This was Ba's way of approving Manu's selfless and dedicated service during her last days.

Kasturba was a wise person who had experienced the world from close quarters. She knew her husband better than anyone else. She was aware of his infatuations. She had called Jaisukhlal, Manu's father, by her bedside on the eve of her death. She advised him to take Manu away and arrange for her studies at his place of residence at Karachi. Manu was inconsolable on account of her separation from Bapu and Ba. To console her, Gandhiji wrote a chit at 4 am to Chi Manudi on Monday, his day of silence: "I felt much worried about you. You are a class by yourself. You are good, simple-hearted and ever ready to help others. Service has become a dharma with you. But you are still uneducated and silly also."[2] As if this was not enough to placate an inconsolable Manu, he added: "I am your mother. Am I not? It is enough, if you understand this much."[3]

For Manu it was like *manna* from the heavens unsought. He used to call her his 'divine gift'. Manu responded in equal measure to his concern for her. She had no mother of her own and Kasturba was no more. It was natural for her to fill up the vacuum by looking upon Bapu as her mother. He responded in equal measure. He would find time from his busy schedule to shower her with questions about her food and sleeping habits as well as her constipation. He kept assuring her that their separation was temporary and advised her to endure it.

Manudi the Obsession

But soon after Ba died, Gandhiji was anxious to have her back to keep him company in jail. Accordingly, he made a formal request to the authorities to grant her special permission to stay with him. He realised the inappropriateness of his request very soon. He wrote a long letter to Manu beseeching forbearance. It had become unendurable for Manu. She was inconsolable. She had imprisoned herself by being out of prison. He started by upbraiding her but ended up by being sentimental. He called her silly but ended up with a confessional note: "We must endure our separation... Stop crying and live cheerfully."[4]

Manu was in the fifth standard studying at Karachi. He had kept in constant touch with her . He advised her to shift to Rajkot for her studies. He recommended her case to Narandas Gandhi and employed a battery of adjectives recommending her case to him. She was described as a simple-hearted, obedient, devoted girl but unfortunately dull in her studies: "She has created a very good impression on me. I have not another girl in our family with the same spontaneous spirit of service that she has. The devotion with which she looked after Ba has captured my heart. She would like to remain with me, but I do not wish it."[5]

After Bapu was released from prison, he was recuperating at Juhu, Bombay. In his letter of 27 May to her, he had described himself as a 'broken reed': "If I were keeping good health, I would not let you go anywhere, but would have given you what I myself could."[6]

He was concerned with every aspect of her life. He was even worried about her sleeping posture. So in January 1945, he made her sleep with him for three nights for correcting her sleeping posture. While he was so protective of her, he was not able to keep her away from prying eyes. This made her feel insecure all the time. She was a sensitive being and that doubly increased her worries. It added to his worries also: "I am very much worried about you. You are always crying and seen restless."[7]

The demands made on her by Gandhiji and the outside world were too much for her. Especially troublesome was the antagonism of Sushila Nayyar, who had been dethroned by her. Sushila had decided to carry on psychological warfare against Manu: "Tell [Sushila] boldly whatever it is. She tells me that she has not stopped you from attending the class because you share the bed with me."[7]

Just a hint by him was enough to announce to the whole world his *brahmacharya* experiments in which Manu was a full participant. She was participating as only a *bhakta* would willingly do. Indeed the *bhakta* in her was prepared to sacrifice her life at the altar of her *ishtadeva* (personal God). But all his soliciting on her behalf did not help her. She admitted to Gandhiji: "[She was] consumed by the fear of the surrounding atmosphere." He had his admonition ready for her: "The world will frighten all those who let themselves be frightened."

This advice had little effect. His appeal to her 'to cast off fears in the sea' didn't help. He spent considerable amount of his valuable time in improving her mental makeup. However, all this was to prove futile. She was not equal to the task. During June 1945, Gandhiji was to stay at Birla House, Bombay, and he sent for Manu to meet him. He was worried to find her in a 'shattered condition'. Her physical condition was a true reflection of her spiritual crisis. Even he was to throw up his hands in utter despair. She had found the burden overwhelming. He felt anguished after reading her letter. He tore it into pieces. Everyone was her enemy beyond the protective *lakshman rekha* drawn by him: "If there was anything private in it, it was your silliness... You wish to go back on your word! Who will trust you then? ...Your letter was silly."[8]

Reading between the lines, it seems quite clear that Manu Gandhi was only a reluctant partner in Gandhiji's *brahmacharya* experiment. She was the youngest among his women associates. She was not even 19 in 1944. She had too much respect for Bapu to refuse him. After all, to shine in the reflected glory of a great man was given to a few men and women in their lives. His charisma also proved to be too powerful a magnet to be deflected artfully.

Developing Coldness

The years 1945 and 1946 were fraught with uncertainty. She was confronted with too many pressures. A certain degree of coldness had developed between her and Bapu. She stayed away from the ashram for considerable periods of time. Gandhi felt hurt when Pyarelal referred to the fact obliquely.

Gandhiji, who had laid claim to being her mother, was keen on knowing everything about her. She was fast reaching the state of puberty. Now he was mystified by the absence of any signs of puberty in her. What was to be done: "She was nineteen. She was faced with a difficult problem. She claimed to be complete stranger to sexual awakening generally associated with a girl of her age. As a [nosy] 'mother' he must know."[9]

Actually Manu was neither deceiving him nor was she unaware of her sexuality. The explanation lies elsewhere. Charisma is a form of sexuality. It emasculates the sexuality of the person responding to a charismatic icon. Bapu was Manu's one point agenda and her entire world. Francis Watson described her thus: "sweetly immaculate as Saint Rose of Lima".

Abnormal Responses

Abnormal reactions and responses are natural to persons placed in her position. Manu was a victim of her name and fame under the shadow of a great man. She must have suppressed her sexuality to compensate for her high-flown status. While normal situations result in normal responses, abnormal situations bring about abnormal responses. Such people live in the unreal world and view it as the normal state of affairs. So here was Manu responding illogically and irrationally to abnormal expectations from him. She had tried to escape the net thrown around her, or, at its worst, she was trying to strike the best bargain with Bapu.

Gandhiji complained to her on March 19 1946, about her laying down preconditions before she was to join him. He saw 'distrust' and 'unhappiness' in her predicament. What greatly upset him was that Manu was blaming him for lack of confidence. He could now read her mind about being consumed 'by the fear of the surrounding atmosphere'.[10]

Bapu employed all kinds of strategies to win her over and break down her resistance. He was now stationed in New Delhi for crucial talks about India's independence. Above all the rest of the things, Manu was on his mind. He shot off a letter to Manu on the eve of his departure for Calcutta and then onwards to Noakhali. He was preparing the ground for her to join him: "Further, I shall be happy if you come over and have a talk with me. I do not wish to put any pressure on you. It is my earnest desire that you should remain a pure virgin till the end of your life and spend your life in service."[11]

Watching Bapu break the resistance gradually should be a lesson in itself. It leaves no option for the other person except to surrender hands and feet bound, completely brainwashed and in the end entreating for total surrender. Manu came rushing to him to Noakhali on 19 December 1946.

Towards Noakhali

October 1946 had been an ominous month for Noakhali. Communal riots had broken out. There was large scale looting, murders, rapes and burning of properties. Gandhiji decided to move to Noakhali (now in Bangladesh) to face the situation frontally. He reached Calcutta by early November 1946. Manu was still on his mind. He wrote to her father Jaisukhlal Gandhi from Calcutta reminding him: "Manu should be with me. But it seems it is now impossible for her to come."[12]

Since Manu was on the move, she read this letter only after reaching Mahua (Gujarat) on 1 December 1946. By that time Gandhi had reached Noakhali. She was greatly moved by the reference in the letter to her. In the meanwhile her father was flooded with an unending stream of letters from Bapu. He was all by himself in Noakhali. He had managed to keep his old associates like Sushila Nayyar, Pyarelal and Amutussalaam at bay.

At the same time Bapu was very solicitous about the safety of Manu. He was equally anxious to have her join him. On the very next day (November 15 1946), he sent a telegram to her father, enquiring about the possible date of her arrival in Noakhali. Things had begun to work his way. Soon after his departure from New Delhi, he sent his supplication to the 'court of last appeal' of Manudi: "I shall be leaving for Bengal, I suppose, in a day or two. I would have been happier, if you had come here before I left. But now, please yourself. I am quite content whatever makes you happy."[13]

The avalanche of letters to father and daughter had their desired result. Now only the terms of surrender had to be drafted. After it was decided that she would proceed to Noakhali, he was in an extremely joyous mood, so much so that he wrote: "I consider you silly... I will... pull your ears when you come here."[14]

Manu negotiated the most favourable deal for herself after reaching Mahua on 1 December. She wrote to Bapu: "I do not wish to come, if you want me to work in some village away from you. On the other hand, I am eager and anxious to be with you, if only you let me help you and look after you... I promise to brave any dangers that might befall me."[15]

Wish Granted

Her wish was readily granted and she was expected to stand shoulder-to-shoulder with Bapu during the period of his stay in Noakhali. Finally he telegraphed the following to Jaisukhlal Gandhi: "If you and Manu are sincerely anxious for her to be with me at your risk you can bring her to be with me." Gandhiji seemed to have overlooked the safety of other volunteers working in far-flung Noakhali villages at greater risks to their lives.

Her reply, dated 12 December, to "Dear and Revered Bapuji" reminded him of an occasion when she was left all alone: "Bapu, I am alone now!" "Alone?", You said admonishing me, 'how could you be alone when I am with you?'"[16]

Jaisukhlal, accompanied by Manu, was on his way to Noakhali. She arrived at his temporary headquarters in Srirampur on 19 December 1946. Gandhiji was thrilled by her arrival but, by way of caution, he forewarned Jaisukhlal of his daughter being tested and stretched to the farthest limit during her entire stay with him. He promised her nothing short of her *agnipariksha*. To her nothing mattered except for union with her dear Bapu. She went rushing to him when she reached his hut and knelt down in *pranam* to him. He was playful in responding to her. He patted her, twisted her ears, pinched her cheeks and said: "So, you have come."[17]

As it was getting dark, he asked Jaisukhlal to leave Manu in his custody and return to the next village of Kazirkhil for his overnight stay. He would not let her father stay in his hut overnight as he explained to him: "This is the holy ground of sacrifice [*yajna*]... I can't let you sleep or have your meals here."[18] Manu was however to share his hut as his equal partner in *brahmacharya yajna* in the climactic event of his stay in Noakhali.

Noakhali Diary

Both of them went to sleep at 9.30 pm. He woke her up at 12.45 am by the clock, with the gentle touch of his hands. He got up again at 3 am for prayers. Manu was woken up at 3.30 am. The countdown to the preliminaries to his *yajna* had begun. He asked her whether she was ready for the test. She gave her undertaking without any questions asked. Both of them went to sleep after talking for half an hour. All this was faithfully recorded in his diary.

He has recorded every bit of information for posterity. He also made it obligatory for Manudi to maintain a daily record of events in great detail in her diary. It was pursued by him from time to time and signed by him. It was quite a scene to find Gandhiji lying down on a wooden bedstead, intently listening to the entries made by Manu, correcting the entries and putting his signature. Manu made entries in her diary in Gujarati and he suggested the Gujarati words *rojanishi* or *nityanodh* for the diary.

He watched her perform the jobs previously assigned to Mahadev Desai and Prabhavati. Manu had some doubts about the value of some of the trivia contained in the diary. He brushed aside her doubts with a wave of his hand. He had no doubts about its historical value. So he told her: "You must make it a point to get your diary read and signed by me. You won't appreciate today the value of my signature in your diary. But it will bear a sure testimony to the fact that I pour forth my whole heart in whatever I tell you."[19] He ended with a benediction: "See I am training you like a mother her beloved daughter."[19]

History apart, the diary is a great human document of two loving human beings in a lonely and hostile environment.

Foundation of Understanding

The 20th of January 1947, laid the foundation of understanding between the two of them. During the next morning there followed a chit to Manu for building further bridges with her: "Stick to your word. Don't hide even a single thought for me. Give a true answer to whatever I ask from you. . The step I took today was taken after careful thinking... I shall certainly reveal all my thought to you."[20]

Manu was willing to bear the burden and face all tribulations that might confront her. He was happy beyond words at her response and responded to her assurances: "If your faith has really gone that far, then you are safe. You will play your full role in this great sacrifice, even though you are foolish. Preserve this… Question me if you cannot decipher my words."[21]

His reverie was suddenly broken. So much had happened between them in the first twelve hours. Now he was ready for his morning walk accompanied by Manu. She washed his feet and then massaged his body upon his return from his morning walk. The massage was followed by his bath. It was now time for a visit by Jaisukhlal before his return home.

He was delighted to inform Jaisukhlal about Manu being 'firm as a rock' in her determination to stick by him, come what may. He told him of his determination: 'as long I am alive' and proclaimed with a flourish: "She may leave me, but I shall never leave her. Nothing can part us but death. And what can death do after all? It can separate the bodies, but is not the soul immortal? It is my cherished desire to draw out all the hidden best in her which I have noticed."[22]

Gandhiji had a magnificent obsession. He wanted to draw the best out of the obedient, devoted, committed and silent Manu. Bapu was trying to discover virtues in her to carve out a split image of himself in Manudi. Manu was the queen bee in this finale of his life cycle. He was to confide to her: "You know this is a holy sacrifice; and our old *Puranic* sacrifices demand perfect purity on the part of the performers. Satanic urges in man such as lust, anger, infatuation, etc have to be totally overcome."[23]

Sheer Poetry

Nature is said to be benign and cruel in Noakhali. Its countryside is lush with vegetation: swaying palm trees, innumerable water channels, green fields and cottages interspersed at regular intervals. Even a serious minded person like Manu Gandhi was deeply affected by the beautiful nature. She let herself go for a moment after she reached the village Palla on 18 January 1947: "All around Nature has attired herself in a costume of the gayest colours. Then there are the villages of Noakhali, sweet and charming. Added to them are the hearty receptions given to us by the simple and sincere village folk of Noakhali. And to crown everything, my constant awareness of my good fortune in having the chance to travel with the saint who pilgrimages barefoot in this stinging and oppressive cold weather. You can now understand why I am at a loss to express the joy I feel."[24]

It was but natural for Manudi to be joyous during the six weeks she spent with Bapu all by herself. She had also been privy to all his secrets. She had walked side-by-side with him, marching from one village to another. She was witness to the making of history and had the good sense to record it on a day-to-day basis for posterity.

Manu shared the room with Gandhi. He would frequently wake her up and share his secrets with her. They must have talked about men and events, his closest associates and the mechanics of his *brahmacharya* experiments. Manu has not said a word about her participation in the Noakhali *yajna*. The loss is entirely of the world.

Manu had her doubts and fears as well, as she was not sure of herself and fearful of adversaries. When the Noakhali sojourn was in its last phase, she began to feel triumphant over what she had been able to accomplish. Her experience of six weeks spent in Noakhali was extraordinary for a teenager.

By the time Gandhiji reached Alunia on 18 February 1947, he decided to call upon a physically handicapped old man living across the Dhakaria river. He was anxious to have a *darshan* of the great man. So Gandhiji decided to visit him on the spur of the moment. He was accompanied by Manu. The boat ride moved Manu: "It was an unforgettable sight—the river running between colonnades of emerald-green trees, the sky a speckless blue and the weather temperate. It was a question of only 5 or 7 minutes to cross the river. But even for that short period Bapuji stretched his limbs, laid his hand on my lap, .closed his eyes and sank into a nap. The boat glided. Now there was only the vast canopy of the sky above, and a long long stretch of water below lapping against the boat. Far away, both behind and in front of us, could be seen large crowds of men in the background of green foliage. A soft and gentle breeze was blowing. In the midst of this enchanting scenery, and at a time when the mellow evening was displaying its most ravishing beauty, I was alone in the boat, except for one boatman who was no company, with one of the world's most exalted souls, with him lying cosily on my lap and with my palm on his forehead. It was just a fleeting five minutes, but a five minutes that were full of bliss for me."[25]

Stalking Terror

The benign nature of Noakhali was deceptive. Fear stalked the land. Even Gandhiji could feel the heat. Manu was to testify to the fact: "In this region ... none dared to utter the name of Rama." Now thanks to the efforts of Gandhi: "*Ramdhuna* and hymns are sung daily all along our route."[26]

The optimism expressed by her was totally unreal. No Hindu dared to open his mouth to tell the truth to him. Gandhiji was taken in by the deceptive calm. No doubt, his endeavours were in a good cause. Not that he had no inkling of the sad situation because on the very next day of Manu's arrival in Srirampur, he confided to her during his morning walk of his fears: "Don't make the mistake of thinking that you have been summoned here simply to serve me. You know that neither a little girl nor an old lady is safe here. So if you, a youngster of 16 or 17 years, bravely resist an attack from ruffians or die in the attempt, I shall dance with joy."[27] On another occasion he warned Manu of their being assassinated during their sleep.

The terror that stalked the land could be gauged from the predicament in which Manu found herself soon after their arrival in Narayanpur on 15 January 1947. Years ago, Mirabehn had given Gandhiji a piece of stone for rubbing his legs during his daily bath. The stone functioned in place of soap which was never used by him. The stone also brought to him memories of old times.

To her horror, Manu was not able to find the stone, which was evidently left at the previous place of residence. Bapu was greatly upset and ordered Manu to walk back to Bhatialpur to fetch the stone. Her request for a male escort was blankly refused. Now the beautiful countryside of Noakhali was forgotten by her. The winding footpaths and thickets of coconut trees could make her lose her way. The lessons imbibed by her about courage and fearlessness were forgotten.

When she arrived at Bhatialpur, their hostess had thrown away the stone. Ultimately it was retrieved. Manu returned safe and sound by noon. In her own words: "I had breathed God's name all the way with an earnestness which, perhaps, I had never felt before at any time in my life."[28] She wept with joy and great relief after going through so much agony. For Gandhiji it was a test in which she had succeeded. Unfortunately he was under a wrong impression. Actually Manu had totally failed because she was stalked by fear every minute of her walking expedition.

Barefoot Mahatma

A new phase of his *yajna* had begun by the time he reached Chandipur. He decided to discard his sandals and walk barefoot from village to village. After all, he was on a sacred mission and *yatra* to indicate his empathy with the fallen people of Noakhali. He considered visiting the victims of communal riots as an act of pilgrimage to sacred places. After all the earth had been sanctified by his visit to Noakhali. To walk with shoes on such a land was an act of sacrilege to him. He also saw in the faces of the victims the image of *daridranarayana* (God of the deprived and downtrodden). It was a difficult enterprise for a man reaching his early eighties.

Exactly at 7.30 am on 7 January 1947, he began his barefoot march with his bamboo stick in one hand and the other hand resting on the shoulder of Manu Gandhi. While passing through groves of coconut and betelnut, he was required to cross rivulets on narrow bridges. Not only was he visiting sacred places on his pilgrimage, he had also declared the human body as sacred. Indeed he had pronounced the human body as the 'temple of God'. On another occasion, he called the human body: "A tabernacle owned by the Lord of all that is, namely, God."[29]

However, he forgot to insure his physical body with God. He was in serious trouble due to his barefoot *yatra*. His soles had bleeding cuts. There was a deep gash at the joint below the great toe. With loving care Manu Gandhi applied *ghee* to his cuts to provide some relief to him. Undaunted, the barefoot saint marched on. Manu shed many a tear over his plight, but she felt gratified at being allowed to accompany him.

Austere Penance

There was no stopping him. On the 22nd day of his march, he was faced with a challenge. The wintry conditions had become intolerable for him. Manu would wash his feet, clean his festering wounds and apply ointment to provide relief at the end of the march, evening after evening. It did not help the matters very much, because by 7.30 every morning he was ready to march again. Nobody had the courage to tell him to wear his *chappals* until the healing process had taken place.

This penance had gone on for full six weeks. The cold had become unbearable by the middle of February. While at Bishakathkali, Bapu woke Manu at 12 am on the twentieth of February, 1947. He was shivering and his feet had gone cold. Bapu and Manu were all alone by themselves with the gusts of cold wind rushing through the hut. Cold winds howled through the leaky thatched hut in which Manu and Bapu had found shelter for the night. In the words of Manu: "There were only two humans—Bapuji and I."

One of the finest tributes to Gandhiji was paid by Manu that night: "It was the darkest night of the month, the new moon night, or the preceding one. All around us was the fearful and awful solitude of darkness in a dense jungle. The blasts of wind howling through the coconut and betel leaves have made the environment quite sinister. But those trees, besides me, the only witness of the austere penance this man of God was undergoing in order to awaken [humanity] in hardened hearts."[30]

Hutless Shelter

There were occasions when no hut was available for sheltering him for the night. In such situations there were no two choices for both of them except to take shelter under a tree in the open. Such was the act of expiation performed by Gandhiji not only in the cause of the victims but also for those who victimised them. His benediction was for all whether they were sinned against or sinning.

The hurdles placed in the way of Gandhiji would have broken the stamina of anyone else. He must not have had any illusions about changing the hearts through his incessant marches, frequent harangues and endless face-to-face dialogues. He had realised very early that his intrusion in Noakhali was not welcome. This became apparent when he moved from Atakona to Shirdi on 19 January 1947. The path for the day was slippery, but undaunted Bapu marched on barefoot.

This time young Muslim lads had decided to show their disrespect to him by throwing excreta in his path. Bapu was seen removing the lumps of excreta on his path with the help of tree leaves. This exercise continued for sometime until noted by Manu, who walked by him. She protested and volunteered to do the job for him. He would not accept any assistance on that account. He had been performing such tasks since his days in South Africa. With a smile on his face, he shooed away Manu and told her in no uncertain terms that cleaning the toilet gave him maximum satisfaction.

Back to Pyarelal

The shadow of Pyarelal over Manu had once again began to loom large. He had been posted to another village away from the headquarters of Gandhiji. He managed to present himself from time to time in Gandhiji's court. He would find time to be alone with Manu during his brief visits. They would chatter away sitting in a corner. Gandhiji did not like the special attention that Pyarelal was to paying to Manu.

Gandhiji decided to rebuke her about wasting time in 'idle chatter'. He warned her about 'bad company'. He also warned her on wearing "tight clothes" like *salwar* and *kurta*. Manu had for the first time started wearing Punjabi dresses because of its convenience in movement. Parasuram had objected to Manu wearing such a dress in Noakhali. Gandhiji must have been feeling insecure with Pyarelal hovering around her. So here was Bapu being protective by laying down the do's and don'ts about dress, hair style and her tendency to gossip.

The presence of Pyarelal in Noakhali was a matter of concern to Jaisukhlal Gandhi. Pyarelal had ardently wooed Manu in the past. Her father had to be reassured by Gandhiji before Manu was to land in Noakhali. Gandhiji had to assure the worried father by promising 'nobody (will) harass… her'. In any case Pyarelal had been posted to a village away from the temporary headquarters. He went to the extent of defending Pyarelal: "[His] eyes are clean and he is not likely to force himself on anybody. I don't think he did anything wrong in placing his ideas before me in the presence of all."[31]

Compromising with Pyarelal

He, however, advised Jaisukhlal to let Manu on her own and work out her relations with others on her own. While he chose to defend Pyarelal, he was remorseless toward his sister Sushila with whom he had recently fallen out. She also considered Manu her rival for the attention of Gandhi. Here he was complaining bitterly to Pyarelal about Sushila. He was equally concerned about the fallout over Manu: "I consider the present spectacle very bad for Manu. I have given my soul to protect her and I am still doing it."[32] He went to the extent of accusing Sushila of committing *adharma* and was prepared to break with Pyarelal, if he were to defend his sister.

He knew how difficult Pyarelal could be by himself alone and a formidable force when in alliance with his sister. The best thing in the circumstances was to bait him by opening his lines of communication with Manu. Here was the compromise that came to be worked out between them: "You have agreed that you and I should never talk [about] keeping Manu apart. You cannot entertain any doubt about her at all. Hence I advise you to convey to her the purport of our talk."

Gandhiji was smart enough to realise that Pyarelal was only a small player and not a competitor for the attentions of Manu. He advised Pyarelal: "Affection can never last till end. It certainly did not last in this case. Hence you must be cheerful and confident and inspire in her as much confidence as possible."

Having prepared the ground, he eased Pyarelal into accepting that God's will was to be fulfilled by having Manu share his bed: "God belongs to everyone. He will do as He wills. I am doing only that. I am having her sleep close to me. She sleeps naked but sleeps soundly. She is to be woken up whenever there is work, be it at 2 o'clock or 3 o' clock. I consider it a very good sign that she is able to sleep like that. I have known it since the Aga Khan Palace days that she is quite unself-conscious. The main thing was she should be with me, in my care and associate with you and learn. That has happened. Now we must all wish that only that which spontaneously occurs to her will happen. Only then will she be completely free from fear."[33]

Suspecting Manu

Whenever Gandhiji used to be worried, he would get up before his scheduled time. Now that the young lady had become conscious of her charms (thanks to Pyarelal), it worried Gandhiji a great deal. He would get up earlier than usual, at 2 am. He woke up Manu on 27 December 1946, at 2.15 am. He has recorded the gist of the conversation with her in his diary: "Made her understand the temperament of... Talked to her about the need for simplicity in clothes and in hair styles, and asked her not to waste time in chats with… or anyone else. Showed her how one's company affects one's character very often."[34]

The mysterious reference in the diary notes is probably to Pyarelal, who was not the only cause for his worries. He had also picked up quarrels with Sushila on 17 December. Parasuram had parted company with him on 1 January 1947. His *brahmacharya* experiments in which Sushila and Manu had become involved during his Noakhali sojourn had come to be widely known among his associates outside Noakhali.

Thakkar Bapa, who was the most respected among his top associates, was on his way to Noakhali. Bapa arrived in Srirampur on 27 December to dissuade Gandhi from proceeding with what he had claimed to be his *brahmacharya yajna* any further. Manu seemed to have gone astray by establishing direct rapport with Pyarelal. All these developments must have cast a shadow over the old man. It was no more an idyllic situation for him.

A feeling of insecurity had taken hold of Manu by reflex action. Gandhiji began to suspect her fidelity and charged Manu with crimes she had not committed. She was too shrewd. She recognised her premier position in the eyes of Bapu and would not risk cheating him. He had to eat humble pie by 10 January 1947. He had by then realised that of all his associates, she was the only one in his entourage to have followed him blindly. Others had in fact deserted him as a lost cause.

He made up for his shortsightedness in suspecting her: "I had accused you, but now I freely admit that it was a totally false accusation... So, I lost sleep. I looked at my watch. It was 2 am. Something within me prodded me. 'You have to wake up Manudi', it said, 'it is your duty to tell her that your mind now accepts her innocence in the affair."[35]

It was not difficult to gauge the working of his mind in those difficult days. He had a troubled mind and hence, "I see nothing but darkness all around. The whole atmosphere is surcharged with lies and untruths... Just observe, however, how God sustains me. Though I sleep at 10 or 11 pm, rise at 2 or 2.30 am, do my work at high pressure and get no rest at all, I carry on somehow! That itself is a wonder. I felt suddenly that lest I disappear from the world shortly, I should give you some idea of what I now feel about you and speak out frankly."[36]

Tribute to Manudi

By now he had begun to recognise her true worth by subjecting her to *agniparikasha*. It took him several years to realise her full worth. She had been his secretary, bathroom attendant, butler, nurse and night companion, with whom he shared his innermost secrets. She attended upon him 24 hours a day for seven days of the week. She sat over conferences with his associates. She maintained a detailed diary of events for him. She had begun to prove herself.

He had now begun to call her 'a noble specimen of womankind'. She was so sacrificing by nature that she found no difficulty in winning everybody to her side. While Kasturba possessed the wife's subtleties, Saraladevi Chowdharani was too domineering, Mirabehn sickeningly possessive, Sushila too troublesome for his comfort and Manudi was as gentle as a lamb who could be led to the slaughter house without a whimper of protest. Bapu was quite satisfied, because he had been able to mould her to his requirements.

He never had any doubts about her devotion, but he was not too sure of her calibre. At times he was impatient with her. She was prone to frequent bouts of illness. This worried him. He was, however, most anxious to shape her into a public figure of consequence. He also had doubts about her potential. After departing from Noakhali he was to reach Calcutta on 1 March 1947. Then he made an accurate appraisal of her: "As for Manudi... She has not outgrown the immature thinking of an adolescent girl. It is very necessary that she should gain an adult's wisdom... She is very simple, gentle and easily duped; but me she serves very well and ardently. She had simply lost herself in service to me."[37]

She felt embarrassed by his praise, but Gandhiji silenced her by saying that he would like the whole world to see us 'just as we are'.

Final Judgement

In the end, Gandhi-Manu relationship cannot but seem odd: a great charismatic personality of our times and a young girl distinguished for her ordinariness. Yet the association was deep and abiding.

In his own words, he lived in the midst of 'suspicion and distrust' and 'exaggeration and untruth'. This was a voice in wilderness losing grip fast, in his last years. Accordingly, his dependence on Manu ('the mere chit of a girl') had grown precariously. But Bapu's constant refrain 'I am with you' did not assure Manu. She admitted to a feeling of constant alienation. At heart she was timid. Just five days before Gandhiji was assassinated, he charged her with failing to realise the potential of his *mahayajna*.

What were his real intentions in pursuing the *brahmacharya* experiment? What was he trying to prove to the world and to himself? There are no clear answers to be discovered in all his writings and pronouncements. It is an enigma wrapped in a mystery. One has to read between the lines to decipher his mind. Perhaps he never lacked courage except in this instance.

He compared himself to a lone passenger journeying, come rain or storm. His inability to articulate his thesis boldly pricked his conscience a great deal. That his close associates like Sardar Patel accused him of committing *adharma* might have dissuaded him from being an open book. In February 1947, he talked of publishing the results of his in-depth research in man-woman relationship. Here he was embarked on uncovering 'the great spiritual mystery' of all times. He pitied those failing to read the true significance of his sacred *yajna* in the cause of *brahmacharya*. Just a few days before his assassination, he claimed to have achieved the state of *nirvana*.

Like all of us he had his moments of self-doubt. Certainly he was no God. He admitted to having committed mistakes. At times he went to the extent of comparing his Noakhali *brahmacharya mahayajna* to a flop show. Thus he wavered between the two extremes of confidence and self-doubt. Who was the real Gandhi?

CHAPTER 21

In the Noakhali Soup

Probably Gandhi was way ahead of his time. He was an open book and the frankest person on earth. His voluminous correspondence, books and contributions to the *Harijan* group of newspapers mirrored his innermost thoughts. His correspondence with his women associates is very voluminous. Manu was encouraged to maintain a diary during her Noakhali sojourn as well as during his last months in New Delhi. He would go through the diary and sign it after carrying out corrections. Thus, we have a graphic idea of what went on at Noakhali. Manu's record is incomplete in one respect. She does not hint a word about her reactions and responses to the *brahmacharya* experiment. Gandhi was, however, not squeamish in this matter. He confessed to the fact in several letters to his associates.

Squeamish *Brahmachari*

Resistance continued to build among his colleagues against his outlandish practices. The hostile responses of Nirmal Babu and Parasuram had prised open the issue. That his *brahmacharya* experiments had become the talk of the town must have reached his ears and he was required to defend himself. According to Parasuram, about 50 critical letters on the subject were received by Gandhi before 31 December 1946. The trickle gradually turned into an avalanche. Finally, he had to throw up his hands in despair and pray to almighty God to rescue him.

Parasuram forced the issue into the open. Gandhi acted fast and shot off a letter to Rajkumari Amrit Kaur, soon after the break took place with Parasuram. He dismissed the concerns of Parasuram nonchalantly: "The main cause I think was that Manu shared the same bed with me."[1]

He defended his *brahmacharya* experiments by asserting that these were conducted in the open. All his associates in Noakhali had known about Manu sharing the bed with him. He failed to recognise the elementary truth that his experiments went against the ethos of the people around him. He had praised Manu's full participation in the experiments. He had singled her out for being totally 'un-self-conscious'. He was living in an unreal world. He had seriously believed that through such practices, he was helping her out of the fear that haunted her all the time.

Manu was a young girl. Imagine her bearing pressures from Gandhi, and Pyarelal, standing up to the hostility of Sushila Nayyar and the disapproval of the whole range of his senior and junior associates and the members of his entire family! It would be too much to expect her to be equal to the task expected of her.

Family at War

His family members were not amused at the happenings. The elder son Harilal was never in his good books. Manilal was living far away in South Africa. Devdas was always resentful of his eccentricities. That left Ramdas, the gentlest of the lot. Gandhiji indeed felt comfortable in dealing with him. He tried to probe Ramdas. He asked Manu Gandhi to write to Ramdas in detail about his laboratory experiments.

In his letter of 10 January 1947, he directed Manu to write a detailed letter to Ramdas 'about her sharing the bed with me'. He also mentioned in the same letter that he intended to bring about changes in 'this programme'. This was nine days after Parasuram threw his bombshell in the form of his accusatory letter of 1 January 1947. Doubts had begun to assail him about fundamental concepts such as *satyagraha*, *ahimsa* and *brahmacharya*. It was to be a cry in the wilderness: "I am still surrounded by darkness. I have no doubt whatever that it indicates a flaw somewhere in my method."[2] His response was indeed unconvincing: "That alone is true which we realise by experience."

Parasuram had forsaken him but he kept hammering on the topic through his correspondence with Nirmal Babu, who, in turn, kept throwing sceptical hints to Gandhi. Parasuram was turning out to be a conscience-keeper not only of Gandhi but also of Manu, Sushila and Pyarelal. Here Parasuram was at it again: "He should see the light of truth as far as his domestic circle[s] are concerned... As far as I am concerned his eyes are blinded by his affection for them."[3] The more Gandhi was subjected to criticism, the more defensive he became, even to the extent of defending the indefensible.

Sleeping Arrangement

The crisis intensified with the passage of time. He was spending a great deal of time in providing explanations. His associates were divided into camps. Those who were vehemently opposed to *brahmacharya* experiments constituted the majority. Others like Satis Chandra (of Banaras), Vinoba Bhave and G D Birla were neutral but not necessarily on his side. Those who were hostile to him had decided to come out in the open. Things were going from bad to worse in February 1947. He now turned to Satis Babu for succour. Known as 'Nanga Baba' he was highly respected. Gandhi set a poser to him about a young girl of 19, 'who is in the place of granddaughter' to him sharing the bed with him: "not for any animal satisfaction but for (to me) valid moral reasons". Would Satis Babu see anything 'bad or unjustifiable in this juxtaposition'?[4] The question had arisen because several of his associates had objected to his sleeping with Manu (the granddaughter of his uncle). He appealed to Satis Babu for a satisfactory answer. He even asked him to take time before responding to him. He must have felt embarrassed and therefore avoided responding to Gandhi.

By this time he was in real trouble with the editorial board of the *Harijan* group of newspapers. Eminent Gandhians like K G Mashruwala constituted the board. The editorial board was assigned the task of editing the newspapers in his absence. The editorial board had dared to edit allusions to *brahmacharya* experiments in Noakhali in one of his pieces intended for publication. He protested. Kishorelal Mashruwala and Narahari Parekh sent a telegram to him in response to his protest over editing of the piece: "Your letter first instance. We relinquish charge *Harijan* papers and correspondence. Charge against Jaisukhlal withdrawn in second letter on learning our misunderstanding."[5] Gandhiji responded with another telegram addressed to Kishorelal

Mashruwala: "SORRY YOUR DECISION. YOU ARE ENTITLED, REGARD IT HASTY. ANY CASE YOU WILL RENDER NECESSARY HELP TILL NEW ARRANGEMENT MADE. WIRED

JIVANJI [D Desai]."[6] Very cleverly Gandhi offered to resume the editorship of the papers to get rid of the troublesome editorial board.

Logical Vinoba

With a storm brewing around him, Gandhi turned to Vinoba Bhave for guidance. Amongst his closest associates, Vinoba Bhave was in a class by himself. An erudite scholar of the Indian tradition, he maintained his distance from him. Indeed his sagacity and wisdom were his assets. Gandhi now turned to him for sympathy as he was in a real soup by this time. Invariably, everyone was upset over his sleeping with Manu. He, however, persisted with the practice: "Manu sleeping with me is not a part of my experiment but is a part of the present *yajna*." He would not hesitate to put forward outlandish arguments in defence of the indefensible: "My mind daily sleeps in an innocent manner with millions of women, and Manu also, who is a blood relation to me, sleeps with me as one of these millions."

His mulishness made life difficult for others and himself in the bargain. He freely admitted to Vinoba Bhave the inconveniences he had caused to others: "Kishorelal's agony is difficult to bear. He is so upset that he is on the verge of breaking down. The same is the case with Narahari [Parekh] and Swami [Anand]. I do not know how the women at Sevagram and elsewhere must be suffering."[7]

His letter of February 10 to Vinoba Bhave elicited a reply on 25 February 1947. There was no comfort in the reply. Vinoba made his disagreement with his mentor crystal clear. His concept of *brahmacharya* found no favour with Vinoba, who put forward the argument that any consciousness of difference between the sexes was 'contrary to ideal *brahmacharya*'. In other words, for any true *brahmachari* to be conscious of different sexes was a total violation of the theory and practice of *brahmacharya*. Logically, for Gandhi to be conscious of Manu's gender was contrary to the basic norms of *brahmacharya*. Thus Vinoba was quick to demolish the edifice built so laboriously by his mentor. Having snubbed Gandhi without having said so, Vinoba Bhave decided to close any further discussion on the matter in future. He knew Gandhi was beyond redemption. He also knew that Gandhi would not listen to any one. His final argument was to end any further argument. If he were a perfect *brahmachari* then he need not test his *brahmacharya*. If he were an imperfect *brahmachari*, then he should not take undue risks by testing it.

From Vinoba Bhave he turned to his friend G D Birla, who was also his financier and benefactor. They had carried on a lively correspondence over a number of years. They were an odd couple, considering the fact that the Birlas were the textile and jute kings of India and Gandhi was a relentless advocate of *khadi*. Here was a machine and a *charkha* living in perfect harmony. Ghanshyam Das Birla was one notch above his associates due to his special status. Gandhi would spontaneously open up to him. He chose to confess to his friend his tale of woe in his letter of 15 February 1947. The revolt among his associates had turned into an avalanche. No longer was it confined to his ashram associates.

It was not merely Kishorelal Mashruwala, Narahari Parekh and Swami Anand who had long faces. The revolt had spread far and wide.

Committing *Adharma**

Sardar Patel was furious. He spoke openly about Bapu indulging in *adharma* by his practice of sleeping with women without clothes. Devdas wrote a letter of strong protest to his father and his strong words were still ringing in his ears. Gandhi did not attach too much importance to the letter of Devdas, whom he still viewed as a child, yet to grow to full adulthood.

The letter from Sardar Patel rankled in his mind due to his sweeping charges. He turned to his friend G D Birla to sustain him in this moment of crisis. He would have liked Birlaji to approve his concept of

---

* The circle of his critics kept expanding much beyond the narrow confines of the Gandhian loyalists. His life style was 'variously described as outrageous, titillating, bewildering, or merely absurd'. (p.260) Nirad Chowdhari was one of his numerous and persistent critics, who in his private communication to Francis Watson left no one in doubt about his scepticism regarding Gandhi's ashram life style : "But, of course very many things [including], Mahatma Gandhi's abnormalities [obsession and hyper-revulsion] were known to all of us. On this score I had nothing but contempt for him- and I was expressing my opinion quite frankly even in 1933, when I had an opportunity to watch him at close quarters. The behaviour of his entourage (especially women in it) disgusted me". (p.267). B R Ambedkar, upon being questioned about Gandhiji's credibility 'from the point of view of his morality'(p.261). The British authorities in India, however, maintained stoic silence over the subject.

Source : Watson, Francis. *The trial of Mr Gandhi*. Macmillan, London 1969.

brahmacharya with no holds barred. This was a cry in the wilderness. So pathetic was his state of mind that he went on repeating his argument like a *mantra ad nauseum* to everyone without convincing a single person: "Whatever I am doing here is as a part of my *yajna*. There is nothing I do knowingly which is not a part and parcel of that *yajna*. Even the rest I take is as a part of that *yajna*."[8]

Very little is known about the mechanics of this so-called *yajna* of Gandhiji. There is a hint of it in his own words conveyed through G D Birla in the same letter: "The point I must make my friend's grasp is this: 'When I take Manu in my lap, I do so as a pure-hearted father or as a father who has strayed from the path of virtue?' What I am doing is nothing new to me; in thought I have done it over the last fifty years; in action, in varying degrees, over quite a number of years."[9]

Having made an objective presentation of a bad case, he suddenly turned around 360 degrees and threw a challenge to the whole world. 'come rain, come fire', he would not change: "Even if you severe all connection with me, I would not feel hurt. Just I want to stick to my dharma, you have to stick to yours."[10] Birla's response is not known.

Risking Perdition

Unfortunately Gandhi was fast reaching a stage which was beyond comprehension, in the last years of his life. The process had its beginning in the thirties and reached its climax in Noakhali during 1946 and 1947.

Human beings have an infinite capacity to hold on to illusions even when they come to realise the real situation. It was now J B Kriplani's turn to be his soul mate. He once again talked of Manu as his granddaughter, "as we consider blood-relations [and she] shares the bed with me, strictly as my very blood... as part of what might be my last *yajna*." The resulting cost was the loss of his 'dearest and earliest comrades'. Notwithstanding the pressures, he was in a nasty frame of mind and was throwing challenges at the whole world: "The whole world may forsake me but I dare not leave what I hold is the truth for me. It may be a delusion and a snare [and a mirage]. If so, I must realise it myself. I have risked perdition before now. Let this be reality if it has to be."[11]

That he had gradually begun to lose confidence in himself is evident from the following letter. The argument did not wash with Satis Chandra Das Gupta, Vinoba Bhave or G D Birla. Acharya Kriplani was the

Congress Party President at that time. He was a known cynic but this time he took pity on Gandhiji: "Sometimes I thought that ... you may be employing human beings as means rather than as ends in themselves."[12] Or, perhaps he liked to treat human beings as guinea pigs to be experiment upon.

God's Eunuch

His area of operation was gradually constricted. Still, there were numerous friends and associates who were blissfully unaware of what was going on in Noakhali. Balkrishna Bhave was one of them. To him he wrote with a flourish: "Probably you do not know that Manubehn (Jaisukhlal's daughter) sleeps with me."[13]

He complained of Kishorelal Mashruwala and other associates boycotting him. They had flatly charged him with *adharma*. He persisted in the practice because for him sleeping with Manu was his dharma. How could he forego his dharma? Wouldn't this be the forsaking of sacred *yajna* in midstream? How could he dare to commit such an impropriety? Would not he set a bad example for others by abandoning his 'last *yajna*?' So ran the plethora of arguments in his mind. He also knew that his persistence had cost him dear friends and associates. He had been unable to convince any person. By this time his own persistence had begun to falter. He had begun to think that there must be some flaw in his practice. Wouldn't it have called for a thorough review of practices? His ego had erected a barrier difficult to cross. He felt so desperate as to go public in Noakhali by speaking about his *brahmacharya* practices during his speeches at public meetings. His audience did not have the foggiest idea of what he was talking about, but his public confession sent a chill down the spine of those who knew.

His first mention of his *brahmacharya* practice came in his speech at a prayer meeting held at Amishapara village on 1 February 1947. It must have taken Professor Bose by surprise. It was his duty to translate his speeches into Bengali. He was stunned into silence and took the precaution of omitting from the translation his practice of having his 'granddaughter' to sleep with him. Gandhiji did not like it a bit. He conveyed his displeasure to Nirmal Babu in no uncertain terms. He decided to repeat the mention of his practice in his speech at a prayer meeting held at Satgharia village on the very next day. The last mention of the practice took place at his public address at Sadhurkhil on 3 February

1947. Gandhiji referred to 'small-talks, whispers and innuendos' going around, of which he was well aware: "He was already in the midst of so much suspicion and distrust, he told the gathering, that he did not want his most innocent acts to be misunderstood and misrepresented."[14]

He had very clearly mentioned in his last public address, the fact of his 'granddaughter' sharing his bed with him. He sought the benediction of Prophet Mohammed, who had 'discounted eunuchs' for their free access to the other sex. Thus he himself became "God's eunuch" because of his voluntary choice to perform his *brahmacharya yajna* in the company of his granddaughter. He also sought the benediction of his audience in the sacred task he had undertaken in Noakhali. As usual, he was defiant of his opponents and he was unambiguous in stating that duty must be performed.

The task that Nirmal Babu had left incomplete at Amishapara remained to be completed. So in his address at Satgharia on 2 February 1947, he referred to his private life. How could he be moral in public life and be immoral in private life? Both of them could not go together. In his third address at Sadhurkhil on 3 February he compared himself to a pilgrim facing all kinds of difficulties on the way to his destination. Nevertheless, he expected to remain undaunted. Severe criticism which he had been subjected to, did not deter him but made him more determined than ever before: "A pilgrim has to bear every kind of life whether rain or water, he must continue in his journey to reach his goal. And I am a pilgrim today. Why should I be afraid of rains or water."[15]

All this reflects on Gandhi and his varying moods. He was defiant, too sure and persistently strident at times. The moods changed in no time. Now he became moody, hesitant and unsure of himself. Then he returned to his self-centred cocoon. The real Gandhi must stand up.

Pyarelal's Obsession

In Shakespearean tragedy, comic relief is provided at regular intervals to bring relief. *L'affaire* Manu Gandhi (with Pyarelal) was undoubtedly a diversion from so much serious business being conducted in Noakhali. Indeed it added to the woes of both Gandhi and Manu with no resultant comic relief. Pyarelal was again agitated. He shot off letters regarding his favourite preoccupation and obsession with the young lady. Though Pyarelal was on field duty, he was anxious to return to the temporary headquarters so as to be near to Manu at all cost. Gandhi tried to put him off for as long as possible without being impolite: "Come if you must... I shall say that you should leave Manu and yourself in the hands of God." It was he who had suggested to Pyarelal to give lessons to Manu: "Manu's intrepidity deserves to be encouraged."[16]

The alarm bells started ringing soon thereafter. Gandhi had been engaged in attempts to balance this triangular relationship by buying peace with Pyarelal. He had brought them together but, he employed equally clever tactics to keep them separated from each other. At the same time, like a watchful guardian, he anticipated trouble well ahead of him. His sixth sense told him so. He did not fail to notice the agitation writ large on Manu's face. He took the initiative to forewarn Pyarelal: "Even if you have Manu's good at heart, she… must be allowed to shape herself... Wake up if you can."[17]

The presence of Pyarelal at the temporary headquarters was enough to disturb the equanimity of Manu. She confided her embarrassment to Professor Bose, who conveyed her complaint to Bapu on 4 February 1947: "I understand that Manu has told you already how, in her distress, she confided to me some portion of her troubles. She told me how she had been steadily losing respect for P [Pyarelal] because the latter had been pursuing her in spite of clear rejection, and how he had even talked of suicide to her on a former occasion. It was also a surprise to me to learn how sister [Sushila] has been pleading and pressing her to accept the love of her brother, even after she knew her mind."[18]

Gandhi talked to Manu over the subject. As there were no assurances coming from her, she received an implied admonition from him: "The more you try, the more complicated the situation will become."[19] The very next day, he told Pyarelal: "Your agitation disturbs me."[20] Now came the turn of Professor Bose. Gandhi brushed aside the complaint and came to the rescue of Pyarelal. He even passed on the letter to Pyarelal for his perusal. He also talked in parables by referring to Pyarelal as 'A' and Manu as 'B' in his reply. The interplay of 'A' and 'B' gave him so much vicarious pleasure.

He discussed the complaint with Manu and the poor girl was made to retract. To Gandhiji, Pyarelal's pining for Manu was an act of purely platonic love. He had an explanation for Pyarelal's conduct which he considered entirely impeccable: "As [Pyarelal's] love is wholly free from animal passion. I have called it poetic. It is not a perfect adjective but I find no better. He once loved a girl with the same passion as he loves B

[Manu Gandhi]. In either case, it was philanthropic. The first came in a flash, the second took two years to discover."[21]

He quoted Pyarelal to the effect of his viewing Manu as a sister or daughter to him, as long as Manu did not change her mind. Going by the age difference, Manu should have been adopted by Pyarelal as his daughter rather than his sister. She did not relish the idea of him being her lover. She did not like being shadowed by him constantly. The lengthening shadow of Pyarelal never left Manu. Pyarelal was equally irreconcilable because he had been rejected as a lover not just once but twice.

The Trio

Poor Manu was in trouble not only on account of Pyarelal, but she was under great pressure owing to a variety of reasons. There was a spate of critical letters denouncing Gandhi's *brahmacharya* practices. She was so embarrassed that she refused to have a peep at the correspondence. Notwithstanding the assurances of Gandhi, there was no peace for her.

Indeed her battles were being fought all alone within her mind. Manu was a teenager who had led a protected life. She found the pressures too much because the letters had started turning abusive and accusatory: "One should not associate with a man who follows immoral ways… He deserves no respect, no matter how highly placed he might be."[22] Any teenage girl who was not thick-skinned enough would have cracked under similar circumstances. The Gandhi-Pyarelal-Manu triangle became complicated with the passage of time. Nirmal Babu was clear in his mind about the complicated relationship: "But if his love for B [Manu] is of the poetic variety, why should he need B's physical presence even within several miles of himself?"[23]

Nirmal Babu mocked at Pyarelal by asserting the spuriousness of his commitment to Gandhiji and his work. Unfortunately Pyarelal was more sinned against than sinning. He was a victim of circumstances. His life had not been made easy by Gandhi. He was starved of the company of women and denied access to the female company under the watchful eyes of Gandhi himself. He would turn starry-eyed and see the visions of Saint Manu Gandhi. Inevitably the news of going-ons in Noakhali reached the ears of Manu's father, Jaisukhlal Gandhi. Gandhi had to assuage him through his letters: "Manu's good will be Pyarelal's good. Manu is firm in this matter."[24]

While all this was going on, there was a letter from K G Mashruwala in the last week of February. Gandhi had arrived in Haimchar and was preparing to move out of Noakhali. He called Nirmal Babu and talked to him about the Mashruwala letter. Manu had translated it from Gujarati for the benefit of Nirmal Babu: "The main charge [in the letter from K G Mashruwala] seemed to have been that Gandhiji was obviously suffering from a sense of self-delusion in regard to his relation with the opposite sex. Manu then related to me the details of what Gandhiji described as his *prayog* or experiment or self-examination."[25] Unfortunately, Nirmal Babu had decided to keep the details of the *prayog* to himself by promising, "But, of this, later". The correspondence between Gandhi and Mashruwala is no longer available. Unfortunately it was destroyed by Mashruwala himself.

Thakkar Bapa

Ultimately the venerable A V Thakkar (popularly known as Thakkar Bapa) had to intervene to resolve the dispute. He decided to visit Noakhali himself in the fourth week of February, 1947 to have a direct dialogue with Gandhi, Manu Gandhi and other associates of Gandhiji at Noakhali. The gentle and unobstrusive Thakkar Bapa spent a week in Noakhali watching the situation himself. He had a detailed discussion with Gandhi on 24 February 1947 at Haimchar and questioned his *brahmacharya* experiments in Noakhali. Indeed his sleeping with Manu was only a part of his *yajna*—sacrifice, penance and sacred duty—that is how he tried to get across to Thakkar Bapa, who however did not hesitate to warn his mentor: "Don't miss the wood for the trees."

Gandhiji viewed his *yajna* as 'the lonely road to God'. In pursuit of this objective, he was prepared to disown all his companions and ready to 'disillusion' his own committed admirers. The argument he put forward to Thakkar Bapa got too complicated at times, especially when he talked of thousands of women, Hindu and Muslim alike, whom he would view as mothers, sisters and daughters: "But if an occasion should arise requiring me to share the bed with any one of them I must not hesitate, if I am the *brahmachari* that I claim to be." Where was the need for such bravado? In response to the question whether he would let others emulate him, he replied in the affirmative, provided it was to be a 'sincere, bonafide, honest endeavour'. He promised to publish the results of his laboratory experiments: "As soon as my research is complete I shall publish the results to the whole world."[26]

There was so much spontaneity in Gandhi's remarks that Thakkar Bapa was successfully bought over by him. He even blessed Manu on the eve of his departure from Noakhali on 2 March 1947. He told her: "I am really delighted with your way of serving Bapu... May God make you happy all your life!" Manu had won him over completely. She also took the opportunity to explain to him about her place in the *brahmacharya yajna*. This was the first time when Manu opened up: "Only after our talk today I have been able to have a deeper understanding of the meaning of what you are trying to do."[27]

Thakkar Bapa was a silent listener. He was, however, not a novice to the game. He was working towards a plan and indeed he achieved it effortlessly. He was extremely persuasive with Manu. She saw merit in his argument: "How could public opinion be defied so blatantly as was sought to be done by Gandhi?" He pleaded with Manu to suspend the practice for the time being. He also prompted her to talk to Gandhi. Manu appreciated the argument. She was successful in persuading Gandhi herself.

Gandhi was not convinced but Manu succeeded in making Thakkar Bapa fall in line with her. It was but natural for Thakkar Bapa to feel grateful to her for the success of his mission. Manu had closed the controversy with one nod of her teenaged head. All the three of them-Bapu, Manu and Bapa—smelled victory. Thakkar Bapa felt elated for making Gandhi fall in line through Manu. Manu gained respect with Bapa for facilitating his task. Gandhi felt elated because he had made Bapa consider his case sympathetically: "But what pleased me particularly was that during my week's stay...I could convince him in regard to many things and he revised many of his views."[28]

The semblance of peace returned after Gandhi agreed to the request of Thakkar Bapa. He was at ease himself. So was Manu at peace with herself. He informed Vinoba Bhave gleefully: "Nowadays Manu does not sleep in my bed. It is... due to a pathetic letter from Bapa. But according to my view it does not make any difference in the situation even if I am practising *adharma*."[29]

He gave similar good news to his friend Horace Alexander: "I suppose you already know that Manu no longer sleeps in the same bed with me.

This departure was made by [Manu] with my full approval in order to please [Thakkar] Bapa who, though he saw absolutely nothing wrong, would appeal to her not to continue [it] while I was in Bihar."[30] Even Gandhiji was a slave to his ego and assented in the same letter: "I do not know but agree with the conclusion. But I did not wish to argue and therefore I promptly agreed." He kept hawking the same line to justify his practice. He made no bones in telling Balkrishna Bhave: "And if we pay exclusive attention to [views of others], we can make no progress... More than this I need not say just now."[31]

Tackling the Family

Now that Gandhi was at ease with his bloated ego somewhat battered, he could turn his attention to his own family. He decided to tackle Sushila Gandhi (wife of Manilal). She belonged to the Mashruwala family by birth and therefore he had to do a lot of explanation to her. He had felt greatly pained because his views and those of Kishorelal were diametrically opposite. Kishorelal Mashruwala was still not reconciled to the situation. The temporary relief provided by Thakkar Bapa was no relief for the likes of Kishorelal, who was bent upon the discontinuance of the practice permanently. He tried to explain the matter to Sushila: "My ideas and conduct are not new. I can say that they go back to fifty-five years ago."

He further added: "It is possible that I might not have been able to express my ideas clearly in my writings or talks."[32] For such a loquacious person like Gandhi it was simply not true. The real reason lay elsewhere. He was hesitant to make any public presentation of his ideas about *brahmacharya*. He was himself on record on several occasions stating that the time was yet not ripe to make disclosures. This does not, however, detract from the merit of the case. Being a great communicator, he should have had the courage to defy public opinion and come out clean on the subject.

Caring for Manudi

After Gandhi left Noakhali for Bihar, he had Manudi on his mind all the time. Now that Thakkar Bapa had drawn a *lakshman rekha* between them, the dividing line was felt more acutely than ever before. It was reflected in his diary, his notes to her and exchange of letters with others. He praised her and discovered many virtues in her which were simply not there. After he reached Sodepore from Noakhali, he still talked of her childlike innocence. He affirmed his lifelong commitment to her, in his diary, after he reached Patna. This assurance was given to her at Srirampur and repeated at Patna: "This girl, who stays with me all the twenty-four hours and serves with distinction should not fall ill. After all I have made her my partner in *yajna*." When she was suffering from appendicitis, he reluctantly agreed for her to be operated upon for the fear that she might die.

She was just one companion left at the fag end of his glorious career. There were very few others, who were left to share his joys and sorrows. He unburdened his innermost thoughts to her. Manu was a patient listener. He had convinced himself that he was surrounded by hostile forces. Manu alone was left to listen to his tales of woe: "I am surrounded by exaggeration and untruth. In spite of my search I do not know where the truth lies. But I do feel that I am nearer to God and Truth."[33]

He was required to pay a heavy price in the end. The climax of sixty years of public service for him was in performing the *yajna* to kill all *yajnas,* and to have the pleasure of Manu's company for twenty-four hours a day. Was it worth the trouble? It is hard to believe that Manu was the ultimate instrument for achieving the ultimate truth for him.

One of the most memorable incidents in their association took place during his stay at Patna on Sunday the 16th of March 1947, at the unearthly hour of 2 am. He was wide awake at that time. He was startled to hear the resonant voice of Manudi reciting the *shlokas* for her morning prayers. She stopped her recitation soon after Bapu called for her.

The next step she took was indeed fascinating to watch. She bent across his mosquito net and held his hand firmly. This was her affirmation, expressing gratefulness to Bapu for all he had done for her. This gesture equalled all the reams of paper Gandhi had used in praising Manu. He stroked her hand lovingly, to calm her frayed nerves. Did the gesture have something to do with the temporary stoppage of the *brahmacharya yajna* during his sojourn in Bihar?

The reverie was suddenly broken. It was already 3 am. Prayer time was nearing. He began his usual routine of brushing his teeth first thing in the morning. Manudi was woken up. It was now time for prayers at 3.55 am. It was yet another day in the lives of Manu and Bapu. Yet the early morning of 16 March 1947, was indeed the most memorable day in the life of Gandhi. History books shall overlook the incident and the date in which it took place as an inconsequential one in the life of a great statesman. One must go through his diary of the same date to understand its full significance.* Shouldn't one be grateful to Manu for making the memorable happening possible? Manu was a good girl and spoke no evil. She saw no evil and heard no evil. She was the Cinderella of the Gandhian world. Such people shall inherit the earth.

The Noakhali sojourn had been a mouthful for him. He began to talk of his death. The theme recurs in his writings in the post-Noakhali period. During his talk with Manudi on 13 May 1947, he welcomed death with open arms while striving for perfect *sthitaprajna* or firmness in judgement and wisdom. While in Noakhali, he had repeatedly talked of both of them being assassinated in bed. He talked of death during the appendicitis illness of Manu Gandhi while travelling through Bihar. Now he had lost all desire for living for 125 years. He would have hated to die a slow and lingering death: "But if I die taking God's name with my last breath, it will be a sign that I was what I strove for and claim to be."[34]

---

* "Today I was wide awake as it struck two. I did not seem to get sleep. Then all at once, I heard Manudi reciting the *shlokas* of the morning prayer. I was startled. I called her a couple of times. Then she was quiet. She did not say anything, but she was frightened. She lifted my mosquito-curtain and held my hand. I stroked her for a few minutes, and asked her to be calm. Now, she became conscious and withdrew her hand" (*Collected works*, 87: Mar.16, 1947, 98, *The Diary*, Patna).

CHAPTER 22

The Last Journey

Manu Gandhi was with Mahatma during his last days in New Delhi. There is a graphic account of his last month in the diary maintained by her, mirroring the picture of political India 'and of the agony and unrest of Bapu's mind'. It is indeed a true picture of those days because Manu was privy to his innermost thoughts. She was his 24 hour companion. She was his daughter, granddaughter, mother, housemaid, chamber maid, secretary, nurse, dietician and companion. Reciprocally, he claimed to be her 'mother' in addition to being her father, besides being her grandfather through blood relationship. It was a loving relationship defying classification by usual standards.

Demanding Routine

Gandhiji would behave like an errant child and refuse to be serviced by any one except by Manudi. He would peremptorily order her about all the time. He would tell her: "[After all] you are my life partner in this great sacrifice."[1] He would wake her up at midnight and keep her awake till the early morning hours. She would help to bathe him. She would shave him until he took his bath. Or he would shave himself and dictate his correspondence from his bathtub. There ought to have been a photograph of him resting in his bathtub with his lady companions waiting upon him.

She would also administer enema to him. While Gandhiji was on fast on 15 January 1948, he was extremely uncomfortable. Manu administered enema to provide relief to him. He liked the operation, but he was greatly exhausted. Manu would panic on such occasions. She would die a thousand deaths everytime he was in bad shape: "I get nervous or break down crying, woe be to me!"[2]

How demanding he would be was to be seen in his daily routine. His day started with his early morning prayers, followed by a brisk walk, massage and bath. Manu along with Abha Gandhi helped him in these chores. He was used to simple meals but to feed him was an exhausting exercise for Manu and Abha. He would have hot water with honey immediately after prayers, followed by two spoonfuls of honey with hot water at 5.30 am. The exercise was repeated at 1230, 1530 and 1900 hours with slight variations. At 1530 mud-plaster was applied to him. His substantial meal was at 9.30 am sharp. On alternative days he would take three light chapatis, uncooked saltless vegetables, 16 ounces of milk, two oranges and one apple. He would take no wheat on the other cycle of alternate days and content himself with three bananas and 16 ounces of milk with an orange or some other fruit. His dinner at 1600 hours consisted of cooked (but saltless) vegetables, a bit of orange or some other juicy fruit taken along with 16 ounces of goat milk. To maintain him was an arduous task requiring perfect knowledge of arithmetic.

His daily routine during his New Delhi stay was chalked out to the last minute. The stream of visitors had to be attended to and Manu was to make sure that no one disturbed him in his sleep or short naps. In the evening, Abha and Manu were to act as 'his walking sticks' to lead him to the prayer ground. His tired feet had to be washed frequently.

Alternate *Shakti*

He would share his agonies and joys with her. With his worries cumulating day-by-day, he would be completely off colour wading through his heavy routine. His condition would turn critical. Only Manu was there to share his troubles. He would not be able to sleep and then he would wake up Manu to unburden himself. There were times when he would dictate to her at the most unearthly hours. All this was too much for her delicate stomach. She kept bad health and this added to her woes. Her troubles were not only physical but also spiritual. What could the poor girl do? She was barely in her twenties. Not surprisingly, she died a premature death in her forties. She survived him by eleven years. She was more dead than alive in the remaining years of her life.

While he was on his way from Bihar to New Delhi to meet Lord Mountbatten, the last Viceroy of India, he confided in her during his train journey on 30 March 1947: "Now mind you, you are my only companion in this ordeal, and I am going to Delhi for the first time. When I decided to go to Noakhali, I had resolved to do or die there and had sent away from me all my companions. But I allowed you to join me in this sacrifice [*yajna*]. You are with me here as you were there... But I am duty bound not to leave you. You also would not wish me to leave you, and so you are coming with me. But remember this will be a severe test for you."[3]

Now on his march to his ultimate destiny, he was in a tearing hurry to complete his unfinished tasks. New Delhi was beckoning him. He had a premonition of his death. He also had a death wish and urge for martyrdom. Thus he was anxious to carry through his *brahmacharya mahayajna*.

Death Wish

Was he placating Manu by assuring her of his lifelong commitment to her? Was he flattering her to be in her good books? Was he not sure of himself while repeating his commitment to her *ad nauseam*? Did he have anything else in his mind? Why was he confiding so much in Manu? Gandhiji had begun to feel isolated and hence insecure. Accordingly, his dependence on Manu increased disproportionately.

Gandhiji had a death wish and probably a fear of death at the bottom of his heart. Already the bomb explosion had taken place. He had no doubt in his mind that the attempt on his life was an inevitable consequence of his views. He confided to Manudi: "I wish I might have to face the assassin's bullet when lying in your lap."[4] The 22nd of January, 1948 was the anniversary of Ba's death. Gandhiji was in a reflective mood. He knew for sure that death was hovering around the corner. While Manudi was engaged in giving massage, he confided to her: "Note down all that I told you this morning and show it to me. Do not yet talk about it to anybody. It was necessary to confide to you all these things. Therefore I have confided them to you."[5]

He had a compulsive desire to reach his version of *nirvana* through his unnatural death. He even had a premonition about his death. He told her as early as May 1947: "And as you are a witness to this *yajna* of mine, I do wish that you should be my witness in this and not go before me."[6] He also reminisced about his dear friends and associates of past to Manu. He was prepared to face death so long as Manu was with him. He seemed to be in a defiant mood by declaring to the world that given a choice he would opt for Manu rather than anybody else.

Gandhi knew perfectly well that he was in trouble. Just a few supporters were left to sustain him till the end. Manu was certainly on his side. Among the public figures, Jawaharlal Nehru alone supported him during his troubled times. His crystal ball told him about Jawaharlal's sincerity, reliability and devotion. During June 1947 Gandhi was singing his hallelujahs. All said and done he saw a child in Manu. For him, Jawaharlal was the same because he had 'the heart of child', and yet he had 'the intellect, learning and power' of outstanding intellectuals and, above all: "He can renounce things as easily as a snake its slough. His tireless energy would put even a youth to shame."[7]

His attachment to Manu proved to be his undoing. Not only did he receive flak from his companions, associates and family members, but he received a flood of critical letters from the public. He simply ignored critical references, except once in a while when he cared to respond to such letters. One complainant rightly pointed out that he was wasting his time by paying too much obeisance to Manu. Gandhi was soon up in arms and came to gallant defence of Manudi. He baffled his other female companions by claiming Manu to be his soul mate: "I wish to uncover to the world a great spiritual mystery similar to that which I have demonstrated concerning truth and *ahimsa*."[8]

Troubled Female

Despite Gandhi's protection Manu was a troubled soul. She was not equal to the task. She was, however, a very sweet person. It was not in her nature to confront anyone. On 21 September 1947, she received a memo from Bapu disapproving of her conduct. It was a rare event. There must have been something troubling him necessitating a rebuke to her, of all things about a *bhajan* badly sung at his prayer meeting. For him the *bhajan* was symbolic of the identity of man with God: "I will not tolerate even a single shortcoming in you."[9] It must be out of sheer pique when on the next day, he wrote a note to her: "I am not angry; I am unhappy. I am helpless if you do not understand my unhappiness."[10]

He would have been content with an apology. To his surprise it was not forthcoming. Finally it was rendered, but he insisted on dictating the terms of surrender: "We two girls [Abha and Manu] were guilty of a grievous error during the prayer yesterday. We wish to purify ourselves by confessing before all of you... We thus insulted our Maker... We sought Bapu's forgiveness and he has forgiven us. But the pain has persisted... We hope that our public confession [at the prayer meeting] will relieve it to some extent."[11] Gandhi was being a difficult child demanding exclusive attention. Admittedly he was a child. And so was Manu. Here were children playing all kinds of games which were meaningful and meaningless at the same time.

Manu was, however, confronted with more serious troubles. Pyarelal was like Banquo's ghost that would not go away. She was troubled because Bapu was yet again going on a fast. She was also troubled on account of: '[Pyarelal] dreaming of his marriage to her at the age of 50. What a stroke of luck!'[12] The unmistakable reference was to Pyarelal, whose persistence in the cause of Manu was too tangible. Gandhi was doing his best to calm her. He told her to take a charitable view of the situation. He pleaded with her to reason out with him face to face: "Just think how you can bring [Pyarelal] round by explaining the true position to him in a loving manner... You have the emotion but not the courage. Put more confidence in yourself and everything will come all right."[13]

All this drama was taking place barely sixteen days before Gandhi was assassinated. It was incongruous of Gandhi to ask poor Manu to act as Mother Courage. He should have ticked off his own secretary for his conduct. That he avoided to upbraid Pyarelal is a great mystery of the life and times of Gandhiji.

Troublesome Devdas

As if Pyarelal was not enough of trouble for Gandhi, Devdas, his youngest son, also added to his woes. Devdas was, however, on the right track. He was one of the most constructive critics of his father, for his *brahmacharya* experiments were anathema to him. He was equally uncomfortable with his father during his stay in New Delhi. Coincidentally, the stinker from Devdas (about Gandhiji's decision to go on fast*) arrived on the same

---

* Gandhiji began his fast on 18 January 1948 and broke it on 28 January 1948 on receiving a signed declaration by various groups and organisations of Hindus and Muslims in Delhi over maintaining communal harmony and peace in the capital. The declaration also proved to be his death warrant after a mere two days.

date when he was trying to cope with intractable Pyarelal. His son's letter brought tears to his eyes. Manu did not have the heart to bring the letter to Gandhi's attention.* The dilemma faced by Manu was faithfully recorded in her diary on 13 and 14 January 1948. On one hand, Manu was worried and, on the other hand, Gandhi was being so solicitous about her to the extent of tenderness in gently pressing her back with his hand. At precisely such a moment, it was instinctive for her to feel concerned about her future. Manu had sung the following psalm in her morning prayer: "The path to God is for the brave, and not for cowards." Actually she did not seem to practice what he had preached to her, for she was not too sure of the protective cover of her mentor remaining for too long.

The day-to-day diary maintained by Manubehn in Gujarati of her impressions of Gandhi during his stay at Birla House, New Delhi is of great historic value. Here is a saga of a grandfather and a granddaughter, a guru and a disciple and of two incompatible comrades experiencing an intense personal relationship amidst tremendous political pressures and strains.

On the night of 31 December 1947, Gandhi told Manu that he was already planning to go on fast by 3 January 1948. This time he intended to fast-unto-death. He was all ears to his inner voice. He also talked of a different course of life for him. Manu was the only one in whom he had confided his new resolve. Even in the midst of so much political activity in New Delhi everything centred around him, he could not take his attention off Manu. He began to talk of injustices done to his "grand-niece of 16 or 17 years", by spreading about her relations with him. How would he recompense her? He had a ready response to her troubles: "If I were your true and holy mother, I would fall asleep in your lap, repeating the name of Rama and talking to you in the natural manner."[14]

In his conversations with her, he went out of his way to ingratiate himself with her. This was his way of expressing gratitude for her participation in the *brahmacharya yajna*, her total devotion and her deliberate underplaying of her association with the Mahatma. He knew

---

* Gandhiji was upset over the letter from Devdas. He replied to his son in the harshest possible terms on 14 January 1948. "I did not like to hear from you or anybody else arguments against the propriety of the fast. That I have listened to you so far is a sign of modesty and patience" (Gandhi, Manu, *Last Glimpses of Gandhi*, 1934).

his end was near and he was in a hurry to repay his debt to her. Besides, it was a most satisfying relationship in which two incompatible persons would find so much happiness in each other. They would forget all the worries confronting them, after they found themselves closeted at night, chattering away their troubles.

Uncertain Future

Gandhiji called his last days as 'the second phase of the great sacrifice', the Noakhali episode being the first phase of the great sacrifice, or *mahayajna.* Manu was once again a partner in this great enterprise. Tears welled in Manu's eyes after hearing his discourse about her association with him.

He was greatly worried about Manu's fate after he passed away. Did he have a clear premonition of the future? What would be her fate and her life without him? Would she be thrown in the dustbin of history, perhaps not even deserving a footnote? Would she be packed off unceremoniously a day or two after he was gone? How was her future to be secured? This concern was equally shared by Manu.

Manu was her own greatest enemy. She was unused to the wiles of the world. She was yet to learn to stand on her own feet. For once, Gandhi was to make a correct appraisal of her. In his note to her, he was to tell her complainingly: "If you were to have more courage, your entire bearing would change. You have considerable capability in you but that this has not been developed fully because of your withdrawing nature. Think over this …. Your timidity is killing you."[15]

Now that death was hovering over him, Gandhiji was in the process of settling all his debts. Undoubtedly he owed a great deal to Manu for the sacrifices she had made in his cause. He recorded a handsome tribute to her in a note dated 23 January, 1948. He took the unusual step of dictating a note to Manu in her personal diary underlining the sacrifices she had made in his cause. He went to the extent of telling her: "Whether in the family or outside, I have not met a girl of your purity. That is why I became a mother to no one but you."[16]

Flattering the Lady

Then he talked of the possibility of another bomb explosion. Indeed he seemed to be excited about the possibility: "I may depart from you, repeating the name of Rama." He welcomed death with open arms and inevitably brought her into picture as more of a hyperbolic gesture on his part: "As for me, I shall think I have won a victory only when you transform yourself from an old woman of seventy, which you look today, into a bloomy maiden of seventeen."[17] He ended his note with a benediction for her: "May your service bear fruit".

Immediately after dictating his note to Manu, he decided to address her father, Jaisukhlal Gandhi. He made a mention of his long talk with Manu on 23 January and recalled her services to him in Noakhali as well. He explained how she escaped certain death from the bomb explosion. He also talked of her great contribution to his great sacrificial Noakhali *yajna*. Accordingly, Bapu owed a debt to her and he was in a great hurry to unburden himself: "You will see that I have settled the debt I owed. She has sent you her diaries. She has made great progress in writing the diary. She takes great interest in writing notes and when I see them Mahadev's face appears before my eyes."[18]

That Mahadev Desai and Manu Gandhi maintained diaries recording their days with Gandhi in contrasting style is to be noted. Mahadev's are a record of his public activities skirting the personal angle substantially, except for the unintended juicy bits about Gandhi's exchange of correspondence with Saraladevi Chowdharani. Essentially, Mahadev's diaries are a record of public activities of a public figure in the process of transforming himself into a *mahatma*.

Manu's diaries are an intense account of private relations of two incompatible persons (both in age and intellect) in the public eye. They are indeed dramatic because they describe the private life of a great man during his final years, lived with intensity at a point of public and private crises.

Isolation Cell

When in difficulty, he would depend upon his conscience. He was being his own prophet. He was thus left with few options but to go on fast to have public attention focussed on him once again. Fasting was his secret weapon on such occasions. He was living in an unreal world. He confided that he was about to see the light. The more he got isolated, the more he believed in himself. On 4 January 1948, he flattered Manu by telling her: "If you are true and holy mother, I shall fall asleep in your lap, repeating the name of Rama." He also confided to her, "I think of all persons I am the most favoured of God."[20] He was now threatening to move to the Muslim quarters of old Delhi to restore communal peace and harmony. This could have been no more than a symbolic gesture. The fact, however, remained that he was trying to rise above his circumstances. Fasting was his way of a symbolic protest. The day had at last arrived. It was 12 January 1948, and it happened to be a Monday. Even when Jawaharlal Nehru and Vallabhbhai Patel had been to see him in the morning, they had no inkling of his crucial decision. He did not care to tell anyone about 'his decision to go on a fast to anyone except his own conscience'.[21]

His decision to go on fast came in a dramatic fashion. His women associates were the first to know about it. Sushila Nayyar was all excited and rushed to tell Manu about his decision to go on fast. All of them were so excited that they immediately went to him. It was his day of silence. He wouldn't talk. He also refused to communicate in writing. He ordained them to get back to their respective duties. Manu was asked to resume her translation work. Drama seemed to have become a substitute for real action and had replaced mature consultation with his senior colleagues in the political field. His having established a direct channel to God, through his inner voice was a matter of his satisfaction, but not for others wishing well for him.

Manu was not at all excited about his decision to go on a fast. This decision had come like a bolt from the blue. Manu had a hunch much before the decision was actually taken. She was very worried and was in low spirits. The announcement of the fast was almost like the end of the world for her. She would have been orphaned, if something were to happen to him. She would have been reduced to a big zero in the event of his demise. She considered the fast an inauspicious sign. After all, he had gone on fast a mere six months ago at Calcutta. The fear of losing Bapu remained immanent in her mind. She shed lots of tears but those were wasted. His placating and flattering served no purpose this time. She was disconsolate. She was even afraid of her own shadow.

Tears of Joy

Bapu had other ideas. He had convinced himself of being 'a prisoner of God' and hence at his mercy and obliged to no one else. It was his usual custom to write notes to his associates from time to time. This time it was his turn to justify his decision to go on fast. As he was about to go on fast on the evening of 13 January, he handed over a letter to Manudi pleading with her to have courage and assuring her: "The whole tenor of my life will change."[22]

On 25 January it was the usual prayer time at 3.30 am. While brushing his teeth after the morning prayer, Gandhiji became very grave and shared his innermost thoughts with Manu. He was referring to rumours floating around town about his relations with Manu. He was hurt but declared her completely innocent. After all she was merely responding to him. She was a passive actor in the drama produced, directed and acted by him. He called upon God as his witness. He did not care, even if public mocked at him. He had reached the end of his tether. It mattered the least to him, whether he was dead or alive.

He was, however, satisfied on one score. His *brahmacharya yajna* in Noakhali (and New Delhi) had reached fruition. It was a clear demonstration of his philosophy of life in practice. Beleaguered as he was, he remained undaunted until the last days of his life: "People may not realise the significance of this sacrifice. Perhaps Manu may not realise it either, because she is too young to entrust me to the future. When I think deeply the consciousness that I have almost fulfilled the main purpose of my life, which is self-satisfaction, dawns upon me."[23] Here was triumph and tragedy at the same time. There were only five days left to the D-Day.

Manu has testified to the fact that Gandhiji's anguish was increasing day-by-day. His cup of misery was brimful on 29 January–a day before D-Day. While Manu massaged his head with oil, he felt giddy and began to cough. He was increasingly concerned over lack of probity in public life. His deteriorating physical state matched his spiritual state of mind. He however returned to the topic once again. His dependence on Manu increased as it happened in his Noakhali days. Again and again he confided in her: "You alone are my partner and helped in this sacrifice... I threw you in the sacrificial fire and you emerged safe and sound."[24] Both Bapu and Manu were becoming sentimental and also isolating themselves from the rest of the world in this process. He refused to resume dialogue with his closest associates and well-wishers. Herein lay the basic flaw in his thinking.

Saying Goodbye

Instead, Manu and mere Manu was his panacea for the ills afflicting him. Come the last day, he talked to Manu while taking a bath. He was virtually bidding goodbye to her without realising it. This time he drew a portrait of Manu without going into any specifics. It was his way of saying a benediction to her: "You are a budding girl of 18. You cannot realise at this stage how much strength of character I have developed in you. From the day you came to Noakhali [on 19 December 1946] till now I have put you to a thorough test and made you pass through trying experiences of all sorts. You may well not realise the value of this today, but keep a permanent record of these words of mine, since they will stand in good stead in your future life, whether I live or pass away."[25]

Gandhi made history and he was also its chronicler. He was anxious for Manu to record every word he uttered. Very few have had their private history recorded so meticulously and without too many embellishments. His place was secure but what about his underlings like Manu who were but forgotten after he passed away? Only the pleasant memories were left of her legacy.

Just ten days before Gandhi was to pass away, she ruminated over her relations with him. She could not contain herself any longer: "Every minute I am overawed with the feeling that in the estimation of Bapu my importance is increasing day by day although he has so many followers, comrades and learned men at his disposal. He has a high regard for me and trains me for public life". The cat was out of the bag. Gandhi was preparing Manu for public life, perhaps on the grandest scale possible. Manu was however fully aware of her limitations: "I am afraid lest I should come a cropper one day... Since he exalts me so high, I may have a downfall someday."[26]

Premonition of Death

Great people live in style. They also love to die in style. They like to be in the public eye. They generate news to be in the limelight. Like ordinary and wary mortals they do not feel any less uncomfortable at the very mention of death. They also have a death wish. Gandhi is also on record for his wish to die at the hands of an assassin. He had said several times, he would be a 'false mahatma' if he were to die a natural death. The sacrifice of his life was the price he was ever ready to pay. His *yajna* in Noakhali was a sacrifice. All his fasts-unto-death were a kind of sacrifice. So was every *satyagraha* movement launched by him. So was his death at the hands of the assassin, a *yajna* to propitiate the gods. Indeed he had offered to hold a dialogue with those who had attempted to throw a bomb at him. Manu was not pleased by his playing with death.

He had a definite premonition that his visit to Delhi would be the closing chapter of his life. He engaged himself in hectic activities on all fronts to make up for lost time. Death had begun to hover over his head. The bomb explosion was an indication of things to come. He was preparing himself for death as his all-embracing and welcome delivery. There are numerous indications to this effect in his correspondence and conversations with Manu Gandhi. When queried by a woman associate, he said, how could one be sure of tomorrow, and indeed who had seen it? Accordingly, he was resigned to his tomorrows. He was gradually turning philosophical. His responses to letters received by him had become brief. Two or three liners were his response to letters received by him. Yet some of his replies were sheer poetry.

In fact he returned to the question, What would happen tomorrow? On the day he was assassinated? When queried about his plans to leave for Wardha, he promised to make his decision known through the radio bulletin at night. He also wrote to Mashruwala on the same subject: "My proposed visit there is still in the air. I have mooted the idea of my staying at Sevagram from 3rd to 12th [of February]... Probably we shall be able to take some decision tomorrow."[27]

The letter could not be posted on January 29. Manu enquired of him and he replied philosophically: "Who has seen tomorrow? If my going is to be finalised, I shall mention after the prayers and it will be relayed in the night broadcast. But the letters should not have been left like it... It may be lapse on the part of someone else but I regard it as a lapse on your part." Here was a prophecy by Gandhiji which came to be true!

Tryst with Destiny

On 30 January 1948, he gave an undertaking to Manu to remain with her in spirit, even after he was dead. He had a tryst with destiny on the same date. He was now ready to meet his Maker in person. He had already seen the face of death after the earlier bomb explosion. As a true *satyagrahi* he had seen visions of Him in his assassin. He could not help bringing in the name of Manu in this connection. He visualised his death by assassination: "While lying on your lap and repeating the name of Rama with a smile on my face."[28]

It had to be Manu and Manu all the way. Manu was mighty pleased because it was a 'wonderful lesson' for her to be close to him, hear him constantly, and, above all, have the privilege of his unlimited and exclusive love. Somehow Manu and death were closely related in his mind. The day before he was actually assassinated, he expansively told Manudi: "And if an explosion took place, as it did last week, or somebody shot at me and I received his bullet on bare chest, without a sigh and with Rama's name on my lips, only then you should say that I was a true *mahatma*. This will benefit the Indian people."[29]

The day was mostly spent in the company of Manu. He was all praise for Manu. He was finding virtues in her which she did not possess. In the late afternoon he had a long session with Sardar Patel. He was getting late for his meeting with the Kathiawar delegation. Manu had to remind him about his appointment. He had put off the meeting with the delegation after the prayer meeting. He was late for the prayer meeting by ten minutes. He had his last meal quickly. It consisted of 14 oz of goat's milk, 4 oz of vegetable juice and three oranges.

This restless spirit was now ready to meet his Maker directly. Manu was to recall that he had asked her to sing a song for the first time: "Whether tired or not..., O man!, do not take rest."[30] He was indeed a restless soul, who had sworn never to take rest for a minute.

Just before his march to the prayer ground, Manu put together his pen, his rosary, his spittoon, the case for his glasses and the notebook for recording his discussion and was ready to accompany him. Bapu was annoyed with Manu and Abha ('his walking sticks') for his late arrival at the prayer meeting. Actually the fault lay with him for his extended discussion with Sardar Patel. Abha had indeed alerted him by picking up his watch and holding it in front of him to remind him of the time. Absorbed as he was in his discussions, he did not pay any attention to her gesture. Thus the entire fault rested with him.

Maniben Patel had to remind him. But he would not pay any attention to her either. Finally he was ready for his historic march to death. Immediately afterwards he was his usual self. He steadied his hands on the shoulders of the two girls. He laughed, joked and exchanged pleasantries with Abha and Manu. He made fun of Abha for serving carrots-the cattle feed-to him for his meal. When reminded of his punctuality, he called Abha and Manu his watchkeepers.

He was as usual walking along the cordoned lane supported by Abha and Manu on each side. Suddenly there emerged a shadowy figure forcing his way out of the crowd towards him. He kept going, unmindful of the presence of two young ladies. He kept walking remorselessly. For a minute Manu assumed he intended to touch Gandhi's feet as a mark of respect. He kept surging forward and wouldn't listen to Manu (who kept murmuring about Bapu being late for his prayer meeting).

She tried to stop him with the movement of her hand. It was no use stopping him. Everything she was carrying in her hands—the notebook, spittoon and the *mala*, fell on the ground. As Manu bent to collect her belongings, the unknown person confronted Gandhi. He fired three shots in quick succession at point-blank range. Gandhi's blood splashed on the young ladies accompanying him. The blood marks were most prominent on the spotless white saris of Abha and Manu Gandhi. Manu heard Gandhi uttering the words 'Hei Ram' and the limp body fell softly on the ground. Gandhi-the history-maker-was no more at 5.17 pm sharp.

Three Versions

There is a slightly different version to be found in Manubehn's *Last Glimpses of Gandhi*. Manu was one of the 'sticks' with the help of which he walked to his prayer meetings. After the spittoon etc. fell from her hands she scuffled with the stout man in *khaki* dress, but she had left him after the rosary dropped from her hand. She bent to pick it up, thus providing a free hand to the assassin. For a moment there was confusion, worse confounded due to the enveloping smoke from the gun. She saw Gandhi's hands folded. Bapu still kept marching forward with his bare chest, until he fell down to ground in a lump. She heard the words "Hei Ra... ma! Hei Ra...' on his lips."[31]

There is a different account of the incident given by Nathuram Godse: "Of the two girls accompanying Gandhiji one was rather close to him and I feared she might be hurt in the attempt. So deciding what to do to avoid that eventuality, I moved forward and uttering the word 'Namaste' (Bow to you), I bowed to Gandhiji with the hands folding the weapon. Moving one step ahead I pushed that girl aside. In the next split second the shots were fired. Weak as he already was, Gandhiji collapsed almost instantly dead on the ground, with the faintest 'Ah!' which arose deep down from his lips: "Gandhiji's indestructible incombustible and unchangeable soul, which was also incapable of being dried, was just vanishing into the elements and I was entering my live *Samadhi* (living death)."[32]

So now we have three versions of the last famous words of Gandhiji. His *Collected Works* describe those as "Hey Ram". Manu Gandhi in her book thinks he uttered: "Hei Ra... m!, Hei Ra...". Nathuram Godse heard the word "Ah!" and that was the end of the matter. This was like the Roshomon story enacted again.

Dustbin of History

Manu's world lay in shambles. The deed was done. Only the formalities remained to be completed. What was left for her, except for his nail clippings which she had deposited reverentially in a box and termed those as "priceless gems"? She had no longer access to his dead body. Others had taken charge of him. She was extended the privilege of resting her head on the lap of Sardar Patel during the funeral ceremonies. She knew very well that the Sardar had never had any love for her. After the funeral ceremony, Devdas brought her over to his residence to console her. Apparently he was most affectionate towards her. Like Sardar Patel, Devdas had bitterly complained to Gandhi about his outlandish *brahmacharya* experiments. His mind was working feverishly to get rid of her as soon as possible.

The death *anniversary* of Kasturba was celebrated with much solemnity on 22 February 1948. It was the deadline determined by Devdas to despatch Manu Gandhi to her home town. She was to be accompanied by Kanu and Abha Gandhi on her train journey back to her home town. She, however, got one opportunity to visit the sight of the burning pier at 2 am the next day. She went to the burning ghat accompanied by Devdas.

The anniversary of Kasturba's death was the deadline set by the determined Devdas. Manu was despatched to her hometown by the late evening train on 22 February. The train was late by two hours. Devdas took Manu aside on the railway platform for an informal chat. He was very considerate to her, but, at the same time, he was anxious to make sure that she kept her mouth shut about her relations with Bapu.

He was particularly concerned about her diary with Gandhi's comments on it. While Gandhiji had viewed the diary as a great historical document, his son Devdas had appointed himself as the censor to suppress it. Devdas was rightly concerned about the possibility of a scandal exploding in public and damaging the name and reputation of the great man.

Devdas had especially targetted Manu: "Not to disclose the contents of my diary to anyone and at the same time forbade me to divulge the contents of important letters."[33] Devdas was being rather unsophisticated in peremptorily ordering her: "You are very young but you possess a lot of valuable literature. And you are also unsophisticated. But since your brother is with you, I have no fear."[34]

She was already forgotten. She went back from New Delhi to Mahua practically unnoticed. Only four persons accompanied her. The team included her father Jaisukhlal, Abha Gandhi, Kanubhai and a lowly attendant. Nobody remembered her thereafter.

Her diaries in Gujarati are a remarkable document of our times. She lived in obscurity after the death of Gandhi, and died comparatively young at forty one– unknown, unwept and unsung. A great many secrets of Bapu died with her. She lived for less than two decades after Bapu passed away. She was more of a corpse than a living person before she actually died. She must have lived on memories which she alone had the privilege of sharing with one of the greatest men of our times.

Who's Who

Adjania, Sorabji Shapurji(1883–1918): Parsi young lad who had earned kudos from Gandhiji for his role in *satyagraha* movement and in 1912 was sponsored for legal education in London by Pranjivan Mehta, died young at 36.

Ambedkar, B R (1893–1956): Dalit icon and father of Indian Constitution, was sceptical of Gandhiji's *brahmacharya* practices and generally opposed to him.

Amrit Kaur, Rajkumari (1889–1964): The Kapurthala princess was always treated with due deference by Gandhiji. He gave her freedom which was not extended to anyone except Saraladevi. He called her a *Rebel* and was a *Tyrant* to her. They exchanged hundreds of letters during 1934–47. She was one of the participants in his *brahmacharya* experiments.

Amutussalaam, Bibi (1907–85): The proud Rajputani from Patiala ('The crazy daughter' to Gandhiji), had a turbulent association with him from 1931 to 1948. He posted more than four hundred letters to her over a period of seventeen years. She was thin, pale and sickly, suffering from TB, piles, asthma, pleurisy, tonsillitis, pneumonia and migraine. Yet, she was bold enough to tackle Pir Pagaro in persuading him to end communal riots in Sind. Amutussalaam was also a participant in his *brahmacharya* experiments.

Anand, Swami: A long-time associate of Gandhiji's, who along with Nathji went all the way to Naokhali to dispute with Gandhiji over his interpretation of *brahmacharya*.

Andrews, Rev. Charles Freer (1871–1940): A classical scholar, missionary, educationalist (St. Stephen's College and Vishwabharti connection) and a friend of Gandhiji. They were 'Charlies' and 'Mohans' to each other. He too was sceptical of his world view.

Asar, Lilavati: The long-time associate of Gandhiji (1929–1948) was a lonely person, slow-witted and extremely quarrelsome, the reason for which nobody loved her. Gandhiji took pains to tutor her personally. Also, one of the participants in his *brahmacharya* experiments, she was no more than a playful kitten providing moments of relaxation to him. Lilavati was marginal in his scheme of things, but he was quite concerned about her.

Bajaj, Jamnalal (1889–1942): The industrialist and philanthropist friend of Gandhiji's, associated with the funding of Sevagram Ashram; he had a fierce spat with Mirabehn over her sickening possessiveness of her mentor.

Balibehn: The sister-in-law of Harilal who looked after his children; could not but resist the temptation to give "three or four slaps" to her drunken brother-in-law.

Balvantsinha: A close associate of Gandhiji. He also became a close confidant of Harilal during his short stay at Sabarmati ashram in the thirties.

Bawazeer, Imam Abdur Kader: The pious Muslim cleric who moved from Phoenix and settled down at Sabarmati ashram along with his family.

Bhandari, Col. M.S.: The genteel Inspector-General of Prisons who supervised the stay of Gandhiji and his associates during their 1942–44 imprisonment at Aga Khan Palace internment camp, Poona.

Bhave, Balakrishna: The younger brother of Vinoba Bhave to whom Gandhiji wrote an enlightening letter on the mechanics of *brahmacharya* experiment.

Bhave, Vinoba (1885–1982): The tallest among the associates of Gandhiji, the wise, scholarly and ascetic *bhakta.* Gandhiji called him a "real pearl", one who had joined the ashram in 1926, "not to be blessed but to bless, not to receive but to give". He maintained a respectable distance from his mentor, and, he considered his *brahmacharya* experiments 'contrary to ideal *brahmacharya*'. Subsequently, he was to compare Gandhi's unconventional practices to Krishna's *Raslila.*

Bose, Nirmal Kumar (1901–72): The distinguished anthropologist was a practising Gandhian, who participated in the Salt and Quit India movements. He was the closest associate of Gandhiji during his Noakhali sojourn chronicling events with cold academic objectivity. Gradually, he became disgruntled with his mentor. Bose has graphically recorded the turbulent Noakhali drama on a day-to-day basis in his book *My Days* *with Gandhi* (1953) and his personal papers deposited in the National Archives of India. He established an ashram at Bolpur near Santiniketan to propagate Gandhi's ideas.

Braj Kishore Prasad (1877–1946): The father of Prabhavati was a distinguished advocate and prominent Congress leader of Bihar, who hosted Gandhiji during the Champaran campaign. The gentleman-lawyer-politician was responsible for arranging the marriage of his daughter Prabhavati with Jayaprakash Narayan.

Cachalia, Ahmed (d.1918): Prominent Gujarati businessman in South Africa, who was an active supporter of Gandhiji and went to jail.

Chowdharani, Saraladevi (1872–1945): She was the true and high-profile love of Gandhiji (1919–20). The whirlwind romance took them all over India. Gandhiji even called her his 'spiritual wife'. The aristocratic lady was the niece of Rabindranath Tagore. She was Gandhiji's hostess during his extended stay for several months in Lahore during Jallianwala agitation. The imperious lady had the distinction of wearing the first *khadi* sari.

Chowdhary, Rambhuj Dutt (1866–1923): He belonged to a rich *zamindar* family of Punjab. During the martial law in 1919, Rambhuj came to be known as the "uncrowned king of Lahore". He had a long association with the Congress party. He was also actively connected with the Arya Samaj. He was a poet, an orator and a media person. He married three times, the third time to Saraladevi Chowdharani.

Cook, George Cram: Nilla Cram Cook's father, a famous theatrical director, had undoubtedly influenced her maverick behaviour and world view.

Cook, Nilla Cram ('N') (1908–82): The most vivacious female who crossed Gandhiji's path, though briefly, in 1933. she represented the bohemian spirit of Greenwich Village. He went completely overboard in his enthusiasm for the American *prima donna*, but ended up branding her the Fallen Woman. Her book *My Road to India* (1939) is her finest testament in the cause of Gandhi and India, as well as feminism.

Dafda, Dudabhai: Dudabhai, the teacher, and his wife Daniben, the Untouchable couple, were admitted to the ashram by Gandhiji in the face of stiff opposition by Kasturba and practically everybody close to him during 1915. He withstood the revolt by adopting Lakshmi, the Dafda girl, as his daughter.

Das Gupta, Satis Chandra: The indefatigable Gandhian from Bengal had organized the entire Noakhali operation during 1946–47 with much credit.
Desai, Mahadev Haribhai (1892–1942): The gentleman-secretary of Gandhiji's was 'adopted' by Kasturba as her fifth son. He joined the ashram as early as 1917. He had difficult times with his mentor during 1935–1938 who accused him of having a roving eye for Sushila Nayyar. The relations were never the same between Pyarelal (Sushila's brother), Gandhiji and him. His diary *Day-to-day with Gandhi: Secretary's diary* (10 vols.) is a faithful record of daily happenings.
Desai, Valji: An academician by background, Valji engaged himself by editing several works of Gandhiji and Mahadev Desai.
Dhupelia, MESTHRIE-Uma: Sita Dhupelia's daughter and academician by profession, she has recently published a voluminous biography of her grandfather Manilal Gandhi entitled *Gandhi's prisoner?* (2005).
Dhupelia, Sita(1928–99): Manilal's daughter was outspokenly critical of her grandfather's maltreatment of her uncle Harilal and her parents Sushila and Manilal. She was a resident of South Africa
Doctor, Jayakunwar (Mehta) alias JEKI: Daughter of Dr Pranjivan Jagjivan Mehta, a close friend of Gandhiji's. She was fondly described by him as 'My only adopted daughter'. She came to stay with him at Tolstoy and Phoenix farms. She was married to Manilal Doctor at the instance of Gandhiji. Her involvement with Manilal, Gandhiji's son, created a much-talked about sex scandal. She was imprisoned along with Kasturba in South Africa during 1913. There were many ups-and-downs in her personal life. Gandhiji was there to sustain her during her subsequent tragic existence in India.
Doctor, Manilal: The footloose and maverick barrister fought for the cause of Indian labour across continents, married Jayakunwar Doctor, twelve years younger to him.
Doke, Rev. Joseph (1861–1913): A Baptist churchman edited *Indian Opinion* and published the earliest biography of Gandhiji, *Gandhi, an Indian patriot in South Africa.* (1909).
Erikson, Erik H: The distinguished psychologist spent considerable time at Ahmedabad, studying mill-labour strike led by Gandhiji. Has published his critical psychobiography, *Gandhi's truth.* (1962).
Faering, Esther (1892–1962): Esther was a pretty Dutch missionary who came to teach at a missionary school in South India during 1916.

She came to spend some time at Sabarmati Ashram and was enchanted by Gandhiji. She decided to join the company of Gandhiji. She also spent a while at Santiniketan. At one point of time, there was almost a daily exchange of letters between her and Gandhiji. His letters to her are interspersed with poetic verses. In one of his letters he addressed her as 'Rock of Ages', quoting from a popular Christian hymn (circa 1775). Eventually she married Dr. E. K. Menon and settled in India.

Fischer, Louis: The American media-man who spent considerable time with Gandhiji to observe him. Has written his definitive biography, *The life of Mahatma Gandhi* (1962).

Gandhi, Abha: She was born Chatterji and married Kanu Gandhi. Both of them were close to Gandhiji for many years. She also participated in *brahmacharya* experiments though reluctantly.

Gandhi, Arun: Manilal Gandhi's son and author of the book on Kasturba.

Gandhi, Chhaganlal (b. 1880): A nephew of Gandhiji, managed Gujarati section of *Indian Opinion* at Phoenix and subsequently functioned as manager of his ashrams in India.

Gandhi, Devdas (1900–57): The youngest son of Gandhiji who was delivered personally by him. The favourite son is on record to have differed with his father over his *brahmacharya* practices and his association with young women. He married Lakshmi (daughter of C Rajagopalachari) in 1933 in spite of stiff opposition from his father and his father-in-law.

Gandhi, Gulab/Chanchal (née Vora)(d. 1918): The beloved wife of Harilal Gandhi, whose early death unhinged her husband for the remaining days of his vagabond life.

Gandhi, Harilal Mohan (1888–1948). Popularly known as Bhai: The eldest son of Gandhiji ('The restless soul'), was called Harilal by him. The 18-year-old married 11-year-old Gulab Vohra (daughter of Haridas Vohra on May 2, 1906). He was never reconciled to his famous father, especially after the death of his wife Gulab in 1918, also known as Chanchi and Chanchal. His tragic life has been best narrated in Dalal, CB *Harilal Gandhi: Ek dukhi atma* (1977) (original in Gujarati).

Gandhi, Jaisukhlal Amritlal: An executive in a shipping firm, he was the grandson of Gandhi's uncle Tulsidas. The only reason for his fame nests on his being the father of Manu Gandhi, the teenage young lady who was one of the closest associates of Gandhiji during his Noakhali, Bihar and Delhi sojourns (Dec. 1946 to Jan. 1948).

Gandhi, Jamnadas: The youngest brother of Chhaganlal and Maganlal, he was a buddy of Manilal Gandhi involved with him in JEKI affair at Phoenix.

Gandhi, Kaniyalal Narandas (1917–86) alias Kanu: The son of Narandas, who along with his wife Abha (*née* Chatterjee) (1925–95) had been associated with Gandhiji since 1934. He joined Gandhiji during his Noakhali sojourn along with his wife. He was also an official photographer to Gandhiji.

Gandhi, Karamchand (1822–85) Also known as Kaba Gandhi (and Kaba Kaka, Kabai Bhai and Kaba Bhapa). He married four times and his youngest wife Putlibai (1822–91) whom he married in 1843, bore him three sons and one daughter, namely Raliatbehn (1862–1960), Lakshmidas (1863–1914), Karsandas (1867–1913) and Mohandas (1869–1948). She was the greatest influence over her son Mohandas Karamchand Gandhi, who was left stranded, searching for bits and parts of Putlibai in three generations of women from Millie Graham Polak (circa 1905) to Manu Gandhi (circa 1946).

Gandhi, Kasturbai (1869–1944) Maiden name: Kasturbai Kapadia (daughter of Gopaldas Nanakji) Also known as Kasturba, Motiba and Ba (mother in Gujarati). She was married to Gandhiji in 1883 and bore him four sons, Harilal, Manilal, Ramdas and Devdas. The hapless illiterate Hindu wife grew in stature gradually as the Mother Courage of our times. She was closest to Gandhiji but kept her distance from him to retain her inviduality.

Gandhi, Khushalchand (1851–1937): The son of Gandhi's uncle, Jeevanlal, he dedicated his four sons, Chhaganlal (1881–), Maganlal (1883–1928), Narandas (1885–1974) and Jamnadas (1895–1949) to the cause of Gandhiji, both in South Africa and India. The son of Narandas, Kaniyalal (Kanu) (1917–86) and his wife Abha (*née* Chatterjee) (1925–95), were closely associated with him as was Prabhudas (1901–), the son of Chhaganlal, who published his childhood memoirs *My Childhood with Gandhi* (1971).

Gandhi, Lakshmi: The Brahman daughter of C Rajagopalachari was married to Devdas, youngest son of Mohandas Karamchand Gandhi in 1933 after much reluctance from both parental quarters.

Gandhi, Maganlal (1883–1928): The second son of Khushalchand was the jewel in the crown of the Gandhian establishment. He had coined the term '*sadagraha*' for passive resistance. He died very young. His death was a great shock to his mentor. Upon his death Gandhiji wailed that 'his heir to my all is no more' and thereby he had been 'widowed' more than his own widow.

Gandhi, Manilal (1892–1956): The second son of Gandhiji, who settled down in South Africa and managed the Phoenix Farm, rather unsuccessfully, after his father moved to India. He kept falling in love with the 'wrong' type of women to the exasperation of his father. Eventually he married Sushila (*née* Mashruwala) in 1927, who passed away in 1988. While he was cowed down by his father, Manilal maintained his independence by default by living away from him. His daughter Sita Dhupelia thought differently. She did not fail to notice that her parents lived their days in a "captive state".

Gandhi, Manuben (1928–69): The daughter of Jaisukhlal, a distant cousin of Gandhiji, whom he fondly called his 'granddaughter'. She was in early teens when she came to live with the Gandhis, and became his closest associate during 1946–48. Manudi was the most pliable of all his female companions in showing readiness to participate in his *brahmacharya* experiments in Noakhali. She has left a graphic account of her days in books and diaries. Her two books *The Lonely Pilgrim* (1962) and *Last glimpses of Gandhi* (1964) are worthy of note. She walked into anonymity after the death of her mentor in 1948. She died unknown, unwept and unsung in 1969.

Gandhi, Prabhudas (1901–95): Son of Chhaganlal Gandhi, he has provided a graphic account of activities at Phoenix Farm, including JEKI-Manilal affair in his book, *My Childhood with Gandhi between 1904–1914*, (1957).

Gandhi, Ramdas (1897–1969): The third son of Gandhiji was a perfect gentleman and true Gandhian in every sense of the term. His father described him as a true *bhakta*. He married Nirmalabehn (also known as Nimmubehn) (*née* Vora) in 1928 at Sabarmati Ashram. She dedicated the rest of her life to Sevagram Ashram after the death of her husband and passed away in the year 2000.

Gandhi, Sushila(1907–88): Coming from the Mashruwala family, the deaf young lady was married to Gandhiji's second son, Manilal, who managed the Phoenix Farm for several decades until its forcible closure.

Gandhi, Uttamchand (died 1869): The patriarch of the Gandhi clan was also known as Ota Gandhi. He had six sons including Karam Chand, the father of Mohandas Karamchand. His personal integrity was his hallmark that distinguished him.

Ghoshal, Jankinath (1840 – 1913): A prominent nationalist leader of Bengal, he organized the 1901 annual session of Indian National Congress, attended by M.K. Gandhi (and by Saraladevi Chowdharani). He married Swarankumari Devi, the elder sister of Rabindranath Tagore and mother of Saraladevi seemingly her mother's literary genes and reformist zeal traveled down to her daughter Saraladevi.

Godse, Gopal: The younger brother of Gandhiji's assassin, Nathuram Godse, wrote a book in defence of his brother. He passed away recently.

Gokhale, Gopal Krishna (1866–1915): Statesman and educationist of the highest order, and political guru of both M.A. Jinnah and Gandhiji.

Gool, Dr A H.: Son of Josub Gool, was progressive in his thinking and provided leadership to Indian community in South Africa along with his enlightened wife.

Gool, Fatima (Timmie): Josub Gool's daughter who fell in love with Manilal Gandhi (and had the support of her family), but was thwarted by Gandhiji in 1926 because she was a Muslim.

Gool, Josub (Yusuf): Leading merchant of Cape Town of Gujarati origin and a leader of Indian community, host to Gandhiji, and father of Fatima Gool.

Horace, Alexander: Member of the British Society of Friends (Quakers), a close friend of Gandhiji and author of a book on Gandhi, *Gandhi through Critical Eyes.*

Jayaprakash Narayan (1902–1979): Jayaprakash, the tallest socialist leader, married Prabhavati in 1920 but was unable to exercise his conjugal rights because his wife had taken a vow of celibacy under the direction of Gandhiji, who even suggested to Jayaprakash to take another wife for himself. The cold war between the three of them spluttered for nearly two decades. JP viewed Gandhiji as a co-conspriator with Prabhavati aligned against him.

Joshi, Chhaganlal: A loyal but sceptical associate of Gandhiji who did not hesitate to contradict him over his public commitment to the ashramites to cease his controversial practice of resting hands over the shoulders of girls while walking.

Kallenbach, Herman (1871–1945): Born in Imperial Germany of Jewish parents, he moved to South Africa during 1896 to practice architecture. He came to be recognised seven years later as a budding pioneer in his land of adoption. He met Mohandas Karamchand Gandhi who changed his entire life. They affectionately called each other 'Lower House'

(Kallenbach) and 'Upper House' (Gandhi). He was affectionately known as Uncle Hanuman by the ashramites. Tolstoy Farm was built on Kallenbach's personal farm near Johannesburg. He was the closest friend to Gandhiji, his brother-in-arms, his financier in early years, his conscience keeper, and, above all, his true apostle, pioneer *satyagrahi* in the right sense of the term, and a *karamyogi* patterned after his mentor. His jail diary maintained by him during 1913 provides a graphic account of the birth of passive-resistance movement and its ideology in South Africa. Kallenbach has been rightly described by his niece as 'a loyal, constant, loving and generous friend of Mahatma Gandhi for over forty years.

Kantak, Premabehn: Premabehn was one of the most aggressive and domineering females who crossed the path of Gandhiji, in whom she also found her substitute father. She came to his ashram in 1929 and moved to Saswad Ashram (near Poona) subsequently because of irreconcilable differences with the rest of the community. Her correspondence with him on *brahmacharya* ended in public controversy after it was published in a book form in Marathi, *Prasad diksha* (1938). Her next book *Kama and kamini* was a fictional piece narrating the odyssey of a Gandhian in search of *brahmacharya*. At one time Gandhiji confessed to Prema to having lost confidence in his abilities to practice *brahmacharya*, after a series of what he termed as 'involuntary discharges' occurring during 1936–38.

Kalelkar, Dattatraya Balkrishna (1885–1981): A close associate of Gandhiji and Tagore, who was outspoken about his failure to practice *brahmacharya* in real life in his hilarious confession to Ved Mehta. He practicsed *coitus interruptus* to overcome his vow of married *brahmacharya*. Sushila Nayyar was engaged to his son, but the engagement broke up thereby generating bitterness.

Khare, Yoga: Pyarelal was completely infatuated with Yoga, who he believed, had responded to his overtures favourably. Her engagement to another person was apparently in connivance with Gandhiji. This made Pyarelal to go mad for a number of years (1936–38). The whole episode assumed comical character in the end.

Koestler, Arthur: The distinguished literateur wrote contemptuously about Gandhiji's *brahmacharya* practice in his book, *The lotus and robot.* (1949).

Kripalani, Sucheta (1908–74): Sucheta and her husband Acharya Kripalani, observed physical (or married) *brahmacharya* from day one of their marriage at the instance of Gandhi. Acharya Kripalani remained sceptical of their mentor's *obsession magnifique* with *brahmacharya* (in and out of marriage). Acharya Kripalani had gently charged his mentor with employing human beings as guinea pigs for his ends.

Lakshmi (1914 – 84): Born to Dudabhai Dafda and his wife Daniben, the 'Untouchable' girl was adopted by the Gandhis in October 1920. She was brought up affectionately by Kasturba after she had defied her husband (along with others) over the admission of the 'Untouchable' couple to the Sabarmati Ashram. Laxmi was all but forgotten after she was married off to a Brahmin boy, Maruti, in 1933. Her progeny, Haridas and Kalpana, have been scored off the Gandhian map.

Mashruwala, Kishorelal (1890–1952): One of the closest associates of Gandhi, who along with Narahari Parekh, Swami Anand and his guru Kedarnath (Kulkarni) was openly opposed to his *brahmacharya* experiments. He corresponded extensively with his mentor on the subject, but committed the impropriety of destroying the correspondence. He was related to Gandhiji by two marriages of Sushila (Mashruwala) Gandhi and Manu (Gandhi) Mashruwala.

Mashruwala, Manu (Gandhi): The daughter of Harilal was a great favourite of her grandmother Kasturba and married into Mashruwala family.

Mathuradas Trikumji: Nephew of Gandhi who along with Devdas Gandhi stopped Gandhiji in his tracks in falling headlong in love with Saraladevi Chowdharani. He also wrote a play on divorce keeping in mind the Sarala affair.

Mehta, Ved: The blind expatriate biographer of Gandhiji was able to obtain, albeit reluctantly, a confession from Abha Gandhi about *brahmacharya* practices in his book *Mahatma Gandhi and his associates* (1977).

Menon, E Kunhi: Medical doctor by profession, married the Dutch missionary Esther Faering and converted to Christianity, followed his wife by performing public service in South India.

Mirabai: The Rajasthani princess who turned Krishna *bhakta* and was celebrated for her lovelorn poetry. Gandhiji re-named Miss. Slade as Mirabehn soon after her arrival in India during 1925.

Mirabehn (1982–): Original name: Madeleine Slade—the admiral's daughter who became the favourite disciple and his close associate in 1925. She said good-bye to India in 1958 and lived the remaining years of her life in Beethoven's beloved forest near Vienna. Highly emotional and attached to Gandhiji, they had a hate-love relation, throughout their long association of 23 years. Eventually she turned to Baba Prithvi Singh Azad, who also rejected her. Her autobiographical work *The Spirit's Progress* (1968) is a true story of pilgrim's progress turning sour in the end.

Morton, Eleanor [real name: Elisabeth Gertrude Stern (Levin)]: The author of one of the few authoritative books on women associates of Gandhiji in her book entitled *Women behind Mahatma* (1969).

Mukerji, Satis Chandra ('Naga Baba' of Banaras): Gandhiji turned to the well-known mendicant for advice on his *brahmacharya* practice; whose reply is not known.

Naidoo, C.K.T (Thambi): Known as "The brightest star" of Indian community in South Africa, he served ten terms of imprisonment for the cause.

Nanakji, Gopaldas (Kapadia): The father-in-law of Gandhiji, Nanakji, was a rich merchant residing sumptuously in Rajkot. He was a close friend of Karamchand Gandhi, Gandhi's father.

Nathji: An old-time associate of Gandhiji, he travelled all the way to Noakhali along with Swami Anand to argue with him over his *brahmacharya* experiments.

Nayyar, Sushila (1914–2001): Sushila had the longest association with Gandhiji as his personal physician and attendant. Being the sister of Pyarelal, she was privy to everything that came to pass around Gandhiji. Her close relations with Mahadev Desai upset Gandhi and Pyarelal a great deal. He is on record to have written 222 letters to her during 1941. The tension between Sushila and Gandhiji was also palpable during his Noakhali sojourn. To her credit, she produced a monumental study (very much strong on documentation) entitled *Mahatma Gandhi* (10 vols.) jointly with her brother Pyarelal.

Parasuram, R.P.: The volatile and sensitive youngmen hailing from Kerala was his major domo (along with Prof. Nirmal Kumar Bose) during his Noakhali sojourn watching minute-to-minute happenings around Gandhiji. Parasuram broke with him over his *brahmacharya* experiments.

He wrote a ten-page long letter of protest to Gandhi on Jan. 1, 1947 and went away from him for good.

Patel, Raoji Manibhai: An old-time associate of Gandhiji who participated in the 1913 *satyagraha* in South Africa and in 1930 civil-disobedience movement in India. Gandhiji was to share his Manilal woes in Jeki affair with him.

Patel, Vallabhbhai (1975–1950): The first Deputy Minister of India, and a long-time and respected associate of Gandhiji, who had accused him of committing *adharma* through his *brahmacharya* practices.

Patel, Vina: Abha Gandhi's sister whose name is also mentioned in the famous 1945 letter of Gandhiji to Munnalal Shah listing names of women involved with him in his *brahmacharya yajna.*

Payne, Robert: The American author of one of the most accomplished biographies of Gandhi, *The life and death of Mahatma Gandhi* (1969). It is full of delectable anecdotes.

Pir Pagaro: The notorious warlord and leader of a religious sect in Sind, was persuaded to call off communal riots at the instance of Gandhian *bhakta* Bibi Amutussalaam.

Polak, Henry Leon (1862–1934): Gandhiji's deputy in legal practice, Henry was a *Chhotabhai* to Gandhiji. He proved to be a jealous husband on account of Gandhiji's obsessive interest in his wife Millie. At one time very close to his mentor, he gradually distanced himself from him on ideological grounds. His detailed letter to Gandhiji about the worldview of Jawaharlal Nehru is prophetic.

Polak, Maud: The younger sister of Henry Polak and favourite of Gandhiji, she functioned as honorary secretary, South Africa British Indian Committee, London.

Polak, Millie Graham (1880–1962) (Maiden name: Millie Downs): Millie came into Gandhiji's life ('the loving sister') after she married Henry in 1905. She went through an arduous life with Kasturba to sustain the joint household. Gandhiji had the best of the times with her during his visit to London, but she had the worst of times during her enforced stay in India during World War I. She was a lady in every sense of the term with a British(dry) sense of humour. Suffering was the badge-of honour for her and her husband during their association with Gandhiji. Her record of their conversations over a decades makes compelling reading in her memoirs, *Mr Gandhi, the Man* (1940).

Prabhavati (1906–73): The wife of Jayaprakash Narayan, who remained celibate throughout her married life, had no stomach for the physical side of married life, as soon as she came into contact with Gandhiji. This decision was the cause of great tension between Jayaprakash, Gandhiji and herself. She preferred to stay with her mentor as his 'devoted daughter' in his Ashram rather than live with her husband. The tug-of-war between Gandhiji and JP was her ultimate destiny.
Prithvi Singh, Azad: Once upon a time a great revolutionary, he came to live at the Gandhian Ashram, after eschewing violence. Mirabehn was to fall in love with him, but she was rejected by him as too domineering.
Putlibai: The third wife of Karamchand Gandhi, a woman of strong character with deeply religious (and ethical) bend of mind, the qualities inherited by her youngest son, Mohandas Karamchand Gandhi. She was the most dominating factor in Gandhiji's life.
Pyarelal (Nayar), Nickname: Baboo: Pyarelal took over from Mahadev Desai after his demise in 1942. The relations between Pyarelal and Gandhiji were disturbed throughout the thirties and forties. His attempts at courting Yoga Khare and Manu Gandhi had come to nought on account of his mentor's determined opposition. Eventually he was to wed a Bengali lady in 1950, two years after Gandhiji passed away. His sister Sushila Nayyar was the third side of the triangle. Gandhiji wrote 448 letters to the duo between 1936–48, attempting unsuccessfully to propitiate both of them.
Rajagopalachari, C: The shrewdest among political leaders of Gandhiji's generation, his daughter Lakshmi was to marry Gandhiji's youngest son, Devdas, after much opposition from him and Gandhiji.
Rajchandbhai (1867–1901) Real name: Rajchandra Rajivbhai Mehta: He was also known as Kavi and Shrimad Rajchandra. He was married to Zabakbai. A jeweller by profession, he was a profound scholar of Indian tradition and the nearest to be accepted as Gandhiji's *guru*. He was a recognised *shatavadhani* (capable of doing hundred things at the same time). Gandhiji termed his writings 'the quintessence of his experiences'. His book, *Sandhya* was a *Bible* for Gandhiji, who proved to be an apt pupil by actually practicing his theory in real life.
Rajendra Prasad: The first President of independent India, he was a close associate of Jayaprakash Narayan's father-in-law, Braj Kishore Prasad and related to him by marriage.

Ramakrishna (Paramhansa): The great saint of Bengal whose views of *brahmacharya* are strikingly similar to those of Gandhiji.
Rolland, Romain (1866–1944): The distinguished French literateur, carried on extensive correspondence with Mirabehn and Gandhiji. He also published a pioneering biography of Gandhi in French, introducing him to Europe.
Rustomjee, Jhalhhoy (Parsee)(1861–1924): Wealthy trader and a leading community leader in South Africa, he was a close friend of Gandhiji.
Sanger, Margaret: The great advocate of birth control, had a verbal dual with Gandhiji on December 3/4, 1935, when they debated over his pet obsession with *brahmacharya*. It was a debate between the respective exponents of birth control and married continence. Perhaps the intensity of the debate had resulted in a prolonged breakdown of his health, which led to his prolonged recuperation in Bombay.
Schlesin, Sonja (1891–1956): She had a Jewish-Russian origin, joined Gandhiji as his novice secretary in South Africa when she was merely 16. She was introduced by his friend Kallenbach. She took complete charge of him including the *satyagraha* movement launched by him. She was constantly at war with Manilal Gandhi after his father left South Africa. Sonja and he corresponded from 1915 to 1947, with his last letter talking of his 'desire' to live for 125 years. Unfortunately, most of the correspondence has been lost irretrievably.
Shah, Kanchan: The Shahs, Kanchan and her husband, Munnalal were considered role models for realising the ideal state of physical *brahmacharya* or *brahmacharya* for married couples. Her husband was singled out due to his submissive nature. Obviously, Gandhiji had not counted on defiant Kanchan, who had earlier walked out on him over his *brahmacharya* experiments under strict laboratory conditions. Kanchan got away lightly after she gave birth to a baby, but not poor Munnalal who continued to be belaboured for the rest of his life.
Shah, Munnalal: Manager of Sevagram ashram, husband of Kanchan Shah, and a (failed) role model for practicing married / physical *brahmacharya.*
Shukadev, Rishi: Shukadev was the son of Vyasa, the legendary chronicler of *Mahabharata*. He was a householder and like Gandhiji had four sons. Shukadeva believed to have conquered the senses so completely as to be pronounced a perfect *brahmachari*. He was the role model for Gandhiji.

Spiegel, Margarete: The absent-minded, naive and slow-witted German professor came to stay in the Ashram in early thirties to escape the Nazi persecution of German Jews. She was too much obsessed with the person of Gandhiji, who, in turn, was bored stiff with her rather too soon. Her proposal to marry Harilal disturbed the equanimity of Gandhiji. She moved to Shantiniketan and finally returned to Deutschland, and died before completing her memoirs.

Swarankumari Devi: Rabindranath Tagore's elder sister and Saraladevi's mother, maintained a saloon for *bhadralok* gentry in Calcutta.

Syed, Ghulam Murtaza Shah: The ex-chief minister of Sind Province and a gentleman to the core, who did not hesitate to resign from the Muslim-League led provincial Government, after being impressed by lone-person crusade led by Bibi Amutussalaam in the cause of communal harmony. He resigned in empathy with 'his dear sister' who had earlier won over the notorious Pir Pagaro to her cause. Her very success discomfited Gandhi and Maulana Azad to no end.

Tendulkar, G D: The official biographer of Gandhiji who published his staid 8-volume biography, sumptuously illustrated with photographs.

Thakkar Bapa: Real name: Amritlal Thakkar (1869–1951): Thakkar Bapa was the most saintly of Gandhiji's associates who travelled all the way to Noakhali to persuade Gandhi through the good offices of Manu Gandhi to suspend his *brahmacharya* experiments in Noakhali. To his own utter surprise Thakkar Bapa was successful in achieving his objective.

Tyabji, Rehana: Coming from the distinguished Tyabji family of Bombay, she devoted her life to the cause of Gandhiji and him personally. She was obsessive about Gandhiji and viewed him as her substitute for Krishna.

West, Ada (Deviben)(b. 1871): Sister of Albert West, she worked as a school mistress at Phoenix during 1913.

West, Albert (b. 1880): A theosophist community leader, he met Gandhiji regularly at Isaac's Vegetarian Restaurant (of onion fame) in Johannesburg. He was to settle down at Phoenix Farm for a while.

Woodroofe, Sir Justice John: Chief Justice by vocation, he was the greatest exponent of the *Tantra* cult. His book *Sakti and Sakta* (1918) is a classic on the subject. Gandhiji had read him while in Yeravda jail and was possibly influenced by him to some extent expounding his *brahmacharya* philosophy.

Citations/References

BACKGROUND NOTE: Mahatma Gandhi was a compulsive letter-writing buff who would write 10–15 or more letters per day. He wrote 245 and 99 letters respectively to Sushila Nayyar and Pyarelal during 1938–41, making it a total of 344 letters addressed to them in four years. He would even jot down notes for his associates residing with him on days when he observed silence. He wrote no monographs in his lifetime due to his busy schedule. Even his *Autobiography* was serialised. He, however, wrote extensively for periodical publications edited by him. Those included: *Indian Opinion, Young India, Navajivan* and *Harijan* group of newspapers in English, Hindi and Gujarati.

All his extant writings have been brought together in one-hundred volumes published by Publications Division, Ministry of Information, Government of India between 1958 to 1994 as per details below:

a) 1–90 (1884 – 1948)
b) Supplementary Volumes (1–10)
   Supp. Vol. 1 [vol. 91] (1894 –1928)
   Supp. Vol. 2 [vol. 92] (1929 –1934)
   Supp. Vol. 3 [vol. 93] (1935 –1941)
   Supp. Vol. 4 [vol. 94]
   Supp. Vol. 5 [vol. 95]
   Supp. Vol. 6 [vol. 96]
   Supp. Vol. 7 [vol. 97]
   Vol. [98] Index of persons
   Vol. [99] Index of subjects
   Vol. 100 Prefaces

His first letter was addressed to his brother Laxmidas Gandhi and it is dated November 1, 1888. It is followed by his London diary of 120 pages. He wrote it when he was only 19. It has been reproduced with spelling mistakes, missing punctuation marks, absent words and mixed paragraphs as in original. His last letter was dated January 30, 1948 (the day he was assassinated)

Collected Works are limited to his own writings. Unfortunately, there is no parallel collection containing letters received by him. He must have received many more letters than he wrote himself. Very few letters received by him have been preserved. However, his letters are almost a complete saga in themselves.

He had a great sense of loyalty towards his colleagues. The intensity of his relationship had its ups and downs, but the association, in most cases, continued until his dying days.

How deeply he felt for others is shown in his correspondence with his women associates. The following table graphically described the situation in respect of individual persons:

Names (Women associates)	Volume References (in *Collected Works*)	Period of Association
Polak, Millie Graham	6 – 51	1906–1932
Schlesin, Sonja	8 – 89	1908–1947
Chowdharani, Saraladevi	16 – 89	1919–1947
Mirabehn	25 – 90	1924–1948
Asar, Lilavati	32 – 90	1926–1948
Kantak, Premabehn	40 – 90	1929–1948
Nayyar, Sushila	44 – 90	1930–1948
Amutussalaam, Bibi	46 – 90	1931–1948
Spiegel, Margarete	52 – 89	1932–1947
Cook, Nilla Croom	53 – 59	1933
Amrit Kaur, Rajkumari	57 – 89	1934–1947
Shah, Kanchan	63 – 87	1936–1947
Gandhi, Manu	73 – 90	1940–1948

The present work is extensively based upon Gandhiji's original writings as collected in his *Collected Works,* First Edition. Those have been cited in the following manner.

e.g. CW: 70 : August 9, 1939 : Patna

Explanation

- The first digit refers to *Collected Works* of M.K. Gandhi ;
- The second digit refers to the volume number of *Collected Works*;
- The third digit refers to the page numbers of *Collected Works;*
- The fourth digit refers to the place from which the letter was sent, or the original source of reference.

Chapter 1: Ode to *Brahmacharya*

1. CW : 79 : Ap.9. 1945 : 360.
2. CW : 70 : Oct. 28, 1938 : 307.
3. CW : 79 : Mar. 6, 1945 : 212–13.
4. CW : 79 : Mar. 11, 1945 : 238.

5. CW : 79 : Mar. 6, 1945 : 215.
6. MEHTA, Ved. *Mahatma Gandhi and his Apostles.* Indian Book Company, New Delhi. 1977, 48
7. BOSE, Nirmal Kumar. *My Days with Gandhi.* Nishana, Calcutta, 1953, 133.
8. SANGER, Margaret. *Gandhi and Mrs. Sanger. Asia*, New York, 1936, 698.
9. PAREKH, BHIKU. *Colonialism, Tradition and Reform: An Analysis of Gandhi's Political Discourse.* Sage, New Delhi, 1989, 204.

Chapter 2: Celibacy in the Indian Tradition

1. CW : 12 : [Mar 7, 1914], 376.
2. CW : 86 : Feb 1, 1947, 420, Amishapara.
3. CW : 30 : Feb 25, 1926: 15.
4. Mehta, Ved. *Op. cit.*, 210
5. CW : 23 : March 17, 1922 : 102.
6. CW : 35 : Nov. 22, 1927 : 289.
7. Pyarelal. *Mahatma Gandhi : The Last Phase V.1,* [pt. 2]. Navajivan, Ahmedabad, 1956, 578.
8. CW : 87: [Mar. 15–16, 1947] : 90.
9. CW : 87 : [Mar. 15–16, 1947] : 92.
10. CW : 87 : Mar 17, 1947 : 103.
11. CW : 78 : [on or after Sept. 5, 1944] : 82.
12. CW : 23 : Mar. 17, 1932 : 102.
13. CW : 67 : June 4, 1938 : 106.
14. CW : 86 : Feb 10, 1947: 453 : Footnote.
15. CW : 62 : Mar 14, 1936: 262 : *Harijan*,
16. CW : 50 : July 11, 1932: 209.
17. CW : 10 : Jan. 20, 1910 : 133.
18. CW : 30 : Mar. 7, 1926 : 86 *Harijan*.
19. Sil, Narasingh. *Ramakrishna Paramahansa: A Psychological Study*, E.J. Brill, London, 1991, 497.
20. *Ibid.*, 47.
21. Gandhi, Manu. *Bapu my mother*. tr. From the original in Gujarati by Chitra Desai. Ed.2, Navajivan, Ahmedabad, 1962.
22. Polak, Millie. *Gandhi and Women* in Shukla, Chandrashekhar, ed. *Gandhi as we knew him.* Vora, Bombay, 1945, 46.
23. Ashe, Geoffery. *Gandhi: A Study of Revolution.* Asia, Vora, 1968, 261.
24. Green, Martin *Gandhi: Voice of a New Revolution.* Continuum, New York, 1993, 114.
25. Gandhi, M.K. *An autobiography, or the study of my experiments with truth.* Ed. 2., Navajivan. Ahmedabad, 1958, 64.
26. CW: 88: June, 88, 1948, 58–59, *Harijan.*
27. Green. *Op. cit.,* 83.

28. *Op. cit.,* 84.
29. SIL. *Op. cit.,* 84.
30. CW : 87 : July, 15, 192 : 58 : *Navajivan.*
31. CW : 34 : Sept. 15, 1927 : 460.
32. SIL. *Op. cit.,* 64.
33. *Op. cit.*.
34. CW : 87 : Mar. 17, 1947 : 108.
35. CW : 84 : June 30, 1949 : 390.
36. CW : 72 : June 29, 1940; 199: *Harijan.*
37. Erikson, Erik H. *Gandhi's truth:on the origins of militant non-violence.* Faber & Faber, London, 1979.
38. Polak, Millie Graham. *In the South African* days *in* Chandrashekhar. *op. ct.*, 249.
39. CW : 35 : Dec. 11, 1927: 378.
40. CW : 70 : Oct. 30, 1939: 312.
41. Koestler, Arthur. *The Lotus and the Robot.* Hutchinson, London, 1949, 149–50.
42. Prabhu, KK. and RAO, U.R., *eds. The Mind of Mahatma Gandhi.* Rev. Ed. Navajivan, Ahmedabad, 1947, Foreword.
43. Sanger, Margaret. *A summit meeting on birth control in* Cousins, *ed., Profiles of Gandhi: America remembers a world leader.* Indian Book Company, New Delhi, 1947, 96.
44. Green. *Op. cit.*, 171–72.
45. CW : 67 : May 7, 1938 : 69.
46. CW : 62 : Dec. 3/4, 1935, 159.
47. CW : 84 : June 30, 1946 : 390: *Harijan.*
48. CW : 62 : May 6, 1936: 290.
49. CW : 62 : Mar 6, 1936 : 372.
50. CW : 62 : May 29, 1936 : 210–12, *Harijan.*
51. CW : 62 : May 6, 1936 : 372.
52. CW : 62 : May 21, 1936 : 428–29.
53. CW : 67 : May 2, 1938: 58.
54. CW : 67 : May 3, 1938: 61.
55. CW : 67 : May 12, 1938: 80.
56. CW : 47 : June 18, 1931 : 9.
57. CW : 86 : Feb. 6, 1947 : 437.
58. Bose. *Op. cit.* , 172.
59. CW : 86 : [before 14, 1946]: 234.

Chapter 3: *Brahmacharya* in Practice

1. CW : 53 : Feb, 13, 1933: 290.
2. CW : 61 : Sept 21, 1935: 436: *Harijan.*

3. CW : 37 : Sept 10, 1928 : 258.
4. CW : 37 : Sept 10, 1928 : 259.
5. CW : 50 : Aug. 18, 1932: 382.
6. CW : 50 : Aug. 18, 1932 : 386.
7. CW : 54 : Ap. 6, 1933 : 311.
8. CW : 61 : Sept. 21, 1935 : 437 : *Harijan.*
9. CW : 61 : Sept. 21, 1935 : 437 : *Harijan.*
10. CW : 62 : [Dec 3 /4, 1935]: 159.
11. CW : 62 : May 6, 1936 : 372.
12. CW : 67 : May 3, 1938 : 60.
13. CW : 67 : May 12, 1938 : 80.
14. CW : 67 : May 7, 1938 : 69.
15. CW : 67 : May 16, 1938 : 84.
16. CW : 93 : May 16, 1938 : 148.
17. CW : 67 : [June 2, 1938]: 104.
18. CW : 67 : [about June 11, 1938]: 118.
19. CW : 67 : June 11, 1938: 117.
20. CW : 67 : June 22, 1938 : 133.
21. CW : 67 : June 12, 1938 : 340.
22. CW : 67 : July 2, 1938 : 149.
23. CW : 67 : [July 15, 1938]: 171.
24. CW : 67 : July 1, 1938 : 147.
25. CW : 67 : July 2, 1938 : 148.
26. CW : 67 : Sept. 13, 1938 : 335.
27. CW : 72 : May 24, 1940 : 91.
28. CW : 70 : Aug. 8, 1939 : 82.
29. CW : 70 : Aug. 9, 1939 : 82.
30. CW : 70 : Aug. 15, 1939 : 82.
31. CW : 68 : Dec. 12, 1938 : 196–97.
32. CW : 93 : Feb. 3, 1939 : 237–38.
33. CW : 67 : Sept 17, 1938 : 355.
34. CW : 67 : July 1938: 166
35. CW : 67 : Sept. 19, 1938: 362–63.
36. Mehta. *Op. cit.* , 201.
37. *Op. cit.* , 203–04.
38. CW : 65 : May 16, 1937 : 213.
39. Shriman Narayan. *Mahatma Gandhi, the atomic man.* Somaiya, Bombay, 1971, 19.
40. CW : 74 : May 13, 1941 : 55.
41. CW : 74 : May 13, 1941 : 54.
42. N.K. Bose Papers: N.K. Bose to K.G. Mashruwala. Mar. 20, 1951, serial No. 42,193,94 National Archives of India, New Delhi.
43. *Ibid.*, N.K. Bose to K.G. Mashruwala. Mar 31, 1951, serial no. 97, *op. cit.*

44. *Op. cit., K.G. Mashruwala*, Ap. 3; 1951, *op.cit.*
45. Nehru, Jawaharlal, *Selected work.* V.6, Orient Longman, New Delhi, 1974, 349.
46. *Ibid.*

Chapter 4: Ba

1. Morton, Eleanor. *Women behind Mahatma Gandhi.* Rainhardt. New York, 1954, 2.
2. Gandhi, Arun. *Kasturba, a life.* Penguin Books, New Delhi, 2000.
3. Morton. *Op. cit* ., 1–2.
4. Meer, Fatima. *Apprenticeship of the Mahatma: A biography of M.K Gandhi, 1869–1914.* Hindustan Sahitya Sabha, 1997, 7.
5. Gandhi. *Autobiography, op.cit.*,204.
6. *Op. cit.* .
7. *Op. cit.* , 161.
8. *Op. cit.* .
9. *Op. cit.* .
10. Parikh, Nilam. *Gandhiji's lost jewel: Harilal Gandhi.* National Gandhi Museum, New Delhi, 2001, 23.
11. *Ibid.*, 28–29.
12. CW : 10 : [Mar. 5, 1911] : 428.
13. CW : 10 : [Mar. 9, 1911] : 447.
14. CW : 9 : Nov. 9, 1908: 105.
15. Erikson. *Op. cit.,* 237.
16. Gandhi. *Autobiography, op.cit.*, 238.
17. *Op.cit.,* 239.
18. Polak, Millie Graham. *Mr. Gandhi, the man.* Vova. Bombay, 1940,102.
19. CW : 9 : [Jan 16, 1909] : 150.
20. CW : 9 : [Jan 28, 1909] : 174–175.
21. CW : 9 : Mar. 11, 1909 : 613.
22. Gandhi, M.K. *Satyagraha in South Africa.* S. Ganeshan, Madras, 1928, 425.
23. Parikh. *Op.cit.,* 426.
24. *Op.cit.*
25. CW : 12 : [before Apr. 19, 1913]: 31.
26. Gandhi, Devdas. *My brother*, Hindustan Times. Feb. 23, 1948.
27. CW : 9 : Nov. 9, 1908: 105.
28. CW : 9 : Nov. 18, 1908 : 105.
29. CW : 9 : Nov. 19, 1908 : 106.
30. CW : 9 : Nov. 9, 1908 : 106.
31. CW : 9 : Nov. 9, 1908 : 105.
32. CW : 96 : [June 21, 1909] : 9.
33. CW : 96 : Feb. 27, 1914: 167.

34. CW : 12: [Mar. 8, 1914]: 380.
35. CW : 96 : Ap. 12, 1914 : 82.
36. CW : 12 : [Mar. 8, 1914] : 379.
37. Fischer, Louis. *The life of Mahatma Gandhi.* Jonathan Cape, London, 1969, 74.
38. *Ibid.*
39. Morton. *Op. cit.* , 30
40. Gandhi. *Autobiography, Op.cit.,* 22.
41. *Op. cit,* 22–23
42. *Op. cit.,* 18.
43. Morton. *Op. cit.,* 74.
44. Gandhi, Prabhudas. *Kasburba in Kasturba Smarak,* Kasturbagram, 1962, 139.
45. CW : 3 : June 30, 1903 : 352–353.
46. Sanger. *A summit meeting, Op. cit.,* 36.
47. Nanda, B.R. *Mahatma Gandhi, a biography.* George Allen and Uanwin, London, 1958–21.
48. Nayyar, Sushila. *Mahatma Gandhi's last imprisonment, the last story.* Har-Anand, New Delhi, 1996.
49. Gandhi, Prabhudas. *Op. cit.*
50. Gandhi, Arun. *Kasturba. op. cit.,* 311.
51. Desai, Narayan. *The fire and the rose.* Navajivan, Ahmedabad, 1993, 238.
52. Bose. *Op. cit.,* 63.
53. *Op. cit.* .
54. Nayyar, Sushila: *Kasturba: a personal reminiscence.* Navajivan, 58.
55. *op. cit.,* 58–59.
56. Nayyar, *Sushila.* Kasturba, *op. cit.,* 85
57. Nayyar, Sushila. *Mahatma Gandhi's last imprisonment* the inside story. Har-Anand, New Delhi, 1996, 339.
58. Nayyar: *Kasturba, op. cit.,* 96.
59. Nayyar. *Last imprisonment, op. cit.,* 339.
60. *Op. cit.,* 340
61. Nayyar, Sushila. *Kasturba. op. cit.,* 97.
62. *Op. cit.,* 343.
63. *Op. cit.,* 345.
64. CW: 77, Mar. 9, 1944.

Chapter 5: Ba, Bapu and Family

1. Rolland, Romain. *Mahatma Gandhi,* S. Ganesh, Madras, 1925, 25–26.
2. Payne. *Op. cit* .,, 381.
3. CW : 13 : Sept. 23, [1915], 128.

4. CW : 18 : [Oct 9, 1920]: 338.
5. CW : 96 : Sept. 10, 1916: 240.
6. CW : 53 : Feb. 13, 1933, 288–89.
7. CW : 53 : Feb. 13, 1933, 289.
8. Mehta. *Op. cit.,* 247–48.
9. Payne. *Op. cit..* , 381.
10. Dhupelia, Mesthrie. Uma, *Gandhi's prisoner etc.,* Permanent Black, New Delhi, 2005, 171.
11. Payne. *Op. cit.,* 644.
12. *Op. cit..*
13. CW: 35 : Nov. 28, 1927 : 339–40.
14. Fisher, *Op. cit.,* 29.
15. CW : 12: Ap. 22, 1914 : 410–11.
16. Dhupelia-Mesthrie. *Op. cit.* , 175.
17. Gandhi, Prabudas. *My childhood with Gandhi.* Navjivan, Ahmedabad, 1957, 190.
18. CW : 11 : Feb. 226, 194 : 359–60.
19. Dhupelia-Mesthrie. *Op. cit..*
20. *Op. cit.,* 175.
21. CW : 23 : May 17, 1922 : 101–02.
22. CW : 30 : Ap. 3, 1926 : 229.
23. CW : 30 : Ap. 3, 1926 : 229.
24. CW : 30 : Ap. 3, 1926: 229.
25. Dhupelia, Sita. *A granddaughter reminiscences in* MEER, Fatima, *ed. The South African Gandhi – An abstract of the speeches and writings of M.K. Gandhi,* 1893–1914. Ed. 2, Metiba, Durban, Ed.2, 1071, 1996.
26. Fischer. *Op. cit.,* 265.
27. Parikh. *Op. cit .,* 44
28. Dalal, Chandanlal Bhagubai. *Harilal – Ek dukhi atma.* Sarva Seva Sangh Prakashan, Varanasi, 1980, 117–36.
29. *Ibid.,* 136.
30. CW : 5 : May 27, 1906,
31. Dalal . *Op. cit .,* 80
32. CW : 72 : Aug 18, 1940: 354 : *Harijan.*
33. CW : 57 : Feb 21, 1934 : 196.
34. CW : 63 : Aug 2, 1936 : 199.
35. Parikh. *Op. cit .,* 76.
36. Dalal. *Op. cit .,* 84
37. *Op. cit .,* 85.
38. *Op. cit .,* 79.
39. Parikh. *Op. cit .,* 71.
40. *Op. cit .,* 99–102

41. *Op. cit*., 102.
42. *Op. cit*., 85.
43. *Op. cit*., 85.
44. *Op. cit*., *103*
45. DALAL. *Op. cit*., 106
46. *Op. cit.* 157–58.
47. *Op. cit*., 158.
48. Dhupelia, Sita *Op. cit*., 1072.
49. Gandhi, Devdas. *Op. cit*..
50. Op. cit.
51. Dhupelia, Sita. *Op. cit*., 1072
52. CW : 12 : [Ap. 22, 1914] : 410.

Chapter 6: Millie and Henry Polak

1. Polak, Millie Graham. *Mr. Gandhi, the man. Op.cit.,* [11].
2. *Op.cit.,* 12.
3. Polak, Millie. *A look at South Africa.* Gandhi-Polak Papers, serial No. 53, National Archives of India, New Delhi.
4. CW : 96 : Nov. 15, 1909: 34.
5. Polak, Millie Graham. *Op.cit.,* 65.
6. *Op. cit*., 67.
7. *Op. cit*., 78
8. *Op. cit*., 79.
9. *Op. cit*.
10. CW : 96 : Nov. 14, 1909 : 32.
11. CW : 96 : Nov. 14, 1909 : 32.
12. CW : 96 : Nov. 14, 1909 : 32.
13. CW : 96 : Dec. 31, 1909 : 41.
14. CW : 96 : Ap. 4, 1910 : 42.
15. CW : 17 : May 15, 1920, 533.
16. CW : 17 May 15, 1920, 533, footnote.
17. Polak, Millie Graham. *Op. cit*., [99].
18. CW : 9 : Nov 11, 1909 : 534.
19. CW : 9 : Sept. 23, 1909 : 430, footnote.
20. CW : 96 : Nov. 14, 1909 : 32.
21. CW : 96 : Dec. 26, 1909 : 39.
22. CW : 96 : Dec. 31, 1909 : 40.
23. CW : 96 : Dec. 31, 1909 : 40.
24. CW : 96 : Dec. 31, 1909 : 41.
25. CW : 96 : Ap. 19, 1911 : 51,
26. CW : 51 : Oct. 12, 1932 : 233.
27. CW : 6 : Oct. 26, 1906: 19.

28. CW : 96 : Nov. 14, 1909 : 33.
29. CW : 96 : Nov. 15, 1909 : 34.
30. CW : 12 : Ap. 19, 1913 : 41.
31. Polak. *Op. cit*., 87.
32. *Op. cit*., foreword, 5
33. *Op. cit*., 85
34. CW : 96 : Mar. 21, [1921] : 177.
35. CW : 96 : Monday [no date] : 307.
36. Polak-Gandhi Papers. *Millie to Henry Polak.* V.3, p.1, serial no. 54, Nov. 14, 1916, 118, *op. cit*.,
37. *Ibid.*, serial no. 63, Dec. 2, 1916, 150–51, *op. cit*..
38. *Op. cit*., serial no. 65, Dec. 20, 1916, 154. *op. cit.* .
39. *Op. cit*., serial no. 67, Jan. 2, 1917, 118, *op. cit.*.
40. Green. *Op. cit*., 29
41. Polak. *Op. cit*., 74.
42. CW : 14 : July 22, 1918 : 497.
43. "ONE WHO KNOWS HIM". *The why and how of Gandhi.* V.6, pt. 2 & 3, Henry Polak Papers, National Archives of India, New Delhi.
44. Desai, Mahadev. *Day-to-day with Gandhi: Secretary's diary* V.1. Sarva Seva Sangh Prakashan, Varanasi, 242.
45. Polak, Millie. *Op. cit*., 151.
46. *Op. cit*., 178.
47. CW : 51 : Oct. 17, 1932 : 252.
48. CW : 96 : Nov. 23, 1939 : 313–14.
49. CW : 79 : Mar. 25, 1945 : 301.
50. CW : 96 : [July 29, 1911]: 63.
51. CW : 96 : Ap. 17, 1914: 183.

Chapter 7: Dictator Sonja

1. Gandhi, M.K. *Satyagraha in South Africa.*, *Op. cit*., 278.
2. Payne. *Op. cit.*
3. Gandhi, M.K. *Autobiography*, 141–42.
4. Paxton, George, D. *Sonja Schlesin, Gandhi and South Africa.* , *Gandhi Marg.* 21, 1999, 328.
5. *Ibid.*, 328.
6. Parikh, Narahari, *Mahadev's early life.* Navajivan, Ahmedabad, 1953, 52.
7. Gandhi. *Satyagraha in South Africa. op. cit*., 275–76.
8. *Op. cit.*
9. Gandhi *Autobiography, op. cit*., 209.
10. Paxton. *Op. cit*., 330
11. Gandhi. *Satyagraha in South Africa. op. cit*., 275.
12. CW : 12 : [on or after June 13, 1947] : 429–30.

13. CW : 15 : Feb 23, 1914 : 97–98.
14. CW : 37 : July 15, 1928 : 66.
15. CW : 54 : Ap. 20, 1933 : 420.
16. CW : 14 : June 23, 1918 : 447–48.
17. CW : 47 : Aug. 18, 1931 : 307.
18. CW : 15 : June 2, 1919 : 341.
19. CW : 24 : Aug 15, 1924 : 580.
20. Paxton. *Op. cit*., 329
21. *Op. cit*., 334
22. CW : 80 : May 13, 1945 : 125.
23. CW : 80 : May 13, 1945 : 125, footnote
24. Pyarelal. *Mahatma Gandhi : The last phase.* V.1., Book 1, *Op. cit*., 102.
25. CW : 89 : Nov. 1, 1947 : 449.
26. CW : 13 : June 23, 1947 : 448.
27. CW : 35 : Dec. 21, 1927, 403.
28. CW : 80 : May 13, 1945, 125.
29. Pyarelal. *Op. cit.*
30. Dhupelia, Sita. *Op. cit*., 1071

Chapter 8: JEKI: 'The Only Adopted Daughter'

1. Polak, Millie Graham. *Mr. Gandhi.* Ed.2, Vora, Bombay, 1950, 115.
2. CW : 11 : [Oct. 22, 1911] : 171.
3. CW : 11 : [Oct., 22, 1911] : 171.
4. CW : 11 : [Mar. 13, 1913] : 487.
5. Gandhi, M.K. *Satyagraha in South Africa. Op. cit*., 372.
6. *Op. cit*., 367
7. *Op. cit*., 373.
8. Erikson. *Gandhi's truth. Op. cit*., 239.
9. Polak. *Op. cit*., 112.
10. Gandhi, Prabhudas. *My childhood with Gandhi. Op. cit.*
11. *Ibid., 116–17.*
12. *Op. cit*., 118.
13. *Op. cit*., 119.
14. *Op. cit*., 120.
15. CW : 96 : [Aug. 15, [1913] : 134
16. CW : 96 : [Aug. 15, [1913] : 134.
17. Gandhi, Prabhudas. *Op. cit*., 118.
18. *Op. cit.*
19. Uppal, J.N. *Gandhi: Ordained in South Africa.* Publications Division, Ministry of Information and Broadcasting, Govt. of India, New Delhi, 1995, 412.
20. Dhupelia-Mesthrie. *Op. cit*., 105.

21. Polak. *Op. cit*., 116.
22. *Op. cit*., 118.
23. *Op. cit*., 119.
24. *Op. cit.*
25. *Op. cit.*
26. CW : 12 : [Sept. 18, 1913] : 171.
27. CW : 12 : [Sept. 18, 1913] : 171.
28. CW : 12 : Feb. 24, 1914 : 356.
29. CW : 12 : [about Feb. 26, 1914] : 359.
30. CW : 12 : [Feb. 26, 1914] : 358.
31. CW : 96 : Feb. 27, 1914 : 166.
32. CW : 96 : Feb. 27, 1914 : 167.
33. CW : 12 : [Mar. 22, 1914] : 395.
34. CW : 12 : [July 19, 1913] : 145.
35. CW : 12 : [Dec. 14, 1913] : 270.
36. CW : 12 : [after Feb. 15, 1914] : 352.
37. CW : 12 : [Feb. 24, 1914] : 256.
38. CW : 12 : [Mar. 7, 1914] : 376.
39. CW : 96 [May 6, 1914] : 186.
40. CW : 96 : [Ap. 12, 1914] : 181.
41. CW : 96 : [May 13, 1914] : 188.
42. CW : 96 : [May 13, 1914] : 189.
43. CW : 12 : [Ap. 22, 1914] : 410.
44. CW : 96 : [May 10, 1914] : 188.
45. CW : 96 : [May 18, 1914] : 190.
46. CW : 36 : Feb. 29, 1928 : 70.

Chapter 9: Esther Faering: The Danish Missionary

1. Larsen, Tine Elisabeth. *Anne Marie Petersen, a Danish woman in South India, a missionary story 1909–51*, ed. By Daniel Joyaraj, Gurukul Lutheran Theological and Research Institute, Chennai, 2001.
2. CW : 13 : Jan 11, 1917: 326.
3. CW : 13 : Jan 15, 1927 : 329.
4. CW : 13 : Ap. 15, 1917 : 364.
5. Wolpert, Stanley. *Gandhi's passion: The life and legacy of Gandhi.* Oxford University Press, 2001, 104.
6. CW : 13 : Dec. 12, 1919 : 106.
7. CW : 13 : Dec. 12, 1919 : 106.
8. CW : 14 : July 22, 1918 : [497],
9. Reddy, E.S, and Terp. Holger. *Friends of Gandhi: Correspondence of Mahatma Gandhi with Esther Faering (Menon) and Annie Marie Petersen and Ellen Harrup,* 2005, Introduction.

10. *Ibid.*
11. Danish Mission Periodical. 87 (49), 1920, 689–99.
12. *Ibid.*, 86 (50), 1919, 923.
13. CW : 16 : Aug. 22, 1919 : 58.
14. CW : 16 : Aug. 22, 1919 : 57.
15. CW : 16 : Aug. 24, 1919 : 59.
16. CW : 16 : [on or after Jan. 16, 1920] : 486 : Delhi.
17. CW : 16 : Jan. 24, 1920 : 499–500.
18. CW : 16 : [Jan. 25] : 1920 : 506.
19. CW : 17 : [Feb. 12], 1920 : 26.
20. Toplady, Angus Montague. *Hymns and spiritual songs for the little flock.* Slow HILL, Bible and Tract Depot, 1932 (Original ed. 1856).
21. *Ibid.*
22. CW : 17 : Mar. 14, 1920 : 90.
23. CW : 17 : Mar. 16, 1920 : 90.
24. CW : 17 : [Mar. 18, 1920] : 95.
25. CW : 17 : [Mar. 19 : 1920] : 98.
26. CW : 17 : Ap. 15, 1920 : 315.
27. CW : 17 : Ap. 15, 1920 : 315.
28. CW : 17 : May [2], 1920: 376.
29. CW : 17 : Mar. 21, 1920 : 108.
30. LARSEN. *Op. cit.* 40.
31. CW : 31 : Mar. 24, 1933 : 2.
32. Gandhi, M K, "My dear child": Letters from M K Gandhi to Esther Faering, ed by Alice M Barnes. Navajivan, Ahemdabad, 1956.

Chapter 10: Euphoric Mirabehn

1. Mirabehn. *The spirit's pilgrim.* Longman, London, 1960, 12.
2. *Ibid.*, 53.
3. Rolland, Roman. *Mahatma Gandhi.* S. Ganesh, Madras, 1922.
4. Sabarmati Gandhi Papers. *Letter from Mirabehn to M.K. Gandhi* V.23, serial no. 10541, May 29, 1925, 134-43,Gandhi Smarak, Sangrahalaya, Ahmedabad.
5. CW : 27 : July 27, 1925, 414–15.
6. Mirabehn. *Op. cit.*, 65
7. CW : 29 : Nov. 26, 1925, 282.
8. Rolland and Gandhi. *Op. cit.*, 46.
9. CW : 29 : Dec. 4, 1925 : 298.
10. CW : 30 : May 15, 1926 : 447.
11. Rolland and Gandhi. *Op. cit.*, 47.
12. CW : 32 : Jan. 3, 1927 : 503.
13. CW : 33 [May 8, 1927] : 298.
14. CW : 33 : Ap. 27, 1925 : 285 : footnote.
15. Gandhi, M.K. *Bapu's letters to Mira,* 1924–48, ed. by Mirabehn, Navajivan, Ahmedabad.

16. CW : 33 : May 12, 1927 : 313.
17. CW : 35 : [Sept. 29, 1927] : 57.
18. CW : 35 : Oct. 2 [1927] : 70.
19. Morton. *Op. cit.*, 150.
20. Sabarmati Gandhi Papers. *Letters from Mirabehn to M.K. Gandhi.* V.47, serial no. 17245, June 7, 1931, 425.
21. CW : 47 : June 24, 1931 : 49.
22. CW : 55 : [May 10, 1933] : 171.
23. Desai, Mahadev. *The diary of Mahadev Desai,* tr. from the Gujarati by Valji Govindji Desai, Navajivan, Ahmedabad, 1953, 63.
24. *Ibid.*
25. CW : 49 : Ap. 8, 1932 : 279.
26. CW : 51 : Sept. 23, 1932 : 134.
27. CW : 51 : Sept. 24, 1932 : 132.
28. Sabarmati Gandhi Papers. *Letter from Mirabai to M.K. Gandhi.* Sept. 24, 1932, *op. cit.*.
29. CW : 55 : May 29, 1933 : 178.
30. Sabarmati Gandhi Papers. *Letter from Mirabehn to M.K. Gandhi.* V.58, serial no. 21086, Ap. 29, 1933, 175
31. *Op. cit.*, serial No. 21169, May 4, 1933,6–7.
32. *Op. cit.*, V.59, May 8, 1933, serial no. 21233,359
33. CW : 49 : Feb. 25, 1932, 157.
34. CW : 52 : Dec. 15, 1932 : 200.
35. CW : 62 : [Feb 13, 1936] : 186.
36. CW : 47 : June 24, 1931 : 49.
37. Mirabehn. *Op. cit.*, 97/
38. *Op. cit.*,
39. COOK. *Op. cit.*, 401
40. *Op. cit.*, 398
41. CW : 73 : Dec. 2, 1940 : 209 : footnote.

Chapter 11: Mirabehn in Low Tides

1. CW : 51 : Oct. 26, 1932 : 298.
2. CW : 62 : [Feb. 13, 1936] : 186: footnote.
3. CW : 62 : [Feb. 13, 1936]: 186.
4. CW : 63 : Sept. 12, 1936 : 275.
5. CW : 68 : Dec. 27, 1938 :250.
6. CW : 72 : May 18, 1940: 75.
7. CW : 73 : Oct. 14, 1940 : 101.
8. CW : 78 : Aug. 18, 1944 :111.
9. Mirabehn. *Op. cit*, 219.
10. *Op. cit*, 220

11. Sabarmati Gandhi Papers. *Letter from Mirabehn to M.K. Gandhi.* V.57, serial no. 20048, Jan.16, 1933, 555–56, *Op. cit.*
12. CW : 53 : Feb. 17, 1933 : 319.
13. Rolland. *Op. cit.*, 206.
14. Mirabehn. *Op. cit.*, 296.
15. CW : 33 : May 12, 1927 : 33.
16. Sabarmati Gandhi Papers. *Op. cit.*, V.58, serial no.21035, Ap.22, 1933, 119.
17. *Op. cit.*, 120.
18. CW : 58.
19. Gandhi, M.K. *Op. cit. , 198.*
20. Mirabehn. *Daily Notes,* Sept. 11, 1938, Nehru Memorial Museum and Library, New Delhi.
21. Prithvi Singh, Azad, *pseud.,*. *The legendary crusader.* Bharatiya Vidya Bhavan, Bombay, 1987, 1230-231.
22. *Ibid.*, 230–31.
23. Baba Pritvi Singh Azad Papers. *Letter from Mirabehn to Prithvi Singh Azad.* Oct. 26, 1939, 7. Nehru Memorial Museum and Library, New Delhi.
24. *Ibid.*
25. *Op. cit.*, Nov. 10, 1939 [1].
26. *Op. cit.*, Nov. 11, 1939 : 5
27. *Op. cit.*, 3–4.
28. *Op. cit.*, 5.
29. *Op. cit.*, Nov. 17, 1939, 3
30. *Op. cit.*, [After Dec. 25, 1939].
31. *Op. cit.*, Mar 23, 1942.
32. *Op. cit.*, Mar. 13, 1943, 3–4.
33. CW : 94 : June 12, 1944 : 118.
34. CW : 94 : June 14, 1944 : 119.
35. CW : 94 : June 23, 1944 : 121.
36. CW : 94 : July 18, 1940 : 130.
37. Gandhi. *Op. cit.*, 366.
38. Mirabehn. *Op. cit.*,316.
39. Gupta. *Op. cit.*, 179.
40. CW : 52 : Dec.15, 1932 : 200
41. Rolland and Gandhi. *Op. cit.*, 457.

Chapter 12: Cook and Spiegel: The Mad Duo

1. CW : 53 : Jan 18, 1933 : 84.
2. CW : 53 : Jan 18, 1933 : 84–85.
3. Cook. *Op. cit.*, 337.

4. *Op. cit.*, 348.
5. *Op. cit.*
6. Green. *Gandhi. Op. cit.*, 334.
7. CW : 53 : Feb. 12, 1933 : 279.
8. Cook. *Op. cit.*, 394.
9. CW : 54 : Ap. 12, 1933 : 381.
10. Cook. *Op. cit.*, 381.
11. *Op. cit.*, 382.
12. CW : 54 : May 17, 1933 : 102.
13. Cook. *Op. cit.*, 353.
14. *Op. cit.*, 385.
15. *Op. cit.*, 395.
16. *Op. cit.*, 394.
17. *Op. cit.*, 357–58.
18. CW : 54 : Mar. 19, 1933 : 102.
19. CW : 54 : Mar. 24, 1933 : 179.
20. Cook. *Op. cit.*,
21. CW : 55 : June 20, 1933 : 209–10.
22. CW : 54 : May 18, 1933 : 121.
23. CW : 54 : May 28, 1933 : 230.
24. CW : 55 : Ap. 23, 1933 : 8.
25. CW : 54 : May. 9, 1933 : 27.
26. CW : 55 : May 8, 1933 : 153.
27. CW : 55 : May 8, 1933 : 153.
28. CW : 55 : May 7, 1933 : 142–43.
29. Cook. *Op. cit.*, 395.
30. *Op. cit.*, 397.
31. *Op. cit.*, 403
32. CW : 55 : May 10, 1933 : 167.
33. CW : 54 : Ap. 10, 1933 : 365.
34. Bhatti, Anil and Voigt, Johaness H. *Jewish exile in India,* 1933–45, Manohar, New Delhi, 1999, 153.
35. *Ibid.* 150.
36. CW : 53 : Feb. 24, 1933 : 389.
37. CW : 53 : Jan. 1, 1933 : 48.
38. CW : 53 : Feb. 24, 1933 : 389.
39. CW : 53 : June 22, 1933 : 216.
40. Cook. *Op. cit.*, 369.
41. CW : 56 : Nov. 24, 1933 : 274.
42. CW : 56 : Dec. 2, 1934 : 298.
43. CW : 58 : June 4, 1934 : 53.

44. CW : 58 : Aug. 16, 1934 : 311.
45. CW : 58 : Sept. 8, 1934 : 428.
46. CW : 58 : Sept. 8, 1934 : 428.
47. CW : 59 : Oct. 17, 1936 : 188.
48. CW : 59 : Sept. 19, 1934 : 27.
49. Parikh. *Op. cit.*, 163–64.
50. CW : 60 : Ap. 22, 1935 : 456.
51. Parikh. *Op. cit.*, 77.
52. CW : 61 : Aug 13, 1935 : 330.
53. CW : 55 : Ap. 29, 1939 : 69.
54. CW : 60 : Jan 16, 1935 : 83.
55. Sabarmati Gandhi Papers. *Letter from Margarete Spiegel to M.K. Gandhi.* V. 59, serial no. 21310, May 6, 1933, 448 *Op. cit.*

Chapter 13: Saraladevi: The Romantic

1. Green. *Gandhi: Voice of a new generation , op. cit.*, 224.
2. Gandhi, M.K. *Autobiography, op. cit.*, 351.
3. CW : 16 : Nov. 25, 1919 : 316.
4. CW : 16 : after Jan. 23, 1920 : 497.
5. CW : 16 : Jan. 27, 1920 : 516.
6. CW : 17 : Feb. 27, 1920 : 53.
7. CW : 17 : Feb. 29, 1920 : 63.
8. CW : 17 : June 4, 1920 : 479.
9. CW : 17 : Ap. 17, 1920 : 318.
10. CW : 18 : July 25, 1920 : 87.
11. Green. *Op. cit.*, 280.
12. CW : 18 : Aug. 10, 1920 : 130.
13. CW : 17 : Ap. 28, 1920 : 353.
14. CW : 17 : Ap. 28, 1920, 353.
15. CW : 17 : Ap. 25, 1920, 340, *Navajivan.*
16. CW : 17 : May 19, 1920 : 429 : *Young India.*
17. CW : 18 : July 7, 1920 : 20.
18. CW : 18 : July, 21, 1920 : 71 : *Young India.*
19. CW : 17 : May 1, 1920 : 365 – 66.
20. CW : 79 : Feb. 1, 1945 : 84.
21. Green. *Op. cit.*, 281
22. CW : 19 : Dec 14, 1920 : 107.
23. CW : 17 : Ap. 19, 1920 : 357.
24. CW : 17 : Ap. 30, 1920 : 359.
25. CW : 17 : Ap. 4, 1920 : 296.
26. CW : 17 : May 2, 1920 : 375.

Chapter 14: Saraladevi in Limbo

1. CW : 18 : Aug. 23, 1920 : 192.
2. CW : 18 : Aug. 24, 1920 : 193.
3. Desai, Mahadev. *Day to day With Gandhi.* V.3, *op. cit.*, 178.
4. CW : 16 : [Dec. 7, 1919] : 334.
5. CW : 16 : [on or before Jan. 16, 1920] : 486.
6. CW : 16 : [after Jan. 25, 1920] : 510.
7. CW : 95 : Jan. 20 [Jan 20[1920] : 27.
8. CW : 16 : [after Jan. 23, 1920] : 405: Lahore.
9. CW : 17 : May 4, 1920: 385.
10. CW : 17 : May 4, 1920 : 385.
11. CW : 17 : May 4, 1920 : 385.
12. CW : 19 : Dec. 4, 1920 : 69.
13. CW : 18 : Aug. 20, 1920: 101.
14. CW : 19 : Dec. 17, 1920: 93.
15. Desai. *Op. cit.*
16. CW : 19 : Dec. 17, 1920 : 137.
17. CW : 19 : Dec. 17, 1920 : 137.
18. CW : 19 : Dec. 17, 1920 : 138.
19. CW : 25 : Aug. 24, 1924 : 37.
20. CW : 56 : Oct. 9, 1933 : 79.
21. CW : 23 : Ap. 13, 1924 : 430–31.
22. CW : 53 : Feb. 5, 1933 : 229.
23. Sanger, Margaret, A summit meeting on birth control in Cousin, Norman. Ed. Profiles of Gandhi, etc. Indian Book Co., Delhi, 1969, 39.
24. *Op. cit.*
25. CW : 50 : June 18, 1932 : 64–65.
26. Nayyar, Sushila. *Mahatma Gandhi, op. cit.*, 309.
27. CW : 87 : Mar. 16, 1947 : 99.
28. CW : 87 : Mar. 16, 1947 : 108.
29. CW : 72 : June 1, 1940 : 120.
30. CW : 77 : June 2, 1944 : 298.
31. CW : 81 : Aug. 19, 1945 : 140.
32. CW : 81 : Aug. 19, 1945 : 143.
33. CW : 88 : June 13, 1947 : 145.
34. CW : 17 : May 19, 1920 : 430

Chapter 15: Prabhavati: The Nun

1. CW : 35 : [Jan. 27, 1928]: 501.
2. Lakshmi Narayan Lal. *India's voice, India's soul.* Hind Pocket Books, New Delhi, 1977.

3. CW : 40 : [Mar. 4, 1929] : 76.
4. CW : 40 : [Mar. 11, 1929] : 129.
5. CW : 47 : July 6, 1931 : 112.
6. CW : 92 : Aug. 25, 1931 : 226.
7. Scarfe., Allen & Wendy. *JP & his biography*. Orient Longman,1975, 111.
8. CW : 92 : June 9, 1934 : 477.
9. CW : 67 : Oct. 12, 1938 : 426.
10. CW : 79 : Nov.11, 1939 : 339.
11. CW : 93 : Ap. 16, 1936 : 58.
12. Ranjan, Sudanshu. *Jayaprakash Narayan*. National Book Trust, New Delhi, 32, 2002.
14 *Op. cit.*
14. CW : 56 : Sept. 24, 1933 : 25.
15. RANJAN. *Op. cit.*
16. *Op. cit.*
17. Lakshmi Nayayan Lal. *Op. cit.*, 72
18. CW : 61 : May 26, 1935 : 105.
19. CW : 61 : June 9, 1935 : 151.
20. CW : 62 : May 24, 1936 : 439.
21. CW : 62 : Mar. 8, 1936 : 250.
22. CW : 67 : Oct. 12, 1938 : 426.
23. CW : 92 : Dec. 4, 1929 : 121.
24. CW : 92 : Nov. 27, 1930 : 228.
25. CW : 92 : Dec. 2, 1936 : 496.
26. CW : 92 : Dec. 2, 1934 : 496.
27. CW : 64 : Ap. 7, 1935 : 61.
28. RANJAN. *Op. cit.*, 34.
29. CW : 93, April 16, 1936, 58.
30. CW : 63, Sept. 13, 1936, 281.
31. CW : 63, Sept. 13, 1936, 281.
32. Jayaprakash Narayan. *Selected works,* ed. By Bimal Prasad, V. 3, Manohar, New Delhi, 2003,100.
33. CW : 87 : May 16, 1947 : 483.
34. Scarfe *Op. cit.*
35. *Op. cit.*, 416.

Chapter 16: Kanchan: The Duvidha Shah

1. Mehta, Ved. *Mahatma Gandhi and his apostles. Op. cit .*, 213.
2. CW : 79 : [on or about Mar. 11, 1945], 239.
3. CW : 70 : Sept. 30, 1939 : 220.
4. CW : 72 : May 27, 1940 : 103.

5. CW : 72 : Aug. 5, 1940 : 355.
6. CW : 81 : Oct. 4, 1945 : 315.
7. CW : 85 : July 27, 1946 : 70.
8. CW : 79 : Mar. 20, 1945 : 273.
9. CW : 81 : Aug. 19, 1945 : 141.
10. CW : 82 : Nov. 3, 1945 : 19–20.
11. CW : 72 : July 31, 1940 : 341.
12. CW : 82 : Nov. 3, 1945 : 20.
13. CW : 72 : May 6, 1940 : 45.
14. CW : 74 : June 10, 1941 : 110.
15. CW : 82 : Nov. 3, 1945 : 20.
16. CW : 79 : Nov. 3, 1945 : 19.
17. CW : 79 : Feb. 21, 1945 : 148–49.
18. CW : 79 : Mar. 15, 1945 : 251.
19. CW : 82 : Nov. 8, 1945 : 42.
20. CW : 82 : Jan. 11, 1946 : 392.
21. CW : 84 : May 23, 1946 : 191.
22. CW : 84 : May 31, 1946 : 245.
23. CW : 86 : Dec. 8, 1946 : 205.
24. CW : 65 : May 16, 1937 : 213.
25. Gandhi, Indira and Jayakar, Pupul. *What I am : Indira Gandhi in conversation with Pupul Jayakar*. Gandhi Memorial Trust, New Delhi, 1986, 22.
26. CW : 85 : Oct. 7, 1946 : 429.
27. CW : 85 : Oct. 7, 1946 : 429–30.
28. CW : 85 : Oct. 7, 1946 : 430.
29. CW : 87 : Feb. 21, 1947 : 3.
30. CW : 88 : June 19, 1947 (4.00 a.m.): 175.
31. CW : 88 : July 9, 1947, 358.
32. CW : 89 : Sept. 26, 1947 : 244.
33. CW : 83 : Ap. 3, 1946 : 358.
34. CW : 79 : Mar. 6, 1945 : 215.
35. CW : 90 : Jan. 19, 1948 : 457.

Chapter 17: Triangular Syndrome

1. Parekh. Narahari D. *Op. cit.*, 53.
2. Morton. *Op. cit.*, 151.
3. CW : 93 : Mar. 26, 1935 : 11.
4. CW : 93 : Mar. 17, 1936 : 57.
5. CW : 93 : May 18, 1936 : 61.
6. CW : 93 : Sept. 19, 1938 : 208.
7. CW : 93 : Nov. 22, 1937 : 128.

8. CW : 93 : Nov. 22, 1937 : 128.
9. CW : 93 : Ap. 16, 1938 : 135–36.
10. CW : 93 : May 11, 1938 : 141.
11. CW : 93 : June 29, 1936 : 68.
12. CW : 83 : Ap. 16 [on or before] 1938 : 137.
13. CW : 95 : [Ap. 1938] 94.
14. CW : 67 : May 16, 1938 : 84.
15. CW : 93 : May 16, 1938 : 148.
16. CW : 67 : May 3, 1938 : 61.
17. CW : 67 : May 2, 1938 : 58.
18. CW : 93 : May 16, 1938 : 148.
19. CW : 93 : Ap. 16, 1938 : 134.
20. CW : 93 : Ap. 16, 1938: 136–37.
21. CW : 93 : May 10, 1938 : 140.
22. CW : 93 : June 5, 1938 : 179–80.
23. CW : 93 : May 8, 1938 : 152.
24. CW : 93 : May 14, 1938 : 143.
25. CW : 93 : May 15, 1938 : 144.
26. CW : 93 : May 15, 1938 : 145.
27. CW : 93 : May 16, 1938 : 148.
28. CW : 93 : May 15, 1938 : 144–45.
29. CW : 83 : May 15, 1938 : 146.
30. CW : 93 : May 16, 1938 : 147.
31. CW : 93 : June 2, 1938 : 170.
32. CW : 93 : May 18, 1938 : 152.
33. CW : 66 : May 31, 1938, 455.
34. CW : 93 : May 24, 1938, 158.
35. CW : 93 : May 26, 1938, 161.
36. CW : 93 : May 23, 1938 : 156.
37. CW : 93 : June 6, 1938 : 181.
38. CW : 83 : June 11, 1938 : 183.
39. CW : 83 : Aug. 12, 1938 : 189.
40. CW : 68 : Oct. 15, 1938 : 109.
41. CW : 68 : Oct. 15, 1938 : 109.

Chapter 18: Sushila in Trouble

1. CW : 93 : July 15, 1940 : 330.
2. CW : 93 : [1938] : 228.
3. CW : 93 : [1938] : 232.
4. CW : 93 : Sept. 25, 1939 : 279.
5. CW : 93 : Aug. 28, 1940 : 353.

6. CW : 66 : May 31, 1938 : 455.
7. CW : 93 : Aug. 28, 1940 :353.
8. CW : 93 : May 23, 1938 : 157.
9. CW : 93 : [before July 7, 1937] : 254.
10. CW : 93 : Aug. 21, 1938 : 267.
11. CW : 93 : Aug. 22, 1940 : 352.
12. Mehta. *Op. cit.*, 203–04.
13. CW : 67: June 11, 1938 : 116–17.
14. CW : 93 : Feb. 14, 1940 : 302.
15. CW : 93 : Sept. 12, 1938 : 204.
16. CW : 93 : July 18, 1940 : 333.
17. Mehta. *Op. cit.*, 201.
18. *Op. cit.*, 203.
19. *Op. cit.*, 204

Chapter 19: The Living Hell

1. CW : 96 : Dec. 5, 1946 : 198.
2. Bose, Nirmal Kumar. *My days with Gandhi.* Nishana, Calcutta, 1953, 133.
3. *Op. cit.*, 107.
4. CW : 85 : Sept. 22, 1946 : 355.
5. CW : 85 : [Sept. 24, 1946] : 370.
6. CW : 86 : [after Dec. 4, 1946] : 195.
7. CW : 87 : May 17, 1947 : 487 : Patna.
8. CW : 86 : Dec. 25, 1946 : 263.
9. Bose. *Op. cit.*, 109.
10. CW : 86 : Dec. 17, 1946 : 239.
11. CW : 86 : Dec. 17, 1946 : 239.
12. Bose. *Op. cit.*, 115.
13. N.K. Bose Papers. *Letter from Sushila Nayyar to N.K. Bose and Parasuram,* serial no. 42, Dec. 19, 1946, 20. National Archives of India, New Delhi.
14. *Ibid.*, 20–21.
15. Bose. *Op. cit.*, 120.
16. CW : 86 : Jan. 2, 1947 : 299.
17. N.K. Bose Papers. *Letter from Parasuram to M.K. Gandhi* , serial no.53 (draft).
18. N.K. Bose Papers. *Letter from Parasuram to N.K Bose, 1947.*
19. CW : 86 : Jan. 2, 1947 : 299.
20. CW : 86 : Jan. 2, 1947 : 300.
21. N.K. Bose Papers. *Letter from N.K. Bose to M.K. Gandhi.* Serial no.53, Jan. 1, 1947, 60. *Op. cit.*.
22. *Op. cit.*, 76.
23. Bose. *Op. cit.*, 184.

24. N.K. Bose Papers. *Letter from N.K. Bose to M.K. Gandhi.* Serial no.55, Jan. 3, 1947, 75, *Op. cit.*
25. *Op. cit.*
26. *Op. cit. Letter from Parasuram to N.K. Bose,* Serial No.60, Jan.12, 1947, 89, *op. cit.*
27. *Op. cit. Letter from N.K. Bose to M.K. Gandhi, op. cit.*.
28. *Op. cit. Letter from N.K. Bose to M.K. Gandhi.* Serial no.73, Mar. 18, 1947.
29. Bose *Op. cit.*, 180.
30. *Op. cit.*
31. *Op. cit.*, 187.

Chapter 20: Noakhali Yajna

1. Gandhi, Manubehn. *Bapu – my mother. Op. cit.*, 4.
2. CW : 77 : Feb. 27, 1944 : 240.
3. CW : 77 : Feb. 27, 1944 : 239.
4. CW : 77 : Feb. 27, 1944 : 239.
5. CW : 77 : May 20, 1944 : 278.
6. CW : 77 : May 27, 1944 : 294.
7. CW : 79 : Feb. 5, 1945 : 96.
8. CW : 79 : July 21, 1945 : 13.
9. Pyarelal. *Op. cit.*, 576.
10. CW : 80 : May 22, 1945 : 163.
11. CW : 85 : Oct. 11, 1946 : 446.
12. CW : 86 : Nov. 4, 1946: 73.
13. Gandhi, Manubehn. *The lonely pilgrim. Op. cit.*, 3.
14. CW : 86 : Dec 2, 1946 : 178.
15. Gandhi, Manubehn. *The lonely pilgrim. Op. cit.*, 5.
16. *Op. cit.*, 6–7.
17. *Op. cit.*, 8.
18. *Op. cit.*, 9.
19. *Op. cit.*, 47.
20. CW : 86 : Dec. 20, 1946 : 245.
21. CW : 86 : Dec. 20, 1946 : 245
22. Gandhi, Manubehn : *The lonely pilgrim. Op. cit.*, 14:
23. *Op. cit .*, 31.
24. *Op. cit .*, 149.
25. *Op. cit .*, 218–19
26. N.K. Bose Papers. *Parasuram to N.K. Bose*, Serial No.60, Jan. 12, 1947, 89. *Op. cit.*
27. Gandhi, Mahubehn *Op. cit .*, 13.
28. *Op. cit .*, 103.
29. *Op. cit .*, 213.

30. *Op. cit*., 225.
31. CW : 86 : Dec. 12, 1946 : 221.
32. CW : 94 : Dec. 22, 1946 : 330.
33. CW : 94 : Dec. 30, 1946 : 333.
34. Gandhi, Manubehn. *The lonely pilgrim. Op. cit*., 48.
35. *Op. cit*., 89.
36. *Op. cit*., 89–90
37. *Op. cit*., 272.

Chapter 21: In the Noakhali Soup

1. CW : 86 : Jan. 18, 1947: 366.
2. CW : 86 : Jan. 10, 1947 : 335.
3. N.K. Bose Papers. [*Parasuram] to N.K. Bose*. Serial no. 60, Jan. 12, 1947, 89, "Lazy Bones] *op. cit.*
4. CW : 86 : Feb. 1, 1947 : 414.
5. CW : 86 : [on or before Feb. 9, 1947] : 452 : footnote.
6. CW : 86 : [on or before Feb. 9, 1947] : 452 : footnote.
7. CW : 86 : Feb. 10, 1947 : 453.
8. CW : 86 : Feb. 15, 1947 : 466.
9. CW : 86 : Feb. 15, 1947 : 466.
10. CW : 86 : Feb. 15, 1947 : 466.
11. CW : 87 : Feb. 24, 1947 : 13–14.
12. Pyarelal. *Mahatma Gandhi, the last phase.* V.1. *Op. cit.*, 582.
13. *Op. cit.*
14. CW : 86 : Feb. 1, 1947 : 420.
15. CW : 86 : Feb. 3, 1947 : 425.
16. CW : 94 : Jan. 19, 1947 : 350.
17. CW : 94 : Feb. 3, 1947 : 362.
18. N.K. Bose Papers. *N.K. Bose to M.K. Gandhi.* Serial no.62, 91, Feb. 4, 1947, *op. cit.*
19. CW : 94 : Feb. 6, 1947 : 363.
20. CW : 94 : Feb. 7, 1947 : 364.
21. CW : 86 : Feb. 7, 1947 : 441–42.
22. CW : 86 : Feb. [13], 1947 : 461.
23. Bose, Nirmal Kumar. *My days with Gandhi.*, *op. cit*.,179.
24. CW : 87 : Mar. 18, 1947 : 110.
25. Bose. *Op. cit*.,160.
26. CW : 87 : Feb. 24, 1947 : 15.
27. CW : 87 : Feb. 24, 1947 : 16.
28. CW : 87 : Mar. 2, 1947 : 35.
29. CW : 87 : Mar. 10, 1947 : 63.
30. CW : 87 : Mar. 25, 1947 : 153.

31. CW : 87 : April 13, 1947 : 272.
32. CW : 87 : April 16, 1947 : 361–62.
33. CW : 87 : April 29, 1947 : 384.
34. CW : 87 : [May 22, 1947] : 522.

Chapter 22: The Last Journey

1. Gandhi, Manu. *Last glimpses of Bapu.* Shivlal Agarwala, Delhi, 1962, 149–50.
2. *Ibid.*, 149.
3. Gandhi, Manu. *Bapu-my mother, op. cit*., 19–20.
4. Gandhi, Manu. *Last Glimpses of Bapu.* , *op. cit*., 234.
5. *Op. cit*., 238.
6. CW : 87 : June 14, 1947 : 150.
7. CW : 88 : July 21, 1947 : 212.
8. CW : 88 : July 21, 1947 : 383.
9. CW : 89 : Sept. 21, 1947 : 212.
10. CW : 89 : Sept. 22, 1947 : 217.
11. CW : 89 : Sept. 22, 1947 : 218.
12. Gandhi, Manu. *Op. cit*., 115.
13. *Op. cit*., 116.
14. *Op. cit*., 29.
15. CW : 90 : Jan. 13, 1948 : 417.
16. CW : 90 : Jan. 23, 1948 : 481.
17. CW : 90 : Jan. 23, 1948 : 482.
18. CW : 90 : Jan. 24, 1948 : 488.
19. Gandhi, Manu. *Last Glimpses of Gandhi. Op. cit*., 27.
20. *Op. cit*.
21. *Op. cit*., 56.
22. *Op. cit*., 119.
23. *Op. cit*., 257.
24. *Op. cit*., 297.
25. *Op. cit*., 302.
26. *Op. cit*., 235.
27. CW : 90 : June 30, 1948 : 520.
28. Gandhi, Manu. *Op. cit*., 234.
29. *Op. cit*., 298.
30. *Op. cit*., 300.
31. *Op. cit*., 309.
32. Godse, Gopal. *Gandhi's murder and after, ed.*, by S.T. Godbole, Surya, New Delhi, 104.
33. Gandhi, Manu. *Op. cit*., 334.
34. *Op. cit.*

Glossary

TERM	MEANING
ADHARMA	Violation of ethical obligations
AGA KHAN PALACE	Located in Poona; Gandhiji's detention camp during 1942–44
AGNIPARIKSHA	Test by fire
AHIMSA	Non-violence
AMALA	Pure
ARDHANGINI	Better half ; wife
ASHRAM	Hermitage
BANIA	Merchant caste
BEETHOVENSTEIN	Woods near Vienna which were the abode of Mirabehn after 1958
BELUR TEMPLE	Famous temple in Karnataka known for its sculpture
BHADRALOK	Gentry (of Bengal)
BHADRAMAHILA	Lady
BHARATI	Bengal periodical published by Saraladevi Chowdharani from Calcutta
BHAGVATA GITA	Poetic dialogue between Krishna and Arjuna in Mahabharata ; a philosophical classic
BHAGVATA PURANA	Religious work devoted to Vishnu
BHAKTI	Religious devotion
BRAHMA	One of the Trinity (the god of creation)
BRAHMACHARI	One observing continence
BRAHMACHARYA	Continence
CHARKHA	A spinning wheel
CHAPPALS	Footwear
CHELA	Disciple

CHOTTABHAI	Younger brother
DANISH MISSIONARY SOCIETY	Danish establishment for promoting the cause of girl education in South India
DARSHAN	Sighting of meritorious person / deity
DHARMAJA	The first born (literal meaning: born of duty)
DHARMA	Ethical duty / obligation
DHED	Untouchable caste (of Gujarat)
DHOTI	Cloth tied around the waist; loin cloth
DURGA	The consort of Lord Shiva
DUVIDHA	Uncertainty; in two minds
GITA GOVINDA	Lyrical poem of Jayadeva in praise of Krishna
GITA RAHASYA	Commentary on the *Gita* by Lokmanya Tilak
GOPI	Milkmaid
HARIJAN	Gandhiji's main vehicle of expression, published in weekly in English, Hindi and Gujarati.
INDIAN OPINION	Multilanguage newspaper published from Phoenix Farm, now closed
KAFFIR	South African tribe
KAILASH TEMPLE	Symphony in stone dedicated to Lord Shiva, located in Karnataka
KALI	The fierce and bloody consort of Shiva.
KAMA, KAMADEVA	The God of Love and Desire
KAMA (verb)	(Sexual) desire
KAMAJA	The second child (literal meaning: carnally born)
KRISHNA	One-in-two playful and statesman god
KUNDALINI	The latent energy leading to ultimate liberation
LAKSHMAN-REKHA	Absolute limit
LEELA	Illusory pageant (of human existence)
MAHATMA	A great soul
MAHAYAJNA	Gandhiji's *brahmacharya* experiences in Naokhali so named; (literal meaning- great sacrifice)
MAHESH	Another name of Lord Shiva
MALECHA	Foreigner; unclean
MANU	The ancient law giver
MARRIED *BRAHMACHARYA*	Practice of *brahmacharya* by married couples
NOAKHALI	Now in Bangladesh, it was worst effected by communal riots in 1946; Gandhiji spent four months during 1946–47 walking barefoot from village to village
NILA NAGIN	Blue snake
NIRVANA	Supreme bless
PARMAHAMSA	Great soul

PARIAH	Outcaste
PHOENIX FARM	An experiment in communal living, near Durban
PHYSICAL *BRAHMACHARYA*	Practice of *brahmacharya* by married couples.
PRAYOG	Experiment
PURUSHA	The eternal man, also a name of Brahma.
RADHA	Krishna's beloved
RAMA	An incarnation of Vishnu; the king of Ayodhya
RAMAYANA	Epic Sanskrit poem by Valmiki
RASALILA	Krishna's dance with *gopis*
RAVANA	Anti-Hero of *Ramayana*
RIG VEDA	The first of the foundation holy books of the Hindus
RISHI	Seer
RISHIYANGA	An ancient seer and renowned brahmachari, a character mentioned in *Ramayana*
SABARMATI ASHRAM	The main centre of Gandhiji's political activities after he returned to India, so named because it was located on the banks of Sabarmati river in Ahmedabad
SAKTA	Shiva cult based on sexual practices
SAMADHI	Trance
SARVODAYA	Ideal society
SATYAGRAHA	Non-violent resistance
SATYAGRAHA ASHRAM	The earliest ashram established by Gandhiji at Kochrab near Ahmedabad
SATYAGRAHI	The one offering *Satyagraha*
SAUBHAGYAVATI	Married woman, fortunate and fulfilled
SEVAGRAM ASHRAM	Gandhiji's headquarters after he moved away from Sabarmati Ashram; located near Wardha in Maharashtra
SHAKTI	The consort of Shiva; a manifestation of female energy
SHIVA	One of the Trinity; the god of destruction
SINHGARH FORT	Gandhiji's favourite resort in Maharastra
SHUKADEVA	Son of Vyasa of *Mahabharata* fame; a renowned seer and brahmachari
SMRITI	Oral knowledge
SHAMBOOMELA	The irreverent event (literally: the festival of Shiva)
STHITAPRAYAN	Firm in judgement and wisdom; a Jaina doctrine
SUFI	Liberal Muslim cult based on renunciation
SWADESHI	Movement advocating the use of native products and boycott of foreign goods

TABERNACLE	Any place of worship that is not called church or temple
TANTRA	Shiva cult based on sexual practices
TAPASYA	The practice of austerities
THIRATANKARAS	Lineage of Jaina prophets; 24 in number
TOLSTOY FARM	1000-acre farm belonging to Kallenbach; Gandhi's first experimental ashram in S. Africa
TONGA	Horse-driven vehicle
TRAPPIST MONASTERY	Located in Pinetown (Natal); a role model for Gandhi's for communal living
TULSI	Holy basil plant
VAISHNAVA	A devotee of Vishnu
VAISHNAVISM	Bhakti cult
VALMIKI	The author of *Ramayana*
VISHNU	One of the Trinity; the god of creation
VOLKSRUST JAIL	Notorious detention place for *Satyagrahis* in South Africa
YAJANA	Sacrifice
YOGI	Male ascetic
YOUNG INDIA	The earliest publication expounding Gandhiji's views after his return to India from 1919 to 1933

Index

D

E

F

G

Girja Kumar is a veteran research scholar. The man behind the Sapru House library, he was born in 1925, in Dera Ghazi Khan (Pakistan); this multi-faceted scholar retired as chief librarian of the Jawaharlal Nehru University Library in 1985. He held many important positions including chairman of the Delhi Library Board (1985-86) and President of the Indian Library Association (1983-85). He was Asso iate, Oriental Division, Library of Congress, Washington DC during 1954-55.

Besides writing for various newspapers and magazines as a book critic, he has to his credit a number of books including the definitive biography of the world-renowned Dr S R Ranganathan and *The Book on Trial, Fundamentalism and Censorship in India*.

Brahmacharya, Gandhi and His Women Associates, based on extensive research, is a biography within a biography. Girja Kumar's second book with Vitasta, *The Indus People* is on his Indus Valley roots and the story of the Indic people of the land of Mahabharata.

Review

Ever since the book was first published in 2006, critics and scholars have attested to Girja Kumar's writing. This book sparked a fresh discourse in Gandhian Studies.

The author does not take sides and deals respectfully with the subject of his study, and that is to his credit. Many Gandhians may object to this work. Some of the passages are revolting indeed. The truth, however, must be faced. As Gandhiji once said: Truth is God.

MV Kamath in *Organiser*

Mother Courage: Kasturba Gandhi with children, 1903
(From Left to Right: Harilal, Ramdas, Ba, Devdas, Manilal)

JEWISH BONDING: Gandhiji, Sonja Schlesin and Henry Kallenbach at Johannesburg in 1913. Sonja was Gandhiji's secretary in South Africa.

Gandhiji's mother Putlibai. He was deeply influenced by her and tried to look for her image in every woman he met.

Esther (Faering) Menon ,
the Danish missionary.
She quit job to join Gandhiji
who called her
the 'Rock of Ages'.

Madelein Slade who Gandhiji
renamed as Mirabehn. Her life
was a pilgrimage in the cause
of the Mahatma.

Sushila Nayyar was Gandhiji's personal physician and attendant. Gandhiji cared a lot about her and her brother Pyarelal.

Rabindranath Tagore's niece, Saraladevi Chowdharani. Gandhiji called her his 'spiritual wife'.

The princess of Kapurthala
Rajkumari Amrit Kaur
was Gandhiji's close confidante.

Bibi Amutussalaam was a proud
Rajputani from Patiala.
She managed to end Pir Pagaro
communal riots and was
closely associated with Gandhiji.

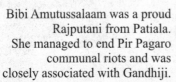

Prabhavati was wife of Jayaprakash Narayan. Gandhiji tried to shape her as a role model for married brahmacharya.

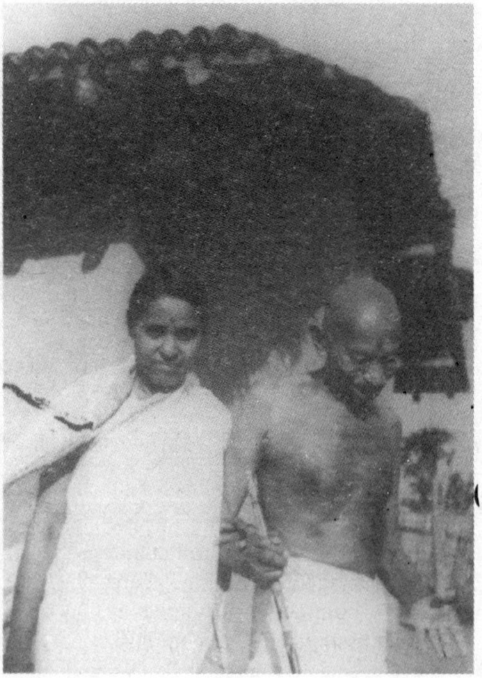

Gandhiji with Premabehn Kantak at Sevagram in 1941. Her correspondence with him on brahmacharya ended in a controversy when it was published in a book form in Marathi, *Prasad Diksha* (1938).

Gandhiji and his 'walking sticks', Sushila Nayyar (left) and son Manilal's wife Sushila (right), after a meeting with the British Cabinet mission in Delhi in 1946.

Sustained and Selfless: Kasturba Gandhi and Gandhiji. Ba was a passive but equal partner in his brahmacharya pledge of 1906.